What Some Expe

"*Can We Dance?* has all the elements every fine ⸏_____ the three guiding points you must follow when proceeding with a relationship—inward with self-reflection, outward with honest evaluation of others, and upward toward the highest spiritual good. Keep *Can We Dance?* as a handy companion on your way to finding and strengthening your relationship."

~ Paul Coleman, Psy.D., author of *How to Say It for Couples: Communicating with Tenderness,*
      Openness, and Honesty

~S ʠ~

"*Can We Dance?* is a wonderful, life-changing book full of amazing wisdom. This is the manual for relationships that the world has needed."

~ Janet Murray, writer, editor, and educator

~S ʠ~

"This spiritually uplifting book provides step-by-step practical instructions and tools for building the foundation of a lifelong relationship with a special person. As a single myself, it is allowing me to get over my fears and develop character strengths that will assist me with a committed relationship. I am also finding it valuable to use the materials in *Can We Dance?* during relationship coaching and while presenting workshops with youth and young adults internationally."

~ Nevin T. Jenkins, 32, conference keynote presenter, workshop leader, and
      relationship coach

~S ʠ~

"This is really great! I love all your ideas, and they are very well expressed. I love the sense of helpfulness and kindness toward the reader—the sincere desire to help him or her. This is a very valuable book. So, so needed!"

~ June Saunders, relationship coach and co-author of *Cultivating Heart and Character, Educating*
      *for Life's Most Essential Goal*s

~S ʠ~

"Character is the foundation of life."
~ John Covey, Director of FranklinCovey Home and Family Division

~S ʠ~

"For those who are really serious about making their relationship work, this book is more than just a good read. It covers so many areas necessary for a good relationship, including the development of friendship, which is the foundation of a great relationship. It is a useful, practical book with stimulating questions for discussion, activities, and worksheets."

~ Fiona McDonald, Manager of Education Services, Relationships Australia (Western)

Can We Dance?

Learning the Steps for a Fulfilling Relationship

Susanne M. Alexander
with John S. Miller

A Both Eyes Open™ Relationship Book

Can We Dance? Learning the Steps for a Fulfilling Relationship

Published by Marriage Transformation LLC
P. O. Box 23085, Cleveland, Ohio, USA 44123
www.marriagetransformation.com; Phone: 216-383-9943

International Standard Book Number/ISBN: 0-9726893-6-2 or 978-0-9726893-6-6
Library of Congress Control Number/LCCN: 2005936822

©2006 by Marriage Transformation LLC, all international rights reserved. Printed and bound in the United States of America by Central Plains Book Manufacturing. No part of this book may be reproduced by any mechanical, photographic, or electronic process, or by any other means, in the form of a photographic or digital recording, nor may it be stored in a retrieval system, transmitted or otherwise copied for public or private use, including on the Internet, without the written permission of the publisher, except by a reviewer, who may quote brief passages in a review. Anyone wishing to translate any of this book into another language must seek permission in advance and obtain written approval. Electronic and hard copy versions of all translations must be provided to the publisher. Thank you for respecting these legal requirements. Your integrity with this spreads a spirit of loving respect throughout the world and makes us very happy!

Marriage Transformation and Both Eyes Open are trademarked terms. See page 470 for extension of copyright notices and permissions.

This book is designed to provide helpful educational information about relationships. The publisher and the authors are not engaged in rendering legal or clinical advice. No information, advice, or suggestions are intended to take the place of guidance from a therapist or licensed professional. If such assistance is required, the reader should seek the services of a competent licensed professional. The authors and publisher shall have neither liability nor responsibility to any person or entity with respect to any loss or damage caused, or alleged to be caused, directly or indirectly by the information contained in this book.

The examples and stories in *Can We Dance?* are fictional, but based on the authors' knowledge, observation, and experience of working with people as relationship or character coaches. The stories provide illustrations of key concepts.

Cover Design:	Matthew Levine (www.neomatthewlevine.hostrocket.com)
Layout Design:	Joyce Ashman and Susanne M. Alexander
Cartoons:	Brenda Brown (www.webtoon.com); Randy Glasbergen (www.glasbergen.com); and Catherine F. Hosack (www.catherinesart.netfirms.com); licensed for use; copyrights held by artists
Back Cover Author Photo:	Steve Petti, new image media (216-514-1835, www.newimagemedia.com)

Acknowledgements

From Susanne M. Alexander: My husband Craig and I joke that writing and producing a book has its similarities to pregnancy and then giving birth to a baby. That means I experience joys, soaring highs, dismal lows, and lots of aches and pains! Craig's love, thoughtfulness, caring, confidence, cooperation, encouragement, flexibility, generosity, gentleness, service, and strength make it possible for me to go through the process of producing books. Without him as my friend, confidante, consulting partner, husband, and prayer partner, this book would not exist in service to all of you. I love you, sweetheart!

From John S. Miller: I thank Susanne and Craig for extending the invitation to me to participate in the writing of this book, for it has been a tremendously valuable personal learning experience for me. I also thank my sister, BonBon, for her profound insights and encouragement. Foremost, however, I thank my courageous wife, Cindy, for her undying support and encouragement through this entire process, for her unswerving belief and moral support to walk with me side by side through all of life's adventures, and for her consistent willingness to fearlessly strive together with me to build a forever friendship-based marriage.

The process of creating *Can We Dance?* required the dedicated, unified effort of many people. We are honored and thankful for the friendship, love, support, and service of a great team of people, who generously provided insights, inspiration, encouragement, advice, edits, content, experiences, proofreading, hard work, time, quotation checking, technical support, graphics, cartoons, photos, financial backing, and testimonials. We extend our deep respect and appreciation to all of you:

Joyce Ashman, Marielle Audet, Kamilla Babahani, Bruce Barick, Michael Bond, Laura Brotherson, Brenda Brown, Don Brown, Ryan Burke, Hillary Chapman, Paul Chapman, Chris Cirvencic, Jennifer Coates, Jane Covey, John Covey, Jim Dalenburg, Frank DeMaria, Gail Duilio, Richard Eastburn, Deb Evans, Yasmin Farhoumand, Craig Farnsworth, Leah Farnsworth, Lu Farnsworth, Carl Fravel, Ron Frazer, Randy Glasbergen, Liz Hendrix, Mike Hillis, David Holzman, Ping Hong, Catherine Hosack, Katrina Jarman, Nevin Jenkins, Daniella Kantorova, Matthew Levine, Linda Kavelin Popov, Sarah Keller, Khalil Khavari, Sue Khavari, Sue Martin, Brenda Maxwell, Shem Maxwell, Neal Mayerson, Fiona McDonald, Jef McDonough, Craig McIntosh, Jenni Menon, Johanna Merritt Wu, Bob Mlakar, Shamsi Modarai, Christina Munk, Janet Murray, Ed Muttart, Kay Muttart, Reggie Newkirk, Phyllis Peterson, Steve Petti, Yakov (John) Phillips, Dan Popov, Carmel Purkis, Harold Rampey, Joretta Rampey, Betty Roth, Nishat Ruiter, Cyprian Sajabi, Nacim Sajabi, June Saunders, Martha Schweitz, Leif Segen, Maxwell Shell, Mead Simon, Jean Taber, Michelle Tashakor, Tina Tessina, Renate Tilgner, Holly Tolles, Ruth Twaddell, Carmen Valverde, Deborah Van Den Hoonaard, Joyce Watanabe, Loretta West, Barbara Whitbeck, Debbie Wilke, Annette Young, Jordan Young, and all of our workshop and coaching participants, listserve participants, and survey respondents.

Table of Contents

Worksheets in Each Chapter

Part 1 ~ *Dance Lessons:* Preparing Yourself for a Great Relationship

Part 2 ~ *It Takes Two:* Creating a Lasting Friendship-Based Relationship

Note: A set of worksheets is available for purchase at www.marriagetransformation.com.

Your Invitation to a New Kind of Relationship Dance

Can We Dance? represents a revolutionary transformation in the way you approach preparing for, seeking, and being in a relationship.

Think of all the people in your life. How many of them have a happy and fulfilling relationship with a partner? We are confident that there is a deep yearning in your heart for a wonderful relationship that lasts, but you may not know how to accomplish it.

Does the following scenario seem too familiar?

> Mark and Stephanie's relationship is getting off to a great start. They met recently at a local seminar, and they were instantly attracted to each other. Almost every evening, they go to movies, restaurants, plays, or other events going on in the city. They are amazed at how well they get along and what a wonderful and sexy couple they are. They are certain they were made for each other.

> Mark and Stephanie begin excitedly sharing the details of their relationship with close friends and coworkers. However, within weeks, they are complaining about each other to the same people. They fight regularly, because they keep making assumptions about what each other is thinking and feeling. One pushes the other to open up more and share their life, but the other resists. They criticize each other, and communication breaks down between them. Soon, they end their relationship in disappointment and frustration.

Relationship advice from friends, relatives, magazines, books, television talk shows, or the Internet often provide more confusion for you than solutions. Currently the media's message is that you have to find "the one right" person in the world for you based largely upon physical appearance. The media portray sexual chemistry and love at first sight as the ideal you have to attain. Mark and Stephanie believed all of this. However, none of these factors provides the essential foundation to make a relationship extraordinary.

Instead, the message in *Can We Dance?* is to prepare yourself for a relationship first and then go into it with Both Eyes Open™. This means clearly seeing and knowing what you expect and need in a relationship and understanding all the important aspects about your partner. Of course, your partner will need to know you thoroughly as well.

A vital part of knowing yourself and your partner is understanding the character qualities you each bring to a relationship as strengths. For instance, these can include generosity, patience, enthusiasm, kindness, or courage. **This book will help you to develop each of your many character qualities and use this knowledge to help you observe your partner's qualities. Character qualities are foundational for the success of a relationship.**

Through expanding your knowledge and participating in activities and reflection, you will gain **vital new skills** that help you to discover a special partner and build a strong friendship and relationship together. Friendship is also a foundational aspect of relationships. **The greater the depth and strength of your friendship with a partner, the stronger your relationship will be.**

You will learn new ways to communicate with a partner, such as how to speak Character Quality Language, and communicate encouragement, support, and love to your partner. You will also understand how to avoid common communication pitfalls in relationships. Society has promised you a quick fix for everything, including finding someone and having a relationship. **In fact, it takes commitment, effort, and excellent communication skills to establish a great friendship and deep love with a partner.**

Can We Dance? is an extraordinary guide to a new and realistic approach to having a lasting relationship. It helps you to make significant new choices in how you and a partner create a relationship.

Here is what can happen if Mark and Stephanie try a different way of interacting:

> Mark and Stephanie's relationship is getting off to a great start. They met recently at a local seminar, and they were quickly attracted to each other. They decide to pursue getting to know each other. Over the next few weeks, they spend time together doing activities they both enjoy, such as going to plays, museums, and restaurants. In addition, they participate in a community service project, exercise together, and discuss the books they are reading. They have meals both as a couple and together with friends and family members. Mark helps Stephanie with solutions for a challenge she is experiencing with work, and Stephanie helps Mark with a problem he is having with a relative. They work through occasional communication challenges together, and they become close friends.
>
> Stephanie wants to see Mark in a variety of settings. It is important to her to observe his character and see that he can be consistently respectful, compassionate, trustworthy, and friendly. To Mark, it is also important for him to see trustworthiness in Stephanie. In addition, he wants time to observe that she is consistently truthful, cooperates easily and readily with him, and, like him, has a strong connection to spirituality and family. They are confident that they are establishing the foundation of a lasting relationship.

Having this type of relationship may seem unattainable, but the answers to these questions are in this book—if you are willing to learn and practice what it will take to create a happy, lasting friendship-based relationship!

Consider what you really want from a relationship. Together you can:

- Develop full partnership with respectful equality between you
- Fulfill your purposes and goals in life
- Encourage each other and help each other to be your best
- Reach your full potential as people who contribute to your families, workplaces, and communities
- Develop a deep and wonderful bond of friendship and love
- Develop communication skills, so you and your partner experience a deep connection between you

You have probably taken more training to get a driver's license than you have to be successful in a committed relationship or marriage. However, a relationship and marriage have far greater impact on your happiness, success, and well-being in life. Relationships can change your life forever. They have long-term implications that require skillful handling. Books, DVDs, CDs, websites, workshops, coaching, counseling, and more are all resources to empower you to be confident in your choices and actions. The more you know, and the more skills you gain, the better the outcome will be.

We are continually fascinated and amazed at how important character, friendship, and communication are to successful relationships. We invite you to begin your adventure in learning new ways to perform the relationship dance. It is time for you to explore yourself, discover a great partner, and create a happy, lasting relationship.

Welcome to your relationship dance class!

Susanne M. Alexander, Relationship and Character Coach with John S. Miller, Character Coach

What Does Dancing Have to Do with a Book About Relationships?
Foreword: by Carmen Valverde, Ed.D.

A professor once said to me, "Dance is such a pleasurable thing to do, that it makes you wonder why there are people who do not like to dance. That would be an interesting question to answer." The same can be said for being involved in relationships in general. Some people are happily married, and some, for various reasons, avoid a committed relationship.

Imagine that you are attending a party or an event that has lively music and dancing. You watch others having fun on the dance floor. You think of asking someone to dance, but you are afraid of rejection. Or, from the other perspective, someone approaches you and asks, "Would you like to dance?" Depending on a number of variables, you will answer either "Yes" or "No, thank you."

You might decline the invitation if you do not know how to dance, or you think you are not good enough to dance with the person. You may not like the way he or she looks or behaves. You may believe that you just do not like dancing—it does not appeal to you. It is also possible that you tried dancing in the past, and you felt awkward, someone made fun of you, you learned more slowly than other students in your dance class and felt inferior, or your dance partner stepped on your toes. Maybe a friend put dancing down and ridiculed people who danced.

The same possibilities exist with your feelings about relationships. It looked like fun, so you tried it. You were hurt, though, and decided that a committed relationship is not for you. You might blame yourself. You might blame your partner. Maybe you never learned to trust others. The truth is, as in dancing, people need to learn how to get along in relationships. There are basic principles to follow and techniques to learn.

First, you need the desire to learn. Just as you might want to know how to dance well, you want to know how to have a fulfilling and love-filled relationship. This book pre-supposes that you do want to learn; otherwise, you would not be reading it. The first step is learning to BE a great partner. In dance, this means learning the basic steps. In relationships, you do this by developing your skills and your character qualities. Personal integrity is important on and off the dance floor. Then you learn the skills to find a lasting friend and partner.

To learn how to dance, you need good instruction, a good example, practice, feedback, correction, encouragement, and more practice. You need to commit time, effort, and energy to the task. You need to master the important principles and techniques of movement and then how to work with a partner. Being with a partner in dance or in a committed relationship requires you to find a special person, and then to have proper positioning, compatibility, connection, and good communication.

Dancing well involves equality and respect, cooperation and communication. There is give and take, leading and following, obeying the rules of the dance floor, and especially kindness and courtesy to your partner and everyone around you. You need to learn the steps, timing, and how to improvise when something or someone gets in the way of you and your partner. With unity between you, when you trip, stumble, or get off the rhythm, you can recover quickly and continue dancing together.

Everyone can dance. The question is HOW WELL do you want to dance? In this book, the authors offer you principles, methods, techniques, steps, and exercises that will help you to develop and improve your ability to dance the dance of relationships. It is worth the effort—good dancing and fulfilling relationships make life worth living.

Dr. Valverde teaches at Rutgers University, New Brunswick, New Jersey, United States. She has been teaching dance for over 30 years, and she met her husband while dancing. She also assisted with the dance metaphors throughout the book.

Understanding the Components of *Can We Dance?*

You may choose to flip past this section, because you want to dive right into the book. However, you might be someone who appreciates seeing a map before heading out on a trip instead. If that description fits you, here is a navigation guide to the structure of this book, as well as why we chose to handle some wording and sources in certain ways.

COMPONENTS OF CAN WE DANCE?

The book has three parts:

- **Part 1 — Dance Lessons: Preparing Yourself for a Great Relationship** emphasizes what you need to do individually to be effective in a relationship, including character assessment and development and assessing your expectations. Ideally you will do Part 1 before you are in a relationship, but you can do it after you have a partner as well.
- **Part 2 — It Takes Two: Creating a Lasting Friendship-Based Relationship** assists you through developing friendships, finding a partner, observing how a partner speaks and acts, building communication skills, and developing a deeper friendship and serious relationship. It is not necessary to have a partner to read and do the activities in Part 2. There are some activities, however, that you will return to when you have a partner or you can do along with a partner or others.
- **Part 3 — The Best Dance: Exploring Powerful Character Qualities** is a reference guide containing the 56 character qualities used throughout the book. It assists you to deepen your understanding and practice of each of the qualities.

Elements in Parts 1 and 2

Identification of Character Qualities

Character qualities such as *confidence*, *honesty*, and *respect* are in *italics* (except in the worksheets) to assist you in recognizing and practicing them. Various forms of the quality are included in this structure, such as *strength* as a form of *strong*. As you notice the italics, you will begin to see how common character qualities are in daily usage.When you encounter an italicized quality, if you want to understand it better, you can turn to Part 3 to read an explanation of it.

Stories and Examples

The scenarios in this book are fictional, but they reflect attitudes, actions, and experiences people have shared with us. People can be single or unmarried at any age, and in any part of the world. Our goal is to serve a diverse audience that spans a wide range of ages and lives around the world. The stories used throughout this book reflect some of this diversity. Each contains principles and behavior for you to learn from, regardless of your age or cultural background.

Learning in Action

Normally, you read a book simply to learn new concepts. However, relationships are not merely conceptual. Therefore, *Can We Dance?* invites you to participate in a more active adventure to learn new insights and skills. Included throughout are: **Questions for Reflection** and various **Activities** (some include **Worksheets**).

The activities and worksheets are wide ranging to involve you physically, mentally, emotionally, and spiritually. Some of the communication activities and tools may feel a bit strange and uncomfortable as you first use them; however, that provides opportunities to *strengthen* such qualities as *courage* or *flexibility*. If you take the time to be thorough with doing the activities, your insights and new skills will benefit you in your relationships. Note that the word is "thorough," not "perfect"! You may also develop your own activities to supplement or replace the ones provided. A few of the activities *encourage* engaging your *creative* side through using "the arts"; such as, collage, poetry, music, or writing. Often using the arts can bring surprising and helpful insights and perspectives.

The majority of the activities are set up for you to do on your own, assuming that you will not necessarily have someone yet who will participate in them with you. However, many you can do with a partner, and some will be ones you will return to when you do have a partner. Remember that where the activity involves someone else, that participant needs to be willing, not pressured. Ideally, your partner will also have a copy of this book and be going through the same process of relationship preparation as you are.

As you set goals for your character development, actions, and what you want from a relationship, you will begin to act, assess, learn, and then change course if necessary. Through this active process, you will learn how to be successful in a relationship. This discovery process is vital. In her book, *The Truth About Love*, Pat Love, Ed.D., says, "Couples who rush through discovery, skipping over the information-gathering process, decrease the likelihood of their relationship going the distance and creating a love that lasts."[1]

Wording Choices

It is sometimes difficult to find words that effectively describe people's roles in relationships, especially when someone is not married. We chose to use the term **"partner"** instead of other choices, such as boyfriend or girlfriend, because it includes the concept of equality and applies across a wide span of ages and various relationship stages.

We have not completely eliminated the concept of **"dating"** or going out on a "date." However, we have largely replaced it with a wide range of activities that focus you on getting to know yourself and a partner in meaningful ways. We have also avoided the term **"breaking up"** to describe the ending of a relationship, because it portrays a shattering of the people and relationship, and there are other alternatives.

This book will **distribute globally**, and many people reading it would not understand some of the popular expressions used in North America. As a result, we have done our best to eliminate them. For the same reason, we have minimized the use of contractions (I'll, won't, don't...) At times, this results in the text seeming a bit formal, but we hope you will agree that understanding is more important.

Grammar rules are controversial and changing, and sometimes they can either assist or hinder readability. We chose to use words such as **"they,"** **"their,"** or **"them"** as substitutes for a constant use of his/her, he/she, and so on. Some may find this substitution equally distracting, and to them we apologize.

We believe that having a *spiritual* connection between partners can *strengthen* a relationship, so at times this book includes ***spiritual* terminology** and *encourages* you to explore and try activities such as prayer, meditation, worship, reading *spiritual* material, and more as possibilities. The words "God," "Creator," Higher Power, or Great Spirit appear at times, but you may use a different term for a *spiritual* force in your life, or you may not believe in this concept at all. Please use whatever terminology fits your beliefs, and any *spiritual* practices that work for you in your life.

Sources

Can We Dance? includes a wide variety of sources, as there is a rich array to draw on about both character and relationships. We use quotations from:

- Philosophers
- Founders of religions, religious leaders, and religious scripture
- Relationship and marriage researchers
- Therapists and counselors
- Authors
- Singles who responded to our informal surveys
- Traditional wisdom

These quotations will expand your perspectives and give you insights into new choices and actions to consider in your life. There are sources, copyright notices, and permissions notes in Appendix B. We *encourage* you to pursue reading many of these original sources to continue expanding your knowledge and skills.

In Part 3, the quotations for "Spiritual Reflection" come from six global religions: the Bahá'í Faith, Buddhism, Christianity, Hinduism, Islam, and Judaism. Quotations from some of these appear at times in Parts 1 and 2 as well. We recognize these as rich sources about character and relationships, and we hope that you find them insightful.

Part 1

Dance Lessons:
Preparing Yourself for
a Great Relationship

Different Dances

As you begin your journey through this book, you will discover that *Can We Dance?* offers many different ways to explore this vital subject. Choose the method that best fits your style, personality, *flexibility*, relationship status, *purpose*, and *commitment* to immersing yourself in a new relationship approach. You can:

- **Dance Your Own Dance -** *Create* and follow your own unique method.
- **Follow the Dance Instructor -** Read the text, reflect on the questions, and do each of the activities (including the worksheets) in order as you read.
- **Understand the Sequence -** Read through the book completely, and then circle back to the beginning to do the questions and activities.
- **Learn Step-by-Step -** Read one, two, or three chapters, do the reflection questions along the way, and then go back and do some of the activities that appeal to you.
- **Get a Friend Involved -** Complete each activity in Part 1 as you read. When finished, use what you learned to find a partner. Read and do the activities in Part 2 together with them.
- **Twirl Energetically -** Jump from each bold, enlarged sentence to the next one to catch the highlights, and do random activities along the way.
- **Stay Light on Your Feet -** Read only the cartoons.

The goal is to learn as much as you can in the ways that work the best for you.

Completing the Worksheets

There are worksheets at the end of each chapter in this section to *help* you to understand yourself better, identify what you bring to a relationship, and *discern* what you are looking for in a partner. Please consider the following when completing them:

- Unless otherwise noted, the worksheets are designed for you to complete by yourself.
- For each worksheet, ask yourself whether it will help you to have involvement with or input from others.
- If you have a partner, you can invite them to complete the worksheet in their own book, or the two of you can use this book for reference and put your answers on separate pieces of paper; it is best if you and your partner do not see each other's papers during the activity, so you do not influence each other's answers.
- If you do not have a partner yet, you can choose to ask a friend or a small group of friends to participate with you.
- If you complete the worksheet activity with someone else, discuss your answers with them when you are each finished.

Basic Footwork:
Understanding Character

Jewel and Grant sit facing each other at a tiny outdoor café across from the Louvre. It is quiet and calm as Paris gradually comes to life and they wait to enter the famous French museum. A waiter delivers cups of steaming chocolate-laced coffee and hot, flaky croissants with fresh strawberry jam. Grant holds Jewel's hand across the table, knowing she is his destiny. When they finish eating, they walk across the street and gaze at the Eiffel Tower in the distance. They each think to themselves, "Is anything more romantic than Paris in the springtime?"

Ah, you probably thought for a moment that you stumbled into a romance novel! You may be tempted sometimes to slip into this make-believe world, and think that being with someone should be endlessly perfect. Relationships are fun, enriching, supportive, and adventurous. But at times, they are also exasperating, confusing, painful, and scary. They take you through the full range of emotions from high to low, and they often include challenges. Just as becoming an *excellent* dancer requires time, effort, and practice, so does preparing for a fulfilling friendship-based relationship. It is not an instant process. Finding and attracting a great partner, and becoming close friends with each other, requires learning more about yourself and developing new *strengths* and skills.

Before you learn to dance with a partner, you begin with learning the basic footwork. Before you are in a relationship, an essential step is learning about and developing your own character. This learning includes understanding what character is, why it is important, and gaining a clear picture of your own character *strengths* and growth areas. When you understand your growth areas, you then take action to develop yourself. As you learn about and develop your character, you will begin to identify what character qualities will *help* you to be successful in a relationship. Character will be the work of the first three chapters of this book.

As the book proceeds, your increasing knowledge of your own character will empower you to identify what character qualities are important for you to see in a partner. When you have a partner, you will learn how to observe their character *strengths* and areas for growth. Knowledge and observation about a partner are vital. The ability for you and a partner to practice character qualities effectively with each other significantly increases *loving* and *unified* communications between the two of you. Practicing character qualities also enhances the ability you and your partner have to establish a happy, lasting relationship.

DEFINING CHARACTER

The word "character" is likely familiar to you, so you may have some understanding of what it means. Consider that it is the sum of all the qualities you have developed throughout your life. These qualities then guide your choices toward causing positive rather than negative outcomes. For instance, are you *honest, compassionate*, and *responsible*? If you act practicing these character qualities, the effect is positive. If, instead, you choose to steal, neglect the needs of others, and avoid paying your bills, all of these choices will have a negative impact on you and others. You will then know these same qualities need *strengthening*, and you can then choose to develop them.

You may not have stopped to think about the wide variety of character qualities. There are actually dozens of them, and you were born with the capacity to develop them all. Think of each of your qualities as a tool in your toolbox. You have the capacity to use all of them over time. You have the choice to use them or not to use them, and you have the choice to use them correctly or not to use them correctly. The more you know about your tools, the more you will use them effectively.

At this point in your life, you are likely *strong* and effective in practicing some character qualities and unskilled or uncertain about practicing others. You develop each quality according to your own willingness, choice, and effort. **The more you develop your qualities, the better you are able to function effectively in the world, and the greater will be your ability to establish a *strong*, happy, and lasting relationship.**

There is a list of character qualities on the following page that represents a selection of common descriptors of character. It consists of key qualities to focus on in your own self-development prior to being in a relationship, those to look for in prospective partners, and those to practice together with a partner.

Most of the qualities on the list will seem familiar to you. However, you will likely learn about aspects of each of them that you never thought of before. As you read about the qualities, you can have a variety of responses. Once can raise a happy memory for you. Another can prompt you to think of a difficult moment in your life when either you or someone you were interacting with did not practice a character quality in an effective manner. You may also react to or make assumptions about some of the qualities. Stay aware of your thoughts and feelings as you begin to study each of them.

The qualities that are the focus in *Can We Dance?* are:

Acceptance	Discernment	Idealism	Respect
Assertiveness	Encouragement	Integrity	Responsibility
Beauty	Enthusiasm	Joyfulness	Self-Discipline
Caring	Equality	Justice	Service
Chastity	Excellence	Kindness	Sincerity
Commitment	Faithfulness	Love	Spirituality
Compassion	Flexibility	Loyalty	Strength
Confidence	Forgiveness	Mercy	Tactfulness
Contentment	Friendliness	Moderation	Thankfulness
Cooperation	Generosity	Patience	Thoughtfulness
Courage	Gentleness	Peacefulness	Trustworthiness
Courtesy	Helpfulness	Perseverance	Truthfulness
Creativity	Honesty	Purity	Unity
Detachment	Humility	Purposefulness	Wisdom

It may be *helpful* for you to pause at this point and read more about all of these qualities in Part 3, beginning on page 406. Remember that throughout *Can We Dance?* the qualities that appear in part 3 are *italicized* to assist you to spot them (except in the worksheets). As you see an *italicized* word, you can then turn to Part 3 and re-check your understanding of it as needed.

Copyright © 1998 by Randy Glasbergen.
www.glasbergen.com

"Looks aren't everything. It's what's inside you that really matters. A biology teacher told me that."

You develop your character qualities over time, influenced by your parents, teachers, family members, employers, partners, the media, and your experiences. **Character qualities shape and influence your thoughts, attitudes, feelings, actions, choices, and interactions with others.**

ACTIVITY

For a week or some other logical period of time, track how often the topic of character or any of the character qualities from this section are discussed in the media, such as television shows, movies, or magazine articles. What are your thoughts and conclusions from this observation?

CHARACTER STRENGTHS AND GROWTH AREAS

Just as when you exercise the muscles of your body, the qualities you practice with the most become *strong*. As they grow and develop, they become an integral part of your personal identity. Don Coyhis of the Mohican Nation says, "We need to realize the seeds we plant in the spring will be what show up in our summer season of growth and will be the fruits that we will harvest in our fall season. We really have a lot to do with what shows up in our lives."[1]

Perhaps you consistently practice *patience*, in part because you learned to wait after school for a sibling, and now you are *patient* as you *help* customers as the manager of a retail store. Even if you are consistent in practicing *patience* in most circumstance, however, there can be moments that test you. When you experience these times, you are less *patient* or even the complete opposite, and you become impatient. Perhaps you have difficulty waiting in lines, or you have difficulty dealing with a family member who annoys you at times. These moments let you know that you will benefit from *strengthening* your practice of *patience*.

You will not be perfect at practicing any of the qualities, and personal growth and change are an ongoing part of life. In fact, character growth really means that you are involved in a gradual process of personal transformation that advances you forward every day. The goal is to be as *excellent* and consistent as you can be—to have high standards for yourself. However, it also includes being able to *accept* and *forgive* yourself when you struggle and slip backward, and then choose to do better in the future.

Again, like your muscles, the qualities that you do not practice very often either stay ineffective or become weak. For instance, if you quit part way through projects when they become difficult, you are weak at practicing *perseverance*, and this is an area for growth. At times, you infrequently practice a quality because it does not seem to have any particular application in your life. Other times, you may not be aware of a quality or understand it. You can also be uncertain about how to practice it effectively.

Perhaps, instead, you flip back and forth between the extremes of practicing a quality effectively and then acting like its opposite as you learn to understand it better. One week you are *compassionate* toward a family member, and the next week you are distant and spend less time listening to the person. You see the effect of both of these attitudes and better understand how important it is for you to be *compassionate* consistently. As your understanding of each of the qualities grows, you will see that you are always in a state of growth and development, moving from weakness and ineffectiveness to *strength* and effectiveness. **The goal for each character quality is to achieve a high level of consistent effectiveness.**

Others can see how well you practice your character qualities as you choose how to speak and act in various situations. **A character quality is a *strength* when you choose to practice it both consistently and appropriately in a variety of circumstances.** Practicing it includes having harmony among your inner attitude, your words, and your actions. For example, you are consistently *purposeful* when working with a partner on tasks. Moreover, you are appropriately *patient* with your words and actions as your partner learns to do something for the first time (and you are not frustrated on the inside!).

Once a quality is a *strength*, it will likely continue to be one throughout your life. *Strengths help* you to:

- Gain and use knowledge [examples: *creativity* and *wisdom*]
- Accomplish goals in the face of opposition [examples: *courage* and *perseverance*]
- Look after and befriend others [examples: *compassion* and *kindness*]
- Reach out to others, make a difference for them, and work well with others in groups [examples: *justice* and *service*]
- Maintain *moderation* in your choices [examples: *humility* and *self-discipline*]
- Connect to the larger universe and provide meaning and purpose in your life [examples: *beauty* and *spirituality*][2]

As you progress through *Can We Dance?*, you will learn how to:

- Assess your practice of character qualities
- Practice the qualities effectively as you make choices
- Evaluate your actions and the effectiveness of your choices
- *Strengthen* your practice of qualities that are weak
- Observe qualities in friends and a partner as they make choices
- Begin to see how you and a partner can practice the qualities together

Your actions and the choices you make in preparing for a relationship, finding a partner, and then maintaining the relationship,

relate fundamentally to both your character and theirs. Because of the longevity and consistency of character quality *strengths*, identifying them in a partner is vital, as is understanding the areas that a partner needs to *strengthen*. As you understand and practice character qualities effectively, you will make better relationship choices.

ACTIVITY
Consider the lives of famous people you admire, and see if you can identify their character *strengths*—perhaps *courage, kindness,* or *perseverance.* You may know that these people were not perfect in many ways in their lives or relationships. In spite of this, you can still name qualities that *helped* them in their faith communities, workplaces, or social activism. Then, look at your parents, other family members, or close friends and identify their character *strengths.* Consider a book or movie you like and the qualities of the people portrayed in them. What qualities from the lives of all of these people do you want to develop as character *strengths* in your own life?

~ *Question for Reflection* ~
What have I learned about character from my family members? From others?

YOUR DUAL NATURE

Throughout your life, you will feel two forces within you that you can allow to pull you either toward doing beneficial actions or toward doing harmful ones. Whichever direction you choose to go significantly affects your life and the success of a relationship. The first force is the desire to *respect* your higher nature or best self, which is composed of your character qualities. Some people refer to this higher nature as your *spiritual* self, and they regard the source of their character qualities as God or believe their higher nature reflects the qualities of God. Whether you believe this or not, you can still be aware of this higher nature within you and the value of understanding and developing your character qualities.

Your higher nature develops as you learn to practice character qualities effectively and apply them to bring about a positive outcome on your own words and actions and in others' lives. A visual image that may *help* to illustrate this part of you is imagining yourself as a mirror reflecting the life-giving and warming light of the sun when you reflect character qualities to others. The more you polish your mirror through paying attention to developing the qualities, the better you will reflect or practice them. The imagery in this quotation may also *help* you to remember this concept: "The light of a good character surpasseth the light of the sun and the radiance thereof."[3]

Some people refer to character qualities as "virtues" or "character traits." The scriptures of the world's religions, the writings of great philosophers, and the work of relationship experts stress the importance of developing these qualities so that relationships work well. For instance:

> "Love is patient, love is kind. It does not envy, it does not boast, it is not proud. It is not rude, it is not self-seeking, it is not easily angered, it keeps no record of wrongs. ... Love never fails...." ~ *The Bible*[4]

> "But indeed if any show patience and forgive, that would truly be an exercise of courageous will and resolution in the conduct of affairs." ~*The Qur'án*[5]

> "Make it your guiding principle to do your best for others and to be trustworthy in what you say." ~ *Confucius*[6]

> "Virtuous action depends not just on what we do but also on doing the right thing for the right reasons, and knowing that we are acting for the right reasons." ~ Blaine J. Fowers, Ph.D.[7]

When you choose to listen to the other force, which is your lower nature or lower self, the result is against your best long-term interests. Your lower nature pulls you toward being self-centered, or to engaging in negative or destructive behavior. You think negatively, and you make choices that harm you or others. You or other people are left hurt or diminished in some way.

Using the same imagery as above, your mirror has dust on it, and you are reflecting less light. Your lower nature connects to the physical or material part of the world, and tends to pull you away from what is uplifting or *spiritual*. For instance, if you listen to your lower nature, you would choose to be greedy and selfish with money you earn, rather than to practice *generosity* with others, a quality of your higher nature. Consider this quotation:

> In man there are two natures; his spiritual or higher nature and his material or lower nature. ... Signs of both these natures are to be found in men. In his material aspect he expresses untruth, cruelty and injustice; all these are the outcome of his lower nature. The attributes of his Divine nature are

shown forth in love, mercy, kindness, truth and justice, one and all being expressions of his higher nature. Every good habit, every noble quality belongs to man's spiritual nature....[8]

Having the best relationship possible requires you to practice your character qualities effectively, and for you to search for a partner who does the same. Neither of you will be perfect, but you will be consistent in practicing your qualities and engaged in the process of character growth. You will then maintain your relationship through acknowledging and *encouraging* character qualities in each other.

ACTIVITY
It may assist you to understand this important concept about your dual nature if you engage your *creative* side. Use various art or building supplies to *create* something that demonstrates the struggle between one's higher and lower natures.

THE POWER OF CHOICE

Throughout your childhood, your parents, or those who raised you, *helped* to form your character with the dynamic power of their example, verbal guidance, and discipline. *Ideally*, they guided you to understand which of your actions were good ones (higher nature) and which ones were harmful (lower nature). Perhaps your father taught you to stay *confident* and *courteous* after losing a game instead of becoming angry. Maybe your mother taught you to speak *respectfully* to your grandparents instead of rudely.

You continued building and learning about your character through new experiences and the choices you made. You may have practiced *commitment* through keeping promises to your friends, and learned from seeing how this *helped strengthen* your friendships. Perhaps you were *compassionate* to a neighbor, and you saw the happiness this brought to them. You might have learned *respect* for school property through the guidance of a teacher. A part-time job may have *helped* you learn to be *responsible*. **While you develop your character throughout your entire life, all these experiences and more formed its foundation by your late teens. This foundation then set the stage for you to continue a lifetime of making choices to develop and adjust your attitudes and actions. Much of this character development occurs within your friendships and a relationship.**

Many additional sources influence your character choices. For instance, the visual media, such as television or movies, often provide you with an array of images. They show people making a wide variety of choices, some of them with positive outcomes, and some more destructive. You can also learn about how people handle character choices through reading newspapers, magazines, books, and stories. As you read and understand the lives of the people you read about, you can compare their choices to your own and those of people close to you. Are the outcomes from their words and actions and yours beneficial or harmful?

You may see people in your school or workplace who sometimes make ethical and *wise* choices that *respect* themselves and others. You also see those who at times choose to be greedy, dishonest, disrespectful, or self-centered. Perhaps a person justifies cheating on an exam, misuses an expense account, or takes property belonging to others. Prominent people throughout the world also show you how to practice character qualities effectively as they make difficult leadership decisions that benefit many people. Other leaders demonstrate poor judgment, and many people are adversely effected as a result. In every situation you observe, you have a choice between following the good example of others and refusing to follow the example of those who are unwise.

If you did not learn how to practice a variety of qualities as you grew up, they are likely weak, and it is even more important for you to focus on personal development work now. **You have the free will to make whatever character and behavior choices you wish, as well as to influence whatever consequences follow. The *wiser* your choices, the better the outcome will be. You have the power to choose how you respond to people and how you treat a partner and others. Your behavior is not dependent upon the behavior of others. You are *responsible* for your own character choices, which include your words and actions.**

When a choice rests on the foundation of a *strong* character, and allows you to *respect* your higher nature and that of a partner or others, the outcome is positive. Consider this quotation from Caroline Myss, Ph.D., about choices:

> Having faith in someone commits a part of our energy to that person; having faith in an idea commits a part of our energy to that idea; having faith in a fear commits a part of our energy to that fear. ... Our faith and our power of choice are, in fact, the power of creation itself. We are the vessels through which energy becomes matter in this life. Therefore, the spiritual test inherent in all our lives is the challenge to discover what motivates us to make the choices we do, and whether we have faith in our fears or the Divine.[9]

As you make choices about your words and actions that include practicing character qualities effectively with others, your self-*respect* and happiness will grow. "Choosing to lead [y]our lives with self-control and self-directedness is at the heart of feeling good."[10] Your self-*respect* and happiness then continue to support you in interacting with others in ways that make an uplifting difference. For example, you can show *kindness* to a sick friend, *courage* when you are fearful about meeting someone new, or *generosity* to a neighbor in need.

ACTIVITY

Pause reading at this point and take some time to complete **Worksheet 1.1: Understanding Your Character Choices**. Remember to be *honest* and *gentle* with yourself in the process of completing it. The goal of the worksheet is not to become self-critical. It is to *help* you with the next step in the process of better understanding and developing your character qualities, which will be the focus of both Chapters 2 and 3. As you complete the worksheet, note any situations that can be part of the focus of your character development work that will be in Chapter 3.

~ Questions for Reflection ~

1. What choices in my life show that I am practicing character qualities effectively?
2. What new choices do I want to make?
3. What scares me about making choices?

MISUSING QUALITIES

In the previous sections, you learned that you can have character qualities that are *strong*, need *strengthening*, or are at any stage of growth between those two states. You are also beginning to understand how your character qualities affect your choices. In this section, you will learn about another dimension of character: misusing qualities. **Misusing qualities is a new, somewhat complex, and yet exciting concept.** A character quality misuse occurs when you are *strong* and effective at practicing a character quality, but you practice it in one or both of the following ways:

- To excess, and/or
- At the wrong time or place

The result from a misuse is usually harm to yourself or others and often arguments, hurt feelings, or some other type of dissension or disunity. For example, you could have the character *strength* of *flexibility*. If you misuse it by practicing it to excess, you might be so relaxed in your life that you never make plans with a partner or set goals. An example of practicing *flexibility* at the wrong time or place is that you agree to escort your partner to her best friend's wedding, but you do not make sure you have a suit to wear, and you do not show up on time to pick her up as agreed. Not only will this degree of *flexibility* cause conflict with your partner, but they will find it increasingly difficult to *trust* you. It would be very difficult for others to work or socialize with you in either of these cases of misuse, and you would likely disrupt your friendships or a relationship regularly. Remember that Part 3 includes explanations to *help* you to practice qualities effectively and understand their misuses.

Moderation and Misuses

One quality that you will apply consistently in resolving misuses is *moderation*. When you practice any quality to excess, practicing *moderation* along with it *helps* you to tone it down. If, instead, you are practicing a quality at the wrong time and place, *moderation* will also *help* you to pause, slow down, and assess what you are saying or doing. **Practicing moderation helps you to adjust your practice of any quality and shift it into being an effective *strength*.** "Moderation is the silken string running through the pearl chain of all virtues."[11]

Moderating a quality does not mean practicing it in mediocrity or "doing it half-way" instead of whole-heartedly. That application is a misuse of *moderation*. Your goal is to be *excellent* in practicing all the qualities through building your understanding of them and making *wise* choices. Practicing *moderation* effectively along with a quality *strength* you are misusing increases the *wisdom* of your choices. For instance, if you learn more about how to practice *flexibility* effectively, and you practice *moderation* as well, you can change how you are practicing this quality. In this way, you can make plans, but you are able to adjust easily to a change in circumstances.

Comparing this concept of misuse to dancing, you gradually learn the dance steps by practicing them correctly, consistently, and with *moderation*. However, practicing excessively or incorrectly can cause injury and frustration. When your legs or arms start to quiver, or you have difficulty controlling your movements or concentrating, it is time to stop and rest. When you are tripping, stumbling, or stepping on your partner's toes, this is a signal that you might need to apply *moderation*. If you look at this concept of misuse from a sports angle, instead, practicing your *strength* appropriately would assist you to play football or soccer well for your team. However, if you take your *strength* off the sports field or out of the arena, and attempt to tackle or interfere with someone, you are likely to cause them an injury.

Here is a story about what can happen when you misuse a quality:

> Paige loves to be *helpful* to others. One day she comes to her friend Gavin's home to *help* him and his elderly father with planting their garden. Normally Gavin's mother plants the flowers, but she is sick in bed and cannot do it.
>
> Gavin explains his mother's garden plans to Paige, shows her where to dig, and indicates where each of the flowers should go. Instead, Paige decides on her own to be *helpful* and starts digging holes where she thinks it will look better to plant flowers. When Gavin comes over to see how she is doing, he is very annoyed to see that she changed his mother's plans, and yells at her to stop. "I was only trying to *help*!" Paige snaps back.
>
> After they both take a few minutes to calm down, they are able to discuss what happened. Gavin explains that it did not work that she made changes in the plans without discussing them. Paige realizes she was being excessively *helpful* and did not think about the consequences of her actions.

In this story, Paige knows the basic dance step of how to be *helpful*. However, she causes a problem when she misuses the quality. If Paige practices *moderation* along with her misuse of this quality, it will ensure that she is not trying to be excessively *helpful*, and that people want and need her *help* before she begins to act.

There are rewards to achieving *moderation* in practicing a quality. Author Linda Kavelin Popov says in *A Pace of Grace*, "When you relax into the virtues of moderation, peacefulness, and contentment, you will find that you no longer digress into scattered, anxious multitasking. Thus, the energy you spend working on whatever task is before you will be far more purposeful and focused."[12]

~ *Questions for Reflection* ~

1. When have I caused harm by practicing a character quality excessively?
2. What can I do to prevent this excessive practice from happening again?
3. Which qualities am I most likely to practice excessively?

Other Helper Qualities and Misuses

Using other qualities in addition to *moderation* as "*helper*" qualities" assists you to adjust your misuse of a character *strength* and make it more effective instead. For instance, in the story above, Paige could have practiced the *helper* qualities of *respect* and *courtesy* and talked through her actions with Gavin before doing them. When misusing *flexibility*, you can practice the quality of *purposefulness* as a *helper* quality. Note, however, that if *purposefulness* is not yet a *strength*, you may need to learn more about it before it can be an effective *helper* quality for you. Gaining knowledge about the correct practice of the qualities is vital. If you try to apply qualities such as *mercy* or *idealism* to *help* with practicing *flexibility*, it would not work as well as *helping* yourself with *purposefulness*.

Here is another example. If you consider the quality of *contentment*, you can see that practicing it allows you to be calm and to *accept* your life. If you are misusing *contentment*, and therefore you are excessively *content* to the point where you are passive about your life, you can draw on *assertiveness*, *purposefulness*, or *responsibility* to *help* you practice *contentment* more effectively. Consider this story:

> Jeremiah, a senior at the local college, adamantly disagrees with how one of his new professors runs the class. Jeremiah misuses *assertiveness* by speaking up loudly in class, criticizing his professor in front of the other students. He says that there should not be daily quizzes, and there should be formal study groups to help students improve their grades. He knows his fellow students are frustrated as well, and he wants to be *assertive* on behalf of both them and himself.
>
> Jeremiah often leaves class feeling unhappy after arguing with the professor in the middle of class. Jeremiah's grades are going down in this course, but he is very sure he is right about his ideas. However, he just does not know how to get his message across effectively. Every time he thinks he is making progress at being calm in class, he *assertively* speaks out instead. He decides that maybe his close friend Sarah can *help* him with ideas.

One evening as Jeremiah and Sarah enjoy dessert at the college cafeteria, he shares his concerns about his situation. Sarah *helps* him to see that he is causing harm by being excessively *assertive*, when what he really wants to do is *encourage* the professor to do things differently. Jeremiah realizes, as they talk the situation through, that he has been making the situation worse with his rude comments and behaviors. He also begins to understand that he has not been fair or *respectful* to his professor, who is new to the college, and who is probably doing his best under the circumstances.

Together Sarah and Jeremiah work through how he can practice *moderation* and other qualities to adjust his practice of *assertiveness*. They decide his professor may listen to his suggestions if he *assertively* requests a private meeting with him instead of criticizing him in class. Jeremiah can practice *respect, tactfulness,* and *courtesy* in both this private meeting and in the classroom. He can be *responsible* for his behavior and apologize for disrupting the class. He also realizes that he can support the professor in being successful at the college by being *friendly*.

You will empower character growth in yourself by understanding the application of this concept of misuse in your life, and you will benefit from being able to spot character quality misuses in a partner as well. As you and a partner *help* each other learn how to practice your character qualities more appropriately, you will be able to communicate together in a common language with common understanding about the same words and meanings. This communication skill becomes a priceless advantage to you in a relationship. *Note:* Chapter 14 will cover misuses in a relationship.

ACTIVITY

Together with a friend or a group of friends, do a quick skit (short impromptu drama) of someone misusing a character quality and causing a problem. Then, do a new skit using *helper* qualities so that the person's words and actions are effective instead. Discuss together what you observed and learned.

~ Questions for Reflection ~

1. When have I caused harm by practicing a character quality at the wrong time or place? What was the outcome? How can I prevent a reoccurrence?
2. When have I practiced a quality both excessively and at the wrong time and place at the same time? What was the outcome? How can I prevent a reoccurrence?

WISDOM OF CHARACTER WORK

As you go through the chapters of *Can We Dance?*, you will increase your ability to identify your own personal character quality *strengths*, weak areas to *strengthen*, and misuses. With your increased knowledge, you will be able to make effective choices and take action to address your areas of growth. You will then be fully empowered to identify a partner's *strengths*, areas for growth, and misuses. You will clearly know what to acknowledge and *encourage* in a partner, and where you have cause for concern in a relationship. You can then powerfully choose the course of your life and the direction for a relationship.

✥ *Encouragement* ❧

You may not be used to reflecting on your words and actions and how they affect others as much as *Can We Dance?* asks you to do. It may be tempting for you to glance at the "Questions for Reflection" that are included throughout the book and not actually take the time to reflect on them and answer them, or pass by the "Activities" and only do a few of them. Our hope is that they will greatly assist you to be ready to have the best possible relationship. We *encourage* you to pause and take the time to do thoroughly as many of them as possible.

Date: _____

Worksheet 1.1: Understanding Your Character Choices

This worksheet will assist you to begin the process of understanding the character choices that you have made, and how they have affected your relationships of all kinds. This includes family, friends, partners, and spouses.

Instructions:

A) On the first table below, note a few actions that you have taken within a relationship that had a positive result. Note the effect or outcome of your actions. Then, identify a character quality from the chapter or Part 3 that you practiced in that situation.

B) On the second table on the next page, note your actions that have had a negative result and the outcome in those situations. Then, identify a character quality you could have practiced that would have improved the outcome.

Positive Actions (Higher Nature)

Action	Effect/Outcome	Character Qualities That I Practiced
Example: Gave girlfriend a birthday present	She felt appreciated and happy	Thoughtfulness Courtesy

Negative Actions (Lower Nature)

Action	Effect/Outcome	Character Qualities I Could Have Practiced
Example: Ignored a friend at a party	He would not speak to me for a week	Friendliness

Questions for Reflection:

1. What did I learn about my actions and character from completing the tables?

   _____

   _____

   _____

2. What improved ways do I want to speak and act with a partner in a relationship?

   _____

   _____

   _____

   _____

   _____

Your Part First:
Discovering Your Own Character

Wendy lives on her own in an apartment building in a small city. She works for an airline, checking in passengers as they arrive at the counter with their luggage and tickets. The job is often stressful, as customers frequently become annoyed or upset with dragging their luggage around, flight delays, or security procedures. She does her best most days to stay calm and courteous, but sometimes she does not do as well. After a particularly difficult day when she becomes discourteous with two customers, Wendy sits at home with a cup of tea to assess what happened. She does not want to blame the customers and make excuses for how she behaved with them. Upon reflection, she realizes that she did not take time to eat breakfast, and she forgot to practice patience along with courtesy with the customers.

Before you attempt to dance, you need to warm up, stretch your muscles, and begin assessing your *strength* and stamina. Moreover, it will *help* you to know what types of music and movement appeal to you. You may also wish to do some initial movements or solo-dancing before dancing with a partner. Mastering basic skills that allow you to control both your body and balance will assist you as you learn to dance correctly.

In the same way, it will benefit you to know your own character very well before you consider being in a relationship. Like Wendy, have you ever realized that you could have interacted with someone better? Expanding your self-awareness and self-knowledge is part of the dynamic process of character development. The process begins with knowing what your *purposes* are in life, and then doing an initial *honest* assessment of your character *strengths* and your growth areas. Knowing your purposes *helps* you to choose how to spend your time and energy in the most productive ways. Knowing your *strengths* increases your *confidence* and self-*respect*. Knowing your growth areas gives you insights into when you are disrupting relationships, and, therefore, when it will be wise to *strengthen* a character quality. When a quality becomes more effective, you then have access to building *unity* with someone.

The more you know about your own character, the better you will be able to monitor and understand your choices. This monitoring will *help* you to assess whether the ways you are speaking and acting with others are consistent with your life *purposes*. Your growth occurs as you expand your understanding of character, practice the qualities, and observe your behavior choices and their effect on others.

As you become more knowledgeable about your character qualities, you will increase your ability to share yourself accurately and *honestly* in a relationship. You will also improve your ability to observe and understand a potential partner's character and assess how you interact together. These are foundations of relationship intimacy. Because of the insight that understanding character qualities will provide to you, you will be able to build a relationship in a *sincere* and *honest* way.

YOUR PURPOSES IN LIFE

Part of the context for why you will choose to develop your character is the set of broader *purposes* you have for your life. **Discerning your *purposes* will cause you to clarify what you want to accomplish in your life and why. This understanding of your own purposes will also *help* you to determine later on if a partner's *purposes* are harmonious with yours.**

Depending on your age, interests, health, and more, you can be spending your time on a variety of activities and goals. When you think about your *purpose*, however, think beyond the day-to-day tasks of your life. What gets you *enthusiastic*? When you think about the future, what draws you into action? What do you *care* passionately about? What is most important to you? What do you want to accomplish? As you clarify your answers to these questions, you will begin to see how effectively practicing character qualities will empower you to achieve your goals.

Copyright 2001 by Randy Glasbergen.
www.glasbergen.com

"I found my purpose in life, my misplaced values, and my inner-child! It's a very sophisticated search engine!"

Rick Warren, in his book *The Purpose Driven® Life*, says that what drives many people is guilt, resentment, anger, fear, materialism, and a need for approval. He asserts that these will not *create* a successful life for you or others.[1] Instead, "…make ye a mighty effort, and choose for yourselves a noble goal."[2] Some positive *purposes* in life can include:

- Fulfilling the potentials of my body, mind, heart, and soul
- Developing my character qualities into *strengths* that benefit others
- Handling challenges well and learning from them
- *Loving* and worshiping a *spiritual* Being and sharing *spirituality* with others
- Achieving consistent employment or *excellence* in a career
- Earning money to support my family and myself
- Being *generous* with what I have
- Having a *loving* and friendship-based marriage
- Being a good parent
- *Creating* a *strong, unified* family
- Being of *service* to others
- Making the world a better place and bringing people together in *unity*

Perhaps these *purposes* will be meaningful to you, or you may have very different ones. What is important is that you are clear on what your *purposes* are, and why they are important to you.

ACTIVITY

Write a statement of your current *purposes* in life. Consider including ones that give you direction and goals in life. What do you consider as "success" in life? What are your roles? What is important? Share what you write with a close friend or family member, and then edit it based on any valuable feedback they give to you. Put the statement somewhere visible where you will see it regularly, and remember to act according to it. After a few days or weeks, reassess whether these are *truly* your *purposes*, and edit the statement as needed. Do you see these as *purposes* that will be with you for a brief period or for a lifetime?

SELF-OBSERVATION AND ASSESSMENT

Once you understand your purposes, it is important to understand the *strengths*, weaknesses, and misuses of your character qualities. Understanding these involves being able to observe and assess yourself. This observation and assessment means that you *discern* what is working well in your life and what is not. *Discerning* includes understanding what you say and do, and the effect that your words and actions have on others. This is not an opportunity for self-criticism, self-blame, or focusing only on the negative. **It is taking an objective view of yourself. This view *helps* you to determine the facts, so that you know what to appreciate and *respect* about yourself, and what adjustments to make in your life.**

As various situations arise in your life, step back and observe your actions and the effects that they have on others. Then answer *honestly* as you ask yourself:

- Are my intentions, words, and actions in harmony?
- What did I do that was effective?
- Which quality did I practice well?
- Where did I misstep?
- Did I not practice a character quality that would have made a difference?
- Did I actually behave ineffectively, or was the other person having a difficult day or struggling with a personal problem, and I was actually effective?
- How could I have spoken or acted differently to elicit a better response from the other person?

Staying balanced with character quality assessment includes remembering to appreciate your *strengths* that benefit others. You may not realize all that is wonderful about yourself and worthy of appreciation. Perhaps you are *trustworthy* with others' money, *loyal* to your friends, or *thankful* for the blessings in your life. Your many positive qualities provide the foundation for building your character further. Each quality you discover that you are already putting to good use is a cause for appreciation. You will see how far you have already come, which will make your goals seem more attainable, and your challenges ahead will seem more easily overcome.

You may find it useful in determining where you could have acted better if you assess whether your words or actions have caused anyone hurt feelings, injury, or insult, much like stepping on someone's toes while dancing. Perhaps a friend was *generous* and shared a special book with you, and you damaged it or did not return it. Maybe you forgot to be *tactful* when giving someone an opinion about new clothing. Negative consequences from your words or actions are significant indicators that you may need to *strengthen* a quality, practice it differently when in similar circumstances, or choose an alternate one to practice.

Negative outcomes are usually obvious. **Any time there is a lack of harmony between you and someone else, and you feel disunity is present, it is a signal to assess whether a useful character quality is absent or**

not being practiced effectively. Dissension or conflict between you and another person can lead to estrangement between the two of you, where you stop having contact or communication. It is important to understand what happened. "The darkness of error is dispelled by the light of truth."[3] You can also pair *helper* qualities with the quality you are struggling with, as discussed in Chapter 1.

Remember, if you do not practice a quality, it becomes weak and may not be available to you when you need it. It is similar to the way a muscle in your body atrophies when it is not used. You may be in a situation that requires *flexibility* and *patience*, which you do not often practice, so you will be unable to behave appropriately. You could also be misusing your qualities and hurting others. Perhaps you are being so *purposeful* that you push your own ideas or plans through without discussing them fully with others. Clearly *discerning* all these aspects of character practice is part of your personal assessment.

When you make mistakes, you will practice such qualities as *honesty, responsibility*, and *sincerity* to assist you with clearing up any problems that occurred. You will also gain insights by assessing how well your efforts worked in resolving these problems. **This process of assessing yourself and handling any problems that result from your words or actions is in many ways one of inner cleansing. Just as you shower or bathe your body, or tidy your home, you can also keep your internal self clean and orderly.** Chapter 3 will assist you with what to do when your actions are harmful.

As you reflect on your thoughts and feelings, assess your actions, and learn from your mistakes, you will see opportunities to act in improved ways. Just as vehicles need regular oil changes and maintenance, so does your character need regular attention. If you fail to recognize the need for vehicle maintenance or follow through with it, the cost of repair will be far greater than if you had done the maintenance regularly. In the same way, you will need to reassess yourself regularly and start fresh each morning with new goals and choices. Over time, you will learn how to practice the qualities in ways that result in smooth interactions between you and your friends, family, coworkers, neighbors, and others. If you are *loving* toward your mother, brother, and cousin each time you interact with one of them, being *loving* will begin to be a *strength*. It is then an effective tool for you to use in a relationship.

What you will begin to notice is that each of your qualities affects your choices, and each choice you make affects your qualities. As you pay attention, you will often see that you practice a quality effectively in some circumstances, but you have difficulty in others. Perhaps you are *courageous* when facing life's challenges, but you are overwhelmed with fear when you have to raise a difficult issue with someone. At times, you are *courteous* toward friends and strangers, but you can be disrespectful and thoughtless with family members.

Okay, this chapter may make you start to feel a bit like an analyst. Take a deep breath and begin to understand just how important it is that you thoroughly know yourself. There are many good reasons to learn self-observation skills. You will be able to:

- Continuously improve yourself, which increases your self-*respect* and your ability to be effective in your choices and actions
- Observe character qualities accurately in others, particularly in a partner
- Tell quite quickly if you are a good match with someone
- Increase your *confidence* and decrease your stress, because you will likely know what happened, why it happened, and what you can do about it

As you increase your *discernment* of your own character, you develop your skill in *discerning* the characters of others. It is important to "…make your ear attentive to wisdom and your mind open to discernment…. You will then understand what is right, just, and equitable—every good course."[4]

Note: Chapter 10 will assist you with learning observation skills to apply with a partner.

~ *Questions for Reflection* ~

Think back over the past few weeks, and then answer the following:
1. What is an example of an action that I took that benefited someone?
2. When did I hurt, injure, or insult someone? How did I feel and respond? What character quality do I want to work on so I do not harm others?

ACTIVITY

Consider and then discuss with someone what character growth has to do with the concept of personal transformation using the quotation below. Then use your insights to create an artistic, dramatic, or musical representation of the concept and share it with someone.

> What is that mystery underlying human life which gives to events and to persons the power of…transformation? If one had never before seen a seed, nor heard of its latent life, how difficult to believe that only the cold earth, the warm sun, the descending showers, and the gardener's care were needed to cause its miraculous transformation into the growing form, the budding beauty, the intoxicating fragrance of the rose![5]

When to Assess Yourself

It is *wise* for your assessment of yourself to be ongoing. This includes paying attention throughout your day as you talk with or work with others. It can also *help* you to take a regular time each day to review your words and actions and see how well they reflected the character qualities. Daily assessment might feel natural to you, or it may seem difficult, so you will benefit from experimenting and determining what timing works best for you. Be cautious about allowing too much time to elapse between your actions and your assessment, however, because you will forget details or may begin to justify any negative actions. "Each one should test his own actions…without comparing himself to somebody else…."[6] Comparing will cause you to shift your focus away from your own *responsibilities*.

When you do an assessment, consider asking yourself these questions:

- How well did I meet my behavior and character goals today (or this week…)?
- When was I effective in practicing character qualities?
- When did my actions cause hurt feelings or some other negative outcome?
- What could I have done better?
- What did I have control over? What could I not control?
- What will I do differently tomorrow?

Your answers will guide you in making new choices going forward.

Challenges with Assessment and Change

You may find that being fully self-aware and assessing yourself is so challenging that you resist it. Even when you are aware that your behavior is causing negative outcomes, you may resist changing. You are used to seeing yourself a certain way, as are others. Assessment can be easy at times, but at other times, it requires *courage, honesty*, and *perseverance*. It takes *humility* to look at yourself *honestly* and to be willing to improve. It also takes *humility* to ask others to *help* you to see yourself better.

Sometimes it may seem easier to make excuses for why you are the way you are or why you do what you

"I'VE GOTTA BE ME . . . BUT I CAN'T HELP THINKING SOMEONE ELSE WOULD BE MORE QUALIFIED!"

do. Other behavior that can get in the way of seeing the issues that are in your life and changing yourself include:

- Rationalizing or blaming others for your behavior
- Lying to yourself or others about your behavior
- Justifying and defending poor behavior
- Holding on to pride
- Refusing to let others *help* you to see your blind spots
- Denying your need for change and growth
- Holding such high standards of perfection that you give up trying to improve
- Having an overly *strong* desire to please others
- Minimizing the issue and thinking that it was simply a small or isolated offense
- Deciding the other person was too sensitive
- Thinking that no one will ever find out that there is a problem

Do not worry about curbing all of these tendencies at once. You may need to give yourself some time to try out a simple dance step before attempting a complex one. Start out with catching yourself making excuses for something you have done, and take *responsibility* instead. Listen for any blaming words in your daily speech that lay the fault for something you did onto someone else. Practice eliminating these patterns and replacing them with positive words that take *responsibility* for your life instead. The investment of your time in this process will provide benefits to you and others in the short-term and the long-term. You will build valuable relationship skills.

Transforming any avoidance patterns you have, and being *honest* with yourself and others, will increase your self-*respect* and assist you to have a healthy and mature relationship. The more you understand yourself, the easier it will be to share yourself *honestly* with another person. If you resist understanding and developing yourself, a partner can feel uncomfortable or uncertain about being in a relationship with you. As Shakespeare said, "This above all: to thine own self be true, and it must follow as the night the day, thou canst not then be false to any man."[7]

For many reasons, perhaps due to fear of rejection, not being certain who you are, or not liking yourself, you may find that you don a mask and pretend to be someone you are not. This pretence holds you back from self-assessment and change. There is a painful outcome to behaving this way, according to relationship educators Drs. Les and Leslie Parrott:

> If we wear our masks long enough, we may guard against rejection and
> we may even be admired, but we'll never be whole. And that means we'll

never enjoy true intimacy. … When what you do and what you say do not match the person you are inside—when your deepest identity is not revealed to others—you develop an incongruent or fragmented self.[8]

People who wear masks often focus on the impression that they make on others and lack the ability to focus on the other person in a relationship. They can become stuck in a pattern of looking for someone else to make them feel good about themselves. If this pattern applies to you, this process of getting to know your character and developing your qualities is particularly important.

Sometimes when you feel somewhat overwhelmed with the task of assessing yourself, remember that it is fine to take small steps, one at a time. It might also *help* you to remember that you are not a student in school being graded nor an employee going through a performance appraisal to see if you deserve a pay raise. You are an individual practicing self-*respect* through choosing to engage in personal assessment and development. While it is important not to use your assessment to be overly self-critical, neither should you ignore issues. Be *moderate* and choose your focus areas. You will overwhelm yourself if you try to address every character issue or develop every quality at the same time. You have a whole lifetime to develop all of them!

The more you develop your qualities throughout your life, the happier and more harmonious all of your relationships will be. You will know the standard of *excellence* you are striving for, without having unrealistically high expectations of yourself. You will also be able to avoid the trap of being severely judgmental about your failures and criticizing yourself for not being perfect. This balance will also assist you to have reasonable expectations of others around you. Susan M. Campbell in *Beyond the Power Struggle*, says, "As you relax your inflexible expectations of yourself, you tend also to relax your expectations of others."[9] This relaxation into *flexibility* then actually *helps* you strive to be your best.

Assessing yourself is simply an opportunity to look at how you are doing compared to an ideal standard. The goal is to be *detached* enough to *discern* a realistic perspective of yourself that will support you in striving for character *excellence*.

~ Question for Reflection ~

What may be getting in the way of my ability to assess myself effectively?

ACTIVITY

Complete **Worksheet 2.1: Assessing Your Character Qualities** to begin an initial assessment of yourself. It will *help* you throughout the rest of the book if you pause and begin completing it now. Completing the worksheet may be a quick activity, or it may take you some time, depending on how well you already know yourself.

If you find you are struggling, then you may wish to mark the page, and keep coming back to work on it gradually. You may want to reward yourself after completing portions of the assessment with a fun activity, exercise, or something relaxing. You can then return to the worksheet and add to it as your knowledge, observation, and assessment skills increase.

Note: As you go through this worksheet, you may become aware of unresolved matters from your past. You will address these in Chapter 3, so noting them now will *help* you with that activity.

SOME ASSESSMENT SKILLS

Some of your assessment will be during quiet and meditative time. Other times, it will be a more active process involving others. Below are some actions you can take that may assist you in your assessment.

Write in a Journal or Diary

Sometimes it is easy for you to keep track in your head of how you are doing, both your positive actions and where you want to improve. However, often you can gain insights and be more systematic with your assessment if you write it down. Writing can focus your attention and *help* you to clarify what is happening in your life, your feelings, and the reactions you have. You can plan and set goals for how you will respond to a situation as part of the process as well. Then, you can record the progress you make toward your goals. Be specific about what actions and words particularly show that you are improving.

You may find it most useful if you write in a journal daily. Some people prefer to write in one weekly, however, and others only when there is something that they are struggling to understand. Experiment with what works best for you.

ACTIVITIES

1. *Create* a journal to record your ongoing character self-assessment and observations, especially focusing on your progress with the four qualities you chose to work on in Worksheet 2.1. Decorating your journal can be a *creative* break from all the thinking and writing! You may also find it works for you to have a sketchbook, drawing tools, and coloring materials to express your thoughts and feelings visually instead of in words.

2. Set a goal to write in your journal every day for a week. At the end of the week, assess whether this frequency benefited you. If not, set a new goal to try a different frequency. After some time has passed, assess its usefulness. Keep experimenting until you discover what works best for you.

Reflect, Read, and Meditate

Even if you have little or no experience in reflective practices, it is easy to start. Meditation can mean taking some quiet time alone to think and reflect upon your character *strengths* and growth areas. You can *discern* if there are any relationship matters that need your attention. Perhaps you will go for a walk in a park, take a bike ride, or simply find a quiet corner in your home and sit in a relaxed position. Meditation is a personal activity, so you will find out what method works best for you. Some people do group meditative practices, such as yoga. However, even when you are in a group situation, your reflection is turned inward.

Once you are in a location that works for you, then you can breathe deeply and calm your thoughts and emotions. Choose what you want to focus on and learn from your reflection. Perhaps you want to see your character *strengths* more clearly. Maybe you need to acknowledge an issue that requires your attention. By focusing and *accepting* your purpose for the meditation, you open yourself to *creative* insights and solutions. It is good to read something *spiritual* or inspirational that relates to your focus area to inspire your *creativity*. You can also pose questions to your inner self and to God and be open to noticing answers or insights that come to you either immediately or in the hours or days after meditating or praying. [See the next section for more on prayer.] Try to be willing to address even the most difficult issues with *honesty* and *perseverance*.

Reflection will *help* you to gain insights into what you did well, where you went wrong, what you could have done differently, and what you will do in the future. You can use this time to determine what your attitude and choices will be in response to a problem or a disunity you are experiencing with someone that is troubling you. You can make a plan about the best way to interact with others. Meditation can bring you to a place of *peace* and serenity and increase your sense of *spirituality* and *contentment*.

Perhaps your mistake, or a situation you have created, occurred because you were operating on autopilot and not paying attention. Maybe you were focusing on your own needs or problems and not paying attention to how you were affecting those around you or noticing their needs. You may have felt so stressed that you forgot to practice your best character qualities and slipped into acting impatient, inflexible, or insincere. After reflecting on your actions, you can make a plan to act differently and put it into action.

Pray

Praying commonly means turning your mind, heart, and soul toward and developing a connection with a loving Creator and having a verbal or silent conversation. Prayer gives you the opportunity to state clearly what is happening in your life, and request assistance or guidance for yourself and others. This process *helps* you to work through understanding whatever is on your own mind or that is burdening your heart and soul as well. You may address issues in your prayers that you are uncomfortable raising with another person. You can seek to understand your attitudes and actions and the reasons behind them more clearly.

You can use your own words or the prayers of your faith. You can choose to pray alone, and at other times, you might ask someone or a group to pray aloud with you or privately for you. Forms of prayer vary among different cultures and faiths, sometimes including music, drumming, prayer beads, and more. Use whatever form works best for you and *respects* others.

Prayer is often an expression of *love* in your heart for the Creator and *thankfulness* for blessings. In its essence, prayer is a mysterious and mystical process. Answers to prayers can come in many ways. After you pray, the answer to a problem that has been troubling you may become clear to you. You can observe how circumstances change and draw conclusions. You can proceed to take the actions that came to your mind as you prayed, and then observe either positive or negative outcomes and be guided by those. You can receive an inner sense of *peacefulness* and serenity about a choice or decision.

The answer to a prayer can be "no," "yes," "wait," or something different. It can be presented to you days, weeks, months, or years later, when you forgot you prayed for it or when you least expect it. *Discerning* an answer often requires action. As you act on thoughts and decisions reached through prayer, the answers will begin to appear. The pace at which the answers appear, however, is usually out of your control, so the process also requires *patience*.

UNDERSTAND YOUR INNER VOICE

As you engage in reflection, you increase your ability to hear your internal dialogue or use your intuition to understand your actions and others' reactions. Are you aware of the conversation, commentary, judgments, and more that go on constantly in your thoughts? **Internally, you combine all your experiences and learning into inner *wisdom* in order to assess what you and others are doing.** In other words, everything that happens around you goes through this filter you have developed from your past. Sometimes your inner voice is just chatter, and you tune it out. At other times, it is important to pay close attention so that it *helps* inform you well and guides your actions.

For example, your inner voice can warn you before you take a potentially harmful action or say inappropriate words. If you do not catch yourself ahead of time, then your inner voice can indicate there is now a problem. Someone's feelings were hurt or they became upset. Your inner voice then becomes your conscience. It assists you to *discern* that something you did was not right or not your best compared to what you have learned is right.

Your inner voice can also signal that there is some kind of imbalance or disunity between you and another person. Sensing this imbalance is similar to pausing to feel where physical pain is located in your body and determining what is causing it. When you tune your inner voice into your higher nature and toward the character qualities, it *helps* you to create what is best for you and guides your actions in a positive direction. Your inner voice can provide guidance and *encouragement* for you to speak and act in positive ways and repeat your successes.

Your inner voice develops its standards based on whatever you have been taught and learned about behavior throughout your life. This input generally comes from parents, teachers, authority figures, and religious guidance. It is also affected by the choices you make and what you learn from them. When you are conscious that your inner voice is raising a concern, you have a number of steps to take in response. You begin with finding out what is going on and why. You take a close look at yourself and the situation to see if your negative words or actions are hurting only yourself, or if they are affecting others as well. Next, accept *responsibility* for your actions and resolve to do better the next time a situation arises. Apologize, or make amends—even if you think you are the only one being hurt. Taking steps to resolve an issue can be very difficult, but when you try to avoid doing so, your inner voice will keep sending you reminders.

There is a caution in how much you pay attention to these reminders, because your inner voice can be more tuned into your lower nature and create negative outcomes. It can urge you to take actions that harm yourself or others, such as lie, cheat, or steal. Perhaps

I've been trying to understand my inner voice, but I think it's speaking another language.

someone from your past taught you that this negative behavior was okay, so your inner voice then misleads you in this direction. Obviously, you cannot use your past as an excuse to justify poor behavior.

There is another way that your inner voice can mislead you. You may have had a rigid upbringing, with excessive rules and strict behaviors. If so, your inner voice might dump guilt on you even when you have done something minor or nothing wrong at all. You might struggle with perfectionism as a result. This trap actually works against your personal growth. "Authentic spirituality means giving up perfectionism for the rigorous process of developing ourselves one thought, one act, one day at a time."[10] If your inner voice is misleading you, it will take concentrated effort and practice to develop the skill of assessing how much validity to place on your internal signals. You need to be fair, *kind*, and *compassionate* to yourself as well as to others. Yes, the character qualities apply to how you treat yourself, too!

Remember that the character qualities are the *true* standard criteria, or measurement to use for your behavior. They are a gauge for you to look at to determine whether you are doing the right thing or the wrong thing, doing enough or too much, or whether your words or actions are justified and defensible or unjustified and inexcusable. They are like a map that can tell you where you have been, where you are presently, and where you wish to be in the future. They are an unambiguous measure against which you can compare yourself, rather than comparing yourself to other people. They will prevent you from saying that you are better than someone else is, or that you are at least not as bad as someone else is.

It is *wise* for you to undertake self-examination but to avoid negative self-talk that weighs you down with destructive criticism. This criticism looks like inner comments such as "I am so stupid!" or "Why don't I ever do anything right?!" If you are very self-critical—which is essentially training yourself to always see what is wrong with you—you are more likely to be critical of a partner or others around you. In this case, you are also less likely to notice and accentuate your *strengths* and those of a partner. If negativity is an issue for you, it may be useful for you to study the qualities of *humility*, *mercy*, and *joyfulness* in Part 3.

ACTIVITY

Make a list in your journal of all the issues in your life about which you are being negative or self-critical. Assess which ones you can turn into positive situations by taking action, and which ones are either minor or too difficult to deal with at present. Make goals to address what you can, and then proceed to carry them out. Make a list of all of the constructive actions you take and their positive outcomes. When you are slipping into negative thinking, re-visit the list of positive actions to increase your self-*respect*. When you are ready, then address the more difficult issues.

Asking Questions

Often after you interact with others, you will quickly spot when you could have practiced a quality in a better way. Sometimes, however, you know there is an issue, but you might feel a bit stuck in figuring out just what is not working for you. It may then be *helpful* to ask yourself some direct and in-depth questions related to whatever quality seems to be appropriate. If you have a *trusted* friend or relative willing to assist you in understanding yourself, you can also have them ask you questions and discuss the situation together. As an example, below is a potential set of questions you can ask yourself about the quality of *truthfulness*, which often requires the *helper* qualities of *tactfulness*, *kindness*, *courage*, and *confidence*.

- When communicating, am I *careful* to stick to the facts and not make up details?
- Do I withhold important information or leave out key details because they might affect how others view me?
- Do I justify lying under some circumstances? When? Why?
- Do I avoid using *truthful* words to deliberately cause harm, injury, or insult to others?
- When I am *truthful*, do I sometimes forget to be *tactful* as well and hurt others' feelings?
- Do I take the time to search for the *truth* when solving problems, instead of rushing to an easy solution?

Here is another example of questions to ask yourself during self-assessment, this time about *friendliness*, which also has the *helper* qualities of *courage* and *confidence*:

- Have I been in a situation where I was *friendly* to only a few people and ignored or stayed away from anyone I did not know?
- Did I remember to practice *courage* and *confidence* in reaching out to someone new?

- Do I sometimes practice my *friendliness* in a self-centered way to impress someone?
- Am I sensitive about including everyone?
- Do I pretend to be *friendly* in order to gain something from someone else?

The key is to step back and put yourself in the role of being an independent observer of your life and actions. This action takes *courage* and *detachment*. When you are too close to a situation, you can only see a small portion of it. When you are close to a mountain, you might only see a handful of rocks and a few trees. When you are a mile away, you can see all of it.

ACTIVITY

Choose one of the four qualities you chose to develop on **Worksheet 2.1**. Write down a list of self-assessment questions about the quality—like the ones in this section. If this is useful, then do the same activity for the remaining three qualities.

Receiving and Responding to Feedback

Often throughout your life, you will receive positive and sincere feedback in the form of compliments and words of appreciation from others. **This feedback lets you know what qualities others see in you as *strengths*.** When you hear words from people that acknowledge your best actions, you have choices for how to respond. *Humility* will guide you to not respond with your ego and become arrogant. However, *courtesy* and *respect* for the speaker, and *respect* for your own higher nature, will stop you from discounting what someone says and *accept* it with *thankfulness*.

"Here! Do me!"

Sometimes understanding your character requires that you have the ability to listen and take seriously some negative feedback you receive from another person. See how this occurs for Jacques:

Jacques is charming and outgoing with the coworkers in his office. He also regularly invites his friends over for meals at his home. However, when he is shopping, he can be superior, demanding, and unfriendly to sales clerks. He believes these people are not worth his time, and as such, they are not important enough for him to be *friendly* toward them. After all, his interactions with them are so brief.

After shopping one day, Jacques' behavior gets to the point that a clerk *assertively* requests he stop being so rude to her. He is initially annoyed and defensive, but this direct feedback prompts Jacques to step back and look at his behavior. He spends a few days thinking through the way he has habitually behaved in stores, and he begins to realize his attitude and actions have actually hurt others. He makes the choice to change himself. For a few weeks, he goes into a variety of stores and practices being *friendlier*. After working on *friendliness* for a few weeks, he meets Yvette at a party. As they talk, he discovers that she is a sales clerk in a department store. He instinctively begins to withdraw from her, but stops himself and stays *friendly* instead. They like each other and agree to stay in touch.

One day, Jacques decides to stop by the store where Yvette works and invite her to lunch. He stands back and watches as customers interact with her. He sees Yvette being *friendly* to them, and they smile and thank her for her assistance. Jacques realizes that if he had not worked on this area of his character, he might have backed off from getting to know Yvette. Now it is possible for them to develop a relationship.

Jacques was able to make progress in this situation because he did not take offense when the clerk gave him feedback. Instead, he chose to use it to prompt reflection and a change in his behavior. This way of responding to others' feedback is not easy to achieve. It will take practice to stop yourself from reacting and becoming defensive, or from attacking the person who makes comments to you. *Detachment* will *help* you to stop your reaction and take the necessary time to evaluate the feedback. With time and reflection, you will be able to *discern* whether the feedback contains *truth* and is useful for you in changing your words or actions. In Guinea they say, "Those who refuse to drink from the well of knowledge will die of thirst in the desert of ignorance."[11]

At times, it may be useful to ask someone for *assertive* and *caring* input about what you are doing. You can approach your parents, friends who know you well, a professor, or an employer. You can also ask for assistance from a professional counselor, therapist, relationship coach, *spiritual* mentor or advisor, or others skilled in giving objective input and guidance. Ensure the people you ask are *trustworthy* and that you are using *wisdom* in raising the subject with the person. Let them know why you are asking them for input, and why you will value it from them. It may work well for you to choose someone to ask for comments who is also very involved in character growth, as they will participate more freely and be less judgmental.

When you approach someone to ask for input, you will use the words or questions that work for you. Possibilities include, "Can you *honestly* share with me your perspective on how I am acting in (whatever the situation is)?" or "How do you think I am doing at developing (the name of a specific character quality)?"

If you are *sincerely* looking for input that will assist your character choices, you are likely to receive useful information that keeps you moving forward. Ask only people who will give you *honest* answers, however, and will not just tell you what they think you want to hear. Ask them to share both what they see you are doing well and where you can improve. Once you receive their feedback, you can practice *discernment* to assess what is useful from it and what is not. You can then take the *helpful* feedback and apply it to grow and change in new and positive directions.

You will also receive feedback at times without asking for it. When this happens, as it did with Jacques in the previous story, how do you respond? You may need to pause and *detach* from any hurt feelings or reactions you have to the person's words. It may *help* you to take a walk, hammer a few nails into a board, punch a pillow, clean your desk or home, exercise, pray, sleep on it, or do whatever supports you in taking time to process the feedback. When you are calm and ready, then you can assess the person's words and learn from what they said. Confucius says, "When you make a mistake, do not be afraid of mending your ways."[12]

It will be difficult at times to view various experiences and input from others as *helpful* for your learning, but it is in your long-term best interest when you can do so. With practice, it will be easier to regard the feedback from someone as a gift that assists your growth.

At times when you make changes, people who are accustomed to your behaving in a certain way may struggle with accepting that you are changing. It will take time for them to *trust* and understand your *commitment* to change. If someone gives you negative feedback while you are growing, assess its validity and *helpfulness*. Be certain that the person is giving you an appropriate message, and they are not simply feeling uncomfortable with you changing. They may be wishing that you would change back to the way you were before, as this is what they are used to.

As you go through the process of assessment and personal change, make sure that you have people who assist and *encourage* you in your efforts. In addition, the more you anticipate, with *humility*, that those around you will support you in changing, the more assistance, affirmation, and confirmation you will receive.

~ Questions for Reflection ~

1. What feedback have I received related to the four qualities that I am choosing to develop?
2. How did I handle the feedback? Do I need to apologize to anyone for my reactions?

ACTIVITY

Contact and express appreciation to someone who gave you useful feedback.

ᶜ Encouragement ᵔ

If you are not accustomed to doing self-assessment, this chapter may have been difficult for you. However, developing the practice of regular self-assessment is vital to your personal growth and relationship success, so your full participation in this process is a major achievement. It will benefit you for your entire life.

Date: _____

Worksheet 2.1: Assessing Your Character Qualities

This worksheet will assist you to understand how effective you are in practicing a wide array of character qualities. As you look at each quality in the list below, visualize situations in your life where you used it, or you could have used it. Make sure to allow yourself the necessary time to think carefully about each quality. This worksheet will provide a foundation for a number of other worksheets in the book.

It will take longer, but this activity is actually most useful if you review the explanations for each quality in Part 3 first (if you have not already done so). You may have a general idea of the meaning of a quality, but you may not be clear on the specifics. Seeing these may open up some deeper understanding and help you to assess yourself with more clarity and accuracy. *Note:* You may also find it useful to refer to the statement of your purposes in life that you created in this chapter to decide which qualities are most helpful to you in accomplishing your purposes.

Instructions:

A) Place a number to the right of each character quality in the "Rating" column (you may wish to use a pencil), using this assessment scale from 1 to 6:
   1 ~ You are very weak at practicing the quality, and your words and actions are resulting in negative outcomes.
   2 ~ You are somewhat ineffective at practicing the quality, and your words and actions result in negative outcomes.
   3 ~ You are familiar with the quality, know quite well how to practice it, but you often struggle to do so effectively.
   4 ~ You are practicing the quality effectively, but not consistently, and your words and actions usually result in positive outcomes.
   5 ~ You are consistently practicing the quality effectively, and your words and actions result in positive outcomes.
   6 ~ You have the quality as a strength, but you frequently misuse it.

   Note: The qualities that are 1s, 2s, or 3s will be good choices for your development plan in Worksheet 3.1. The qualities that are 4s or 5s will be good ones to include on Worksheet 7.2 where you list what you bring to a relationship. The qualities that are 6s will be addressed in Worksheet 14.1. As you go through this worksheet, you may also become aware of unresolved issues from your past. You will address these in Chapter 3, so making a note of them will help you with that activity.

B) After you have done an initial assessment, it may be useful to share your findings with someone who knows you very well, such as a close friend or relative, which will give you further insights.

C) Answer the questions below the list of qualities, and finish marking the qualities as instructed next to the questions.

✓ or ✗	Character Quality	Rating	✓ or ✗	Character Quality	Rating
	Acceptance			Idealism	
	Assertiveness			Integrity	
	Beauty			Joyfulness	
	Caring			Justice	
	Chastity			Kindness	
	Commitment			Love	
	Compassion			Loyalty	
	Confidence			Mercy	
	Contentment			Moderation	
	Cooperation			Patience	
	Courage			Peacefulness	
	Courtesy			Perseverance	
	Creativity			Purity	
	Detachment			Purposefulness	
	Discernment			Respect	
	Encouragement			Responsibility	
	Enthusiasm			Self-Discipline	
	Equality			Service	
	Excellence			Sincerity	
	Faithfulness			Spirituality	
	Flexibility			Strength	
	Forgiveness			Tactfulness	
	Friendliness			Thankfulness	
	Generosity			Thoughtfulness	
	Gentleness			Trustworthiness	
	Helpfulness			Truthfulness	
	Honesty			Unity	
	Humility			Wisdom	

Questions for Reflection:

1. Which qualities are clearly my strengths? Put a check mark (✓) next to them on the worksheet.
2. Which of my qualities are too weak to use effectively in a relationship? Put an ✗ next to them.
3. Which four qualities do I now want to focus on developing? Circle them. *Note:* You will use these four qualities to complete Worksheet 3.1 in the next chapter, and you will refer back to them throughout the book.

Stepping Forward: Developing Your Character

Pierce runs three miles over roads and hills most mornings by himself. One day, his younger sister, Annette, who runs in the evenings, asks Pierce if she can begin exercising with him. He blurts out, "No way!" and tells her she is too much of a grouch in the mornings to be good company. As Pierce runs alone the next morning, he thinks over his conversation with his sister and how hurt and unhappy she looked at his response. He begins to regret that he was so rude. They are not as close as they used to be, and he could have been friendlier to her. Maybe running together would give them an opportunity to rebuild their relationship. Pierce calls Annette, apologizes, and invites her to run with him the next day. She is willing to forgive him, and they are able to peacefully spend time together.

At this stage in your dance lessons, you are now beginning to understand your *strengths* and abilities. You have tried out some steps with others, so you are gaining insights into where you need further instruction, practice, and skill development. You are learning through action with the *help* of a good teacher or coach, who is willing to give you feedback and *encourage* you forward into more difficult steps and dances.

Practicing dance steps over and over again allows you to master them. So it is with your character. Some days you might think it would be nice if your self-development were complete—no more getting impatient, fearful, or rude. However, it is more realistic to expect that your life will be a process of continuous improvement.

Remember that knowing and developing your character is essential as preparation for a relationship. Gradually you will become more consistent and effective with each good choice you make. A key to remember is that even small changes can have a significant effect on you and your interactions with others.

Sometimes change is difficult, and progress takes willingness and *perseverance*. Often, you realize you need to change to respond to difficulties or after you have made poor choices. Ongoing assessment, *encouragement* from people you *trust* and *love*, apologizing, practicing *forgiveness*, and making amends are all aspects of personal development. Sometimes you also benefit from remembering to lighten up and not take yourself so seriously. Often the best way to handle mistakes is with a sense of humor.

Even when you become an *excellent* dancer, and you have found a consistent partner, it *helps* if you go dancing from time to time so you stay familiar with the steps. If you do not keep your skills sharp, you may begin to think that you need a better partner, when really you just need to improve your own dancing. In the same way, developing your character requires awareness and regular practice, which in turn supports a relationship.

MAKING THE CHOICE TO CHANGE

Often you may know you need to change something about yourself and want to do it, but you are unsure how to accomplish it. You may even see it as something that is difficult or impossible to do. Actually, anyone can change their behavior or replace a bad habit with a good one with consistent effort and *perseverance*.

Before you are in a relationship, it is important to focus on your own development, so you are ready to be an *excellent* partner. Once you are in a relationship, then you can involve your partner in supporting your development efforts.

Small, Consistent Steps

When you think about changing yourself, you may be afraid that you will fail, that others will ridicule you, or that you will appear foolish. You may also spend your energy saying to yourself and others that you cannot change. It is important to acknowledge your fears and overcome your resistance, both of which are roadblocks in the way of your progress. It will take *courage* to make changes in spite of them. The key is being willing to take action and then stepping forward into the process.

Sometimes you have simple and minor adjustments to make in how you interact with others. Are you familiar with the Butterfly Effect? Meteorologist Edward Lorenz discovered that small changes have profound effects on complex systems like weather. He speaks of the potential for a butterfly flapping its wings in one country to cause a tornado in another one. Therapist and author Michelle Weiner-Davis describes the connection of the Butterfly Effect to relationships: **If you make even small personal changes, they can significantly affect the quality of a relationship and a partner's behavior in response over time.**[1] If you then make larger and more consistent changes, the effect will be even greater.

For instance, have you ever noticed that when you *courteously* invite someone to take your seat on a bus or train, or let someone in ahead of you in a line, they and others are more willing to do the same? You have probably also seen that if you offer a *friendly* smile to someone, that person is more likely to smile at the next person they encounter. Mother Teresa said, "Peace begins with a smile."[2]

Your character assessment from Chapter 2 now gives you information about what you may wish to change. Making changes now hinges upon your choice to make improvements. Consider how this process works for Jenita:

> Jenita rapidly writes in her journal about the incident with her manager earlier in the day. "I completely lost my *patience* and was rude to Malcolm when he wanted me to do the weekly report in a different way," she writes. Resting her pen on the notebook, she pauses to reflect about what happened. She realizes that forgetting to set her alarm clock made her hurry, skip breakfast, and arrive late at work. She understands this one small mistake resulted in her struggling with *patience* the entire day. She picks up her pen and begins writing about what she can do and say to let her manager know she regrets her behavior.
>
> Jenita then decides to step back and look more broadly at other areas of her life where *patience* has been a problem. She starts to notice a pattern of conflicts that happen when she rigidly insists that something should be done her way. When she does this, she also becomes impatient with others. She then realizes that this pattern was also a factor with her manager. Jenita's assessment and insights *help* her to identify that practicing the quality of *flexibility* will assist her to be more *patient* with people. She decides to pair these two qualities together in her work relationships for the coming week. She realizes it is also important to put a note next to her bed that reminds her to set the alarm clock. This action will prevent her from getting up late again.

Jenita is making a choice to change, and she has a plan in place to begin the process. She will succeed as she takes action to accomplish the plan, reassesses her progress, and *perseveres* until she becomes consistent with being *flexible* and *patient*.

Some changes will take more time, because you are "unlearning" a habit at the same time as learning a new one. Making the choice to change requires a willing heart, conscious effort, and concentration. The younger you are, the easier it will likely be to make a change, but personal growth happens throughout your lifetime.

~ Questions for Reflection ~

1. When I think about making changes in myself, how do I feel or react?
2. What can be the positive outcomes from changing?

ACTIVITIES

1. Complete **Worksheet 3.1: Character Development Plan** to set goals to improve the four qualities you chose to work on when you completed Worksheet 2.1.

2. Put the four qualities for growth you selected from Worksheet 2.1 and used for Worksheet 3.1 onto small pieces of thick paper or cardboard. Place them in a small bowl or bag. Each morning, pick one to focus on practicing that day. At the end of the day, assess your words and actions related to the quality. When you are in a relationship, you can *encourage* your partner to choose a quality to practice for the day as well. If you see or talk to each other at the end of the day, you can then discuss how your practices of the qualities went. Any time you identify another quality you want to focus on, you can add it to your container.

Perseverance Is Required

Learning to dance requires *perseverance*. It can take many lessons and extensive practice to learn the most difficult moves. With your own personal development, even when a behavior or character issue is long-standing, you can also make progress if you *persevere*. "Spiritual growth is not automatic. It takes an intentional commitment. You must *want* to grow, *decide* to grow, *make an effort* to grow, and *persist* in growing."[3]

Dan Popov, Ph.D., of the WellSpring International Educational Foundation, talks about the importance of *commitment* and change as a part of planning for a happy and productive life. He says:

> Your choices matter, so make a commitment and choose a new path, even if you are uncertain about where it will lead you. Be aware—if the path is familiar, it is not a new one. Only if you give your effort your full

100 percent commitment, will you be able to assess its value effectively later on. Involve others by telling them of your commitment and asking for their assistance—show them how it can benefit both of you. Call on the spiritual power of prayer and allow yourself to be guided forward.

Your commitment and choice to take a new path in your life may result in a period of turmoil; it will call for conscious awareness and regular effort before it begins to feel right. At the first difficulty along the path, you may be tempted to retreat to a more familiar path, but persevere, be determined, and hold your commitment with integrity. Guidance, confirmation, and support come when you are in action. Observe what is happening and be honest with yourself. Growth is positive change. Be patient, flexible, and graceful—change will come—little by little, day by day.[4]

Some days you will notice that you are making more progress than on others. Sometimes you will even feel as if you are going backward, but that is all normal in the process of change. It will often happen that you take two steps forward and one back in the dance of making changes.

If you are struggling with the concept of changing or developing your character, you can try making other smaller changes instead to *help* you gain *confidence*. This way you can also experience *perseverance* and learn about your adaptability and *flexibility*. One possibility you can consider is making a change in your daily routine or schedule. Perhaps you will change the time you eat breakfast, the order in which you do two activities, add in an exercise program, or something similar. See how long it takes until the new pattern feels "normal" and routine.

ACTIVITIES

1. Make one small change in your environment, and see how long it takes you to adjust to it. Changes could include moving a piece of furniture, changing a picture on the wall, or moving your socks to a different drawer. Making this change will *help* you to adjust your expectations and understand that change in a partner or yourself will take some time.

2. Identify a habit that you want to change. Set up a supportive structure to *help* you to be successful, and *persevere* for a few weeks. This structure can include marking goals in a planner, talking to someone regularly who hold you accountable for your progress and *encourages* you, planning weekly rewards, and more. This activity is an opportunity to be *creative*. Assess your progress throughout the process.

SUCCESS IN CHANGING

So, what *helps* you to improve your dance technique? What will *help* you to be successful in developing your character? The sections that follow will provide you with some supportive steps for taking action to have "high-quality" behavior.

Focus on Your Strengths

Your *confidence* and self-*respect* build as you notice what you do well and acknowledge when you are effective at practicing a character quality. **It is also *wise* to practice self-*encouragement* and affirm that you are a person with a body, mind, heart, and soul worthy of *respect*. This practice will assist you with building relationships, as you will be more appreciative and *encouraging* with a partner if you act this way with yourself.** For instance, if your manager at work asks you to try a new and difficult task, you can draw on *courage* as one of your *strengths* to *help* you *accept* and complete the task. If a partner is in a similar situation, or is having difficulty with an issue that you have experience with handling well, it will be easier for you to offer *encouragement* and input.

It is best to choose someone as a partner who is as involved in personal growth as you are. You will find it beneficial if you both have the desire and determination to practice many positive behaviors and character qualities consistently. Involvement in personal growth includes the ability for both of you to listen to what *wisdom* your inner voices offer and to self-correct or adjust after feedback or when experiencing challenges. If a potential partner is not interested in their personal development, and you are involved in this process, the relationship will be challenging and frustrating for you at times. It may also cause the relationship to end.

An image you may find *helpful* in *honoring* your *strengths* is seeing your qualities as gems. Throughout your life, you dig out rough-looking rocks from the mine of your character and clean, cut, and polish them into *beautiful* gems—character *strengths*. These gems are the gifts you then have to contribute in a relationship and to others. As you give these gifts away to others, you will find that these same gifts will be given back to you. You will find that you are "...a mine rich in gems of inestimable value."[5]

Remember to practice *moderation* as you acknowledge your *strengths*. This step is about increasing your self-*respect*, not about building up your ego so you can brag about how good you are. Practicing *humility* will *help* you to maintain balance as you achieve progress. Recognizing, in addition, that your actions are not always the best, *helps* you to see that you and your character are works in progress.

ACTIVITIES

1. Identify four specific precious gems that you think are attractive, such as a diamond, emerald, sapphire, or ruby. You may find it assists you to locate photos of them in a book, magazine, or on the Internet. Look back at Worksheet 2.1, and choose four of the character qualities that are your *strengths*. Match each one of these with a gem. Then as you practice each quality, visualize the beautiful gem that you associate with it. For example, you could associate ruby and *justice* together. Every time you are *just*, fair, or fight for *justice* on behalf of someone else, you will visualize a sparkling red ruby.

2. Think of each of the four qualities that you want to develop (Worksheet 3.1). Then identify four people who each practices one of the qualities effectively. The person can be deceased or still alive, real or fictional, famous or a close friend. Assess what each of them did or are doing that demonstrates the quality you associate with them.

Try New Activities and Experiences

Each day you choose what to do with your time and energy. These choices reflect your priorities—what you believe is most important, such as friends, work, *spiritual* activities, family, education, community *service*, hobbies, home maintenance, entertainment, money, sports, or pets. When you have a partner, they will be on your list as a priority as well. These priorities provide you with many opportunities for personal growth. Take a moment to look back at the statement you wrote of your *purposes* in life (see Chapter 2, page 38) and see if the ways that you use your time and energy reflect them. If not, then you can make adjustments to have them be in alignment.

To carry out changes in your life, you may need to try new activities and experiences, as well as make new friends. These can give you the opportunity to practice new interactions, thereby *strengthening* qualities that may be weak, such as *acceptance, courtesy, generosity*, and *friendliness. Service* to others is one key activity that develops your character. "Sensitivity to the feelings and needs of others and a willing disposition to help and serve are hallmarks of a person committed to the path of spiritual development."[6] Your choices for what kinds of *service* to do will vary widely. You can look to your civic community, neighbors, religious leaders, family, education system, and more for possibilities.

As you make promises to participate in activities, you can practice *commitment*, which indicates to others that you are *trustworthy. Strengthening* your ability to make *commitments* supports relationships, and reduces misunderstandings and serious disagreements. [*Commitment* will be covered in depth in Chapter 5.]

Another way to *strengthen* weak qualities is to develop an awareness of the people you associate with regularly. If you start to notice that someone urges you to behave poorly, or you act differently around them or change yourself inappropriately to be with them, you will be *wise* to spend less time with that person. If you are around someone who is openly unsupportive and critical of your choice to develop yourself, then you may want to reconsider being around the person at all. You can then choose to spend more time with people who set a positive example and *encourage* your development. With *courage* and *self-discipline*, you can practice the qualities you want to develop and learn each time you try.

Note: Chapters 8 and 9 include many activity ideas.

~ Questions for Reflection ~

1. How am I using my time? Am I happy with my choices?
2. What qualities can I *strengthen* specifically through *service* to others?

ACTIVITIES

1. Look at one of the four qualities you are choosing to develop (Worksheet 3.1) and choose a new activity that can support its development. For example, if you want to work on *patience*, you can learn to do needlework and create a small wall hanging, or perhaps restore an old car. If you want to work on *friendliness*, you can plan a social occasion at your home. Try out your chosen activity and assess if it gave you good opportunities to *strengthen* the quality. If it did, consider repeating the activity or something similar. If it did not work well, then try a new activity.

2. Find or design a project that requires you to ask others to *help* you and all of you to work *cooperatively*. Projects can include such activities as building something, doing community *service*, making a quilt, cooking a complex meal for someone, beautifying a piece of property, putting on an event, or many other options. Before you begin the activity, choose the qualities that you want to focus on improving throughout the project. You may choose to share the qualities with your team members, and ask them to assist you with your development process. Invite the others involved in the activity to choose a quality to practice as well. [You may need to show them the list from this book.] At the end of the project, assess what you learned and what personal growth happened. How did your qualities benefit others?

Get Help

Your own *wisdom*, as well as your ability to understand how to handle character quality development, will grow with time and experience. If you want to speed up the improvement process a bit, however, look for guidance from someone who has valuable experience to share. Perhaps they are very skilled at a quality you are developing, and they will be willing to *help* you with some advice, insights, or *encouragement*.

To keep your character qualities *strong* and effective, it *helps* if you associate with people who are *committed* to *excellence,* set a good example for you, and *encourage* you. It may *help* you to remember this thought from Buddha: "A man that stands alone…may be weak and slip back into his old ways. Therefore, stand ye together, assist one another, and strengthen one another's efforts."[7] You do not generally learn about and develop your character in isolation from others; often your best "teachers" are the other people in your life. This includes a partner. As French novelist Henri Stendhal once wrote, "One can acquire everything in solitude except character."[8]

There are many potential sources of assistance when you are working through personal development and troublesome issues. Research and the recommendations of others will guide you to the best resources for you to try and that you can afford. They can include relatives, friends, *spiritual* advisors, teachers, relationship or life coaches, therapists, counselors, or support groups. Various educational opportunities, such as workshops or informal study groups, can be beneficial as well, as you can interact there with others facing similar challenges. You may resist seeking or asking for assistance if you have a *strong* streak of independence (or stubbornness!). In this case, asking for *help* can be a great opportunity to practice the qualities of *acceptance* and *humility*. Try not to view asking for *help* as a sign of weakness, as doing so takes *courage* and *wisdom*, and it will assist you to build *strength*. Reaching out to others also gives them the opportunity to practice qualities such as *helpfulness* and *compassion*.

Note: If you have an active addiction, identify the supportive steps that assist you in managing your life to minimize harm to yourself and others. For addiction to substances such as alcohol, drugs, or food (eating disorders), self-management may include involvement in a 12-Step support group. Someone struggling with Internet pornography might add electronic controls to the computer to restrict access to certain sites, and they would be *wise* to also see a therapist specializing in sex-related matters. An excessive shopper may need to limit the amount of money they carry or credit cards they use.

ACTIVITY
Identify a person in your life who is willing to *commit* to being a listening partner for you, and request that they assist you with your work on your four specific qualities (Worksheet 3.1). Make promises to that person about the actions you are going to take. Agree on how often you will speak to each other.

Handle Difficulties

One way your character develops is through facing, handling, and growing from the difficulties and crises that occur in everyone's life. In fact, a crisis can often transform someone's life in dramatic ways. **It will assist you in your character growth if you take advantage of problems and treat them as valuable learning experiences.** For instance, if you face a difficult decision about what to do with a family problem, you can practice character qualities to solve it, and *strengthen* your ability to practice them in the process. If you or someone close to you has an accident or injury, it becomes an opportunity to practice qualities such as *patience*, *compassion*, or *courage*. Illnesses can challenge you or a relationship, as can addictions. Both conditions will draw on your character *strengths* and invite you to engage in personal growth.

If there has been a problem between you and another person, identify which character quality will be particularly useful in resolving the situation. Spend time visualizing what it might be like to interact with someone while practicing that quality effectively. Affirm internally that you have the ability to proceed in a positive way. Then consciously practice the quality along with your words and actions.

Whatever the challenge, you can use it to *strengthen* your maturity and your *spirituality*. Difficulties can remind you to practice *thankfulness* for the blessings you do have and turn to *spiritual* sources for assistance. Relying on prayer can focus you outwardly on a source for comfort instead of internally on the problem. Sometimes you may lapse into denial, try to escape from problems, or blame others instead. Here is a perspective on behaving in a different way from author Joan Barstow Hernández:

> In contrast, the spiritually mature person faces whatever problems arise with relative calm and decision. He recognizes and acknowledges whatever faults he may have committed which have contributed to the problem and accepts and forgives the errors made by others. He doesn't get bogged down in talking about who caused the problem or waste energy defending himself. He concentrates on searching for a good solution, using prayer for

divine guidance, meditation, and consultation with others. Then he willingly cooperates in carrying out the actions necessary to apply the solution.[9]

You may believe that problems are negative occurrences to avoid, but they are actually learning experiences. "Men who suffer not, attain no perfection. The plant most pruned by the gardeners is that one which, when the summer comes, will have the most beautiful blossoms and the most abundant fruit."[10] Challenges give you opportunities to grow and develop. For every crisis, it is possible to have a personal victory through handling it and becoming *stronger* for the experience.

ACTIVITY

Create a computer screensaver or another visual object to remind you of a quality. When you are going through a difficult time, use what you *create* to inspire you to *persevere* and learn from the experience. Alternatively or in addition, you may also be able to find a song, poem, or quotation that *encourages* you.

Lighten Up

Humor and laughter will happen naturally, as you go through character growth and make mistakes. They *help* you to stop taking yourself so seriously. If you can find the humor in your efforts or in what happened, you might gain more clarity in spotting what direction to go next. You may be able to assist others to laugh along with you as well. **When you are able to be happy and *joyful*, your heart is lighter and you are able to participate more fully in all of life. The more you practice your character qualities effectively, and the more *love* you feel for others, the easier it is to be in a state of happiness.** Do you remember your higher and lower natures as discussed in Chapter 1? Happiness comes from your higher nature, not your lower one. Your lower nature will have you focusing on negative thoughts about everything that is wrong in your life and with the world.

Detachment from anxiety and *thankfulness* for blessings *help* you to be happy, even when there are challenges in your life. While you may think of *thankfulness* as related to your feelings, it is more than that alone. Even when you do not "feel" *thankful*, you can generate *thankfulness* by specifically identifying what is positive in your life that you are grateful to have. Consider this point of view from author Linda Kavelin Popov:

Without thankfulness people would stay focused on negativity. They would do nothing but whine and complain. They would miss the beauty of life and the power of learning, especially during difficult times. ... No matter how difficult or dark things become, there is always light. There is something to learn in every painful situation. In fact, sometimes when you look back at a really hard test in your life and realize what you learned, that is when you feel the most grateful of all.[11]

You can also increase your happiness by being less self-centered and exploring how to make others happy. Can you practice your *creativity* to surprise and delight someone? Can you think of a way to make someone genuinely laugh? Having a *thankful* and happy approach to life enhances your ability to develop your character qualities.

ACTIVITIES

1. Plan a fun activity and invite friends to join you. If you know that you tend to be too serious or overly concerned with details for something that you plan, ask someone else to plan something fun that you can participate in. You can then consider getting involved in part of the planning to gain experience in planning in a light-hearted way.

2. Make a list of 10 people or aspects of your life that you are *thankful* for, and share it with a partner, friend, or relative. You may find it *helpful* to review this list daily, or whenever you start thinking about the negative aspects of your life. Consider adding graphics or decorating the list and posting it in a visible place in your home as well.

3. At the end of each day for a week, identify something funny that happened during the day. If possible, share the stories with a partner, friend, or relative.

DEVELOPING AFTER POOR CHOICES

Sometimes the need to change becomes obvious after you make a mistake or cause hurt, insult, or injury to someone. There are a number of actions you can take to restore a situation, such as making an apology, making amends, or seeking *forgiveness*. When someone has hurt you, then offering your *forgiveness* to them also *strengthens* your character.

Make Apologies and Amends

When you assessed your character and choices in Worksheets 1.1 and 2.1, you probably identified a few times when you caused harm with your attitude, words, or actions, and you never took action to resolve the matters. You may have broken a promise to a friend, been uncooperative with a coworker, disrespectful to a parent or teacher, unfaithful to a partner, cheated on an exam, lied to someone, or any of a wide range of actions from your lower nature. These are all opportunities to assess your character choices, make apologies, make amends, and set development goals.

Whether you have made one mistake or many, you are still capable of attempting a new and better choice next time. You learn as much, if not more, from your mistakes, failures, and challenges than from your successes. You can choose to learn and *persevere* in your character transformation, determined not to make the same mistake again.

It takes *humility*, *honesty*, and *courage* to listen to your inner voice, admit when you are wrong, and take the necessary actions to address any situations you have caused. Whatever actions you choose in order to make amends, it is important to be *sincere*. You must be able to express an *honest* feeling of regret about what happened and convey a *true* desire to do things differently in the future. Your goal is to restore *integrity* to a situation or relationship through appropriate words and actions.

It may be immediately clear to you what *responsible* and constructive actions you need to take to resolve the situation you caused. If not, you can have a conversation with the person most affected, and together choose a path that restores the situation to a state of *integrity* and *justice*. Obviously, if the issue is that you owe someone money, you will likely have to pay it back. Sometimes, of course, what you owe to a person may involve much more than money. It may require asking them to give you another chance to prove your *loyalty* and *friendship* to them. In essence, the person gives you the opportunity to start over. The key is changing your words and actions, both with the one you harmed and with everyone else, to prevent any recurrence of poor behavior in the future.

There also is a type of wrongdoing that is so severe that it will be best for you to make amends by practicing *detachment* and staying away from the person you harmed. Avoiding contact could be best if you have threatened someone's life or well-being, or if the person is adamant about not associating with you further. At times, however, you may be able to address the situation with the intervention of a legal mediator or counsel, or through a religious leader or religious institution.

Many people in the world belong to 12-Step support group programs, particularly people who are struggling with alcohol or other addiction problems or their family members. These programs include the instruction to make a list of all persons the participant has harmed, and become willing to make amends to them all. Once this step is complete, then part of their recovery program includes making direct amends wherever possible, "except when to do so would injure them or others."[12] This is good advice generally.

ACTIVITY

Make a list of everyone you have harmed where the situation has not been resolved and what specifically you did that you regret. [*Note:* You may have begun to make the list while doing Worksheets 1.1 and 2.1]. This activity may take some time to think about, so simply start a list, and keep coming back to it to add names and situations. Being effective at this activity will require a high level of *honesty* and not making excuses for yourself or blaming others for your actions.

As you are ready, or once you are sure your list is complete, make a plan for addressing the items on the list as appropriate, and then begin taking action. Assess each situation, and determine whether you think it is complete for you. Remember that it is very important to do your best to avoid doing anything that is likely to cause further harm. If the person you have harmed is unreachable or has died, you may find it works to complete the issue through prayer or by writing the person a letter.

Note: This may be a difficult activity to complete, so be *encouraging* and *kind* to yourself, and seek assistance as needed. Keep in mind that the goal is to develop yourself, clean up past mistakes, and move forward, not dwell on your faults or inadequacies.

Request Forgiveness

Apologizing and making amends to solve any problems that you have caused focuses you on you being *responsible* for your actions.

Part of the cause likely included a weak or misused character quality, and it will *help* you to be clear which quality to strengthen or adjust. For a situation to be fully resolved, however, the person you harmed needs to *detach* from the hurt and *forgive* you. The challenge in this is that the response to your request for *forgiveness* is in the hands of the other person. All you can do is request it and then practice *detachment* yourself. **Receiving *forgiveness* from the person you harmed is something you cannot expect, but it is a gift when it occurs.**

You may resist asking for *forgiveness*, even knowing that what you did was wrong. However, *forgiveness* will assist you and the other person to put the incident in the past. Depending on your beliefs, you can begin with asking God to *forgive* you, then *forgive* yourself, and finally go to the one that you offended and ask them to *forgive* you. **Self-forgiveness is a key part of the process. When you hold self-directed anger or criticism inside, it freezes part of your life in the past mentally and emotionally, and it can make you anxious and even physically ill.** Take *responsibility* for yourself and your choices, but do not condemn yourself and punish yourself endlessly.

Once you are ready to request *forgiveness*, it is best to do it in person. Otherwise, a phone call is probably the next best thing. A written request is also possible, and it might *help* you to organize your thoughts before speaking to the person. (Be cautious about putting in writing deeply personal information, if the person you are giving it to has a history of being untrustworthy and could use your written words against you or to cause problems for you.) If appropriate, *trustworthy* family members, teachers, advisors, or *spiritual* leaders may also be able to assist you and the other person to resolve the matter. Whatever method you use, *thoughtfully* choose your words, so that you do not make excuses nor offer self-justifications to minimize your behavior. Be brief, clear, and *sincere*.

It is also *wise* to choose the best time and method to talk to the person, rather than simply taking action in a hurry to make yourself feel better. Your inner discomfort is a definite signal that you need to take action, but the other person may be more open to *forgiving* you and *accepting* your amends if you are *wise* in how you handle the situation. You and the other person may be in a more open and constructive frame of mind if you have both tended to your well-being, such as by eating and being well rested first. You may find it *helpful* to pray separately or together as well. It is also *wise* to set up the environment so that the two of you are not distracted by interruptions from people or ringing telephones.

Forgiveness is an act of _mercy_ that allows healing to happen between you and the other person and a restoration of at least some

unity. However, the outcome from your request for *forgiveness* is never certain. The person you approach may not feel you deserve *forgiveness*, may see it as a burden, *forgive* you even before you ask, do it instantly when you ask, refuse to consider it, or may simply need time to think and pray about it. Often *forgiveness* takes time, and the person you harmed has the right to decide on the timetable, no matter how painful the situation is for you when it is unresolved. Be certain you do not burden the person by trying to make them feel guilty if they do not offer you *forgiveness* right away.

While you need to be prepared to *accept* a rejection of your request for *forgiveness*, if you are truly *sincere* in your request, and you are willing to make amends, hopefully the other person will *forgive* you. Whether the person does, or does not, you can be at *peace* with yourself if you have made your best effort. It is important to have a tranquil conscience, heart, and soul.

ACTIVITY

Create or find a meditative space where you can spend time reflecting about your actions, self-*forgiveness*, and who you want to ask to *forgive* you. Consider playing some music that *helps* you to be *peaceful* and feel inner healing.

Give Forgiveness

In the previous section, you requested *forgiveness* because you had harmed someone. At times, however, you will be the person who was harmed, instead. The same principle applies that *forgiving helps* to bring closure to an issue and assists both people to move forward. However, in this case, the *responsibility* shifts back to you again. What character qualities will *help* you to practice *forgiveness* with another person?

Natalie Jenkins is quoted in *The Power of Commitment* as saying that when someone hurts you, *forgiveness* is "...*giving up your perceived right to get even. It is a strategy for making things right again that does not involve revenge.*"[13] **When someone harms you, you have a choice to hold onto your hurt or to let it go by *forgiving* them. *Forgiveness* is not the same as ignoring the situation or saying that what happened was okay. The initial problem still needs to be addressed—just as you are *responsible* for your own actions, so are others for theirs.**

Forgiveness frees you from holding against the person what they did. Drs. Les and Leslie Parrott say that *forgiving* is choosing to reject "...vengeance, renounce bitterness, break the silence of estrangement, and actually wish the best" for the other person.

They also say, "Forgiveness is not for the faint-hearted. Our sense of justice usually recoils at the thought of this unnatural act. Only the brave forgive."[14] In other words, it takes *courage*.

In a relationship situation, when you refuse to *forgive* your partner, you stay stuck in the past and in the pain. You make it difficult to focus on your partner's best qualities. Your relationship cannot fully move forward. Consider this perspective:

> When you forgive, you need to do more than say the words and mean them. You also have to extend a forgiving, helping hand. To truly forgive, you need to be gracious to your partner. Being kind and generous as well as granting pardon will put you back on the same footing and keep your love strong.[15]

***Forgiveness* is directly connected to a person's sensitivity to *unity*.** The more *committed* you are to maintaining harmony, the more you will not be able to tolerate disunity for any length of time, and instant *forgiveness* becomes possible. This ability to *forgive* instantly is not easy for most people, however, so take the time that you need, but work toward increasing your ability to do it quickly.

It is important to be aware, however, that your *forgiveness* needs to be *sincere* and in *integrity*. It is not *wise* to *forgive* someone automatically just because the situation is difficult, or because you feel unhappy that the other person is regretful. If you say you *forgive* someone, while you are still holding onto considerable anger, sadness, or pain from the incident, the situation will not be resolved. Some inner healing needs to happen first.

Once a situation is resolved, then it is important that you leave it in the past and do not bring it up again. Reminding someone about the situation can indicate that you did not completely *forgive* the first time. Keeping a record of each other's wrongs will harm your relationship. Unless, of course, you want to write down a reminder to avoid bringing up issues from the past!

❧ *Encouragement* ❧

These three initial chapters have significantly expanded your understanding about developing your character—an essential component for preparing for a relationship. You have gained worthwhile insights into new concepts and into yourself. You are doing great work! Think of something you want to do to reward yourself—and do it—you deserve it for all your concentrated effort!

Date: _____

Worksheet 3.1: Character Development Plan

This worksheet will assist you to create a character development plan in preparation for being in a relationship. This plan is laid out as a structured process to get you started. However, developing your qualities is actually an ongoing endeavor that happens as you are ready, and as you interact with others. However, this activity will help you to increase your awareness of your thoughts and actions, and make development of your character qualities a conscious choice.

Instructions:

A) Fill in the form below with your four character quality development goals from Worksheet 2.1. Note why the quality and its development are important to you.

B) To help you progress, write down four specific actions you will take to develop each quality. Select target dates for beginning to work on each of them. Then, mark down dates when you will assess your progress on each action. Note these dates in a calendar or in whatever reminder system works for you.

C) When you are ready to assess your progress, you can talk to others, look over your journal notes, assess your behavior, and meditate and reflect on your words and actions. Think carefully about how people responded to you. Then fill in the Signs of Improvement sections. Note any new actions that you now want to take.

Quality to Develop:		
Why?		
Development Actions:	**Start Date:**	**Assess Date:**
1.		
2.		
3.		
4.		
Signs of Improvement:		
New Actions to Take:		

Quality to Develop:		
Why?		
Development Actions:	**Start Date:**	**Assess Date:**
1.		
2.		
3.		
4.		
Signs of Improvement:		
New Actions to Take:		

Quality to Develop:		
Why?		
Development Actions:	Start Date:	Assess Date:
1.		
2.		
3.		
4.		
Signs of Improvement:		
New Actions to Take:		

Quality to Develop:		
Why?		
Development Actions:	Start Date:	Assess Date:
1.		
2.		
3.		
4.		
Signs of Improvement:		
New Actions to Take:		

Questions for Reflection:

1. What are family members, friends, or others noticing and saying about my improved actions? (Ask them if you do not know.)

   _____

   _____

   _____

2. Where do I need further improvement?

   _____

   _____

   _____

   _____

3. What other insights did I gain from this activity?

   _____

   _____

   _____

   _____

Slips, Trips, and Falls: Choosing, Learning, and Moving On

Marcie's marriage ended in divorce three years ago after countless arguments about everything from money to sex. After grieving the loss of the relationship and feeling like a failure, it took a lot of effort for her to feel emotionally whole again. She prayed, recommitted to her goals in life, and took an art class to boost her confidence, creativity, and self-respect. As she healed, she became involved with caring for animals at a local shelter. Now, Marcie is focusing less on her pain and is feeling well balanced in her life. She begins attracting the notice of her new neighbor William, but she initially declines his offer to go out to dinner. She is still somewhat concerned that any relationship she has will end the way her marriage did. But William is persistent, and she gradually begins to appreciate his honesty with her and his responsibility and consistency with his job. He really likes the sparkle in her eyes, her shy smile, and the courteous and helpful way she treats others in the neighborhood. Marcie finally practices courage and agrees to spend time with him.

As you continue your dance lessons, you approach the point where you are considering the possibility of choosing a consistent partner. Your concerns begin to arise as you look ahead, and your previous experiences prompt fears to arise.

If you were choosing a dance partner, some of these thoughts might run through your head: "Will I be able to choose someone who is equal in ability? Will they really enjoy dancing with me? Will I dance as poorly now as I did in the past? Will we be able to dance smoothly and in harmony on the dance floor? What will I do if the person wants to rush fast into being partners and participate in a dance contest before I am ready?"

You may have learned to dance well by yourself, but you are unsure about dancing with someone else. You want to make this *commitment*, but you are afraid your partner will betray your *trust* and not fully participate. You have seen friends having problems with their partners, and you may have slipped, tripped, or fallen down with partners in the past and wonder if it will happen again.

Many factors can leave people without having experienced or observed relationships based on character and friendship that function well. These factors include the high divorce rate, children being born outside of marriage, children being raised by only one parent, addictions, mental illness, abuse within families, forced marriages, and culturally common but damaging family behaviors.

Depending on your experiences, you may not have acquired the necessary knowledge, skills, and *confidence* to find and establish a healthy relationship with a partner. If you come from a difficult family situation, or if you have gone through a negative relationship, you may also be afraid of failure. You may be unsure about how to be part of *creating* a happy, healthy, and successful relationship. The chapters in the rest of this book will assist you with learning how.

It is possible, instead, that you have come from an intact and functional home where you gained a clear understanding of relationships from well-functioning parents in a good marriage. You may also be considering a relationship for the first time. If these situations describe your life, then this chapter may only be of slight interest to you, and you will simply skim it.

However, no matter what your background is, if you have ever been in a relationship, you may have had experiences that are affecting your ability to be a full participant in a relationship now. Part of what assists you in going forward is understanding your previous relationship choices, their consequences, and any difficult experiences that occurred.

You may not have understood the warning signs that were present in the relationship, or handled them in a way that worked well. You may have chosen to act in ways that were not consistent with your higher nature and therefore did not *respect* your best self (Chapter 1). Understanding what happened will *help* you to avoid repeating the same mistakes.

Discerning what trips you up or stops you from fully *committing* to a relationship may feel uncomfortable or difficult. However, *accepting* what is in your way, *honestly* understanding it, and *courageously* overcoming it will empower you to move forward. Taking positive steps, no matter how small they are at first, gives you opportunities to learn, grow, and become *stronger*.

The more *confident* and *responsible* you are about addressing your challenges, the greater the possibility that you will have a relationship that works well for both you and a partner.

RELATIONSHIP CHOICES

Sometimes your relationship choices or your life experiences affected you or have left you with concerns. Perhaps a relationship has ended, but you feel as if it is incomplete, and you are uncertain about beginning a new relationship. Understanding and resolving issues from the past are vital actions in ensuring you are ready to move forward.

Relationship Concerns

Sometimes people feel pain because of their experiences, and they express concerns like these:

> "My parents just divorced, and I am afraid of going through the same pain."
>
> "I tried marriage, and it just did not work out."
>
> "I got engaged, but my partner decided commitment was not for them."
>
> "I want a partner, not someone who treats me like a servant or punching bag."
>
> "I want someone who shows me respect and does not run and share everything from our relationship with friends."
>
> "My father abused me, and I do not know if I can get over it and be in a relationship."
>
> "I was married for a long time before my spouse died, and I do not know what it will be like being with someone new."
>
> "My best friend just broke up with her boyfriend, and she is devastated. I do not want to go through that."
>
> "I need someone who will not only love and accept me, but also loves and accepts my child."
>
> "I dislike all the drama that goes on in my friends' relationships."[1]

Very few, if any, experiences are so severe that healing is impossible. You can learn from what happened, gain new knowledge and skills, and have a healthy relationship.

Resolving issues and healing from the past does not mean that feelings from the past will not recur. They do for everyone at times. No matter how much healing and focusing on the present and future you do, there will still be times when something happens, and you feel anxious or concerned. For instance, a friend or relative gets divorced or has difficulty with a partner, and this causes you to look back on your own life. Incidents can also trigger memories from your past, such as accidentally calling a new partner by an old partner's name, or causing an argument because you assume a new partner is reacting the way an old partner would have. However, you can recognize when the past causes an incident in the present and practice your character qualities from Chapters 1 and 2 and your skills from Chapter 3 to respond effectively to the situation. As necessary and appropriate, you can apologize, make amends, or request *forgiveness*.

~ *Questions for Reflection* ~

1. What are my concerns about being in a relationship?
2. How am I letting my past affect my future relationships?

ACTIVITY

If you had a relationship that is still causing you problems, or you have unresolved feelings about parts of it, it may *help* you to *create* a calm, meditative area or focal point in your home. When you are upset and experiencing negative emotions about the past or any other issue, physically being in or visualizing your meditative area or the focal point you *create* can assist you to calm your emotions and clear your thoughts. Possibilities for you to *create* include a corner of a room in your home that you decorate, a place outside in a garden, or a small attractive reminder that you set on a table. You can *create* a small healing garden or a table centerpiece by using water, rocks, wood, shells, flowers, clay, plants, or other natural materials.

Empower Your Future

For everything that happens in your life, your mind *creates* a story about it that includes your interpretation of the experience. Even small incidents can become part of the storybook in your mind that describes your past. Sometimes when something bad happens, the event itself only lasts a few minutes. However, your memory of it and all your decisions based on its significance can dominate your life for years…or decades. These decisions can be about yourself or about actions you will or will not take in the future. Your past then *creates* your present and your future.

As you look to your future, you may have difficulty recognizing that you have power and influence whereby you can *create* it the way you choose it to be, rather than it being a result of your past. For instance, you have complete authority over your own self in how you choose to interact with other people. You may be more likely to refer back to the story of your life and see the evidence that raises your anxieties or fears concerning how you treat others or how you respond to others. You may conclude that you cannot be successful in a relationship. But you need not be discouraged.

Remember your lower nature from Chapter 1? If you put it in charge of reading your life's story, every little bad thing that happens to you is grounds for you to be pessimistic. You can become trapped in the past by building a storehouse of "evidence" in your mind that predicts you will fail at a future relationship. You could feel self-pity, sorrow and regret, vengeance toward parents or previous partners, and pain. You can act like a victim.

The lower nature drives people to be self-centered and self-focused. It causes them to view each incident only from their own perspective. It causes them to ignore the needs of others, and it interferes with their ability to be in good and healthy relationships. The lower nature becomes the fuel for a life full of regrets and excuses.

If you hang onto the negative evidence that predicts you will fail, it fuels your fear, affects your present situation, impedes your growth, and projects the past into your future. Taken to an extreme, it will be impossible for you to be in a relationship successfully. It is like driving a car forward while only looking in the rear-view mirror. In effect, it *creates* a future where you have a reduced ability to have and maintain healthy relationships. It is important to understand your past and learn from it, but dwelling on the past will only prevent you from *creating* a positive future for yourself. Nor will it benefit you to internalize all the blame for the failed relationship or place all the blame on your partner. The question is, do you want your lower nature to be dictating your future and running your life? Or do you want to pursue a life based upon your higher nature?

Consider this situation:

> Jeremy was married for twelve years to Breeana, and they had two children together. Breeana often drank heavily and complained about whatever bad things happened. He felt sorry for her and kept trying to take *care* of her. She denied she had a problem, however, and repeatedly refused to get *help*. Jeremy kept trying to make life better for Breeana, but nothing worked. After a particularly bad night, when Breeana's behavior threatened the safety and well-being of both him and their children, Jeremy separated from her and later divorced.
>
> On an evening a year and a half later, Jeremy and his mother sit on the porch of her home drinking iced tea. Jeremy raises the question of whether to date again, and his mother expresses willingness to look after the children if he is ready to do so. In the months after the divorce, he had gone out a few times with a woman that he met while bowling with some friends. At first the relationship seemed promising. But soon her smiling charm could not cover up that she had the same drinking problem as Breeana. He tried to *help* her for a few weeks, but he was unsuccessful, and he stopped seeing her. He wonders if he will continue to choose poorly.

For Jeremy to move forward beyond his concerns, he will need to understand why this relationship pattern reoccurred and make new choices.

Stop Repeating Patterns

Sometimes when you have experienced difficult behaviors or conditions in a parent or partner, you may believe that these are

normal for relationships. Or, you could think that a terrible situation is what you deserve and that you cannot have anything better than this. Building your *confidence* and self-*respect*, and developing the other character qualities, will *help* you to turn around this belief. You may also find it useful to re-visit some of the assessment and development practices from Chapters 2 and 3.

Sometimes when you end a relationship, you end up very quickly involved with someone new who has the same problems as your previous partner. This repeating pattern can occur when you do not look below the surface of the person, and you subconsciously recreate a familiar experience. It is possible that familiarity is less scary than changing direction.

Copyright 2004 by Randy Glasbergen.
www.glasbergen.com

**"My last boyfriend said I'm a control freak.
Do you think I'm a control freak? If so, say yes."**

When the same problem occurs in more than one relationship, it is also possible that you have not identified what attracts you to someone. In the case of Jeremy in the previous story, he is drawn to take *care* of women, so he is attracted to people with problems. Once he understands that this is a pitfall for him, he can handle relationships differently. Here is what could happen:

Jeremy decides to join a singles group that meets in the social hall of a nearby religious congregation. One of the women quickly begins conversing with him. As they participate in the group, she talks about needing someone to *help* her repair her house, drive her to the doctor, and manage her finances. This time, Jeremy recognizes the warning signs that this woman is looking for someone to take *care* of her, and he backs off.

A new woman, Alisha, joins the group shortly after, and she and Jeremy strike up a friendship. She has a child close in age to one of Jeremy's. Alisha has moved on in her life after her divorce, and she is capably handling her life. She also wants someone to share it with her. As their relationship deepens, this time Jeremy knows he is making a better choice.

Another pitfall that can cause you to end up in a negative repeating relationship pattern is assuming that you know how to handle relationships well if you have been in several of them or have been previously married. **However, unless you have learned the key lessons and gained new relationship knowledge and skills, you may simply repeat negative or destructive patterns.**

If you are unable on your own to overcome this challenge of repeatedly ending up in destructive relationships, you will then be *wise* to obtain some professional or support group assistance to *help* you to end this pattern. *Note:* You can find support groups through the Internet, in telephone books, and in newspapers.

ACTIVITY

In order to increase your *confidence* in being successful in a relationship, it will be useful for you to interview parents, friends, relatives, or others that you perceive have healthy and successful relationships. Ask them what has *helped* them to stay together, what obstacles they have overcome and how they did it, and what lessons they have learned from the mistakes they have made. When you have gathered the notes from your interviews, go through them thoroughly and extract the information that is most *helpful* for you to remember.

Relationship Warning Signs

You may have missed some of the warning signs in your previous relationships. Look over the list below and see if you can now see what was happening with your partner. Keep in mind that this list reflects situations where your partner was **not receiving treatment, actively seeking to change, or sincerely asking for *help*.** Even if your partner was getting professional assistance, they may not have been successful in overcoming their problems or improving. Consider these problem areas:

- Major character flaws (Indicators can include habitual lying, laziness, or chronic disrespect toward you or others)
- Constant complaints or victim-mentality; regular dwelling on emotional trauma or difficulties from previous experiences
- Jealousy, possessiveness, or controlling tendencies; insecurity or a lack of *trust*
- Argumentative, adversarial interactions; frequent character attacks and conflicts

- Physically violent tendencies
- Emotionally or verbally derogatory or abusive
- Negative attitude and criticism toward self, partner, parents, or others
- Major hypocritical gap between stated beliefs and actions
- Insistence on having sex as a way to solve, forget, or ignore problems
- Substance abuse or addictions (Indicators may have been slowed responses, extreme mood swings, unexpected absences, failure to keep agreements, or financial problems)
- Sexual abuse or addictions (Indicators may have been viewing pornography, or demanding or participating in excessive frequency of sexual experiences)
- Physically harmful or risky actions
- Mental illnesses (Indicators may have been depression, excessive emotional withdrawal, compulsive lying, excessive and unreasonable anger, paranoia or unreasonable suspicions, very high levels of anxiety, eating disorders, unexplained constant or rapid shifts in emotional expressions, unreasonable reactions to normal stress, abuse of or addiction to alcohol or drugs, suicide threats, or repeated abusive and damaging comments or behavior)
- Eating disorders (Indicators may have been harmful binge or avoidance eating habits, sudden or frequent weight gains and losses, or compulsive food rituals)
- Relationship was not a priority; excessive time alone or with others such as friends and family after committing to being partners; partner repeatedly left out of activities and plans
- Excessive flirting with other people; unfaithfulness
- Difficulty keeping a job; expectation of others paying the bills

Other issues may have been signs of problems and disruptions in your couple relationship rather than in your partner. These include:

- An overly dependent relationship with each other (or others), especially when one or both of you were addicted to or abusing substances or each other in some way; deep involvement in each other's problems and attempts to fix them; loss of identity due to excessive focus on someone else's problems
- Relationship began because of something negative in common and did not move beyond this
- Incompatible or polarized views on basic values about faith, family, career, and finances
- Mutual attraction was fading or absent
- Mental, emotional, or physical abuse

- Inability to meet many of each other's expectations
- Regular attempts to change each other
- Constant and sometimes public criticisms, judgments, and corrections of each other
- Frequent personal changes only to please each other
- Boredom, disinterest, or having little to talk about
- Lack of communication
- Serious faults regularly overlooked, and assumptions made that they would get better later

"I'm sorry, Max, but bells didn't go off when I first met you. They were more like police sirens, as a matter of fact.

In a healthy relationship, both of you actively develop your character qualities, so reflect on whether this development was occurring in your previous relationship. If your character development slowed or ceased happening, that was a warning sign. **If you found that your *honest* self-expression and *creativity* were stifled, or if it was becoming harder for you to be *joyful, compassionate*, or *purposeful*, you may have been in a harmful relationship. Another negative indicator would have been either of you changing just to make the other happy, to get something from the other, or to keep the relationship from collapsing, while one or both of you were miserable in the process.**

Note: Your concerns may be more with your parents than with previous partners, especially if it was parental abuse that contributed to you having difficulty maintaining your relationship. Handling the effects of parental abuse or abandonment is somewhat beyond the scope of this book, although much of what applies to partners can assist you. If you are resisting being in a relationship due to serious problems in your home growing up, professional assistance is *wise*.

~ *Questions for Reflection* ~

1. What warning signs of significant challenges do I now see that occurred in my previous relationships?
2. What warning signs have I seen in relationships of others close to me?

Warning Signs Related to Sex

If you had sex in a previous relationship, it would have been a warning sign that your relationship was unwise or having difficulties if your partner:

- Pushed you unwillingly into sexual intimacy or certain sexual acts
- Said that they could not be sure that you *loved* them unless you had sex together
- Said that they deserved sex from you because they gave you a gift, a great date, or some other action
- Insisted that your relationship could not grow further without sexual intimacy
- Threatened to leave you if you did not participate in sexual activities
- Was unfaithful to you by having sex with someone else as well
- Failed to inform or protect you and gave you a sexually-transmitted infection or disease (STI/STD)
- Failed to take the necessary actions to prevent pregnancy
- Showed signs of sexual addiction
- Used sex as a distraction to avoid resolving problems
- Needed sex to boost self-worth or *confidence*
- Could not find anything to talk about, so used sex to fill the time
- Was overly forceful and/or violent
- Used drugs or alcohol to lower inhibitions
- Used pornography to become aroused
- Obsessed and fantasized over sex and regularly masturbated

Of course, it was also a warning sign if you did any of the above rather than your partner. **Any of these signs also indicate that sex may have distracted you from building a friendship-based relationship.**

~ *Question for Reflection* ~

Was there anything related to sex that was a warning sign of problems?

Resisting Warnings and Ending the Relationship

When a relationship was not going well, you may have held on to it because you were trying hard to practice certain character *strengths*. For instance, *compassion* or *kindness* could have led you to stay in a relationship and keep *forgiving* your partner's very poor behavior. In fact, you may have been misusing your character qualities instead (Chapter 1). *Moderation* and *detachment* could have assisted you to approach the situation in a different way. Another example is that you could have been doing your best to practice *loyalty* or *perseverance*, qualities that are appropriate in a relationship normally. If you misused these qualities by practicing them to excess, however, you may have prolonged the relationship and caused harm to you and your partner.

You may have handled warning signs in a number of ways. Since you invested time and energy into a relationship, you may have been tempted to deny or ignore anything that would have invalidated your efforts or ended it. Perhaps you tried to convince yourself that the situation was minor, temporary, or not important enough for you to be concerned. You might have concluded that anything could be overcome with a large amount of time, effort, and *patience*. You might have decided that perhaps you were being too sensitive or intolerant. Maybe your partner's behavior was similar to that of a family member or friend, so you convinced yourself that it was okay. Your partner justified or made excuses for their behavior, and you went along with their explanations without questioning them.

"Kenny hasn't spoken to me in six months, he won't return my calls and he goes out with all my friends. Do you think I should break up with him?"

Alternatively, you could have misused *helpfulness*, and your response could have been to tackle the issue aggressively. You may have tried to rescue and fix your partner or to solve their problems for them. This tendency to want to fix a problem can be particularly common if you were raised with a parent who seemed to need regular rescuing, or if you were taught that aiding someone is always the best thing to do for them. Remember that you can misuse *helpfulness* when you practice it in a way that actually causes harm.

When you are in the mode of desperately trying to solve problems, you may persistently try to find solutions on your own, even when the other person is not motivated to seek assistance, get better, or change. Maybe you sought counseling solely with the goal of *helping* your partner, instead of truly seeking assistance for yourself and ensuring that you looked after your own best interests as well. You gave your partner chance after chance to make changes. You focused so much on trying to solve the issue, that you neglected your own well-being and *responsibilities*. If you attacked the problem aggressively, you may have caused resistance in your partner, which actually kept the problem more firmly in place.

There may be many other factors that caused you to stay in an unhealthy relationship, but at some point, you realized that your efforts were not working. You saw the toll it was taking on you to be in a relationship that was harmful or just drained you of your *joy* in life. You may have then decided that the relationship needed to end.

Ending the relationship might not have been easy, however. While trying to end it, perhaps you:

- Behaved in underhanded, conniving, or poor ways that angered your partner so that they backed out of the relationship without you having to initiate the ending
- Compromised your needs and acted in desperate ways to hang on
- Blamed and lashed out at your partner for things that they did or did not do
- Disempowered yourself by acting like a victim instead of taking *assertive* action
- Panicked at the thought of being alone
- Felt anger that the relationship was not better
- Worried so much about what the other person would do in response that action was impossible
- Went into a deep depression because the relationship was ending
- Quickly moved to end the relationship and tried to put it behind you without having any necessary closure communications with your partner or going through learning and understanding from it
- Went in and out of denial that the relationship needed to end

As you look at the reactions above, notice how many of those that applied to your actions came from your lower nature (Chapter 1). What do you wish you had done instead? What could have *helped* you? Do you need to practice self-*forgiveness* or *compassion* with yourself or with your previous partner? What else would *help* you now?

Alternatively, perhaps you were able to practice your character qualities effectively and approached the situation from your higher nature. Then your actions were closer to the following list. You were:

- *Honest* first with yourself and then with your partner about your thoughts and feelings
- *Kind* and not deliberately hurtful
- *Courageous* and *assertive* in speaking up for what you needed and what was right for you
- *Respectful* toward your partner's well-being and rights and requested the same from them
- *Self-disciplined* in expressing your emotions and responses
- *Detached* from the emotional reactions you had to your partner's choices
- *Responsible* about any actions needed to bring closure to the relationship (handling financial issues, dividing photos, returning belongings…)
- *Respectful* of boundaries for any ongoing communications between the two of you or between your (now former) partner and your family or mutual friends

Even if your partner deliberately tried to make a break-up painful for you, you were only *responsible* for your own choices. You chose to respond with *courtesy* and *respect*, even if they did not.

The next step is to learn from your actions and experiences, and the following section will *help* you to do this.

~ Questions for Reflection ~

1. How did I handle problems that arose in relationships?
2. How did I speak to and act with a partner while ending a relationship?

LEARNING LESSONS FROM EXPERIENCES

You will benefit from learning whatever you can from a relationship experience. If you examine the book of your life from the point of view of your higher nature, you see a very different picture than you did when you looked at it from a lower nature standpoint earlier. Author John Kolstoe says this about the importance of understanding:

> Everybody has problems. Some people call them tests, difficulties, trials or tribulations. Those who like to put a positive spin on the unpleasant call them

opportunities, challenges, learning experiences, stepping stones or special gifts. … Psychologists say that understanding is the most important single step in reducing anger and that great frustration comes from not having a clear understanding of a situation.[2]

You can look at a situation through your higher nature by *carefully* applying the character qualities. You can practice *discernment* and *honesty* to see what there is to understand from your experiences. *Compassion* and *acceptance* will *help* you to see that everyone did the best they could under the circumstances with what they knew at the time. *Responsibility* makes it possible to acknowledge your own role in whatever happened, and whether something bad happened for which you had no accountability but you still felt guilty. *Love* and *unity help* you to see the good in your experiences and feel *contentment* and *peacefulness* with others and yourself.

Even after very bad relationship experiences, it is likely you can still spot something positive. Applying all the qualities mentioned in the above paragraph as you look through a previous relationship is especially vital if you still have contact with the person who hurt you in the past, and you want to feel *peaceful* in your interactions with them. This process is especially important if you have children together, as they will feel better about their parents and themselves knowing that the relationship had some positive history and was not all bad.

As you look at your past and yearn to have a different future, assess your story for what lessons are useful. If you can learn from it or gain pointers about what new knowledge and skills you need to develop, then it is valuable. Otherwise, *detachment* from it will be *wise*. Achieving *detachment*, however, is a process. It often takes understanding the past, acknowledging your fears and concerns, seeing where you set up obstacles that trip you and make you fall, and reorienting yourself in a new direction.

Learning from Your Previous Partner

You might consider having a serious conversation with your former partner about what did not work. This action will take *courage*, but you can learn valuable information for your next experience, if the person is open to having the discussion, and it is safe and *wise*. Look at your motives carefully before having this conversation to be sure that you are not using it to attempt to rekindle the relationship or to prove that your former partner was at fault. Then, communicate your motives to them, indicating that you simply want to learn from the experience. The feedback from them will be most useful if it is specific. *Assertiveness* and *courtesy* will *help* you to request that your former partner be as detailed as possible in response to your questions.

Before the conversation, it will be useful for you to write down some potential questions to ask. A relative or friend might be willing to suggest ones to ask as well. Some to consider are:

- What did I do that you disliked and why?
- What did I do in the relationship that was positive, and why did you appreciate it?
- When did you feel that I did not understand or *accept* you? What did I do at these times that prompted you to feel this way?
- Which of my habits or communication methods caused you problems?
- Where did you find that we were not compatible?
- When did I hurt your feelings, make you upset, or trigger you to feel angry?
- What could I have done differently to make this relationship work?
- What character qualities did I seem to be weak in practicing? What character qualities in me do you appreciate?
- What do you see as the primary reasons for the ending of our relationship?
- Is there anything from our relationship that is incomplete for you? What can I do that will *help* you to bring it to closure?

If you practice *detachment* in the process, it will *help* you with hearing, *accepting*, and appreciating any difficult feedback or comments your former partner offers. Be *respectful* of their opinions, and avoid becoming defensive or trying to justify your own behavior. Note that the questions invite both negative and positive feedback. It is important to *discern* what went wrong, but also *discern* what went right. Once you have the feedback, then you can go through it and assess its usefulness. Some comments will only apply to that relationship, but others may suggest changes for you to make in yourself or in how you speak and act with a new partner.

~ Questions for Reflection ~

1. When I look objectively at a former relationship, what was missing? Where could I have made different choices or behaved differently?
2. What expectations for this relationship did I have that my partner did not meet? Did I communicate them? Were they fair and reasonable?
3. How have I handled the endings of previous relationships (including a marriage)? What were the challenges I experienced in the process, and what did I learn?
4. If I need to end a current relationship, do I want to do it differently than in the past? How do I choose to speak and act that reflect self-*respect*?

ACTIVITY

Create a relationship-ending ceremony to do on your own or with close friends or relatives that assists you with saying goodbye to someone. You can use candles, music, write and burn a letter, burn correspondence, loudly pop a few balloons, do something physical that releases energy, let a balloon go into the air, write a poem, or whatever is meaningful and appropriate for the relationship, circumstances, and whatever feelings you need to release.

If you have not been in a relationship, then consider whether there is someone else important in your life, such as a parent or a grandparent, who has died or left your life. This activity can also assist you with these if you are still feeling incomplete about the situation, have unexpressed emotions, and you are looking for closure.

Learning from Reflection

Unresolved feelings or issues have a tendency to resurface in subsequent relationships. These can cause confusion and negative reactions both in you and in a new partner. Therefore, it is best to understand and resolve your current feelings about a previous relationship and the choices you made in the previous relationship. This resolution then empowers you and frees you to *create* a successful relationship along with a partner in the future.

Some insights into why a relationship failed might only be possible with the passing of time, the calming of your emotions, and lessons and experiences gained in the future. As you go through this learning process, various activities may assist you to sort it all out and *discern* insights. These can include reflection, journal writing, prayer, meditation, exercising, or writing poetry or music.

Buddha describes the importance of meditating on serenity, "…in which thou risest above love and hate, …and regardest thine own fate with impartial calmness and perfect tranquility."[3] In meditation, you draw on insight, rather than on your outward vision. You may find it more *helpful* to do physical movement while you reflect, such as cooking, cleaning, building, repairing, or gardening.

However you choose to do your processing, this reflection time will also give you the opportunity to decide how you will act differently in a new relationship.

Seeking Closure

For you to move powerfully forward after a relationship, you need a sense of completion and closure. Below are some steps to consider taking.

- Fully assess the previous relationship, including all the character-related and communication issues, and determine any additional lessons you can learn
- *Discern* any still unresolved issues from the past that are triggering *strong* emotions or reactions in you, and take steps to bring them to closure
- Discover what you did or did not do that contributed to the failure of the relationship
- Determine what you will do differently in a future relationship
- Look *carefully* at what attracted you to the person and whether it was actually something lasting and substantial, and whether you will use it as a criteria in the future for choosing a new partner
- Determine if there are any communications that have not occurred and you want to make them, or whether there are any outstanding actions you need to take that bring closure (not revenge!)
- Seek *justice* if there are outstanding legal issues with a previous partner
- Obtain professional counseling, *spiritual* guidance, and/or join a support group to assist you to heal from any lingering issues; professional input is especially important if there was abuse of any kind in the relationship
- *Forgive* your previous partner (and their family and friends) and yourself
- Make apologies and amends as needed, appropriate, and *wise* [see Chapter 3]
- *Detach* and let go of resentment, hurt feelings, and anger that anchor you to pain from the past
- *Detach* from any thoughts you are having that your previous experiences mean you will have a negative experience in the future

If you decide that there are communications that you want to have to bring closure to a relationship, consider a few cautions. Be aware that there are some circumstances where it might be unwise, damaging, or unsafe to be in direct communication with someone from your past. If you have any concerns of this nature, please consult a professional counselor or *trusted* advisor before taking action. Remember, too, that you can always pray or write in a journal, which can assist you with resolving your feelings left from the relationship. If the topic is very confidential, consider shredding or burning anything that you write down (which may also *help* you to find closure).

Never impulsively send a letter or email to someone without keeping it private for a number of days as you reflect upon whether what you have said is *wise*. You may also find it useful to share any letter you write with a *trusted* friend or advisor for input before sending it. They can also assist you to be clear about your motives for the communication.

If the relationship that ended was long-term or deeply emotional, you may look to your friends, family, and *spiritual* sources for support. Praying, either by yourself or with others, can be very *helpful*. Personal development workshops and seminars can assist you with looking forward instead of holding onto the relationship and its accompanying emotions.

You may need to receive professional counseling or speak with a *spiritual* advisor to resolve lingering issues and heartache. These can provide a safe and confidential place to express your feelings and assist you with moving on. You will need to allow yourself time to express whatever feelings are occurring for you, such as grief, anger, or disappointment.

If you do not *detach* from a previous relationship, energy that is better for you to direct elsewhere may drain away. You might find yourself performing poorly at your job or in school while you are dedicating so much mental and emotional capacity to reacting to your sustained attachment to the past.

Use prayer, *wisdom*, and discussion with *trusted* others to do what is best for your physical, mental, emotional, and *spiritual* well-being. It will take new thoughts, actions, and emotions to shift your focus toward the future. You will then begin to gain skill in *discerning* which friendships and relationships in your life are truly deserving of your *commitment* and *loyalty*.

~ Questions for Reflection ~

1. What partners have I chosen who have turned out to be poor matches for me? What did I learn from them?
2. What partners have I chosen who turned out to be good matches for me at the time, even if we are not together now?
3. How did I know that a previous partner was a good match for me?
4. What difficulties have come up in my relationships? What did I do to cause them?
5. What have I learned from previous experiences that can *help* me to make better choices now?
6. What am I learning from listening to the promptings of my inner voice, feedback from others, books, and new experiences that are improving my life and character and that will make a difference in future relationships?

ACTIVITIES

1. Complete **Worksheet 4.1: Learning from Relationships** to assess a specific previous relationship and what you can learn from the experience.

2. Complete **Worksheet 4.2: Cleaning Up Previous Relationships** to identify actions you can choose to take to bring closure to a previous relationship.

3. Imagine a cluttered area of your life—perhaps your office, bedroom, garage, workshop, closet, or car—as a relationship from the past. See it filled with piles, trash, dirt, and perhaps with items in need of repair. In your mind, tidy, organize, or clean the area as needed, and repair what is broken. While you visualize doing these actions, reflect on moving forward from the cluttered and unhappy past into a new and happier future. Think about how you will behave differently in the future, so this area of your life or a future relationship does not end up in this state again. If you have an area that is actually in poor condition, you may wish to do this as a hands-on activity instead of as a mental visualization.

Staying Connected or Not

Detaching from the past may be especially difficult if you and your previous partner still interact with each other, for instance due to a child or financial issues. This *detachment* is also difficult if you work with, go to school with, or live near each other.

The better you can stay in the present and communicate clearly during interactions with your previous partner, the greater will be your ability to move forward. If you keep recreating the past or reliving the pain, you may be stuck in it for a long time. The shift to a more positive outlook will be neither easy nor instant. It will be a process. But, you can accomplish it successfully. Author Dan Millman, in his book *Living on Purpose*, says:

> Be gentle with yourself; trust the process of your life. … Perfection is not a prerequisite for life on earth. While we live, we continue to make mistakes and learn from them. We were born not to be ideal, but to be real—not to become someone else, but to become ourselves. We have all made a mess of things, but nothing is less important than the score at halftime. By accepting our humanity we awaken our spirituality. Acknowledging our failures may be the greatest triumph of all.[4]

It may be difficult but possible to have a platonic friendship with a former partner if you choose to handle the transition out of a

relationship with *dignity* and *respect*. Previous sexual intimacy between you can complicate the ease of remaining friends, however. It can also be more difficult when your relationship was very serious, and there was a deep emotional bond between you. When your heart was deeply connected to someone, *detachment* will be difficult. You will likely need time apart for healing and recovery before being able to assess whether an ongoing friendship is even possible. You will also be *wise* to *discern* if attempting to be friends will simply lead the two of you back into being together, and your relationship and difficulties will resume.

As you assess whether to maintain a connection with someone after a relationship ends, it is also *wise* to think about the future. Be very clear about why you want to maintain the connection. How might another partner or potential spouse respond to you still being close with a previous partner? Will a new partner have legitimate concerns about you potentially resuming an emotionally or physically intimate relationship with your previous partner? Will you still feel a *strong* emotional connection and continue to take care of the previous partner's needs in some way? This matter is complex, as you may value your friendship with the person and want a new partner to *trust* you. If the two of them do not get along, however, you may have to make the difficult decision to choose one or the other. [See Chapter 12 for more about jealousy and mistrust.]

~ *Questions for Reflection* ~

1. Have I stayed friends with someone after a relationship ended? What made it possible? What worked well?
2. How have subsequent partners viewed this previous relationship? Has jealousy been a problem? How have I handled that?

MOVING FORWARD

It is *wise* to give yourself some time to heal from an ended relationship before considering entering a new one. It is important to be especially cautious about being in a continuous cycle of relationships that start, last briefly, and end. This pattern can cause you to hold yourself back mentally and emotionally in a relationship, because you always expect it will end. People often use the term "break up" to describe a relationship ending. Breaking something usually results in jagged and scattered pieces that are difficult to put back together. The more something breaks, the more difficult the mending process becomes. It will be *wise* to end this pattern of regular "break ups" in your life if it exists.

You may be reluctant to have a relationship again after a painful ending. You may think you are doomed to repeat your mistakes. You may reason that it is better to be alone than to risk going through the pain again. However, it is likely that the pain of isolation and cutting yourself off from *love* will be worse, and trying again with increased knowledge and skills will be better. **Unfortunately, one of the results of negative relationship experiences for many people is a struggle with or an inability to *commit* to a future partner. However, avoiding *commitment* actually sets you up to fail in a relationship.** Chapter 5 will *help* you to explore fears you may have about *commitment* and what you can do to address them.

As you work through the process of preparing for a new dance partner, you might be tempted to decide that it is too difficult and want to step off the dance floor. You may slip back into hoping that something mystical will happen, and your future will work out without you making an effort. Finding a partner is not a passive activity, however. If you sit around waiting and hope that someone perfect will show up and invite you to dance, you just might end up alone.

Overcoming Your Fears and Anxiety

Fear can definitely stop you from moving forward if you do not recognize and address it. Susan Jeffers, author of *The Feel the Fear Guide to Lasting Love*, puts it this way:

> Fear causes us to protect ourselves, to rigidly hold on, to close our hearts, …
> and to spread our free-floating anger to all members of the opposite sex.…
> The reason why we seldom realize that fear is getting in the way of love is
> that fear has an amazing ability to hide itself behind other emotions, such as
> anger, blame, judgment and the like.[5]

When you recognize that you are in the middle of feeling a high degree of fear or anxiety about being in a new relationship, it can be difficult to think rationally. Here are some steps that can assist you in the process:

- Breathe deeply, meditate, pray, visualize a *peaceful* place, or physically go to a place that makes you feel calm and happy
- Write in a journal what you are afraid of and what is causing your feelings
- Think back to your childhood and note the evidence you have gathered throughout your life in support of your fears
- Reaffirm what you have learned from each of your relationship experiences
- Interact and spend time with friends and relatives who have healthy and stable families

- Take personal *responsibility* to learn the knowledge and skills needed for successful relationships
- Work on building *confidence* and lessening your fear of *commitment*
- Assess what new skills you are learning that will *help* you to handle experiences differently in the future

One new tool that you now have, which you may not have had in your toolbox with a previous relationship, is the ability to recognize and evaluate both your own and another person's character qualities. This new skill will significantly increase your ability to choose a partner with whom you can have a *strong* and lasting relationship. Recognizing that you have this tool will *help* you to lessen your fears of being hurt again.

~ *Questions for Reflection* ~
1. Do I say "no" to invitations from potential partners when I really want to say "yes," because I am afraid that I will fail again?   2. Do I say "yes" or "no" appropriately to potential partners out of *respect* for my needs and wishes?   3. What character qualities will empower me to lessen my fears and anxiety?
ACTIVITY
Write down your exact fears and anxieties. For each one, trace as many of the causes and reasons for it as possible. Pretend that you are a good friend or a relationship coach and write down how you would advise someone with these fears to handle them. Share your fears and advice with a *trusted* friend, relative, counselor, or advisor. What practical steps can you now take to move forward?

CONFIDENT VIEW OF THE FUTURE

If you need assistance with moving forward, there are a number of character qualities that you can practice:

- *Commit* to having a partner
- Be *courageous* in identifying and facing your fears while staying in action
- Use *discernment* and *honesty* to empower yourself to understand what stops you from fully participating in a relationship and what you can do to address your fears and concerns
- Be *truthful* and *honest* in getting to the heart of what you are thinking and feeling

- Be *kind* and *gentle* with yourself, and move at a pace that *respects* your needs
- *Persevere* to prevent you from giving up when the process becomes difficult or uncertain
- Practice *spirituality* to *help* you include prayer and *spiritual* guidance in the process
- Be *idealistic* to *help* you identify what is vital for you in a relationship, while realistically *accepting* that no relationship will measure up to every specific expectation
- Be *patient* with yourself and the process of moving forward into a relationship, recognizing that your fears may not go away entirely

As you draw on these qualities, your *confidence* will build, and your fears will lessen. *Confidence* will *help* you to stay *committed* to learning the knowledge and skills that will assist you to be successful in finding a partner and building a relationship. This success will especially benefit you if the person turns out to be a potential marriage partner.

As you gain new insights about relationships and learn new skills, you will more quickly identify if you are entering a potentially successful relationship or not. The more that you learn how to observe a partner's character effectively, the less reason you will have to fear making a misjudgment. [You will learn more about observation skills in Chapter 10.]

The more thorough and *careful* you are with the process of choosing a partner next time, the more enjoyment you will have in the selection process, and the less likely you will be to go through another painful ending. You are gaining tools and knowledge now that you may not have had before, and this will necessarily have an impact on the way that you think, speak, and act in the future. You can have a *strong*, healthy, and lasting relationship.

There are many different ways to become an active participant in your search for a partner, and many of the remaining chapters will provide you with details about them.

❧ *Encouragement* ☙

This chapter may have been difficult for you as you reflected on previous relationships. If so, it may be beneficial to take a break, and do an activity to refresh and rejuvenate yourself. We hope that after doing the valuable work in this chapter, you are also feeling increasingly *encouraged* and *confident* about moving forward.

Date: _____

Worksheet 4.1: Learning from Relationships

This worksheet will assist you to assess and understand a previous relationship you have had. You will also determine what you have learned from the experiences you had while in it.

Instructions:

A) Note below which relationship you are assessing. Use your journal or a piece of paper to assess more than one relationship if needed.

B) Think about both positive and negative experiences, and what there is to learn from them about how you speak and act in relationships.

I am assessing my previous relationship with _____.

My Character and Theirs

1. I practiced these character qualities effectively with my partner:

   _____

   _____

   _____

   _____

2. I was weak in practicing these character qualities:

   _____

   _____

   _____

   _____

3. I was accurate in spotting these qualities in the person's character:

   _____

   _____

   _____

   _____

4. I initially missed or discounted these character issues:

   _____

   _____

   _____

   _____

Relationship Behavior

1. My negative words and actions that disrupted our relationship were:

   _____

   _____

   _____

2. My positive behavior that enhanced our relationship was:

   _____

   _____

   _____

3. Warnings signs in the relationship were:

   _____

   _____

   _____

4. I handled the warning signs in this way:

   _____

   _____

   _____

5. The following communication issues occurred:

   _____

   _____

   _____

6. I will take these steps to improve my communication skills:

   _____

   _____

   _____

7. I learned these lessons from this relationship that will help me in the next one:

   _____

   _____

   _____

   _____

   _____

   _____

Date: _____

Worksheet 4.2: Cleaning Up Previous Relationships

This worksheet will assist you to clarify and resolve issues from previous relationships that are holding you back from entering a new and healthy relationship. Assessing your previous relationship(s) with Worksheet 4.1, may have prompted you to discern some unfinished and lingering issues or incomplete communications from them. The goal is to move forward with confidence and freedom from unfinished issues. While this worksheet is about relationships with previous partners or spouses, also be aware of any unfinished communications from your relationships with others, such as your parents, that you may need to complete.

Instructions:
A) Answer the questions below as honestly as possible.

B) **Consider these cautions:** Be aware that there are some circumstances where it could be unwise, damaging, or unsafe to be in direct communication with someone from your past. If you have any concerns of this nature, please consult a professional counselor or trusted advisor before taking action. Remember, too, that you can always pray or write in a journal, which can assist you with resolving the issues from the relationship. If the topic is very confidential, consider shredding or burning anything that you write down (which may also help you with closure). Never impulsively send a letter or email to someone without keeping it private for a number of days, as you reflect upon whether what you have said is wise. You may also find it useful to share any letter you write with a trusted friend or advisor for input before sending it.

1. Which previous relationships still raise feelings of regret, anger, resentment, and/or strong and lingering attachment in me?

   _____

   _____

   _____

   _____

   _____

2. What will I do to resolve these feelings? (Examples: pray, apologize, forgive, communicate with the person, seek counseling, write in a journal, or do whatever brings you clarity and resolution)

   _____

   _____

   _____

   _____

   _____

3. What communications are undelivered? Have I left something important unsaid? Do I want to request or give forgiveness for something? Is there an apology to make? Is there a misunderstanding to clear up?

_____

_____

_____

_____

_____

4. What, if anything, prevents me from handling the communications in question 3? What assistance do I need? What will I do to find it?

_____

_____

_____

_____

_____

5. What else do I want or need to say to people or do to resolve an issue or feel peaceful about the past?

_____

_____

_____

_____

_____

6. These are the actions I took and the outcomes that occurred (may need to wait awhile to see and understand the outcomes):

_____

_____

_____

_____

7. How do I feel now? What else do I need to do?

_____

_____

_____

_____

Gaining Confidence:
Claiming Commitment

Vance has made it a personal policy to make no relationship commitments. Through his work and religious faith, he has met several women in many different cities. He communicates with them on a regular basis, whether through email or on the phone. Once in awhile, he flies to visit one of them. However, he likes to keep the conversation light and casual, avoiding serious topics like relationships, and certainly not talking about marriage. Whenever the discussions turn serious, he quickly changes the subject, and he may even spend less time with that friend, fearing that she wants more than their friendship. Recently, he has spent more time with one friend in particular, Shirina. He enjoys going to movies or attending drumming circles at a local coffee shop with her every Sunday evening. She begins sending him email messages commenting on how much she appreciates him keeping his commitment to meet each week. She also comments on his dependability with his work assignments and university coursework. He begins to wonder if he might have the ability to make a commitment after all.

In the previous chapter, you began to empower yourself and eliminate what was in the way of choosing a dance partner. You are gaining momentum in moving your dancing forward. However, a significant fear could still be in your way—that of making a *commitment* to a dance partner. When you avoid *commitment*, and you are unwilling or unable to *commit* yourself to a partner, it can prevent you from choosing someone at all. If a person in your life is a potential partner, you are unable to explore what is possible about dancing together. In the same way, fear of *commitment* can stop you from *creating* a relationship. Fear can either keep you hiding in your home so you do not meet people, or you may socialize constantly and have only very superficial contacts with others.

Perhaps you do take the next step and ask someone to dance with you. However, *commitment* is still an issue. When two partners dance together, one leads and the other follows. The leader must *commit* to making their movements clear and definite. If the leader does not *commit* to a movement or step, the follower cannot follow or tell the direction of the dance. Then, they go nowhere. In a relationship, lack of *commitment* prevents you from being satisfied and happy. You are unable to give your partner your full attention, which interferes with building a bond between the two of you.

This chapter will *help* you to understand your fears and assist you to increase your *confidence* in making *commitments*. Making *commitments* is a skill to develop, just the same way as you are developing your character skills and will develop your communication skills later in the book. You may actually be surprised at how skillful you already are at making and keeping *commitments*.

One *commitment* that you will explore in depth in this chapter is your own personal choice about whether to engage in sexual activities before marriage. You will understand the choices that are possible to make, and then *commit* to the ones you believe are best for you in the present and in the future.

THE PRACTICE OF COMMITMENT

Commitment **is a vital practice within a relationship that** *helps* **you and a partner to focus on developing as a couple. When you** *commit* **yourself to someone as a partner, it is easier to stay** *faithful,* **assist a partner with their** *purposes* **and goals, and determine whether the relationship is one that will last. When you are uncommitted, other potential partners can distract you, and your energy is dissipated in wondering about the relationship.** An uncommitted person acts like a "dance butterfly" and flits around from flower to flower with multiple dance partners. They can be *excellent* dancers, and dance *beautifully* with other *excellent* dancers, but they do not *commit* to a permanent partner.

Dancing with just one partner changes the nature of the dance. If you want to have a deep friendship-based relationship that has the potential for marriage, *commitment* is a vital factor. You can never accurately answer your questions about the relationship you are in, unless you *commit* to it. The act of making a *commitment* makes it possible to fully observe each other, learn about each other's character, and assess the relationship accurately. In other words, making a *commitment* causes action and exploration of each other that will not occur otherwise. You behave differently, events happen, and people assist you because you are *committed*. Consider this perspective:

> Until one is committed there is hesitancy, the chance to draw back, always ineffectiveness. Concerning all acts of initiative (and creation), there is one elementary truth, the ignorance of which kills countless ideas and splendid plans: that the moment one definitely commits oneself, then Providence moves too. All sorts of things occur to help one that would never otherwise have occurred. A whole stream of events issues from the decision, raising in one's favor all manner of unforeseen incidents and meetings and material assistance, which no man could have dreamt would have come his way.[1]

Commitments are made in stages, and each one is a choice you make. Initially, you *commit* to be friends, and then if that is going well, you *commit* to be exclusive partners (or you work on both at the same time!) If your initial *commitment* to be partners goes well, then you move forward and *commit* to court each other, during which time, you seriously consider marriage. If this courting stage is harmonious, then you *commit* to engagement. Finally, there is the biggest *commitment*, to *create* a happy, lasting marriage.

At each stage of a relationship, you and a partner also make *commitments* for how you will speak and act with each other. This chapter will guide you through your personal *commitments* related to sexual intimacy. Other chapters will address *commitments* such as agreeing to meet certain expectations, how you choose to communicate with a partner, and how you and a partner will get to know each other. Each *commitment* that you make provides skill practice. However, each can also prompt uncertainty or fear.

FEAR OF COMMITMENT

At times you may feel scared when you think about making a *commitment* to finding a partner, being someone's partner, or about the relationship becoming serious. You may identify with some of the concerns of these people:

"I was deeply hurt by the last person who lied to me."
"I am afraid of not ending up with the right person."
"Many people I know are divorcing, and I am scared it will happen to me."
"I do not let people get close to me, because it is difficult to trust them."
"Sometimes my choices do not work out well."
"I do not know how to find someone special."[2]

You may feel pulled in different directions. You may know what it feels like to be lonely, yet feel safer not taking the risk of beginning a relationship. You may know how challenging it is to make effective decisions alone, yet be glad you do not have to negotiate with someone else. You may long to be with someone, yet not want to face the possibility of rejection. You want someone who knows you almost as well as you know yourself, and someone who *loves* and *accepts* the real you. However, it is often difficult to go forward and share yourself with another person in the face of negative experiences or present concerns. Depending on the level of fear or concern you have, it may hold you back from being in a relationship at all, or make you hesitate about *committing* exclusively to someone.

Sometimes, even though your emotions feel very real, your fears are actually groundless and come from your imagination (which is a misuse of the quality of *creativity*!). Other times, your fears are based upon actual occurrences in your life. Evaluating your observations and experiences related to the *commitments* and promises the people in your life have kept or not kept will *help* you to understand how fear, distrust, anger, or other responses shape your attitude toward others.

If your parents, other relatives, or close friends have gone through separations or divorces, you may be skeptical about your own ability to keep a relationship *commitment*. If you have been on the receiving end of betrayal or too many broken promises, how does that affect your *trust* in others? If you are suspicious of everyone because of the actions of one untrustworthy person, which is an unrealistic conclusion,

Copyright 2006 by Randy Glasbergen. www.glasbergen.com

"You have a 30 year mortgage, a 5 year car lease, and a lifetime gym membership...but you're afraid of commitment?"

it will negatively affect your ability to develop friendships and a close relationship with a partner. If you have gone through negative experiences, it is more empowering if you use them as motivation to discover what will work in relationships instead.

An unfortunately common expectation these days is that most relationships will be short-lived, even when you hope for them to last. You may believe that even marriage is a throwaway commodity at the first signs of difficulty. **Cohabitation and divorce rates are high in many places in the world, and this factor may have affected your attitude toward *commitment*.** Think carefully—do you want to have a healthy, happy, and lasting relationship? What are you willing to do to maintain one? Working through this book is a significant step in that direction, and you have started with the most important component already—character. The more knowledge and skills you gain, the fewer fears you will have, and the more empowered you will be in *creating* a lasting relationship.

Part of empowering yourself to make a *commitment* to someone is changing how you interact with others. Any of the following can signal that you are avoiding *commitment*:

- Holding people at an emotional distance
- Agreeing to meet someone and then not showing up
- Making promises half-heartedly or without intending to keep them
- Having a pattern of indecisiveness or uncertainty
- Entering into a sexual relationship with someone you do not know or have little in common with beyond physical attraction
- Avoiding communication with a friend or partner

- Talking a lot about doing things but not taking action
- Being deliberately unattractive, such as by wearing ugly clothing, gaining excessive weight, or not keeping good hygiene
- Having frequent misunderstandings with people about who agreed to do what
- Looking around for another partner while being with someone else
- Having multiple partners at the same time
- Going on a continual series of very brief dates
- Being very critical of a partner for not meeting overly high expectations
- Avoiding answering the phone when friends or potential partners call, or ignoring emails or other types of communication
- Changing contact information regularly and not sharing it
- Choosing unsuitable partners
- Leaving and coming back to the same partner repeatedly
- Living with someone without marrying them
- Being disloyal or unfaithful in serious relationships

Can you begin to see how any of these patterns might indicate that you have a resistance to *commitment*? "The moment you believe you can do something, power seems to stream into you; the moment you believe you cannot do it, you have lost more than half the battle, you seem to be drained of the force necessary to do it."[3]

Commitment actually can be natural and easy if you are clear about whom you are, what you value, and do your best to choose a partner who effectively practices character qualities and is compatible with you.

ACTIVITY

Set a goal each day for a week to make and keep three small and simple promises. Notice what is easy or difficult about being consistent and keeping your word.

~ Questions for Reflection ~

1. What scares me about *commitment*?
2. How do I act when people break promises to me?
3. What are my fears about divorce?
4. What do I think led my parents or friends to go through breakups or divorces?
5. How might I avoid similar outcomes without avoiding relationships?

COMMITMENT TO PARTNERSHIP

Another factor that can prevent you from *committing* to a relationship partner is excessive individual independence. You may think that life is easier if you are on your own and you do not need to involve anyone else in your choices and decisions. You can independently decide to buy something, travel, or change jobs without having a discussion first with a partner, and no one holds you accountable for your actions. This independence can be a lonely position, however, and you do not have the benefit of gaining perspectives from someone else who knows you well. You lose the rich opportunity of having a special companion and working in partnership on character growth, eventually establishing a family within marriage, or having someone to be with during retirement years.

If you move into a serious relationship with someone, and from there to marriage, your relationship success becomes dependent upon your ability to be a *cooperative* couple. This *cooperation* means moving from being self-centered to allowing someone to share in your choices and decision-making processes, and learning together what is best for both of you. This shift may not be easy, even when you want to make it. *Cooperation* between you and a partner can be as simple as discussing plans to spend an evening together, or it can be as difficult as whether one of you should accept a job transfer to another location. You may need to *strengthen* the quality of *cooperation* if you have been used to having your own independence.

The National Marriage Project 2005 report on "The State of Our Unions," links family breakdown to a "trend of modernity." It says, "Basic to this trend is the growth of a modern form of individualism, the single-minded pursuit of personal autonomy and self-interest, which takes place at the expense of established social institutions such as marriage."[4] The report continues by saying that this trend expresses itself in various countries in high rates of divorce, cohabitation, and solo parenting, as well as in fragile families. Although you may not necessarily be considering marriage at this stage, this is valuable knowledge in *helping* you to shift your behavior to support your long-term relationship success.

Some ways that you can ease away from being overly independent and learn partnership skills are to:

- Identify someone else's need for assistance and act to meet it appropriately
- Participate on a team or committee that requires you to engage in group decision-making sessions
- Offer a friend or partner equal turns with you in deciding on activities to do together

- Ask someone to *help* you with a task or project or to give input on it
- Look after a child with someone for a few hours or days
- Pray for others

You will think of many more ideas as you begin to focus on the actions you can take to have an outward-looking and *unity*-building focus with others.

~ *Questions for Reflection* ~

1. When is it important for me to act independently? Why?
2. When am I able to *cooperate* with others?
3. What aspects of partnership appeal to me? What aspects do I resist?

ACTIVITY

Choose and carry out an activity that you would enjoy and that requires *cooperation* from others. Notice when you have a tendency to take over and do tasks yourself rather than involving someone else. Notice when you are successful at working with others in *unity*.

BUILDING COMMITMENT CONFIDENCE

If you assess your life, you may actually be surprised how good you are at making and keeping *commitments*. When you clearly think through the implications of a promise and your ability to fulfill it, and then make the promise to another person, you are making a *commitment*. You make a pledge inside of yourself to do something, state the *commitment* aloud to someone else, and then act in agreement with your words. You have probably done this many times in your life.

Consider Charlotte's experience:

> Charlotte says regularly to her friends that she wants to get married, but she keeps going through short-term relationships instead. She is starting to realize that her behavior is counterproductive to achieving her goal. She notices that she gets very excited about being with someone, but once the relationship starts, she loses interest. She starts to criticize him and begins to sabotage the relationship. She starts to think about the next potential partner instead of being with her current one. The positive feeling of capturing a man's interest is so powerful, that she keeps going into new relationships to achieve it.

Charlotte enlists her best friend, Karensa, in assisting her to change this pattern. She makes a *commitment* to herself to act differently, and then makes a firm promise to Karensa to work on it. Charlotte asks Karensa to speak up if she sees her slipping backward into old behavior. When Charlotte meets Brian a few weeks later, she knows he is special. She decides to go slowly and focus on building a friendship with him.

After Charlotte and Brian have been getting to know each other for a few weeks, Charlotte and Karensa are working together *creating* photo albums. Charlotte starts talking about feeling restless and wanting to either push Brian faster in the relationship or get out. Karensa reminds Charlotte of her *commitment* to act differently this time. She asks Charlotte about what she likes about Brian to *help* her remember that she wants a relationship, not a brief conquest.

As you look back over your life, you will likely see that you have made regular *commitments* to yourself. In the story, Charlotte is making a *commitment* to herself to handle her relationship with Brian with a higher level of *integrity* and *responsibility* than she has in the past. How do you feel when you keep a *commitment?* When you keep your promises, you often increase your self-*respect*, thereby increasing your ability to make *commitments* to others. Some personal *commitments* that contribute to your well-being can include eating healthy food, reading a good book, praying regularly, watching less television, spending less time on the computer or cellphone, taking a class, exercising, or meditating.

You have also had considerable practice in making and keeping *commitments* to other people. From the time you were very young, you have had opportunities to make and successfully keep promises. To your family, friends, teachers, faith leaders, employers, or civic leaders, repeatedly you have said you will do something, and then you did your best to complete the task. You valued and kept your word and experienced the benefits that resulted. You also learned along the way that breaking your promises resulted in negative consequences. These consequences then trained you and reinforced for you the importance of keeping promises and only making ones that you can fulfill. You may have also learned how to renegotiate ones that became difficult to keep.

Keeping promises prepared you for making increasingly significant *commitments*. When you were younger, you may have promised to return a toy or book you borrowed, clean your room, do your school homework, take care of a pet, or prepare a meal for your family. As you grew up, you gained opportunities to be successful at longer-term *commitments*. For example, you may have enrolled in college, signed an employment contract, volunteered for a *service* or development project, or taken out a loan on a car. You could also have *committed* to a particular religion or *spiritual* practice with the intent of being involved with it for life. All of these choices involve agreeing to do something for an extended period, and they include the understanding that there will be a mutual exchange. Each party involved in the agreement gives and gets something, whether it is money, learning, participation, character development, or other benefits. An exchange also happens in a relationship—you and a partner both benefit from mutual *commitments*.

When you *commit* to dance with a partner, you will have many opportunities to observe how both you and your partner behave. Do you both show up at the agreed time and place? Are you both wearing clothing that is appropriate for the occasion? Did you both practice the agreed steps, so you can tango, waltz, or salsa dance together?

Reducing Your Fears

You can address your fears and concerns about *commitment* in a variety of ways. You can try making and keeping small promises and work up to larger ones. You can pray, meditate, and ask for *spiritual* assistance. You can also focus on the potential positive outcome. When you are able to overcome your fear of making a *commitment*, or practice *courage* when you are feeling fearful, it opens the possibility of being in a great relationship. With *commitment* as a regular practice in your life, the following outcomes are possible:

- You and others learn you are *trustworthy*
- You *respect* yourself and experience a feeling of satisfaction
- You are relaxed and happy instead of feeling guilty and uncomfortable about disappointing others
- You are able to be *truthful* about your actions
- You are able to maintain a bond of *love* between you and others
- You can focus on deepening a friendship with a partner
- You communicate more openly and effectively
- You are more likely to *assertively* work through and resolve a problem with someone rather than run away or be destructive toward your relationship

These positive outcomes can lessen the fears and concerns you have about *commitment* in general, and assist you to be *courageous* and *commit* to a partner.

Note: This section addressed a fear of *commitment*. However, in some places and circumstances, relationship and marriage practices are strict and rigid. Parents, cultural customs, or religious beliefs may force a couple into *commitment*. In these circumstances, couples may conform to these external demands, but they are unhappy with their partner. *Ideally*, *commitment* will involve free choice for both partners.

ACTIVITY

Take a few minutes to reflect realistically and *honestly* on your history of keeping—and breaking—*commitments* to yourself. See if you notice any patterns throughout your life. Then complete **Worksheet 5.1: Making Commitments**. Use it to assess your recent history of being able to make and keep *commitments*.

~ Questions for Reflection ~

1. What value do I see in *commitment*?
2. How can I reduce my fears?
3. What positive outcomes can happen if I *commit* to a relationship?

COMMITMENT AND SEX

Physical intimacies, including sexual touch and intercourse, have become the norm in dating relationships in many parts of the world for people of all ages. When you care for someone, the pull to be physically intimate can be very *strong*. You do want to know that there is a spark of attraction between you and a partner. **However, it is clear that sexual touch alters relationships.**

Sexual intimacy while you and a partner are getting to know each other, or as a method of getting to know each other, increases the difficulty of objectively assessing a partner's character. It shifts the focus onto physical attraction rather than exploring and developing the other far more important dimensions of your friendship-based relationship.

As you read the sections that follow, think about the sexual choices that you have made previously, what choices you are *committing* to today, and what your *commitment* is to yourself and to a future partner. In a world where sex is so pervasive and prominent, the choices will often not be easy ones for you to make or stay *committed* to fulfilling. You may feel confused at times, change your *commitments*, or try new choices. These sections present you with a foundation for whatever you choose to do.

Defining Sex and Intimacy

Sex is primarily a physical act of intimate touch, but it has mental, emotional, and *spiritual* components. Some people define sex from a physical standpoint as occurring only when there is sexual intercourse. However, it is actually broader than that, because it includes any intentional contact that arouses a sexual response, whether you are by yourself or with a partner. Therefore, sex also includes actions such as:

- Talking explicitly about sex
- Listening to sexually explicit musical lyrics
- Viewing sexual images (pornography or some television shows and movies)
- Reading books that arouse the desire to have sex
- Fantasizing and masturbating
- Manual sex as a couple
- Oral sex

If you choose not to engage in sex in a relationship, it includes avoiding all of these above actions and more. Even couples who make the choice to have sex will be *wise* to have *respectful* limits that eliminate engaging in a number of these activities. As you think about your choices, you will also assess which ones are more likely to develop your lower nature rather than your higher one (Chapter 1), and therefore reduce your self-*respect*.

Note: Refer back to Chapter 4, page 85, for the behaviors related to sex that can be warning signs in a relationship.

Copyright 1999 by Randy Glasbergen.
www.glasbergen.com

"LAST NIGHT MARTY AND I GOT VERY INTIMATE . . .
WE REVEALED OUR INTERNET PASSWORDS
TO EACH OTHER!"

Sex and intimacy are concepts that are often paired together. They can be connected, but they are also quite different. Intimacy is an emotional feeling of familiarity and closeness that is based upon the shared and accumulated experiences between two people. These experiences include every aspect of life. Couples build intimacy by openly and *honestly* sharing the full range of their thoughts and feelings on a variety of topics. Intimacy includes sharing experiences that build connection and closeness. Some of these experiences can be responding to a challenge together or *helping* each other with tasks.

~ *Questions for Reflection* ~

1. What is my general attitude toward sex?
2. What does sex mean to me? What are the sources of my information?
3. Do I know enough about sex and its consequences to make informed choices? Where can I gain more information if necessary?
4. What are my understanding, expectations, and needs about intimacy?
5. How can a partner and I develop non-sexual intimacy?

SEX AND CHARACTER

A significant challenge that occurs when you choose to be sexually intimate with someone, particularly early on in a relationship, is that you do not really know the person with whom you are sharing such physical intimacies. Consider this perspective:

> When we feel attracted to someone, it's natural that we want to express that attraction physically, initially through a hug, a kiss, holding hands or physical proximity. However, if these initial, physical expressions of affection become frequent, intensify, and come to play a prominent part in the relationship, they can quickly grow into a force which binds the couple together emotionally and which makes objectivity about one another's qualities difficult to achieve.[5]

Objectivity is challenging to hold onto when you and a partner are having sex. When you have fully "given" yourself to another person physically, you then want confirmation that you have made a good partner choice. As you get to know your partner, you then may minimize serious issues, make excuses for your partner's misbehavior, or not even see problems that are there. Sexual involvement can also make it more difficult to raise concerns or leave a relationship when you do see serious character issues in a partner.

Chelsea and Hunter experienced some of these difficulties:

> Chelsea and Hunter meet for the first time when they sit next to each other on a flight from their hometown to another city. He is on his way to visit family, and she has a business meeting to attend. They have a lively conversation throughout the 3-hour flight and feel definite attraction to each other. They are able to meet for dinner at their destination city, and they get together for a date upon their return

home. At the end of the date, Chelsea invites Hunter into her apartment. After having some coffee, they begin kissing and touching each other very provocatively. Their passion continues and climaxes with them having sex.

For their next date, Hunter takes Chelsea to the horse racetrack. He keeps excusing himself to go place bets on various horses, most of which lose their races. Hunter becomes increasingly and loudly angry at his streak of bad luck, but Chelsea comforts him. At the end of the night, Hunter has lost hundreds of dollars, but Chelsea reasons to herself that this was probably just a one-time event. She convinces herself that he probably will not get this angry over other things. Chelsea stays the night with him, and she tries to assist him to forget his losses by having sex with him again.

When the couple goes out the next time to a concert, they include Chelsea's sister Charlene and her boyfriend. Chelsea and Charlene talk loudly throughout the concert, making it difficult for anyone around them to focus on the music. Hunter is angry, both at their behavior and at being ignored all night, but he does not want to say anything to Chelsea that might prevent her from staying overnight at his place. He knows Chelsea and Charlene have not seen each other in awhile, and decides to ignore their rudeness.

Very early on in their relationship, Chelsea and Hunter are establishing a pattern of ignoring serious issues, in part to protect their sexual relationship. They are discovering character and behavior problems in each other that may sabotage the relationship, but they are putting their feelings of physical attraction first and not addressing the issues.

Sex without *commitment* and *love* becomes meaningless and unsatisfying. When the satisfaction of immediate desires becomes the primary function or focus of a relationship, you may ignore or not communicate your long-term expectations and requirements of each other. This type of uncommitted sexual encounter interferes with getting to know each other mentally, emotionally, and *spiritually*.

When you physically touch someone, or they touch you, there is an emotional and memory imprint. The more touch there is that feels good, the more you want it to continue. The memory imprint then becomes *stronger*, as do the ties you will likely feel with the person. **This physical intimacy can set up the illusion in your mind that you and a partner are very close with each other, when you actually are not. One of you may be thinking that having sex means you are in a *committed* relationship, while the other could be focused only on enjoying the physical experience.** If the relationship then ends, you may still have the desire for more touch that feels good. This desire can set you up to be in an unwise cycle in subsequent relationships of seeking physical contact when you do not know a partner well.

Physical intimacy can be especially tempting when you are in a long-distance relationship, because it can be very difficult to avoid sexual contact when you visit each other. This difficulty is especially the case if you end up staying in the same place together. Your emotions are already high from being together after time apart, and it may feel natural to be physically intimate as a result. You may think that because you do not see each other often, that having sex will make your reunions even better. However, it is already more difficult when you are geographically apart to keep "both eyes open™" so you clearly and accurately observe a partner's character. Having sex is likely to cloud your vision even further and make sex more important than is *wise* at this stage in your relationship.

~ Question for Reflection ~

How can having sex affect my ability to know a partner's character?

ACTIVITY

Have a discussion with a friend who has had sex with a partner and explore how it affected their relationship.

SAVING SEX FOR MARRIAGE

Ultimately, within marriage, sex is a bonding act of *unity* between all aspects of two people. The *strong love* and deep intimacy between the couple make sex more mutually pleasurable, gratifying, and *unifying*. Consider this perspective from author Justice St. Rain:

> Spiritual and emotional intimacy develop in stages. We go from strangers to acquaintances, to activities partners, to friends, to close friends, to intimate friends. "Instant spiritual intimacy" is a fallacy. It is a popular myth because it is very easy to project our fantasies on people rather than wait to see if a person's inner reality matches his or her outer appearance. "We have so much in common…we think so much alike…It was love at first sight." No matter how much we *want* these things to be true, we can't know that they are until we spend some time together. If they are true, then the time we spend confirming our initial impressions will be a source of great pleasure

and fond memories. But if we are mistaken, we will be grateful that we "looked before we leaped." We may tell ourselves we have fallen out of love just in time to avoid a bad relationship, but in fact, we never loved to begin with.

Physical intimacy also develops in stages, and these stages should *follow* rather than precede their spiritual counterparts. "Instant physical intimacy" is really a form of *exposure*. There is an adrenaline rush that comes from laying ourselves out naked on the table (emotionally or physically) that has nothing to do with knowing, caring or moving closer, but a great deal to do with our deep longing to be known and accepted. If we do not establish our emotional safety first, then the vulnerability inherent in exposing this longing will only increase our fear and decrease our true intimacy.[6]

There are compelling reasons for you to consider choosing to wait for marriage to have sex. Laura M. Brotherson, a certified family life educator, identifies the following reasons as some of those that relate to saving sex for marriage:

- Indicates *trustworthiness*
- Provides a profound sense of accomplishment
- Builds *confidence* and self-*respect*
- Avoids emotional turmoil and heartache [also known as "relationship drama"]
- Avoids regret
- Develops *self-discipline*
- Shows maturity
- Provides physical and emotional safety from sexually-transmitted infections or diseases (STIs/STDs) and unwanted pregnancy

Brotherson expands on some of these points with the following focus on one's character [See Part 3 for an explanation of the word "*purity*"]:

Those who save sex for marriage may share something in common with those who run a marathon, or who climb Mount Everest—a huge feeling of accomplishment. The enduring satisfaction of having accomplished something difficult, often in the face of great adversity, provides a solid foundation for the soul, and a continuing reservoir of genuine contentment and confidence. The quick thrill of succumbing to a sexual experience pales in comparison to the permanent thrill of overcoming great odds to maintain sexual purity for marriage. A profound sense of accomplishment can also come from starting over, at any point, to remain sexually pure until marriage.

...Withstanding the pressures to engage in premarital sexual activity bolsters one's confidence—especially knowing that such an accomplishment can be difficult. The personal thrill of succeeding at something that many say can't be done adds strength to one's confidence and abilities. Confidence in self provides a quiet strength and assurance against the winds of adversity that attempt to blow us over.

Respecting oneself, and others, enough to wait to engage in sexual relations only within marriage also builds self-respect. To respect oneself means to appreciate, to esteem highly, to love. As [people] face life's challenges with resolute determination to save the gift of sexual intimacy for marriage, they develop greater respect for themselves. Self-respect is thus a cause and a result of remaining sexually abstinent before marriage.[7]

For many people, there is also the *spiritual* significance of sex within marriage to consider. *Ideally*, marriage includes a *strong* connection between the hearts and souls of two people. When sexual intimacy includes practicing all of the character qualities, such as *confidence*, *flexibility*, *patience*, *generosity*, and more, the higher natures of the couple are part of sexual intimacy.[8] Remember, Chapter 1 indicated that your higher nature can be referred to as your *spiritual* self. In addition, intercourse becomes an act that affirms the fundamental *unity* in the marriage.

Many people view all sexual acts as special or sacred between spouses, as described below. Consider this perspective from author Tim Alan Gardner in *Sacred Sex*:

> It is important to acknowledge that God could have arranged the whole reproduction thing any way He wanted: a hidden button, a super-secret handshake, or some unique facial exchange that brought about conception. Really, He could have. But instead, He designed sex. He must have had a good reason, but what is it? The answer, in short, is that God wanted sex to be a lot more than just a really fun thing for wives and husbands to do together. And He wanted it to be more than an extremely enjoyable way to populate the planet. He had a far loftier goal in mind. God designed marital sex to be an encounter with the divine. Sexual intimacy…was never intended to be experienced solely in the emotional and physical realms. Rather, it is to be a spiritual, even mystical, experience in which two bodies become one. God is present in a very real way every time this happens.
>
> Sex really is holy. It's a sacred place shared in the intimacy of marriage.[9]

Does the significance of sex between spouses mean that if you have already had sex before marriage, it will be impossible to have a satisfying sex life within marriage? Perhaps not; however, it may be more difficult, take more *acceptance*, and be more challenging to establish healthy sexual intimacy. These may especially be the case if you have regrets about not waiting, or if you have had multiple partners. **If you have already had sex, you can also choose a different course for your future. It is never too late.**

You might think that you need to try sex before marriage to ensure that you and your partner are sexually compatible. However, if the two of you have some sexual difficulties together, or the experience does not quite meet either of your expectations, you and your partner may end what could have been a great relationship. A *committed* married couple is more likely to try options such as discussion, seeking therapy, reading *helpful* books, praying, and working together to resolve any sexual challenges that arise.

Alternatively, you could experience great sex before marriage, when there is the emotional excitement that often accompanies having an affair, only to discover that this goes away once the relationship becomes more established. The initial thrill evolves into emotions that are more realistic. You may see this change as a sign that the relationship is failing, rather than as a natural process as your *love* deepens and matures. The best place to explore physical intimacy is within a *committed* marriage. Otherwise, there is danger in mistaking sexual gratification, and the accompanying emotions of attraction, for the lasting, *committed*, and more enduring *love* that is based upon friendship and character.

If you were sexually active in the past, and you are considering making a different choice now, then it may assist you to look back and understand why you made your previous choices. If you find it a challenge understanding the past or making new choices, talk to a close friend or counselor, pray for *detachment* and *self-discipline*, meditate, or seek supportive family members or groups.

As you assess what choice to make about sex before marriage it may assist you to ask yourself some key questions:

- What do I regret from previous sexual choices
- What regrets do I know that others have?
- What do I not want to regret in the future?
- What are my beliefs about sex before marriage?
- What cultural norms, religious scripture, or family rules guide my choices?
- What difference will my choices make to my current or future children?

These are not easy questions, so you may need to pause and reflect on them or write in your journal about them. You may also find it beneficial to talk about them with a *trusted* friend or family member, *spiritual* advisor, or counselor.

ACTIVITIES

1. Complete **Worksheet 5.2: Assessing Your Perceptions and Commitments about Sex** to explore your thoughts about sex. It is fine to do this activity on your own. If you already have a partner, then you may wish to involve them in completing the worksheet with you. You may also find it *helpful* to discuss your answers with a *trusted* friend or relative.

2. Use popular magazines to find and cut out pictures of people projecting love, sex, intimacy, or words that reflect these themes. Create a collage by gluing them onto a large sheet of paper or cardboard. Discuss with your partner or a friend the various images in the collage and the expectations and feelings that arise for you in looking at them. How are your perceptions of sex and intimacy shaped by popular media? By your family? By other sources? Are these positive or negative influences?

   Note: If you are struggling with your sexual responses to magazine photos, please practice *discernment* and *wisdom* to determine whether doing this activity will be *helpful* or harmful for you.

~ Questions for Reflection ~

1. What do I think and feel about sex before marriage? What do I think and feel about waiting until marriage?
2. Why would I have sex before marriage? If I have sex before marriage, might I regret it later?
3. Why would I wait to have sex until marriage?
4. If I have already had sex with either a previous or current partner outside of marriage, do I want to make a different choice now? Why or why not?
5. What assumptions and expectations about my future with someone will I make if I have sex with them?
6. If a relationship ends after I have been physically intimate with a partner, how will I feel about my choices and myself?

SUPPORTING THE CHOICE TO WAIT

It is a common myth that people cannot control their sexual impulses and actions. This view has become a widespread misconception. With such a belief, it is little wonder that many give in to sexual temptation. You must believe it is possible to save sex for marriage, in order to be able to do so. Also, it is obviously possible, because there are people

who do it successfully. This is when *commitment* and *strength* apply. If you believe that you can save this special gift for marriage, and then choose to do so, you will increase your chances of success.

If you choose to wait to have sex until you are married, it will be *wise* to have a plan to support your choices. One of the main ways to support your *commitment* is to fill your life with activities that make a positive difference for you, your family, and your community. *Spiritual* activities and resource people can also provide support and balance for the pull to be sexually involved with someone.

You may have to change some of your habits and routines to avoid temptation. Start by clearly identifying what leads you toward thoughts or actions that involve sex. Then, it will *help* if you assess your lifestyle and determine where making changes will assist you. These changes may include:

- Minimizing time alone with a close friend or partner
- Choosing to be with different people and in new situations
- Disposing of magazines, books, or movies that lead you to think about sex or to masturbation
- Avoiding going to Internet sites that include sex
- Get involved in activities that keep your thoughts away from a focus on sex

Your choice requires you to be *strong* in your convictions and *courageous* in speaking up about your *commitment* with a new partner. Dr. Paul Coleman, author of *How to Say It for Couples, Communicating with Tenderness, Openness and Honesty*, recommends that you have specific phrases in mind to say to a partner that you practice ahead of time. Being tentative in your statements will not benefit your relationship, because your partner will be confused about your convictions. Dr. Coleman *encourages* making the statement clearly and firmly, framed by a positive and reassuring message. For instance, you might say, "You are very important to me and I love you. But I firmly believe it is best that I wait before becoming sexual with you."[10]

You will also think about how to be clear in communicating your new *commitment* to a current partner, if you have one. Unless your partner is also *committed* to the same new behavior, your change in perspective will be difficult for them to *accept*. Do your best to be consistent with your message, but also recognize that you may slip backward at times as you learn new behavior. Simply re-*commit*, try again, and *persevere*. It is important to have a partner who has *sincere respect* for you and your choices.

Part of what will be difficult is that your partner may choose to leave the relationship because you are no longer being a sexual partner for them. Is it important to you to remain with someone you *care* about, despite the fact that they are not willing to *respect* your heart-felt choices? Or will you remain *true* to yourself and your *wise* decisions? What can you do to stay *strong* and handle this choice in a way that *respects* your *integrity*?

Be cautious that you do not try to rush prematurely into marriage as a response to this dilemma. Marrying just for the sake of *committing* to saving sex until marriage will not give you the benefit of practicing your *self-discipline*, self-*respect*, *courage*, and genuine *commitment*. If you are not ready to be married, making that choice will also not solve your challenge, but will rather compound your difficulties.

~ Questions for Reflection ~

1. What is my personal *commitment* about having or not having sex with a partner?
2. What boundaries do I have or want to have for myself related to me touching someone else or allowing them to touch me?
3. What changes do I need to make in my life to reduce temptation?
4. How can I communicate my *commitment* to certain choices about sex to a partner?

ABSTINENCE

Abstinence is a concept that means refraining from indulging any kind of appetite. One of the ways it applies is to sexual appetite.

In this context, it includes not having sexual intercourse or participating in other kinds of sexual touch, such as fondling breasts or stroking someone's genitals. Participating in even light sexual touching essentially gives someone permission to touch every part of you. Abstinence is saying "no" to having sexual contact with someone before marriage.

When you feel intensely about someone, you want to

Copyright 2005 by Randy Glasbergen.
www.glasbergen.com

"MOM SAYS I SHOULD PRACTICE ABSTINENCE. I'M GOING TO PRACTICE ABSTAINING FROM YARD WORK AND HOUSE WORK AND BABYSITTING MY SISTER. THAT WAY I'LL BE REAL GOOD AT ABSTAINING IF SOMETHING ELSE COMES ALONG."

try every possible way of being close. Your initial instinct may be to do this through touch. It is better to first develop an emotional and *spiritual* bond. This bond provides a *strong* and lasting connection between two people. If you have not already established *love* and *commitment* within your relationship, sex can actually make the painful lack of genuine emotional intimacy more pronounced, frustrating, and upsetting.

Infections and Diseases

One of the important values in choosing abstinence is that it protects your health. Every time you intimately touch someone in a sexual way, from a health and biological perspective, you are not only having sex with them, but you are potentially exposing yourself to anything that their previous partners have had. With each sexual partner you have, concerns such as sexually transmitted infections/diseases (STIs/STDs) increase. Dozens of varieties of STIs/STDs are at epidemic proportions globally, across all ages from teens to seniors, and for both genders.

Some of these conditions can be transmitted through skin or bodily fluid contact other than intercourse. Many do not have obvious symptoms, or the disease could still be in a dormant stage without symptoms. This lack of symptoms can lead to a person becoming infected without even knowing about it. Consequently, they can spread the disease to others without even finding out that they were the cause of the transmission.

Some STIs/STDs are treatable, but some are incurable with treatable symptoms. STIs/STDs can, in some cases, destroy the physical ability to have children in the future, require surgery, or lead to serious illnesses or even death. If you have been sexually active, it is essential to practice *responsibility* and be tested for these conditions before starting a sexual relationship with a new person or getting married.

Although the following paragraph is from a book addressed to women, it makes points that apply to both genders:

> There are now a bevy of sexually transmitted diseases to worry about from herpes to AIDS. It seems that infected bodily fluids are now classified as a concealed weapon, and you're forced to have an awkward talk before he conceals his weapon inside of you. You need to ask the guy you're thinking of having sex with if he's been tested for AIDS, if he's ever used intravenous drugs, … and how many sexual partners he's had. … And if you don't question him at all, it can kill you. As if that's not enough reason to become celibate, there's also the issue of pregnancy to deal with.[11]

The interesting thing about STIs/STDs is that they are of no issue whatsoever to two individuals who are totally monogamous and *faithful* to each other for a lifetime.

┌───┐

~ Questions for Reflection ~

1. What do I think about abstinence?
2. Have I made the *commitment* to be abstinent? Why or why not?
3. How has being abstinent affected the lives of people I know?

└───┘

Pregnancy

Along with the questions that arise between couples of whether to "do it" or not on the first date, the second date, or before marriage, comes the possibility of conceiving a child. Pregnancy is sometimes the unavoidable result of sexual intercourse, often due to failing to use birth control or not using it properly. **It is important to uphold the standard of not having sex with anyone with whom you would not want to share the *commitment* and *responsibilities* of lifelong parenthood.** If learning the right dance steps with your partner is a challenge, imagine how much more difficult it would be if you were carrying a baby as you learn to dance! The admission price to that dance is costly for everyone involved.

If you had a child without being married to your sexual partner, you may now have a child to raise, have given one up for adoption, or have had an abortion. Depending on the circumstances, how you handled a pregnancy brings up such profound and complex emotional issues as future fertility, guilt, grieving, unwillingness to have children with someone else, how to handle child support, or ongoing contact with the child.

For teens in particular, it is important to remember that any sexual involvement can lead to pregnancy—birth control methods are frequently not effective. The *responsibilities* of parenthood can severely disrupt your life, change your plans forever, force you to take on adult *responsibilities* prematurely, disrupt your education, or leave you economically challenged for many years into the future.

For adults, the risk of pregnancy might still be an issue, and birth control methods can also fail adults, but you may be old enough and prepared to be a parent if pregnancy does occur. This view of pregnancy may cause you to think that there is no reason to abstain from sex. You may be *confident* that, if you use contraceptives and lower your risk of pregnancy or disease, there are no other issues to consider. Actually, there are many other serious considerations, particularly if the father chooses not to be involved in the child's life. Raising a child alone is not easy, children do better in a family with two biological and married parents, and it is a lifetime *responsibility*.[12]

At times, some women deliberately seek sexual intercourse and pregnancy because they believe it will *create* someone who will *love* them. This choice is an indicator that the person's self-*respect* is probably weak, and they will benefit from *strengthening* their character qualities. Others see pregnancy, consciously or subconsciously, as a way to force their partner to stay with them or to provide them with long-term financial support. Again, this choice does not show *respect* to either partner, and it can cause long-term harm to the child from having an unwilling parent or from being raised in an unstable home.

~ Questions for Reflection ~

1. Am I prepared for the *commitment* to be a parent?
2. If I choose to have sex, what will I do to prevent pregnancy?

CHASTITY

Chastity is a less-familiar concept that includes abstinence, but it goes beyond sexual acts outside of marriage. It includes making *respectful* choices about such aspects of your life as your thoughts, clothing, and entertainment. These choices *strengthen* your ability to willingly and *joyfully* wait to have sex until you are married. Buddha says, "Abstain from impurity, and lead a life of chastity."[13] When you choose and *commit* to *chastity*, you do not spend your time on sexual activities and preoccupations and instead fill your life with useful activities that fulfill your *purpose* in life (Chapter 2). **The focus on having sex lessens when you balance it with all the rest of your life.**

Chastity is a quality of your higher nature. It *encourages* modesty, which can, in part, involve wearing clothing that covers areas of your body normally reserved for sexual experiences. This modesty does not mean that you dress in unattractive ways, but it does mean avoiding dressing in ways that prompt you to act more sexually seductive or that are deliberately provocative to others. *Chastity encourages* you to avoid actions that prompt sexual thoughts in others.

When practicing *chastity*, you avoid making comments to someone that include sexual innuendos or suggestions. Your choice of activities also excludes those that prompt sexual thoughts and responses, such as explicit movies or television shows. You also avoid putting alcohol or drugs in your body, which can lower your inhibitions and reduce your ability to make choices that are self-*respectful*.

At times throughout history, people have believed that *chastity* applies only to females and that it is impossible for males to practice it. In fact, it is a character quality that applies to and benefits both women and men. **Couples who practice *chastity* together *strengthen* their *equality*.** If you have already been sexually active, but you understand that abstaining and being *chaste* have value in your life, you can choose to change your behavior. While you cannot regain your physical virginity once you have lost it, and it is difficult to stop having sex once you start, you can choose to claim abstinence and *chastity* from this point forward. However, you may need to spend time becoming clear in your mind about your decision and possibly dealing with feelings about your previous choices.

As with abstinence, *chastity* includes maintaining *faithfulness* to your future spouse. You *commit* to reserve sexual behavior and energy to apply with your marriage partner. Consider this perspective from Rúhíyyih Rabbani in *Prescription for Living*:

> Chastity—one of the rarest of all...gems in the world to-day—means to conserve your personal sex powers, so intimate in nature, capable of conferring so much beauty on your life, for their proper expression which is with your life partner, your mate, the one who with you will share home, children and all the glad and sad burdens of living. The decency, the spiritual cleanliness of marriage, the essential humanness of it, are enhanced a thousandfold by chastity on the part of both men and women, previous to their unions. Their chances of successful marriage are also far greater, for they will then share with each other, in every way, the new life they have embarked upon. Comparisons will not be drawn, over-emphasized appetites on the part of one or the other will not have been cultivated which might mar it, and above all, they will have put sex into its proper place, where instead of stampeding the emotional nature of the individual (as it does at present to so marked a degree), it will fulfill its natural function in rounding out life and contributing to its normality and healthfulness.[14]

One of the concepts in this quotation is "stampeding the emotional nature of the individual." Often when you are feeling increasingly drawn to another person, your desire for sex with them also increases. As you focus on these feelings, or surround yourself with peers or other influences that promote sex, the feelings grow. Having sex can begin to feel emotionally essential. In a stampede, animals behave impulsively and are out of control, trampling whatever is in their way. If control is an issue for you, the key is to know and do what assists you in maintaining *self-discipline*.

In reflecting on her struggles with *chastity*, author Lauren Winner in *Real Sex, The Naked Truth About Chastity*, comments that *chastity* does not come naturally to her. She says, "In my attempts to live chastely, *prayer* has been key. It may sound hokey, but I have prayed regularly that God would re-shape my heart and my desires so that I would want the things He wants for me."[15]

You have *stronger* control over your thoughts and physical needs when you practice *chastity*. It keeps your mind clear of physical passions that cloud your judgment about a partner or your relationship. Like every quality, however, you can misuse it. *Chastity* only works well when you practice it in a gentle, *spiritual* context. Without this approach, you can become rigid, self-righteous, and judgmental about both your own and others' sexual choices.

Part of the gift of practicing *chastity* is that a "…person who is in control of his sexual impulses is enabled to have profound and enduring friendships with many people, both men and women…."[16] This control liberates people as they stop behaving in ways that prompt jealousy or mistrust.

Chastity, *helped* by *responsibility* and *purity*, also assists you to avoid spending your time on frivolous activities that waste your time. However, it includes choosing to be involved in activities that bring you and a partner genuine happiness, *joy*, and humor. **Practicing these qualities is not about being perpetually serious about life, but *joyfully* embracing the best of it. It is about choosing to *respect* your own higher nature and that of a partner, and not spend time focusing on or developing your lower nature** (Chapter 1).

Therapist Agnes Ghaznavi puts *chastity* in a broader context as she looks forward into a future where more people will choose to practice it:

> Human beings will evolve both individually and collectively: the practice of chastity by both sexes will create a protection for individuals and society as yet never experienced in the history of mankind. It will strengthen people's character, their sense of responsibility for other people's intimate character, feelings and bodily impressions. Nobody will feel the right to transgress another person's intimacy without permission. People will…also be much more conscious in their sensations and enjoyment, and thus will not be carried away by their instincts…..[17]

Just as Ghaznavi does, Mary Baker Eddy, the founder of the Christian Science Church, looks at the greater impact of *chastity*. She says, "Chastity is the cement of civilization and progress. Without it there is no stability in society…."[18] Stability is increased with healthy, well-functioning families that include *faithfulness* and monogamy as values.

Chastity allows you to make choices that show *respect* for yourself and others, and allow important aspects of your relationship to blossom.

~ *Question for Reflection* ~
What supports me in being abstinent and practicing *chastity* when I am in a relationship with someone?
ACTIVITY
Write a poem, a song, or an essay about whatever challenges you face in making choices about abstinence, *chastity*, and sex.

✂ *Encouragement* ✄

For many people in our global society, both making a *commitment* to a partner, and the choice to wait to have sex with a partner, are major challenges and accomplishments. This chapter shares choices that may be difficult for you to put into practice, but you can succeed. You may struggle at times with which ones to make, and you will learn from the ones that you do make. With consistent effort and *perseverance*, you can make the choices that increase your *respect* for yourself and bring you genuine long-lasting happiness.

Date: _____

Worksheet 5.1: Making Commitments

This worksheet will assist you to assess your ability to make and keep commitments. These commitments may or may not be related to relationships, but they will help you to see whether you have the ability to make many kinds of commitments.

Instructions:

A) Record some of the short-term commitments you have made in the last few weeks, such as a medical appointment. Indicate the promises you have made, such as agreeing to meet a friend for coffee or to play a game together.

B) Also, record some of the long-term commitments you have made in the last year, such as leasing an apartment, buying a car or home, developing a talent, coaching a sports team, registering for college, or paying off a loan.

C) Note whether you kept or are keeping each commitment. This includes such actions as showing up where and when you said you would, making payments, or being consistent with your participation.

D) Examine what prevented you from keeping the agreement, if this happened, and what assisted you to keep it, if you did. Structures that assisted you may have been keeping a calendar, using an electronic banking service, setting your cellphone to provide a reminder, or involving a friend to encourage you.

Commitment/Promise Made	Kept?	What Prevented You?	What or Who Assisted You?

Questions for Reflection:

1. What excuses and reasons do I habitually use for not making or keeping commitments?
   a. ____ I did not have time
   b. ____ It was not important
   c. ____ I had more important things to do
   d. ____ They were not really expecting me
   e. ____ I am a busy person
   f. ____ Something came up
   g. ____ Other: _____

2. If I have to break a commitment, do I communicate with the people to whom I have made the commitment, and re-negotiate it instead of missing it? ____Yes ____ No
   Why or why not? _____
   _____

3. What will assist me to communicate with another person when I cannot keep a commitment that affects them? _____
   _____

4. How do I feel when I break a commitment?
   _____

5. How do I feel when someone breaks a commitment that they made to me?
   _____

6. What will assist me to keep commitments? _____
   _____

7. What difficulties have I successfully overcome to keep commitments?
   _____
   _____

8. What have I learned from this review about how I break commitments ?
   _____
   _____

9. What have I learned from this review about how I make and keep commitments?
   _____
   _____

Date: _____

Worksheet 5.2: Assessing Your Perceptions and Commitments About Sex

This worksheet will assist you to understand all the different associations you have related to sex. It will also help you to make commitments about what sexual activities you will choose not to participate in prior to marriage.

Instructions:

A) Reflect, and then complete the first list with all the words that you can think of that relate to sex and sexual experiences.

B) Reflect, and then complete the second section with the activities you will do your best not to engage in before marriage.

Words Related to Sex

_____   _____
_____   _____
_____   _____
_____   _____
_____   _____
_____   _____
_____   _____
_____   _____

Sexual Activities You Are Committed to Not Participate in Before Marriage

_____   _____
_____   _____
_____   _____
_____   _____

Questions for Reflection:

1. What insights did I gain, or what did I learn about my attitudes and experiences related to sex? _____

_____

2. Why am I committed not to participate in the sexual activities that I wrote down?

_____

_____

Both Eyes Open: Discerning Your Expectations

Nazzy puts the next batch of bread in the oven at her bakery and sighs with fatigue. She never realized how hard it would be to run her own business, handling not only the baking, but also the finances and finding regular customers. On a rare day off, Nazzy goes for a walk in a neighborhood park and meets Ned. As they chat, she finds out that Ned has just finished a business management degree. Nazzy's need for help with the business, and her expectation that a relationship will also give her a business partner, motivates her to consider a relationship with Ned.

You are gaining *confidence* as you resolve many of the issues from your past and begin to make a *commitment* to your future. Now it is time to understand why you want to dance with a partner and what you expect from them. Do you want someone who only dances once a year on a special occasion, or do you want someone who dances through life every day? Do you want someone highly skilled in specific dance steps, or does it work for you to have someone who simply holds you and sways to the music? Do you want to lead or follow? Or would you rather share this role?

You likely have an array of complex reasons for wanting to be in a relationship, and you will have expectations of a partner as a result. Some may be realistic and beneficial. Others, however, may be unrealistic and result in a relationship full of heartbreaking disappointment and difficulties. You might be immersed in a romantic myth about finding the one perfect partner on the planet for you. This romantic view can prevent you from finding a partner or cause you to avoid *committing* to someone who can be a good partner.

Discerning what you are picturing for your future, and making any necessary adjustments to your views and expectations, is an important process. Taking the time to understand your expectations will *help* you to choose a partner who may realistically be able to meet them. Together, you and your partner will discuss what expectations you each have and how to meet them. This discussion is a key part of communication in a relationship. You can determine whether you and your partner will meet each others needs, whether you need to adjust your views, or whether you will choose to find a new partner.

As you look at your expectations for a partner, and how you want the two of you to interact together, you will also assess what you think, believe, and feel about relationships generally. This assessment includes understanding what you learned from your parents, as well as evaluating what you believe about such concepts as "soul mates" and "living happily ever after." You may not be aware of the extent to which various relationship ideas promoted in books and the media have affected how you approach and act within a relationship.

EXPECTATIONS

You may have heard the popular relationship advice that you should not have expectations of a partner. This perspective is unrealistic, unwise, and potentially destructive to a relationship, because it communicates that anything your partner does is fine with you. This myth has developed because people have experienced unhappiness from uncommunicated and unmet expectations. **In fact, expectations can be useful in a relationship, if they are clear, fair, reasonable, communicated properly, and the individuals involved agree willingly to fulfill them.**

Sources of Expectations

From all your experiences and observations, you have come to various conclusions:

- How you will behave in a relationship
- How you would like a partner to behave
- What you expect to happen between the two of you
- What having a friendship-based relationship looks like to you

You will learn more about friendship-based relationships in Part 2, but you can be thinking about this new concept as you consider your expectations. In the past, and still in many cultures and places in the world, being friends with someone that you are in a relationship with is unusual. **However, establishing a friendship with a partner will contribute to the *strength* and happiness of your relationship.** Consider what being friends with a partner will include for you. What will you appreciate about having a friendship with a relationship partner? What will you expect from such a relationship?

Your parents or whatever relationships you observed while growing up are a main source of your expectations. If your parents were not or are not friends with each other, then it may be difficult to imagine what that kind of relationship looks like. In that case, you may actually gain more understanding from observing peer friendships.

Other expectations can arise from what you observed with your parents. You can assume that something that happened between them is what should or does happen in all relationships. Perhaps your parents hugged each other every time they greeted one another. Maybe one parent made all the financial decisions for the family. They may have had good communication or barely spoke to one another. **Whatever their pattern, your awareness of your parents' habits and choices will influence your expectations of what will or will not happen in your own relationship.**

As you have participated in relationships or marriages, you have noticed what worked for you and your partner and what did not. **From these experiences, you have then developed further expectations for what should and should not happen in a future relationship.** This understanding is valuable to an extent, as you now have a greater perspective of your own needs. However, it is unwise to assume that because something happened one way in a previous relationship that it will work that way in a future one. What makes one partner happy will not necessarily be the same for someone else. Nor will you interact with a new partner in the same way.

Books, newspapers, or magazines that you have read; radio shows that you have heard; or movies and television shows that you have watched, have also influenced your expectations. You might surmise from some of them that you should expect to have a partner who looks outstanding all the time, is wealthy, and is endlessly passionate. Of course, any problems that arise will be resolved in pages or minutes, and the relationship will have a happy outcome. None of this scenario matches real life.

You can also have expectations that originate with the cultures you have lived in. For instance, relationships within a culture can have many similarities that reflect attitudes about gender *equality* or dominance. The roles and responsibilities that you act out can be the ones that you saw everyone do. Based on cultural norms, you can expect certain behavior from a partner, or your partner can assume it is appropriate to behave certain ways at key transition points in your relationship. Couples may behave one way when they are friends, but differently if they are serious partners. Marriage would cause yet another shift.

If you are now living in a culture other than the one you knew while growing up, or if you have friends or a partner from a different culture, you may find that what you expect from others does not occur. You can also behave in a way that you have learned, and it causes an issue with your partner. *Discernment* of your expectations, then, is very important. *Note:* More about intercultural relationships is in Part 2.

Discerning Expectations

Even though it is important to determine your expectations, it can be difficult at times to distinguish them. Because they originate from your lifetime experience, they might simply seem to you as part of the normal way everyone behaves or should behave. The key for you, therefore, is to listen to your inner voice and understand what you think is normal for a relationship (Chapter 2). In addition, you will look for what did not happen in relationships you have observed or experienced, but you think should have happened. *Discerning* and understanding are vitally important. Consider this quotation from Bahá'u'lláh:

> This gift [of understanding] giveth man the power to discern the truth in all things, leadeth him to that which is right, and helpeth him to discover the secrets of creation. Next in rank, is the power of vision, the chief instrument whereby his understanding can function. The senses of hearing, of the heart, and the like, are similarly to be reckoned among the gifts with which the human body is endowed.[1]

These questions can assist you in your personal exploration of expectations:

- How did your parents treat each other?
- How should men and women treat each other in a relationship—mentally, physically, emotionally, and *spiritually*?
- What specific behaviors do you consider expected and normal between partners? (Think of *courtesies*, how money is handled, behavior with family…)
- What do you think about *faithfulness* and sexual behavior?

- What *spiritual* or religious behavior will you expect to see in a partner?
- What benefits do you assume will come from a relationship?
- How should differences of opinion be handled?
- How should emotions be expressed? Anger? Frustration? *Love*?

You might have expectations for how a partner behaves around other people. These expectations can include examples such as not flirting with someone else, using polite table manners, and not leaving you alone for long periods in a group setting. What are your motivations behind these expectations? Do you want the person to behave in these ways so that you will look good? Because these actions show that the person *respects* you, and you made a good choice of a partner? Because these actions reflect character qualities such as *courtesy* and *faithfulness*? Relate this to why you might want to dance. To be close to a partner? To show off your skills? To gain attention and applause? Because you *love* to move to music? Because you like to see your partner smile?

As you clarify your expectations, it will be useful for you to make a written list of them (Worksheet 6.1). You will then go through a process of *discernment* to test their validity. You may find it *helps* you to discuss them with a variety of people and gain their perspectives as part of the process. **Your goal is to determine which expectations are realistic, reasonable, or beneficial for you to have in a relationship, and which ones are actually unrealistic, unwise, or unimportant.** Some factors to consider in assessing your expectations are:

- Why the expectation is important to you
- Whether the behavior benefits only you, or whether it also benefits a partner
- What ways the behavior affects you and a partner physically, mentally, emotionally, or *spiritually*
- Whether you can *accept* the behavior in yourself or in a partner
- Whether the behavior moves the relationship forward
- How the behavior affects others besides you and a partner
- The consequences or outcome of the expectation not being met
- Whether you can be *detached* from the expectation or not
- Whether you can adjust and modify the expectation or not

As you think through your expectations and apply the above criteria to them, remember to eliminate ones from your list that you will not request of a partner. **As you develop a list of expectations, you can also begin to define your boundaries, which are actually *strong* expectations for what you want a partner to *respect* about you and your life.** Boundaries let a partner know very clearly what you will have a great deal of difficulty *accepting*. You draw a boundary line when you identify, protect, *assertively* defend, and prevent a partner from crossing into certain areas of yourself or your life. For instance, perhaps due to previous abusive experiences, there are some types of verbal interchanges or physical touch that you do not allow to happen around or to you. Other areas for boundaries can include your time, physical living space, or beliefs, as well as how much emotional negativity you will *accept* from others. Consider this story:

> With papers spread across her desk, Kadisha is working on a detailed database project for work when her phone rings...again. She glances at the phone, back at her project, and then pauses. She sees on the caller ID that it is her new boyfriend, Jorge. Every day he calls her to say hello and ask how her day is going. That is the first call. During his other three to four calls throughout the day, he may ask her what movie she wants to see that night, or when she will be finished at work. While she enjoys talking to him, she is no longer able to focus on her work, and she must often correct errors before finishing her assignments.
>
> Kadisha realizes that not having a boundary around calls at work is really starting to make her annoyed. She answers the phone call, and keeps it brief. After work when they meet for dinner, she raises her concerns with Jorge. She explains that she appreciates hearing from him, but his phone calls interrupt her concentration and disrupt her work. She suggests that she call him on her lunch hour and before she leaves the office. He agrees, but asks that he be able to call her when it is urgent. She agrees to try this plan to see how it will work.

As you can see in this story, you will sometimes discover your boundaries from your experiences. You and your partner may also need to try various solutions before you agree on one that will work well for both of you.

ACTIVITIES

1. You will complete **Worksheet 6.1: Understanding Expectations** in stages. At this point, pause and complete Instructions A and B on the worksheet.

2. Complete **Worksheet 6.2 Setting Personal Boundaries** to assist you to identify which ones are important to you to set and communicate to a partner.

Considering Reasonable Expectations

Some expectations are not just yours as an individual but are common for a large number of people or for particular circumstances. If someone invites you to go to a dance, for example, it is a reasonable expectation that you will dance together and not simply sit and watch others move around the dance floor. Depending on the culture of the event, however, others might expect you to dance only with the partner you arrived with, or they may want you to change partners frequently. Some may even keep men and women separate. If you do not follow the expected behavior for the event, others will likely give you negative feedback.

There are also some general relationship expectations that consistently *help* maintain *unity* and prevent problems. These can include:

- Being in communication with each other regularly
- Growing in intimacy
- Treating friends and family members with *respect*
- Being *honest* and *faithful*
- Obeying the civil laws of your country
- Practicing good hygiene
- Practicing *equal* partnership

Even when you and a partner have commonly held expectations, you may have different interpretations of them. For instance, on the last point above, you will discuss and *discern* what you and your partner both mean by "*equal* partnership." In dance, it means that both partners have the same skill level and are capable of maintaining balance between them. In a married couple, the two partners can have different roles and responsibilities, but have mutual *respect* and decision-making between them.

What will practicing *equality* mean for you and a partner? Sharing who pays for activities? Discussing important issues together? Praying together? You and a partner will work out the application of this quality as you go through experiences together.

As you clarify the expectations that are important to you, be clear whether you expect a partner to be involved in personal growth and development and to what extent. However, be *careful* not to set such a high standard of perfection that almost no one can meet it. As an example, you might think cleanliness as an aspect of *purity* is very important, and you interpret this as rarely having dirty clothes or hands. Your partner might agree with this interpretation at times. However, they may think that there are many times when it is appropriate to be dirty, such as while gardening or doing a project. You and your partner will then need to discuss and agree on the standards that work for both of you and how they might vary depending on the circumstances.

It is also good to recognize that your positive attitude toward a partner and their behavior will affect whether they will be willing to try meeting your expectations or not. William Lederer writes about the Law of Expectations in his book, *Creating a Good Relationship*:

> The way you *think* about a situation (the way you expect it to turn out) will determine how you behave vis-à-vis that situation. ... If, for example, you expect that an event will turn out well for you, you probably will behave with certitude and optimism. Even your facial expressions, stature, and speech will reflect your attitude of positive expectation.[2]

~ Questions for Reflection ~

1. What are my expectations for my behavior in a relationship?
2. What are my expectations of a partner?
3. If I have an expectation that is realistic and important to me, what can I do to *encourage* a partner to meet it?
4. How will I respond if a partner refuses to meet an expectation, or if they are unable to meet it?
5. Do my expectations reflect *equality* between women and men?

ACTIVITIES

1. For the next step in completing **Worksheet 6.1: Understanding Expectations**, complete the first part of instruction C on the worksheet by checking off what you think are your realistic expectations. It is best to use a pencil, as you will likely need to edit and erase some of your answers later.

2. Choose a few love songs that reflect various expectations of relationships. Do any of them include realistic perspectives? What do you think these are? Share the songs with a friend or partner, and discuss with them how the songs influence both of your expectations.

EXAMINING UNREALISTIC EXPECTATIONS

The sections that follow will assist you to determine before being in a relationship whether some of your expectations are unrealistic. In some cases, however, you will only become clear about an expectation's validity as you discuss it with your partner and try it out in a relationship (as appropriate and timely).

As you consider being in a serious relationship and then potentially marriage, some expectations that tend to be unrealistic include the following:

- I will be in a perpetual state of bliss
- I will be loved and respected automatically and all the time regardless of my words and actions
- I will get my own way
- I will be taken care of
- I will be free of parental restrictions
- I will never be lonely
- Marriage will end my miseries, and my spouse will be the solution to all of my problems
- I will have a perfect spouse, and my spouse will satisfy all of my needs
- Love for each other is all we ever need to see us through problems
- Having children is the answer to improving a relationship[3]

Not only are there unrealistic aspects to each of these, but many of them will only be fulfilled if you are taking actions to develop personally or to meet your own needs. For instance, it will be difficult for a partner to *love* and *respect* you if you are not behaving in a way that is *lovable* and self-*respecting*. Having children is an expected outcome for most marriages, but they are not a means for solving problems. You may also live in a culture where it is common for people to decide to have a child before marriage simply to have someone who will *love* them. Either of these circumstances sets children up in fragile circumstances, often without the stability of a happy two-parent family. The children, in turn, are likely to repeat their parents' actions.

How might you test an expectation to see if it is realistic or not? Ask your friends? Your parents? Observe others' relationships? You will find it valuable to discuss your expectations fully with people close to you. If you do end up questioning some of your expectations, you may resolve your concerns through coaching or counseling, talking to experienced couples for insights, reading books about relationships, gaining more information on the Internet, and practicing the qualities of *acceptance*, *flexibility*, *humility*, and *contentment*.

ACTIVITY

For the next step in completing **Worksheet 6.1: Understanding Expectations**, complete the second part of instruction C on the worksheet by checking off what you think are your unrealistic expectations. It is best to use a pencil, as you will likely need to edit and erase some of your answers later.

Then do instructions D and E.

The "Only One Soul Mate" Myth

Some unrealistic expectations are engrained in the general culture. **"Soul mate" is a commonly used term that often misleads people into believing the myth that there is only one "right" person in the whole world to be their mate.** M. Scott Peck writes in *The Road Less Traveled*:

> The myth of romantic love tells us, in effect, that for every young man in the world there is a young woman who was 'meant for him,' and vice versa. … We have met the person for whom all the heavens intended us, and since the match is perfect, we will then be able to satisfy all of each other's needs forever and ever, and therefore live happily forever after in perfect union and harmony.[4]

The view of only one ideal soul mate, and that only one possible relationship can work, can be a contributor to relationship breakups and divorces. After a serious disagreement with a partner, or being attracted to someone different, you might start thinking that your partner is not really your soul mate after all. This disillusioned view prompts you to return to the never-ending quest for the one and only "*true love.*"

This quest can lead you to pursue attraction to a series of people, or involvement with multiple people all at the same time instead of *committing* to just one. You can also repeatedly leave relationships instead of working through normal challenges and growing from addressing them.

You can tell that you likely believe in this myth if you notice that you say something similar to these statements:

"I will know if he is the right person when I meet him."
"I am just waiting for the right person to walk into my life."
"I am confident that I could *commit* to someone if I could find the right person."
"I am looking for the right person to make me happy."
"I am afraid of making a mistake and *committing* to someone, and then finding out that they are not my soul mate."[5]

Actually, many people are possible choices for you in creating a satisfying friendship-based relationship that grows into a successful marriage. Not everyone is a possible choice, however. In order for a relationship to work well, most or all of the following will have to exist:

- Significant amount in common
- The desire and ability to be together in harmony and *unity*
- A *commitment* to find solutions through *cooperation* in spite of obstacles
- An *honest* and *accepting* friendship
- A *strong* bond of *love* and the ability to treat each other in a *kind* and *loving* way
- A well-established foundation of character qualities
- An agreement to nurture and develop the relationship
- Effective communication skills, and interactions with mutual *respect* and *equality*
- A mutual *spiritual* connection
- A *commitment* to have an exclusive and *faithful* relationship
- Genuine physical attraction

While the idea of just one soul mate is *truly* a groundless myth, couples often will develop a *strong spiritual* bond between them. Particularly in marriage, couples feel as if they have mated their souls together, and this is appropriate. **The caution in this section is for you to avoid the mindset that there is only one possible person for you in the world and that you will never be happy or fulfilled until you find that one person.**

~ Questions for Reflection ~

1. What are my beliefs about "soul mates"?
2. How do these *help* or prevent me from being in or *committing* to a positive and lasting relationship?
3. How is this concept different from having a *spiritual* connection with someone?

Fairy-Tale Romance

Another expectation that can trip you up is believing in the myth of "a perfect relationship." This occurs when you are so immersed in the notion of fairy-tale romance that you believe fate or magic will handle all of the details. You might think, "Something magical will happen, and I will be with the right person for me. Then we will live happily ever after." Your thought is that when, where, and how you and your Prince or Princess connect should be totally random, and it will be perfect when you do, with fireworks and theme music included.

Do you remember the story of Cinderella and her Prince? Enjoying dance after dance together is all the preparation that they do for deciding to marry each other. Here is an alternative perspective on their relationship to consider:

> No matter that Cinderella has been socialized to feel at home among the kitchen ashes and would have no idea how to behave in the pomp and circumstance of the royal court. No matter that Prince Charming has grown up in an entirely different culture and acquired its education, tastes, and manners. No matter that the two of them know nothing about each other's attitudes toward the roles of wives and husbands. All they have in common is a glass slipper and a foot that fits it![6]

Moreover, Cinderella was raised by an abusive stepmother, dominated by cruel stepsisters, her father died before she matured, and she has had little exposure to a functional marriage and family. **Expecting your life to unfold like a fairy tale will hinder you in creating a lasting friendship-based relationship on the firm foundation of two well-developed characters.**

ACTIVITY

Ask a friend (or partner) to participate in this activity together with you. Choose a romantic fairy tale and read it aloud together, or watch a television show or movie that portrays a romance. Discuss the impact that stories like this have had on your beliefs about relationships. Alternatively, you can do this activity on your own, and reflect afterward instead of having a discussion.

Discussing and Changing Expectations

You and a partner will benefit from discussing the expectations you both have. You will negotiate and agree on the ones you will each meet, and conclude which ones you will not fulfill and why. This process may take some time, and you may have to try meeting an expectation to determine whether you can make it work.

Your discussion, agreement, and fulfillment of expectations as a couple will *help* prevent either you or your partner becoming upset and angry about unmet expectations, and assist both of you to maintain *unity*. For instance, you might expect your partner to call when running late to meet you, but they see being late as routine behavior. If you and your partner have not discussed this topic, and your partner is then late and does not call, you will become annoyed, which will affect your relationship.

When there is an unmet expectation, you then have to spend time discussing the situation, and work through *acceptance*, *forgiveness*, and so on as appropriate to restore *unity*. You will also be *wise* to decide on how to handle a similar situation in the future. Causing situations that require resolution diverts your energy as a couple into problem solving unnecessarily. There will be enough opportunities to practice problem solving without causing new ones. It is much more fun to meet a partner's needs and experience their appreciation, than it is to handle upset emotions resulting from disappointment.

When you discuss expectations with a partner, it is best to approach the topic in ways that *help* ensure a successful outcome. This approach can include:

- Being open and *accepting*
- Being willing to consider other perspectives
- Treating your partner with *equality*
- Using exploratory language, such as, "I wonder if...," or "Would it be better if...," rather than words that say your partner is "wrong" in their perspectives
- Being *flexible* about and *detached* from the outcome

At the end of the discussion, either of you can shift your positions, agree on a solution that works for the two of you, or agree to disagree *peacefully*. You can decide to experiment and try out some new behavior for a while. This process of agreeing on expectations is a learning-in-action effort, because you will try out new ways of interacting, reflect on the outcome, and determine together what to try next. You may also find out that you are both so different in what you want from each other, that it is best to stop the relationship early in the process.

Once you and your partner have tried out your expectations (as appropriate and timely) and agreed on them, you and your partner will assume that expectations will continue to be met. Part of your ongoing discussion with a partner, therefore, is whether the two of you are willing to continue the behavior. It is common to hear married couples complain that behavior they appreciated before marriage stops after the wedding. What are you each *committed* to continue doing?

Your expectations will also change as your relationship goes through various stages. What you expect from a casual acquaintance will be different from what you expect from a close friend with whom you are in an exclusive relationship. For instance, if a casual friend does not call you for a few days or weeks, you may not notice. However, if you are in a close relationship with someone, and they do not contact you or respond to your phone calls, you will likely be upset or concerned. How serious and *committed* your relationship is will also influence how motivated your partner is to meet your expectations, and your willingness to meet theirs. Consider how expectations change for this couple as their relationship does:

> Oliver and Stacey meet at a meditation and yoga class held at a community center in their city. They start meditating and doing yoga together once a week in between class, and they become friends. Their lives are busy, and initially they do not do much together other than the sessions and an occasional meal.
>
> As time goes on, however, their relationship deepens, and Oliver and Stacey meet each other's families and begin doing more together. When Oliver's grandmother dies, however, he does not let Stacey know until after the funeral is over. She is very upset about this, and she clearly lets him know that she is disappointed he left her out of this major occurrence in his life. She shares with him her perspective that a relationship should include supporting a partner when difficult situations occur.

In this case, Stacey's expectations have changed with the relationship becoming more serious, but she did not communicate them. Oliver also did not stop to think about how his actions might affect Stacey. This incident is a warning sign for them to pause and communicate what new behaviors they want to accompany their current circumstances.

ACTIVITIES

1. To *help* you identify your expectations, and whether they are realistic, go through magazines that show photos of couples doing activities together. Which photos draw you toward them? Which ones match your expectations for a relationship? Can you distinguish between pictures that are realistic and ones that are not? Share the ones you chose with a friend, explain why you chose them, and find out their opinions. What did you learn from this process?

2. Complete **Worksheet 6.3: Creating a Relationship Vision** to begin visualizing a future relationship.

~ *Questions for Reflection* ~

1. What fears do I have about discussing expectations with a partner?
2. What expectations do I have that are vital for a partner to fulfill?
3. How do I (will I) react when a partner does not meet my communicated and agreed-to expectations?
4. How do I (will I) react when a partner does not meet my uncommunicated expectations?

MOTIVATIONS FOR BEING IN A SERIOUS RELATIONSHIP

Closely linked to your expectations are the factors that motivate you to want to find a partner and be in a relationship. Of course, you then expect that your partner will try to fill your needs or will have similar motivations. As with expectations, some motivations can support you in having a great relationship that leads to marriage. Some of these positive motivations can include wanting to:

- Express a deep *love* and appreciation for someone and receive this in return
- Have children and share the *joys* and *responsibilities* of parenthood and family life
- Be of *service* to others with someone
- Share mutual purposes and goals in life
- Have a fulfilled life full of learning and growing together with someone
- Share a deep and long-term friendship
- Develop a *spiritual* bond with someone

Other motivators will cause you long-term challenges. Some of the motivators that can cause difficulties throughout a relationship include:

- Feeling desperate and thinking that any relationship will be better than being alone
- Wanting a parent for your children but not really a partner for yourself
- Wanting a partner's children or family more than the partner
- Wanting someone else to "fix" you and fill an internal emptiness, so that you do not have to do your own personal development work
- Wanting to "fix" someone else
- Fear of hurting the other person if you end a relationship
- Fear that a partner may do something drastic if you end the relationship
- Wanting to run away from problems, or wanting someone to handle your problems
- Guilt that you are not giving your parents a son-in-law or daughter-in-law
- Guilt that you are not giving your parents grandchildren
- Wanting to have someone just to cook, clean, and take care of your home
- Wanting someone to take care of you emotionally, physically, and financially, with no intention of meeting a partner's needs
- Pressure from friends or family rather than a *sincere* desire to be with someone
- Concern about having a relationship before physical aging affects the ability to be a parent or a fully functioning partner
- Wanting to be distracted from stress at school, home, or work

Only you can determine if your motivations are right for you, taking into consideration your history, experience, the situation you are in, and your needs. It will take being very *honest* and *discerning* about what is in your mind and heart. What might be a poor motivation for someone else might work for you and a partner. As with expectations, you and your partner must be *honest* about what motivates each of you to be together and agree on its value.

The two sections that follow offer you some detailed perspectives about the motivations of wanting to fix or be fixed, and about the pressures of timing.

Avoiding "Fixing"

You may be looking for a relationship with someone, but you have the unrealistic hope that he or she can fix whatever you perceive is wrong with you and therefore make you complete. This perspective will make it difficult to *create* a partnership, and it is more likely to result in a situation where you are dependent on the other person. The same concern arises if a partner comes into your relationship with many problems and expects you to be the solution to them.

A relationship works best when it consists of two healthy, independent individuals who are willing to work *cooperatively* together. This view does not mean that either of you are perfect, or that you cannot assist each other with healing from previous experiences. You both can still turn to each other for support and assistance during difficult times. However, if you have both achieved a state of *integrity* or wholeness in your lives, you will build your relationship from a firm foundation of mutual *strength*.

What you expect from other people affects your choice of a partner. You then try to determine if a potential partner can meet your expectations. Consider this situation:

> For years, Camilla stayed awake in her bedroom at night and listened to her parents argue. The topics ranged from money issues to disciplining their children to household chores. Their relationship deteriorated even further when her mother discovered her father stole money at work and risked his job. The yelling, crying, and arguing just kept increasing. As a 12 year-old child, Camilla promised herself she would never be in a relationship like her parents.
>
> Camilla is now dating a wonderful man named Nikkos. She tells him she believes *honesty* and *trustworthiness* are very important, and she is unwilling to compromise about this in any way. Unlike Camilla's parents, Nikkos' parents *love* each other very much and support one another completely. They raised him to have a high level of *integrity* in his life. As his relationship with Camilla deepens, Nikkos becomes

concerned that he may not meet Camilla's expectation of being perfectly *honest* and *trustworthy* all of the time with money. He tries very hard, but he knows that sometimes he pays his bills late, and he does not remember to always report his tip money from his restaurant job on his income tax forms. He wonders how this behavior will affect their relationship.

Camilla's expectation of Nikkos is so high because she essentially expects him to "fix" her past. But, if Nikkos in any way varies from her expectation, she will be upset and may break off their relationship. Essentially her expectation is valid, because she expects him to be *honest*. However, he will not be perfect at fulfilling this expectation, and she is leaving no room for him to ever make a mistake and still *accept* him.

If you expect that a partner will completely take care of you, will never let you be lonely, will meet all of your needs, and will solve all of your problems, you will be consistently disappointed. None of this stance is realistic, since your partner, spouse, and anyone else, cannot possibly be perfect or satisfy all of your needs. You are essentially *responsible* for meeting your own needs, although a partner can assist you in the process and fulfill many of them. Happiness is increased with a wonderful relationship, yet being happy is really a personal choice. Your partner cannot "make" you happy.

It is unwise to expect a partner to do your personal development work for you. For example, some important goals to consider accomplishing before you are in a serious relationship include:

- Clarifying and establishing key character *strengths* in yourself
- *Accepting* and being comfortable with yourself
- Healing from the past as much as possible
- Learning about the components of a functional, healthy relationship
- Expanding your friendship skills, such as keeping confidences, practicing *loyalty*, and sharing
- Developing the ability to handle your own wellbeing
- *Creating* a *purpose* and vision for your life
- Solidifying your fundamental *spiritual* and religious beliefs and values

In dancing and in life, partners have to know what they are doing and have mastery of the basic steps and movements to be successful. Both people must have an *excellent* understanding of the principles and techniques of how to lead and follow. Each partner has a role, and each partner is equally *responsible* for the successful execution of the steps and movements. Also, there is continual adjustment to each other, because you are linked together. To make the movements work smoothly, as well as leading, the leader follows the follower. As well as following, the follower leads the leader. This mutuality of movement is very subtle and requires sensitivity to your partner. However, if both try to lead or initiate a change in position or direction at the same time, conflict arises, and the dancers become unbalanced.

Partners are *responsible* for learning their own parts in the dance. You cannot make someone a great dancer just by taking that person in your arms and moving the right way. They would be going through the motions and might appear to be a participant, but they are only guaranteed to do so as long as you carry them along with you. There is no "magic wand." There is no time where one partner carries the other throughout the entire dance.

However, sometimes one partner knows different variations and patterns of movement that the other partner has not learned. One person can teach the other, if they already know the basics. For example, as a follower, you can dance patterns that you had not previously learned, because you know how to follow certain principles and rules of dance movement. If your leader is a clear leader who follows the same rules and principles of movement, and you are a good follower, you can execute the movements correctly. You then dance smoothly as partners.

Choosing to be in a relationship creates learning opportunities as you interact with each other, participate in activities, and spend time with others. You and a partner engage in the process of learning how to blend into being a team, while still *respecting* that you have individual rights, *strengths*, abilities, needs, and choices. You and a partner will each have character *strengths* that the other does not, and you both learn from and balance each other at times. You will also have skills that a partner does not have, and the same is *true* in reverse. Perhaps one of you will drive, and the other will navigate. One of you might plan an activity, and the other will lead in carrying it out. A partner can meet some of your needs, but not all of them. Together you will determine whether you can dance well together once you each know the basic steps, and determine what "dancing well" means for the two of you.

ACTIVITY

Find something that is broken or damaged and try to fix it. As you work on the project, visualize trying to fix a partner. Reflect on what it feels like to regard someone as "broken" and the process of trying to fix another person. Assess why this approach does not work well.

Timing

Changes that are happening in your body over time may be another relationship motivational factor for you. As you get older, your biological ability to be a mother or father of healthy children and take care of them effectively diminishes. Eggs and sperm can both deteriorate in quality over time, and your children can become high-risk to have birth defects. Pregnancy can also be more difficult as women get older. People who postpone having a serious relationship to finish education and establish a career, or who have married and ended up divorced or widowed, may face these concerns.

It is appropriate to pay attention to timing in finding a relationship, so this awareness of the changes in your body is fine. Where you may get into trouble is if you feel so desperate to find someone quickly, that you are not careful in choosing an appropriate partner. Pressuring a partner to have children before they are ready, or before your relationship is firmly established as a stable marriage, can also set you and your children up for long-term difficulties.

Your parents, other relatives, or friends might be seeing you get older and pressure you to find a marriage partner, or regularly try to set you up with someone they know. They may have a variety of reasons, from wanting to see you happy to hoping you will produce grandchildren, nieces, or nephews for them. To an extent, you can regard their words and actions as supportive and *loving* assistance. When people know you well, they can often actually spot someone who can be a good partner for you. Therefore, before dismissing your friends' and family's assistance, look to see if their actions provide you with an opportunity to meet someone. If their pressure becomes constant, unreasonable, or negatively starts to affect your relationship with them, then you may need to practice *assertiveness* and request that they stop being so insistent.

Another challenge as you age is that your appearance changes. If you are used to considering someone as attractive based solely on physical attributes, as popular culture presents, it may be difficult for you to face either your own aging or that of a prospective partner. **It is important to *detach* somewhat from a physical response to someone so that you can get to know them as a person. Attraction may then grow based on other factors. As is *true* at all ages, character and personality will need to weigh heavier in the equation of whether to have a relationship with someone than physical attributes will.** This is not to say that you do not consider physical attraction as important in your relationship. It simply means that you need to balance attraction with the person's potential to be a great friend and companion. **Everyone has a mind, heart, and soul, not just a physical body.**

Another aspect of timing is the choice to accomplish certain tasks before finding a serious relationship and considering marriage. Many people think that it is important to complete such tasks as finishing school, establishing a career, buying a house, and establishing themselves financially first. There is nothing essentially wrong with this plan. However, another perspective to consider is that there is important growth and development that happens between a couple when they go through these tasks together. If you work with a partner through these tasks after marrying, you may learn skills and develop your relationship as a solid foundation that then prepares you to be effective spouses and parents.

~ *Questions for Reflection* ~

1. Why do I want to be in a relationship?
2. What do I think a relationship will provide for me in my life?
3. Is being married an important goal for me? Why or why not?
4. Are there any motivating factors in my life that will cause me problems in a relationship or marriage?

✎ *Encouragement* ✍

If you are someone who prefers to be spontaneous in life, or if thinking through your expectations seems challenging or even annoying, stop for a minute to think about why we ask you to do this. Conflict between partners sinks relationships. *Discerning* your expectations, communicating them, and agreeing on them with a partner, sets you up for a successful relationship. We are *committed* to *helping* you to do this!

Date: _____

Worksheet 6.1: Understanding Expectations

This worksheet will assist you to clarify what expectations you have about relationships and a partner. It is also a place to track your conclusion about whether each expectation is realistic or not, after you have investigated it.

Instructions:

A) In the first column of the table on the next page, identify the mental, emotional, physical, and spiritual expectations you have of a relationship and a partner. Use additional paper if needed. Consider whether you have beliefs that a partner should behave in certain ways. Be as specific as possible. Use the bullet points below to consider a broad range of possible expectations. Feel free to add others.

- communication frequency and quality
- religious/spiritual practices and beliefs
- diet
- cleanliness
- orderliness
- children
- celebrations
- education
- families

- community/civic service
- sharing responsibilities and equality
- resolving arguments
- decision-making
- time with friends
- handling problems
- drug/alcohol use
- smoking
- sports or recreation

- intimate touching and sex
- time spent together and apart
- money
- living location
- lifestyle
- clothing
- work commitments
- career paths
- exercise

B) Complete the second column with the source of or reasons for your expectations.

C) In pencil, review each expectation and check off the ones you think are realistic. Go back through the list and check off the ones that you think might be unrealistic.

D) Read books, talk to friends and relatives, and observe various couples to determine how they act toward each other. Use what you learn to help you evaluate whether your expectations are realistic, and change any check marks as needed.

E) Complete the fourth column with the reason for your final conclusions.

Expectations of a Relationship & Partner	Why?	Realistic?			Reason
		Yes	No	?	
Example: Men and women should agree on everything	I dislike arguing		✓		Different opinions
Example: I should always receive expensive presents	The more it costs, the more it means		✓		Not financially responsible
Example: Major decisions should be made together	I saw my parents behave this way	✓			Shows equality and respect

Expectations of a Relationship & Partner	Why?	Realistic?			Reason
		Yes	No	?	

Date: _____

Worksheet 6.2 Setting Personal Boundaries

This worksheet will assist you to set your personal boundaries in a relationship and understand why they are important to you.

Instructions:

A) In the "Boundary" columns, identify the subject area for your primary boundaries, such as time, touch, contact, communications, personal space, or beliefs.

B) In the "Request" columns, state the specific boundary that you request a partner to respect.

Boundary	Request	Boundary	Request
Ex: Physical touch	Ex: No tickling	Ex: Beliefs	Ex: Respect my worship practices

Questions for Reflection:

1. Why are these boundaries important to me? _____

_____

_____

2. When will it be most timely to communicate my boundaries to a partner?

_____

3. How will I respond if a partner oversteps a boundary once? Multiple times?

_____

Date: _____

Worksheet 6.3: Creating a Relationship Vision

This worksheet will assist you to visualize yourself and a partner functioning successfully in a relationship in order to clarify what is important to you.

Instructions:

A) Go to a quiet, meditative place. If you wish, pray and/or play some music. Spend a few minutes in this location envisioning yourself in a relationship. How are you acting in this relationship? How is your partner acting? What are you doing together? If you are already in a relationship, then do your best to detach from it and focus on what is important to you. Note some of the key parts of this initial vision on the lines below. You may also wish to be creative in expressing your vision by composing a poem or song, or drawing or painting pictures to illustrate it.

_____

_____

_____

_____

B) Consider many relationships that you have observed. What do you see in them that you admire or dislike? Note these in the space provided below.

Positive Aspects of Couple Relationships	Negative Aspects of Couple Relationships

Questions for Reflection:

1. Which of the positive aspects above do I want to see in my own relationship?

_____

_____

_____

2. What else specifically and realistically describes a successful relationship for me?

_____

_____

_____

_____

_____

_____

4. What actions will I take to expand my knowledge of how relationships succeed? (Examples: interviewing parents, talking to adults you trust and admire, taking a course, reading relationship books...)

_____

_____

_____

5. After considering my original vision, and what I have now learned, what is different about my vision of a relationship now?

_____

_____

_____

_____

_____

_____

_____

_____

_____

_____

_____

Partner Possibilities: Determining a Match

Radley pauses on his hike through the woods and sits on a fallen log. "It has been five months since Cynthia and I ended our relationship," he thinks. "Mum and Pop have been after me to find someone new, and I think I'm ready. Perhaps it's time I let them introduce me to their new neighbor they like so much. Mum says she is friendly and helpful to them, getting them food from the grocer's down the street when the weather was bad. This time I have a much better idea of who will be a good partner for me and who will not. If she does not match up after I take some time to see if we are compatible, I know I can move on. After all, no way do I want to repeat my mistakes from the past."

You have learned basic dance steps and worked through some fears and expectations about dancing. It is now time to determine how to identify a partner you want to dance with consistently. Finding a dance partner is a process that may happen suddenly, but it is more likely to happen over time as you clarify what you are looking for in someone.

To *help* you determine what you want in a partner, you may choose to dance with a number of different people. This process can teach you what to look for, what you like, and what you do not like. However, a number of factors may reduce the number of people you dance with before you find a great match. These include your *confidence* in and *discernment* of what you have to offer, your clarity about what you are looking for in a partner, and your ability to observe others effectively.

If you are at a dance, and you want to find a good partner, you watch the behavior of the dancers on the dance floor. Some people just show off and do not pay attention to their partners. A good partner in the leader role will sacrifice fancy steps to be considerate and save a partner from a collision. Sometimes, you watch a person on the dance floor, and they look good. Then, you dance with them and find out that it will not work, because they have tense arms and a tight grip. You want to find someone who enjoys doing the same kind of dancing you like to do, and you will feel most comfortable with someone who has a similar level of skill as you do.

Your experiences with friends and partners, as well as observing or participating in relationships, *help* you to clarify what you want in a partner. Understanding yourself and identifying what you are looking for in a partner empowers you to make choices that work out well. Since you have previously assessed your own character and grown to understand yourself better, you can now begin to apply those skills to assessing the character qualities of potential partners. You are gaining a better idea of which qualities you may be attracted to the most.

Your primary goal from this chapter is to clarify what you are looking for in a partner. Of course, this clarification will include the character qualities you consider vital. Other aspects of a person affect your choice of a partner as well, such as their personality, culture, and education. Your clarity about all these aspects and more, and their priority to you, will *help* you to choose a partner who is a good match for you.

THE DISCOVERY PROCESS

This chapter presents a method that can aid you in finding a partner who is a good match for you. It will include making a detailed description of the person. This method may seem a bit too practical and unromantic for you initially, but we *encourage* you to try it. **This method is really about including some practicality into your relationship process, not necessarily eliminating some of what you are already doing—unless, of course, it is not working! The goal is to harmonize idealism and realism together.**

It is best to describe what you are looking for before you are in a relationship. Otherwise, you may be tempted to edit your description to match up with your current partner and actually lose sight of what is most important to you. Or, you may try to change the person to match your description, which will likely sabotage the relationship. **If you already have a partner or a potential one, this chapter will challenge you a bit. As much as possible, try to *detach* from specifically thinking about this person and still complete the activities.**

You might have a clear vision of what you want a partner to be like, or you may have very few ideas. You may simply be certain that you will recognize a good fit when you see it. **Remember, however, that relying on random chance will likely result in a series of relationships that are unhappy and dissatisfying.** If you do not know who you are or what you are looking for, then you can end up with someone who does not meet your needs. In Zambia, they say, "Look carefully where you are going or you may end up where you do not want to be."[1]

Completing the activities in this chapter will take time and serious thought. Remember, your goal is to increase the possibility of *creating* a future that includes a successful relationship. When you are specific and realistic about what is important to you in a partner, you are more likely to find someone who fulfills your expectations and needs.

As you consider being in a relationship, you will imagine what it is like and how to describe someone. You can think about what you are each doing separately and together. For example, you want a partner who is an outgoing business manager who

likes to spend time one evening a week with you *compassionately* tutoring children. Perhaps you would rather be with someone who is an architect and builder who practices *creativity*. Or, you imagine being with someone who is as *enthusiastic* about attending car races or other spectator sports as you are. Perhaps your potential partner enjoys working *cooperatively* with others to organize fitness and sports activities for family and friends. Think about the character qualities you want in a partner. How would someone with those qualities interact with you and others? What might they be doing with their life? What will the person be like who can be a genuine partner for you?

You will also consider the personality traits, life skills, or interests that you bring to the relationship, and the ones you want a partner to have. Think about why you make the choices about a potential partner that you do, as well. Is it so that you will have something in common? Because you lack an aspect and hope the other person will balance you? Does the person have to resemble a favorite parent? There is no exact recipe for success in this process, but it is important to think about your choices. Harmony in a relationship requires that you and a partner have a significant amount in common. This quest for harmony does not mean that you should be the same, however. Two almost identical people can become bored with each other or have difficulty getting along, especially if they have the same bad habits or annoying personality traits.

You also might discover that you value a certain aspect of a person because it was a predominant trait in close family members. Harville Hendrix, Ph.D., writes about this phenomenon in *Getting the Love You Want,* "What we are doing, I have discovered from years of theoretical research and clinical observation, is looking for someone who has the predominant character traits of the people who raised us. Our old brain…is trying to re-create the environment of childhood…to heal old childhood wounds."[2] If a parent has died, and you remember them as "perfect," it can be difficult for a partner to measure up to an ideal image you have. If you had a difficult relationship with a parent, you might hope to recreate a new and better model with a partner.

No matter how specific you are and careful you are in the discovery process, there is always an element of mystery. You may not see ahead of time that someone who is different from what you specified in some way is actually a great match for you. Perhaps you thought that finding a partner who is as serious as you would be a good fit, but after you meet someone, you realize that you need their fun-loving nature to lighten how you approach life.

If you believe in a personal God who is interested in your happiness and in your relationships, you will also have *confidence* that answers to prayer and meditation will guide part of choosing someone and building a relationship. However, God will most likely guide you in an appropriate direction if you are in motion, rather than just sitting and waiting. There is *help* along the path, but the decision and journey is ultimately yours. You have a mind, heart, body, and soul, which give you the ability to be a *responsible* and active participant in the process. Leaving it up to God to do *all* the work may be presumptuous on your part. You have the freedom of choice to take action.

ACTIVITIES

1. Think about your parents or those who raised you. List the predominant character qualities and personality traits for each of them. Be cautious that you do not list an aspect you wanted to see in a parent, but it was actually absent. Note which aspects about your parents are what you also want to have in a partner, and why they are important to you. Which aspects are unwise in a partner? Why? Think carefully about whether any unresolved issues you have with your parents are affecting what you are looking for in a partner. How will you resolve the issues?

2. Visualize going shopping for a car and about how this is similar in some ways to choosing a partner. Decide whether you want a new car or a used one. Do you want to be with someone who has never had a partner or one who has never been married before? If you are open to finding a used car, what kind of condition must it be in? Re-furbished or needing a lot of work? Are you comfortable working through previous relationship issues with a current partner? To what extent? Consider how you will find the vehicle. You can use the "want-ads" or go out visiting various car dealers. You may prefer the method of buying a car from a *trusted* friend. You could participate in Internet matching or ask your friends or family members to *help* you find a partner. It is important to know what type of car you are interested in buying. How do you minimize unpleasant surprises after your purchase? Do you know what you are looking for in a partner?

> ## ~ Questions for Reflection ~
>
> 1. What are the advantages and disadvantages of searching actively for a partner?
> 2. What are the advantages and disadvantages of being inactive and waiting for an appropriate person to show up in my life?
> 3. What goals do I want to set, so that I am actively involved in finding someone?
> 4. Who do I want to assist me with preparing myself and finding someone?
> 5. How much time am I willing to spend searching for a partner?
> 6. Where will I look for someone?
> 7. How will I maintain a positive attitude throughout the process?
> 8. How will I know when I have found a likely partner?

CHARACTER QUALITIES IN A PARTNER

As you have been learning about character, and working on your personal development, you have probably been thinking about what qualities are important to you in a partner. **It will *help* you to assess whether you want a partner to have any of the same quality *strengths* as you do, such as the ability to be *respectful* or *loyal*.** This understanding of what you want is important to know, because both of you being effective in practicing a quality can contribute to the viability of your relationship. If you practice *faithfulness*, for instance, and a partner is weak in this quality, your relationship will be constantly unstable and will most likely fail. A partner's weakness in other qualities may not cause as many problems.

There are times, however, when your knowledge of yourself will lead you to conclude that you should look for someone who has *strengths* in some areas that are growth areas for you. A partner can be effective at practicing a quality that balances you at times when you practice a quality selfishly or inappropriately. For instance, you may be very *creative* and *enthusiastic*. At times, your energy is extremely high, and you push yourself very hard and burn out. In this case, it may *help* you to have a partner who is *excellent* at practicing *moderation* and *peacefulness* and who, as needed, can gently assist you to slow down and be calmer. It will be *wise*, in this circumstance, however, to ensure that a partner has some ability to practice and appreciate *enthusiasm* and *creativity*. Otherwise, in offering you balance, they might accidentally stifle your personal expression.

There is no set formula for you to use in choosing the qualities you want a partner to have. After all, you will draw on your experience and knowledge of yourself and your needs, which are different for everyone. Think through *carefully* whether there are any qualities that are vital for you to see in a partner. In other words, if someone does not value or practice them effectively, and has little desire to develop them, you should probably not be in a relationship together. **Some qualities provide a stable foundation for every relationship, regardless of your background and experience, including *truthfulness, trustworthiness, courtesy, faithfulness, loyalty, love, respect,* and *unity.*** The more you and a partner are both able to practice these qualities in your relationship, the *stronger* it will be. It is a fairly simple recipe for success!

As you begin building a relationship with someone, it will take concentration and determination to stay focused on character. You may become so deeply involved in the emotional experience that you lose your ability to see what is happening. Picture yourself and a partner on a dance floor if you are both so intensely focused on each other that you cannot clearly see each other's behavior or the other dancers around you. You bump into other people on the dance floor, arms and legs flinging about without regard for who you hit, or you twirl quickly, resulting in a collision. Can you notice if your partner is *courteous* to the other dancers? Or whether you are being *responsible* for where you put your feet? Can you both be *helpful* to each other in the movements? Will you stop and apologize for a collision?

Character awareness and knowledge are what will support you as you make relationship choices. Rabbi Dov Heller, a marriage and family therapist, says you are headed for trouble if you "…focus more on chemistry than on character. Chemistry ignites the fire, but good character keeps it burning."[3]

Learning about your own character qualities, those of someone else, and then *discerning* how your characters interact—or dance—together will help you to make *excellent* choices. For instance, in the following story, Todd benefits from paying close attention to Melissa's behavior:

> Melissa and Todd work at different companies in the same city. They meet when their managers nominate them to work on a community project to improve the city's schools. The meetings are fun, and they enjoy eating dinner at a local restaurant afterward. As they get to know each other better, they find they are attracted to each other. Melissa really likes how *courteous* Todd is with her, and Todd appreciates Melissa's outgoing and cheerful personality.
>
> After a few weeks, Todd notices that Melissa keeps telling the committee she has completed assigned tasks, but she admits to him later that she really has not done the work. She also tells him about how she occasionally calls her manager and lies about being sick, so she can do something fun. Todd values *truthfulness*, and he

feels uncomfortable about Melissa's dishonest behavior. As they continue to work together and see each other, Todd realizes that he cannot *trust* what Melissa says to him. From their discussions, it is clear to him that she is unwilling to change this aspect of herself. He decides *respecting* his values is more important to him than pursuing a closer relationship with her. He keeps working with her on the committee, but they do not spend as much time together.

Todd's *discernment* about his own values, and his observation of Melissa's character, allow him to assess that she will not work for him as a partner. When either you or a partner is weak at practicing a quality, there are usually negative behaviors that become friction points in the relationship. These can include such behavior as laziness instead of *purposefulness*, rudeness instead of *courtesy*, or domination instead of *equality* and *respect*. Remember to refer to Part 3, which provides you with specific information that will *help* you to identify if someone has a character quality as a *strength* or if it is weak or misused.

ACTIVITIES

1. Complete **Worksheet 7.1: Character Qualities in a Partner** to *help* you to identify your character priorities.

2. Throughout a one-week period, observe others and identify people practicing the top ten qualities you chose as priorities in Worksheet 7.1. Reflect on whether you are able to observe the qualities in others skillfully, or if this is an area for you to develop your abilities (*Note:* Chapter 10 is about observation skills).

~ Questions for Reflection ~

1. What behavior in a partner will I most appreciate?
2. What poor behavior in a partner will most likely be an issue for me?

DESCRIBING YOURSELF AND A PARTNER

There are almost endless ways of describing someone, so you will likely think of many possibilities before narrowing your descriptions of yourself and a potential partner down to the essential elements. As you begin to think about how to describe someone, remember that it is unwise to be too specific about a physical attribute in a partner, unless it is something that is truly an "essential" item. **While in some cases physical attraction may bring you together as a couple, it will not be**

enough to keep you together. Think carefully about intellectual, social, emotional, and *spiritual* characteristics instead of, or in addition to, physical ones. There must also be attraction and harmony between the two of you that comes from your hearts, minds, and souls.

Below are short lists of ways you might describe yourself or describe what you are looking for in a partner. They are provided as an example only, so use your imagination to go far beyond these ideas. Start thinking about everything that makes you or a potential partner unique.

- Effective listener
- *Responsible* with money
- Musician
- Non-smoker
- Mature in handling difficulties
- Prays frequently
- Fair-minded with *excellent* judgment
- *Courteous* and *loving* toward parents
- *Trustworthy*; keeps *commitments*
- Positive attitude toward community *service*

Some personality traits can be:

- Introvert (need to have regular quiet time or time alone to re-charge energy)
- Extravert (need for social time with other people to re-charge energy)
- Adventurous; risk-taker
- Cautious
- Decisive
- Serious
- Playful; fun-loving
- Affectionate
- Cheerful
- Optimistic

Note that you may think a trait is positive or negative depending on whether you value it or not.

Some of the ways that you describe a partner will be the same ways that you describe yourself. Other times, you will describe someone quite different from you. Sometimes differences can be good and necessary. **No two people are exactly alike, and differences often add variety and opportunities for growth in a relationship. However, it is important to be very cautious about being**

in a relationship when there are clear differences that are resulting in, or will obviously result in, regular dissension or disunity. If the differences between you and a partner result in destructive fights, it will be difficult, if not impossible, to build a deep and lasting friendship-based relationship. Can you be harmonious about your differences, or are they highly disruptive to your relationship instead?

It is also important to spend time thinking about what behaviors or traits you may choose to avoid in a partner. Your avoidance may be because you do not feel you have the *strengths* or resources to handle it, or perhaps some other genuine reason. For instance, someone may have bad habits or physical aspects that will make it difficult to sustain a relationship. You might not be able to stand having someone around you who is always messy or who has poor hygiene. You might also find it very difficult or physically impossible to care for the needs of someone with a serious medical condition.

Prioritizing the Details

As you describe another person, you will think through what is most important to you and what is less so. In some instances, what you identify as a requirement for a partner will be "essential," and there can be little or no budging, compromise, or discussion about it. If the person does not have that requirement, then you will either not begin a relationship with them, or you will end it quickly. You can maintain a friendship,

but the person will not be a partner. Other aspects about a person might be very important, but you have some *flexibility* in negotiating with the person about how these aspects will work or not work in a relationship. Yet others aspects of a person can be great to have, but they are not essential for you in a partner.

It will *help* you to describe another person if you take the time to assess what is important about you that you bring to a relationship. You are not simply looking for a person who matches a written description. You are looking for someone who is a good match for you. This activity will also assist you to clarify what to share about yourself with a partner.

A Partner's Purpose in Life

One area that is important to explore is what you want a partner to value as their *purpose* in life and what kinds of goals you want them to have. Remember that you identified your own *purposes* in Chapter 2, so you have that as a reference. Referring back to your own work will *help* you to see what you consider as positive *purposes* in a partner and what will be compatible with yours.

I've been rethinking my purpose in life. Flying around, spreading disease, and drinking blood just isn't very rewarding for me.

A *purpose* may adjust somewhat with time and experience, but often stays consistent throughout a person's life. Goals, on the other hand, will change regularly over a lifetime, but you can learn much about what is important to a person by understanding their goals in the present. If you are going to be in a long-term relationship or marriage with someone, it is *wise* if you appreciate and are in agreement with the person's *purposes*, and you are willing to participate in assisting them to achieve their goals. Of course, this works in reverse as well. You will want a partner's support of your purposes and goals.

As you get to know someone, and you observe the kind of life they are living, you might question some of their motivations and *purposes* in life. Remember, "...man's supreme honor and real happiness lie in self-respect, in high resolves and noble purposes...."[4] You are in "both eyes open™" mode, which means to focus on seeing the whole person clearly. If you see someone consistently doing the following actions, for instance, you will be *wise* to pause for thought before pursuing a serious relationship with them. Consider if they:

- Do the least amount of work possible
- Engage in frequent self-centered activities and do not include others when appropriate
- Cheat or steal from others
- Put effort only into making money, or work only to earn money for fun, and do not balance work with a relationship and activities
- Delight in getting away without consequences for inappropriate or illegal actions

- Have minimal interest in character growth
- Blame others for their circumstances in life
- Look for the faults of others and regularly criticize them

How negatively you view these behaviors and the person's purposes and goals will depend on your values and goals in life and the extent to which the behaviors are occurring.

When you have a partner, you can *encourage* them to write down or share what they see as their *purposes* in life, which will *help* the two of you to discuss them together.

~ *Questions for Reflection* ~

1. How will I be able to tell if I meet someone who can support my purposes and goals?
2. Am I willing to support the purposes and goals of a partner?
3. What types of purposes might be difficult for me to support?

ACTIVITIES

1. Complete **Worksheet 7.2: Describe Yourself** to *help* you identify and focus on what you bring to a relationship. You may wish to copy over your character quality *strengths* from Worksheet 2.1 and include them as well. See activity 3 on the following page if you need ideas for what to write down.

2. Complete **Worksheet 7.3: Describe Your Ideal Relationship Partner** so you begin to clarify what you are looking for in a partner. It will be a good idea to revisit this worksheet regularly as you meet new people, because you will add, edit, or delete items on it as your observation skills improve and your experience with relationships grows. You may wish to use pencil or put your list in a computer to make it easier to edit.

   Be cautious, however, that you do not delete a requirement simply to make your list artificially match up with someone. Also, be aware of who else is around as you complete your list, because you may accidentally describe that person—or their opposite—instead of objectively describing a potential partner.

   After you have made your lists of what you are looking for and what you do not want, then share them with people you *trust*. Someone else may spot items to add or delete, or they may know a person who matches your lists before you do. See activity 3 on the following page if you need ideas.

Continued...

ACTIVITIES *(continued)*

3. It may assist you in determining items to put on the worksheets for this chapter if you engage your *creative* side. One way to do this is to create collages. These are posters made from cutting and attaching words and pictures from magazines with glue onto a large sheet of paper or cardboard in any pattern you wish. You can also use markers or other art supplies to draw or write around the pictures (or simply use drawing materials if you do not have magazines handy). Each collage focuses on a particular subject area. In this case, you have five potential ones that you can do separately, or you might choose to combine one or more of them. Focus on doing whichever one(s) match any worksheet where you are having difficulty generating ideas. Consider these possibilities:

   a. Who you are and what you bring to a relationship
   b. What your character *strengths* look like in action
   c. What your relationship partner is doing (consider home, school, work, community, spiritual activities, recreation…)
   d. What your partner's character *strengths* look like in action
   e. What you do not want to have in a relationship

   Transfer any insights you gain from doing the collages to your worksheets, and consider sharing your collages with others to learn more. You might like to invite friends to do the whole activity with you. [*Note:* If you feel resistance to doing an activity like this, you may need to draw on *courage* or some other quality to discover the benefits from participating.]

YOUR WORKSHEETS IN ACTION

As you meet new people and develop friendships, you will keep in mind all that you have written on your worksheets. You now have a clear way to assess if you want someone to be simply an acquaintance or a close friend and partner. It will *help* you in this process if, as you get to know someone, you focus on asking appropriate questions or participating in activities that give you clear information about whether the person is a good match for you. There will also be more about building friendships and relationships in Part 2 of this book to assist you with this.

Sharing Your Requirements

When you are in a relationship, you may choose to share what you put on your worksheets with your partner. You can also simply raise and discuss specific points from your lists together. Some topics will come up naturally in the course of building a friendship with someone. Sharing your worksheet will be most comfortable if your partner is engaged in a similar process, but you might find it beneficial in either case.

If you are with someone who is able to be very *honest* and is comfortable with you being direct, you can determine quickly if someone is a good relationship partner for you by discussing your requirements, needs, and expectations.

However, a caution with sharing a requirement with someone you are just beginning to know, is that they may pretend to match your requirement, because they are attracted to you.

There may be some sensitive items on your worksheets as well, and you will only bring these up when your relationship has progressed beyond the initial stages. Chapter 12 will *help* you with understanding when you can consider someone is *trustworthy* enough to discuss personal and sensitive topics.

As you discuss with someone whether they have a quality, or whether they believe in something that is important to you, ensure that you both have the same understanding of it. You may have different interpretations of the same requirement. For example, the requirement "takes care of physical well-being," to you could mean taking vitamin pills and exercising three times a week. A partner could interpret it as avoiding smoking and not drinking excessive alcohol. Full and *honest* discussion paired with observation will *help* you to make sure that you are not inaccurately assuming that someone has what you are looking for, or eliminating someone as a potential partner unnecessarily.

A caution about being balanced in relationship-hunting activity is also timely here. Remember to practice *moderation* and not be so involved in searching for a relationship that you appear desperate or frenzied! It is also important to remember to hold onto hope. St. Clement of Alexandria once wrote, "If you do not hope, you will not find what is beyond your hopes."[5]

> ### ~ *Questions for Reflection* ~
>
> 1. Once I have decided what is important in a potential partner, what will *help* me to stay focused on looking for and finding someone who matches what I have written on Worksheet 7.3? How can I avoid settling for being with someone who does not meet my needs?
> 2. How do I feel about sharing who I am with someone else? What might *help* me to be open and *honest*?
> 3. When can it be unwise to be open and vulnerable to someone? When can it be unwise to share with someone what I am looking for in a potential partner?

EXPECTING A PARTNER TO CHANGE…OR NOT

No one stays the same throughout the span of a relationship or marriage. Interests, jobs, activities, physical appearance, roles, and *responsibilities* all shift regularly. The more a person learns and grows, the more they change. **If you choose someone totally based on factors that have a high probability of changing over time, such as physical appearance, you may be setting yourself up for disappointment.** Think carefully about what prompted you to write down a descriptor of a partner that is temporary. Are you expecting the relationship to last?

If you want a lasting relationship, character will be one of the most stable and solid indicators for choosing someone. Remember that once someone habitually demonstrates effective character qualities, they are likely to continue to practice them consistently. If you want someone who will be a straightforward communicator throughout your relationship, find someone who is *assertive* and *honest*. If you see in a partner a high degree of *forgiveness* toward other people, when it comes time to *forgive* you, it will probably happen. If you see *courage* as one of their *strengths*, it will probably be present in the future when challenges occur. It is the same for every character quality.

You will cause yourself heartache and frustration if you see something in the other person that you do not like, and think that you will simply change that person with some time and effort. You may be able to influence the person to choose to change and develop a character quality or act differently, but you cannot hold the expectation that you will be successful. In order to influence another person successfully, they must already be motivated to improve, and you must already be practicing some amount of the positive behavior yourself.

If you are unhappy because someone is rough instead of *gentle* and thoughtless instead of *thoughtful* about paying attention to your needs, it is not likely that increasing the seriousness of your relationship will suddenly change that. If a partner is chronically disrespectful, and this makes you feel unhappy, you cannot count on them to change just because you are together. Set an alarm bell to go off in your head if you hear yourself thinking, "I know they will change later" or "If I *love* them enough, I'm sure they will change"!

© Randy Glasbergen.
www.glasbergen.com

"Of course I can accept you for who you are.
You are someone I need to change."

As you read the following story, ask yourself whether Althea is likely to change her pattern of responding to people she considers incompetent:

Tom and Althea are seriously focused on getting to know each other, and Althea asks him to accompany her to a family reunion out of town. It is a big event that her family holds every five years. Althea stays at her parents' home, and her mother books a room for Tom at a local hotel they use regularly for family or friends coming in from out of town. The first night, there are a few problems with Tom's room. He decides to be *patient* and not complain during the night. The next morning he asks to move to a different room. Because there will not be one available until later in the day, the desk clerk suggests Tom pack his belongings and leave his suitcase at the desk. Hotel employees will move it to his new room when it becomes available.

Althea picks Tom up for the reunion events, they have a fun and social time together, and she brings him back at the end of the day. He discovers at this point that his suitcase is gone, there is a different desk clerk on duty, and no one from the hotel is certain which room is his new one. Tom sits *patiently* in a nearby chair, waiting for the desk clerk to locate his suitcase and room. Althea, however, begins complaining loudly to the hotel personnel that the situation is intolerable. She calls the clerk a rude name, phones her mother, explains the situation, and then punches the speakerphone button. Her mother starts yelling at the front desk clerk as well. As Tom observes Althea, and listens to the interaction, he starts to wonder if this is a relationship he wants to continue.

You and a partner will influence growth and change in each other, if you are both open to this as a dynamic process. Tom can share his concerns with Althea, and she might choose to change. Just as easily, however, she can decide her behavior was appropriate for the circumstances and tell Tom that he was not *assertive* enough.

Think about how you feel when you are with someone who is constantly trying to change you and says it is "for your own good." It does not take long before you begin to feel annoyed or angry. If you try to change a partner, they will likely end up resenting you for your efforts, and they may stubbornly refuse to change in response. **If you are frequently trying to change significant aspects of the person you are with, that is a good sign to consider walking away.**

You cannot expect someone to change, nor can you choose a partner based on the hope that change will happen, if you want to have a happy, lasting relationship. It is especially important to avoid this expectation the older a partner is and the more set in their ways they are. However, if you are still in your teens, and both you and a partner have limited life experience, you may need to look at the situation somewhat differently. **Be conscious of whether someone has the willingness and potential to develop a quality or way of behaving in a relationship, and simply has not yet had the opportunity or training to learn how.**

Note: You may have the habit of always trying to look for anything negative you can find in others, no matter how small, and attempt to fix them. This focus can be an indicator that you have some personal development work of your own to do on *acceptance, humility, love,* or *respect.*

ACTIVITIES

1. Look back at Worksheet 7.3. Are there any items that you listed that will change frequently over the span of a relationship? Do you want to leave them on there or delete them? Why or why not?

2. Ask a friend to request that you change something minor about yourself. What feelings and thoughts occur to you in response? How do you respond to your friend?

~ *Questions for Reflection* ~

1. How do I respond when someone tries to change me?
2. Do I try to change others? Why?
3. In what ways do I attempt to change people?

Accepting A Partner

If you cannot change someone against their will, what is there left to do? **Once you discover who someone is and what is important to them, you are faced with the often difficult task of *accepting* them just as they are (and are not).** The person may be perfectly happy as they are and have no desire or interest in changing any aspect of themselves that you do not like. **Once you have *accepted* the person, you have choices to make.** Can you be with them as they are, or will you make the decision to move on? If there is a character issue involved, *acceptance* from you could actually free the other person to work on personal development. Attempting to force them to change, instead, could stifle them and cause them to resist change. Or, nothing you do could make a difference, because the person is unwilling or unlikely to change. Good communication and observation will *help* you to sort all this out. You will learn many useful skills in Part 2 that will assist you.

Boris said that he wanted to see some change in our relationship, so I gave him two ten dollar bills for a twenty.

Consider how Dameon interacts with Palomi in the situation below, the likelihood of Palomi changing, and the potential consequences if she tries:

Dameon notices Palomi's warm smile and great sense of humor right away, as well as her choice to obey her parents' strict guidelines for her. Conservative and protective, Palomi's parents only permit her to see Dameon on Friday or

Saturday evenings, with a 10 p.m. curfew, and receive limited phone calls during the week. As someone who socializes freely, Dameon often struggles to *accept* her parents' wishes. Palomi, however, is adamant about her *respect* for her parents and her *commitment* to do what they require. He thinks it is not good for Palomi to be so attached to what her parents want.

One evening as they browse in local shops, Dameon pushes Palomi to ignore her parents' wishes and see him more often. He wants her to sneak out of the house to meet him and stop being so concerned about her parents' standards.

Dameon appears to be unwise in expecting this major change from Palomi, especially since he is trying to get her to break her parents' *trust* and disobey them. If the couple pursues their courtship while his focus is on changing her, especially if it requires her to go against her fundamental beliefs and character qualities, Palomi will become unhappy and estranged from either Dameon or her family. She is also unlikely to change enough for Dameon to be happy. Could the relationship survive under such circumstances?

Many steps are important for you and a partner to go through as a couple. As you develop a close friendship and spend time with someone, you have the opportunity to explore how the two of you interact and where you are compatible and where you are not. The best time to decide if you can *accept* someone is before you become serious about the relationship.

MATCH OR NO MATCH

When you are considering a potential partner, or you are already in a relationship with a partner, you will assess what you bring to the relationship and whether the person matches what you are looking for. You will determine if the match is close enough that the two of you can move forward and continue to get to know each other. As you interact together, you may discover aspects that are important about the person that you did not consider in your description, and you will add them to your list.

Alternatively, your heart might pull you toward someone at times, but your mind objects that they do not match your description. This struggle is a signal to step back, assess why you are attracted to the person, and re-assess what you have written. It is possible that you need to pull away from the relationship, or you may reconsider the item and decide it is a *flexible* one. For instance, your partner may be *enthusiastic* about going on regular picnics, and you do not care about them one way or the other. You will happily go on them throughout your relationship, however, because they make your partner happy. You find real *joy* in watching your partner having fun.

Sometimes when you feel attracted toward someone, they are in fact a poor partner for you. There can be chemistry, but no substance

that will support a lasting relationship. If someone clearly does not match your description in key areas, then you will be *wise* to step away from the attraction and assess your choices. It will also be a good time to seek input from someone *trustworthy* who knows you well.

After you have made a good friend or been in a relationship, it is a good idea to revisit Worksheet 7.3 to see if your requirements have changed. This review does not mean that you edit your worksheet in an unwise way to match another person, but rather use this as an opportunity to learn from your experience and self-assessment.

~ *Questions for Reflection* ~

1. After I spend time with someone, and I realize that they do not match the list I made on Worksheet 7.3, what might I do with the relationship?
2. How might it affect me in the long-term if I drop important things from my list of what I want in a partner so that my list fits someone I meet?
3. When is it appropriate for me to practice *flexibility* with my requirements?

✺ *Encouragement* ✺

You are doing extraordinary work. Remember that approaching relationships in this systematic way is a revolutionary shift, and it may be uncomfortable at times. *Perseverance* will *help* you to keep going. It is also important at this stage to remind you that relationships are fun, wonderful, romantic, *joyful*, and special. We are *committed* to *helping* you to include new methods in your life that will assist you to *create* a high-quality, happy, and lasting relationship!

Date: _____

Worksheet 7.1: Character Qualities in a Partner

This worksheet will assist you to identify the character qualities that you believe are most vital for a partner to practice effectively. Once you are in a relationship, you will re-visit this list to assess whether your partner matches your priorities. If you are already in a relationship, try to detach from specifically thinking of your partner, and focus on what is important to you.

Instructions:

A) Read through the entire list of qualities below. If you need to understand a quality better, refer to the detailed character quality explanations in Part 3.

B) Imagine yourself in a great relationship. Think about what activities you and your partner are doing together and with other people. Imagine what character qualities are helping the two of you to have positive experiences.

C) Put the numbers 1-10 **in priority order** for the **10 qualities** that are the most important ones for you to see in a partner. When you are in a relationship, return to this worksheet to discern if your partner matches the list.

	Acceptance		Faithfulness		Peacefulness
	Assertiveness		Flexibility		Perseverance
	Beauty		Forgiveness		Purity
	Caring		Friendliness		Purposefulness
	Chastity		Generosity		Respect
	Commitment		Gentleness		Responsibility
	Compassion		Helpfulness		Self-Discipline
	Confidence		Honesty		Service
	Contentment		Humility		Sincerity
	Cooperation		Idealism		Spirituality
	Courage		Integrity		Strength
	Courtesy		Joyfulness		Tactfulness
	Creativity		Justice		Thankfulness
	Detachment		Kindness		Thoughtfulness
	Discernment		Love		Trustworthiness
	Encouragement		Loyalty		Truthfulness
	Enthusiasm		Mercy		Unity
	Equality		Moderation		Wisdom
	Excellence		Patience		

Questions for Reflection:

1. Why did I choose the 10 qualities that I did?

   1 - _____

   2 - _____

   3 - _____

   4 - _____

   5 - _____

   6 - _____

   7 - _____

   8 - _____

   9 - _____

   10 - _____

2. How do these 10 qualities relate to my qualities on Worksheet 2.1?

   a. What connection or overlap is there between them?

   _____

   _____

   _____

   _____

   b. Would a partner and I be too much alike? Too different?

   _____

   _____

   _____

   _____

   c. What qualities in a partner would balance my qualities or moderate qualities that I sometimes misuse? Are there any changes to make to my priority list?

   _____

   _____

   _____

   _____

   d. What else do I notice?

   _____

   _____

   _____

   _____

Date: _____

Worksheet 7.2: Describe Yourself

This worksheet will assist you to write down a detailed description of yourself. Taking time to do this thoroughly will help you to be sure that you know yourself well, and it will give you a clear picture of what information you will share with a partner.

Instructions:

A) Using the list below for ideas, describe yourself and what you bring as a unique individual into a relationship (refer to Worksheet 2.1 for character strengths). It is best to de-emphasize your physical attributes, unless something is very important about you that will affect a relationship. For instance, you could list a serious illness or physical limitation. Possible ways to describe yourself:

- character strengths
- relationship experience
- needs
- dislikes
- major goals
- life purposes
- values
- family history
- habits (personal and work)

- likes
- commitments
- fears
- personality traits
- attitudes
- financial assets
- behaviors
- cultural customs
- spiritual or religious beliefs and practices

- dreams
- education
- hobbies
- work experience
- appearance
- physical ability
- activities preferences
- sense of humor
- limitations and boundaries

B) You can write a list of what you bring to a relationship on the lines below, or you may find it easier to write your description in autobiographical story form using a computer, your journal, or a piece of paper.

_____

_____

_____

_____

_____

_____

_____

_____

_____

_____

_____

_____

Date: _____

Worksheet 7.3: Describe Your Ideal Relationship Partner

This worksheet will assist you to describe an ideal relationship partner. If you are already in a relationship, do your best to detach from your partner and focus on what is important to you. You can write your description in story form, if this is the method that you used in Worksheet 7.2 to describe yourself. However, if you do so, then use this worksheet to prioritize the key descriptors you write down for what is important for you in another person. This description will not include character qualities, however, which you already identified in Worksheet 7.1. When you are in a relationship, return to this worksheet and assess how well the person matches your requirements.

Instructions:

A) List in detail your description of a potential partner. See Worksheet 7.2 for a list of ideas, and refer back to the text of Chapter 7 for ideas as well. You may wish to use a pencil, since you will edit the list over time.

B) Note what is vital about your potential partner for the two of you to be in a relationship. Mark those items as "Essential." Be specific and realistic. Limit yourself to a maximum of 5-10 essential items. If you are identifying more than 10, consider how realistic your expectations may be.

C) Note what is important to be present in your partner, but through discussion and some change on both of your parts, you can adjust your requirements. Mark those as "flexible."

D) Note what items you would enjoy very much in a partner, but they are less important. Mark those as "great, but not essential."

Description	Essential	Flexible	Great, But Not Essential

Description	Essential	Flexible	Great, But Not Essential

There may be bad habits or physical aspects of someone that would make you and a partner a poor match. List below what you do not want in a partner:

_____

_____

_____

_____

_____

_____

_____

_____

_____

_____

_____

_____

Questions for Reflection:

1. What insights have I gained about what I want and do not want in a partner? Did I identify any patterns? Surprises? Limitations?

_____

_____

_____

_____

2. Have I completed this list with a particular person in mind, or when I was with certain people or in certain environments? Who? How has that affected the content? What adjustments do I now want to make?

_____

_____

_____

3. After discussing this list and any concerns I have about my choices with at least one person that I trust, is there anything I now want to change on my list?

_____

_____

_____

Part 2

It Takes Two:
Creating a Lasting
Friendship-Based
Relationship

Guidance for Completing Worksheets

As with Part 1, there are worksheets at the end of each chapter in this section to *help* you to understand yourself better, identify what you bring to a relationship, and *discern* what you are looking for in a partner. Please consider the following when completing them:

- Unless otherwise noted, the worksheets are designed for you to complete by yourself.
- For each worksheet, ask yourself whether it will *help* you to have involvement with or input from others.
- If you have a partner, you can invite them to complete the worksheet in their own book, or the two of you can use this book for reference and put your answers on separate pieces of paper; it is best if you and your partner do not see each other's papers during the activity, so you do not influence each other's answers.
- If you do not have a partner yet, you can choose to ask a friend or a small group of friends to participate with you.
- If you complete the worksheet activity with someone else, discuss your answers with them when you are each finished.

"Sometimes it's smooth sailing and sometimes they sink. That's why they're called relation*ships*!"

First Dance:
Establishing a Friendship

Jasmine and Varun work together at a local coffee and tea shop. They banter and tease each other, vie to serve customers first, and trade stories about college classes. Both are working on their graduate degrees at the same university, and they plan to become teachers. They meet at the library once a week to study together. When Jasmine is sick and misses a day of classes, Varun takes notes for her. Similarly, a few weeks later, when Varun learns that his father has died, Jasmine holds his hand while he grieves. She drives him to the airport so he can fly home. She also talks to the professors about the reason for his absence, and takes notes to share with him when he returns.

You now have a firm understanding about your capabilities as a dancer, and what you are looking for in a dance partner. Now it is time to see if you have a friend who is available to dance with you, or whether you can find a new one at the next dance you attend. You may dance with a number of people as you determine whether someone is a good match for you as a friend and potential partner.

From a relationship perspective, it is time to look carefully at your acquaintances and friends to see if there is someone you already know who can be a match for you. If there is not, then finding someone will involve widening your circle of friends and activities. Changing your life in this way will take *courage* and a sense of adventure. It is also important for you to practice *discernment* and *wisdom* in choosing how to meet others. Meeting new people is a dance that at times may thrill you, and at other times may leave you with bruised toes. The outcome, however, will be new friends and potential partners.

Friendship is an essential element in any happy and lasting relationship. Have you ever heard someone say that they are "just friends" with another person? Not only does this minimize the value of a good friendship, but it may also indicate that you have not thought about friendship as the foundation of a relationship. As you interact with people, you may start out as good friends, and then attraction grows between you. Or, you may feel a spark of attraction first, and then your friendship grows as you spend time together.

If you begin with attraction rather than friendship, it is important that you quickly assess whether you can also be *excellent* friends. Being friends with someone—free of the drama that sometimes accompanies intense attraction—gives you both the opportunity to get to know each other in a variety of circumstances over time. It also *helps* you to observe each other's character qualities and interactions both together and with others.

As you build a friendship with someone, you will start to share your thoughts, beliefs, fears, joys, and your life's story with them. Typically, you will share less significant things with someone you first meet. In developing a healthy friendship, *trust* and emotional intimacy will build as a gradual part of the process of getting to know each other. The more *trust* between you and your friend, the more you will share.

FRIENDSHIP-BASED RELATIONSHIP

Relationship experts John Gottman and Nan Silver define friendship as "…a mutual respect for and enjoyment of each other's company." They also say, "These couples tend to know each other intimately—they are well versed in each other's likes, dislikes, personality quirks, hopes, and dreams. They have an abiding regard for each other and express this fondness not just in the big ways but in little ways day in and day out." Their research also shows that "…happy marriages are based on a deep friendship." This suggests that you will be *wise* to ensure that you develop a firm friendship with someone before a relationship becomes so serious that it may lead to marriage.[1]

If you pair a relationship with a friendship that has provided you with mutual support and understanding, and you decide at some point to marry, the foundation of your marriage is likely to be much *stronger*. You will already have had the practice of being companions, confiding in each other, supporting and *helping* each other through difficulties, sharing your *joys*, and turning to each other for fun and relaxation. *Ideally*, you will be closer to your spouse than to any other human being.

Describing Friendship

The common saying of "If you want a friend, be a friend" has great validity. **The better a friend you are willing to be, the more likely it is that you will have wonderful and lasting friendships.** Your friendship skills then assist you to have a friendship-based relationship. When you think about being in a close friendship, how do you describe it? Some aspects of it can be:

- Ability to share *honestly* about both positive and difficult matters; good communication

- Acknowledgement of positive qualities in each other
- Ability to spend quiet, *peaceful* time together
- Play, fun, and laughter
- *Acceptance*; ability to be oneself rather than putting on an act
- Support and appropriate sympathy or empathy during difficulties
- *Enthusiasm* about individual and shared achievements
- *Loving, spiritual* connection
- *Encouragement*
- *Loyalty*
- *Trust* that shared information will not be used hurtfully against each other
- Reliability; *trustworthiness*
- Ability to suspend judgment and not jump to conclusions
- Affirmation and approval
- Common and bonding experiences and memories
- Shared goals
- Working together on projects
- Agreed boundaries and expectations
- Shared interests
- Opportunities to learn together
- Ability to disagree *peacefully* and constructively
- Dedication to be of *service* to others together
- Ability to reconnect easily even after being apart
- Motivational feedback or nudging that influences the other to go forward
- Attitude of *forgiveness* and willingness to grant another chance
- *Respectfulness* and *equality*

To achieve the above requires that you and your friends be willing to grow as people as you build your friendships. Through interactions with your friends, you can learn:

- What is *helpful* to others
- What is hurtful to others
- How to communicate effectively
- How to share thoughts and feelings *honestly* and speak *truthfully*
- How to share possessions
- How to *respect* the boundaries and limits of others and yourself
- What triggers intense emotions
- How to disagree *peacefully*
- When and how to tease

- When and how to be serious
- How to keep what is shared as private
- How to *trust*, and be *trustworthy*
- When a friendship is constructive
- When a friendship is harmful or damaging
- How to communicate without speaking negatively of others
- How to observe and acknowledge character qualities in another person

Beginning and then maintaining a friendship is often not easy—it takes *commitment*, time, attention, *caring*, and sharing of one's self with the other. It takes shared experiences, such as spending time talking, learning skills, playing sports, being together in a variety of activities, doing community *service*, or participating in *spiritual* or religious occasions or activities. Poet Kahlil Gibran says, "And let there be no purpose in friendship save the deepening of the spirit."[2] **Being a steadfast and *loyal* friend requires *patience* and the ability to communicate, understand, *forgive*, and resolve any unpleasantness or disagreements.**

As you find and develop new friendships, be wary of people who want to set up exclusive friendships and then behave as if being with people other than those who are already their friends is a waste of time. **Genuine *friendliness* is an open and inclusive quality that brings people into a circle of caring. Genuine *loyalty* does not make unreasonable demands upon the *loyalty* of others.** A friend should not ask you to do something against your beliefs, values, or nature and justify it as asking you to be *loyal* or *loving*.

If your friendship transitions into a relationship, maintaining the friendship is important. **Keeping your friendship *strong* will *help* you to handle the changes that come with new experiences and expectations.** Author Agnes Ghaznavi comments, "As time passes and the relationship is subjected to tension and stress from all sides—personal and social—friendship becomes essential to strengthen the relationship against the forces that are tending to undermine it. Friendship also constitutes a refuge in times of stress or unhappiness."[3] Think of maintaining a car as an analogy for this experience. If you want to take a car on a long trip or one that will have hills to climb, you will make sure that the basic car care is completed, such as an oil change and putting enough air in the tires.

Consider the couple in this story:

> Margie and Frank, whose spouses have both died, recently moved to the same retirement community. One evening, they notice each other at the weekly community cookout and end up having a great conversation. For hours, they sit

by the pool and talk about their children and grandchildren, beliefs, a common interest in historical documentaries and biographies, where they grew up, concerns about retirement, and movies they enjoy. They laugh more than they have in a long time, and they end the evening looking forward to the next time they will be together.

As they spend time with each other, Margie and Frank continue to deepen their friendship. Their topics of conversation broaden and deepen. They participate in more activities, and they begin to develop a relationship.

Genuine friends are gifts in your life, because they are a reliable presence and source of *respect* and *encouragement*. They are only a phone call, email, visit, or step away. Friendships take effort and *care* to maintain so that hurt feelings, jealousy, or neglect do not cause them to fade away. Some friendships have such *strong* emotional or *spiritual* connections that they last through difficulties, geographical distances, and separations.

The dances you will do with friends are fun and lively, interspersed with breaks to get to know each other. You can have simultaneous friendships with a number of people. **You may choose not to be in an exclusive relationship with someone at this stage. This gives you the advantage of getting to know many different people without romance as a factor.** It can work well to socialize in a group, rather than just with one other person. Participants have the opportunity to become acquainted with each other in an easy and safe social environment. If there are no exclusive couples or pairings during activities, you can interact *respectfully* with each person, and get to know the characters of many people simultaneously. Focusing on friendship gives you the freedom to learn skills and get to know people, without tripping over all the expectations and complexities of a closer relationship before you are ready to be with a partner.

ACTIVITIES

1. Complete **Worksheet 8.1: Appreciating Friends** to expand your understanding of what is best about having good friends in your life.

2. Take photos, create a collage, or write a poem or song that demonstrates what a great friend is like. Consider choosing a specific friend for your focus.

3. Interview a friend about what they appreciate in you as a friend. *Encourage* them to be very specific and to include your character qualities.

~ *Questions for Reflection* ~

1. Am I able to *create* and maintain friendships? If not, what holds me back?
2. What specific actions have I done to maintain friendships?
3. What makes me a good friend?
4. Who are my good friends, and what do I value about these friendships?
5. What is my history of friendships with the opposite gender? With the same gender? What have I learned from both?
6. What challenges have I experienced with friends? What have I learned from these?
7. What roles do *spirituality*, religion, and God play in my lasting friendships?
8. Do I share my *spirituality* openly with my friends? Do I have friends that do not approve of me sharing it? How does that make me feel about the friendship?

CHARACTER AND FRIENDSHIP

Friendships advance through various levels. According to author Bill Gothard, two people start with being acquaintances, progress to casual friendship, proceed to close friendship and fellowship, and finally become intimate friends. He speaks of the final stage of intimate friendship, which is "...based on commitment to the development of each other's character."[4]

As you interact with your current friends and gain new ones, getting to know their characters is an important task. Generally, friends can relax and be themselves, which *helps* to make it clear what qualities a person has as *strengths* and their areas for growth. **There is a greater tendency for friends to behave naturally around you, not try to impress you, and not fear losing their relationship with you. Exclusive romantic relationships with little or no foundation of friendship, on the other hand, have a greater fear of loss attached to them.** Discussions or disagreements that are lively between friends, when they happen between romantic partners, can become emotionally charged or difficult.[5]

Being attracted to each other's character qualities is an excellent way to begin a friendship. Consider this story:

> Noam and Lesley meet when they are assigned to the same team for the spring beach cleanup in their city. They quickly begin talking and joking with each other. Picking up the debris accumulated after a number of winter storms, as well as other assorted trash, is hard, sweaty, and dirty work. As they move around the beach together with their teammates, Lesley notices how quick Noam is to *cooperate* with

others in picking up the larger, heavier pieces. Meanwhile, Noam notices Lesley's *confidence* as she becomes a leader in the group, and how *persevering* and *encouraging* she is as the group gets tired. Lesley smiles in appreciation as she watches Noam *thoughtfully* hand out water bottles to the group members when they take a break.

Noam and Lesley start an *excellent* friendship from a foundation of *respecting* each other's best and *sincerely* practiced qualities. They also gain valuable insights by watching each other as they interact with others. The *discernment* of each other's qualities during this activity *helps* to solidify the experience into a *strong*, positive memory for them both.

On the other hand, as you get to know someone, their actions can raise concerns for you. If someone is consistently disrespectful, irresponsible, discourteous, and other similar poor behaviors, you need to listen to your inner voice and consider *detaching* from the person (Chapter 3). Unless your friend is able and willing to engage in serious change, going forward and developing a relationship with someone who mistreats you as a friend is highly unlikely to turn out well.

You can gain additional understanding of someone's character by learning why someone chooses the friends that they do. To be popular? To have a companion for activities? To have a life-long bond? To hold onto intimacy that began in a previous relationship? Consider this quotation from Joan Barstow Hernández:

> Becoming acquainted with a person's other friends and trying to understand what he has in common with them also contributes to a deeper knowledge of his character. Friends usually share some values. Therefore, if you do not see the qualities in a person's friends, which you think you see in him, it may be an indication that you do not yet know him very well, or that you have an idealized concept of him.[6]

A friendship-based relationship can also provide a safe place to influence the development of each other's character qualities, if you both agree to this practice. As you grow closer to each other, you can talk freely and provide *gentle* and *tactful* feedback, support, and understanding about character challenges. In an established relationship between close friends, your *caring* feedback and discussion becomes an important factor in character growth. "Genuine service demands that we speak the truth in love. We do not serve each other by avoiding one another's weaknesses."[7] **When a genuine friend offers *loving* and *compassionate* feedback, it is much easier for you to *accept* it, because you are *confident* your friend knows you well and has your best interests in mind.** In a friendship-based relationship, you both *help* each other.

Remember as you and a friend or partner *encourage* each other's character growth, however, that you avoid slipping into fault-finding or focusing too much on the other person. Your primary focus needs to remain on your own character. It is important to:

> …resist the natural tendency to let our attention dwell on the faults and failings of others rather than on our own. Each of us is responsible for one life only, and that is our own. Each of us is immeasurably far from being [perfect]…and the task of perfecting our own life and character is one that requires all our attention, our will-power and energy. If we allow our attention and energy to be taken up in efforts to keep others right and remedy their faults, we are wasting precious time.[8]

The description of friendship listed earlier in the chapter includes many character qualities—*caring, truthfulness, faithfulness, enthusiasm, loyalty*, and more. Friendship with a relationship partner includes appreciating each other's best qualities. Author and researcher Blaine J. Fowers, Ph.D., writes about "character friendship" as the ideal and lasting friendship. He says:

> …it is based on the friends' recognition of each other's good character and on the shared pursuit of worthy goals. … [T]hey are brought together because they recognize each other's good qualities—the character strengths that make it possible for them to seek the good together. … [C]haracter friends work together as a team or a partnership to achieve their shared goals. … [M]utual happiness is a by-product of shared commitment and teamwork….[9]

As you develop your friendships, you can practice your character qualities in ways that benefit both you and your friends. Practicing mutual *courtesy, generosity, kindness, respect,* and others will deepen your appreciation for each other.

~ *Questions for Reflection* ~

1. When has a friend's effective practice of character qualities made a positive difference in my life?
2. When have a friend's character challenges been a problem for me?

ACTIVITY

Begin a new journal book or a new section in your journal with a focus on friendship. On the top of several pages, put the name of a friend. Below each name, list the character qualities you appreciate in them. You can start this journal with the two people you listed on Worksheet 8.1.

As you gain new friends, add them to your book and begin to observe and list their qualities. Think about whether these friends reflect the qualities that you want in a friendship-based relationship partner. Remember Part 3 is a reference for you.

YOUR CIRCLE OF FRIENDS

Finding a friend who can become a partner requires a shift in perspective. It takes *courage* to open your attitudes and life to new experiences. **Having a partner is unlikely to happen without looking at the people you already know in different ways, and adding new people to your group of friends.** Besides *courage*, it takes time and energy. Are you willing to step into the adventure?

Current Friends

As you consider finding a partner, you will begin by looking at your current friends to see if one of them really does match your relationship requirements (Worksheets 7.1 and 7.3). Throughout this process, it is possible that you will see someone you already know through new eyes, and that the person may be willing to be more than a friend. Sometimes, however, it is more difficult, as in this scenario:

> Martin and Gayle have been good friends since they were in elementary school. Together, they rode bikes, played basketball, and ate cake at birthday parties. They went camping with their families, sat through an after-school lecture and detention for passing notes to each other, failed geometry, and marched in the high school band.
>
> During their senior year of high school, Martin begins dating a new student named Lissa. Gayle had recently begun wondering about whether the two of them

should go out together, and she is confused and unsure how she feels about his relationship with Lissa. She worries she will lose Martin's friendship. After hearing from him about his relationship, she begins to wonder if she should speak to him about wanting to be more than just his good friend herself. She prays, talks to her parents, and asks Martin to meet her in the park near their homes.

As they sit on a bench, Gayle explains to Martin that she has been struggling with mixed feelings about him having a relationship with Lissa. She realizes she might have some feelings for him that go beyond being good friends. She asks his thoughts about whether they could be romantic partners. Martin does not say anything for a couple of minutes. He does not want to hurt her feelings, but he decides to be *honest*. He replies that he values their friendship, but he just does not think of her that way.

Gayle is upset and disappointed. They talk awhile longer and end up agreeing to have some time apart. They know that their friendship is changing, but they agree to continue maintaining it as best as they can in the future. For now, they both agree to give each other some time to consider and explore relationships with others.

When you feel you are ready to start looking for a potential partner, it is good to also look beyond your immediate friends and widen the circle of those you know. Doing this will *help* Gayle realize that she can still have a close friendship with Martin, but not depend on him as a relationship partner.

~ *Questions for Reflection* ~

1. Have I had a friendship that became a relationship? How did that turn out? What challenges were there? How did I resolve them?
2. Have I had a relationship that did not start out as a close friendship? How did that turn out? What challenges were there? How did I resolve them?
3. Is there a friend currently in my life who is a potential partner? What makes them a good choice?
4. What will I have to do to shift a friendship toward being a relationship? Am I willing to do this?
5. What are my concerns about shifting a friendship into a relationship? How can I address them?

Widening Your Circle

Where can you look for new acquaintances? Would people you find in these places be potential friends or partners? How can you look for someone? Would the method you are considering be a good way to find someone? You, like Emily in the next scenario, are *responsible* for initiating a variety of relationships in your life and being aware of each person's partner-potential. Observe how she does this:

> During her first year of college, Emily often spent much of her time avoiding the drinking and partying her friends were involved in, and she was often lonely. Now that she is in her second year, she wants to be more involved in college life. She attends a meeting about forming a choir group that will be part of a new drama production.
>
> Emily quickly begins to develop friendships with the other choir members, including Dennis and Chuck. Together, they talk about the latest computer games, the quirky old films at the local theater, and which professors they think should never retire. As they spend more and more time together, she realizes she has many common interests with Dennis and Chuck, and they both have potential as relationship partners.

Emily will have to be clear about her values and be sensitive in order to maintain her friendships with both Dennis and Chuck. If she attempts to develop a serious relationship with both of them at the same time, it is likely someone will become hurt and the situation difficult.

Be open-minded as you look for new friends. You do not yet know what your partner will look like. Avoid letting assumptions interfere with your approach. In Tanzania, they say, "Milk is exactly the same whether it comes from a black cow or white one."[10]

Think about whether you are limiting your relationships through holding onto biases, prejudices, or stereotypes related to race, religion, culture, education, age, or socio-economic status. When you make choices based on these, you are actually making choices using false information that you are assuming is *true*. Do the people you associate with all think and believe almost the same thing? What can you gain from expanding the diversity of those you associate with as friends? The more broadly you look, while still *respecting* the qualities and other needs you identified in Chapter 7, the more choices you will have in potential partners. [See Chapter 13 about differences between partners.]

It is best to avoid looking for friends solely because they can relate to your own set of issues or difficult history. This can include such backgrounds as being raised by a single parent or being previously married to an alcoholic. Limiting yourself with criteria like these may unnecessarily eliminate a suitable person as a friend or potential partner. This relationship choice can also lead you to match yourself with another person based upon your problems and weaknesses rather than on your *strengths*.

~ Questions for Reflection ~

1. Am I willing to look for new friends?
2. What restrictions do I put on my choices of potential friends?

Building Your Confidence

You may be very *confident* about your ability to meet new people and develop new friendships. However, instead of feeling that way, you may struggle with *confidence* and may be scared or uncertain about meeting new people. Think carefully about your fears, and whether you want them to control your future. Then, do your best to practice personal initiative, *courage*, and *strength*, and take small steps forward.

Remember the discussion about your inner voice (Chapter 3), that can turn to either your higher or lower nature (Chapter 1)? When you meet new people, you have a choice of connecting your thoughts to your higher nature, which will have you practice *friendliness*. Or, you can connect your thoughts to your lower nature, which can stop you from interacting with others, or turn the experience in a negative direction. For instance, your lower nature can cause your inner voice to remind you of painful social experiences from your past, even back to your childhood. Examples are:

- I am not good enough
- They will not like me
- I do not belong here
- I am really on my own

You can see that when you are thinking such negative statements, it will be difficult for you to be close to other people. These thoughts act as a barrier between you and others. If you turn your inner voice to your higher nature instead, you have access to all the character qualities. You will be empowered in a highly transformational way.

When you are facing a social situation, one specific way to put this practice into action is to choose qualities that you want to focus on when you are interacting with others. These qualities might not yet be *strengths* of yours. However, when you say them as part of an affirmation to yourself, it builds your *confidence* in practicing them. Then, as you actually use these qualities in small, safe situations, your *confidence* will grow until you can claim them as *strengths*. Examples of internal positive affirmations are:

- I am *strong* and *confident*
- I am *peaceful* and *friendly*
- I am *loving* and *compassionate*

You can repeat these statements to yourself ahead of time, as well as when you begin to interact with someone new. These inner affirmations will *help* your efforts to go more smoothly, but it will take practice and repetition to be comfortable with them.

Meeting New People

If you choose to widen your circle of friends to find a partner, then you will determine the best way to make it happen. There are many possibilities, and some are listed below. Depending on your circumstances, social skills, interests, and experiences, you may have reservations about some of the options. Some will simply not work for you. However, do your best to practice *confidence* and *courage* and try as many of them as possible. Keep in mind that your best resources for meeting new people are family members, friends, coworkers, or other acquaintances.[11]

Ways to Meet New People
- Be prepared to say "hello" first to someone, and then get to know them through asking interesting questions

- Listen carefully for what you can learn from others
- Spend time doing group activities that you truly enjoy and will like to do in the future with a relationship partner
- Ask your friends and relatives to introduce you to others
- Enroll in college, university, or community education classes
- Get involved with arts-related activities, such as classes or volunteering at art museums, concert halls, or theaters
- Organize or be involved with intramural sports at school or college
- Join hiking or camping organizations
- Go to a park and invite people to play some kind of game or sport with you
- Take a yoga or aerobics class
- Attend dances or take dance lessons
- Buy a dog and begin to walk it around the neighborhood or local park
- Participate in poetry workshops or *creative* writing retreats
- Go to a car, boat, or home and garden show
- Join a choir, choral group, band, or musical ensemble
- Work with other tutors to *help* students in an after-school or weekend program
- Facilitate or join a *spiritual*/religious study group
- Participate in conferences, workshops, *spiritual*/religious sessions, or retreats
- Coordinate or volunteer your time with a community *service* project
- Join a committee addressing a civic or social issue

Possible Places to Consider (Almost Anywhere!)

- Fitness gym or health club facility
- Picnic's with the families of friends
- Religious places of worship, *spiritual* centers, and gatherings
- Shopping center or stores
- Coffee shops or restaurants
- Neighborhood associations
- Sports activities or events
- Hardware store
- Movie rental store
- Hobby-related groups
- College or civic clubs
- Social or activity areas where you live
- Friend or relative's wedding
- Laundromat
- Library

- Comedy club
- Toastmasters International meetings (to learn public speaking and leadership)
- Workplace (*Note:* This could be against some companies' policies.)

<u>Other Options</u>
- An Internet discussion group
- A single's group
- Established dating *services*
- Personal ads
- Internet dating or networking sites

The Internet can *help* you in a number of ways. You can find someone interesting through an electronic discussion group. Many sites that connect people together offer screening tools that *help* you to match up with someone effectively. Some people find that an online matching *service* can make finding someone more efficient. However, be cautious that you do not just rely on someone's online profile as a way of getting to know them.

If someone you meet lives far from you, it is still possible to stay connected electronically. In fact, interacting with someone you meet online, or meet and then stay in touch with over the Internet, can slow down the physical side of the relationship process. This can give you time to get to know each other better without in-person physical attraction sidetracking you. If you are communicating primarily by email or instant messaging with someone, make sure that you include symbols or comments that clearly convey your feelings. It can be difficult at times in communications for someone to tell when you are joking or upset, since they cannot hear your tone of voice.

At times, you can meet someone under unusual circumstances. Perhaps this could be during a crisis or somewhere outside of your normal environment. The experience itself can create a bond between you and someone else. It can appear that you have a lot in common with the person, or it could seem that you are very close very fast. It is a good idea to have encounters with each other under new or everyday circumstances to test whether the connection between you is actually real or lasting.

As you make new friends, it is good to arrange circumstances for your friends and family to get to know them as much as possible. This *helps* you to see how your friends treat your family, and gives your parents the opportunity to know the characters of your friends.

Your parents probably know you very well and have extensive relationship experience. If they also know your friends and potential partners, they can be effective in guiding you through relationships that develop. If you are communicating with a friend or partner on a mobile phone or via the Internet, you may notice that it is easy for your relationship with someone to progress to a serious stage without your parents being involved. *Respect* for your parents and being *creative* will *help* you to find ways to connect everyone together instead.

~ *Questions for Reflection* ~

1. What efforts have I made to establish new friendships?
2. What are my favorite activities to do with friends?
3. How many close friends do I want? Will I want a partner to prefer the same?

Community Service

One way to meet and get to know people that you may not have considered is community *service*. This can be through a long-term *commitment* to an ongoing project, or occasional involvement in one-time events, such as responding to a disaster. People who volunteer their time tend to be effective in practicing the character qualities of *compassion*, *generosity*, and *responsibility*.

As people focus on *helping* others, they can also *strengthen* such qualities as *courtesy*, *flexibility*, *encouragement*, *kindness*, *love*, *patience*, and *respect*. Being of *service* brings out the best in you. So, if you find friends who are involved in *service* or who are willing to be, you may see them demonstrating character qualities that you value. Ensure, however, that you have *pure* motives and are *sincerely* interested in volunteering and not engaging in it solely to meet someone.

As you move into having a relationship with someone, it can *strengthen* your friendship to continue being involved in *service*. At the beginning of a relationship, you can easily become very focused on your own thoughts and emotions, as well as on the other person. **Volunteering and *serving* others expands your view beyond yourself and focuses your attention on how your actions affect others.**

This outward orientation provides opportunities for you to contribute *generously* to others in your community. Consider this quotation from philanthropist Dale Carnegie, "Do every day a good deed that will put a smile of joy on someone's face."[12]

Note: You will explore this topic further in Chapter 9.

ACTIVITIES

1. Complete **Worksheet 8.2: Widening Your Circle of Friends** to help you see ways to expand the number of people you know who are potential partners.

2. Identify someone you would like to get to know better. Invite them to participate with you in an activity that you will enjoy doing and that supports developing a deeper friendship. After the activity, consciously identify what new information you learned about your friend and yourself. Reflect on whether the person has potential to be a relationship partner for you based on your completed Worksheet 6.3. If you do not have enough information to know the answer, then initiate another activity, and reflect again at the end of it.

FOR CAREFUL THOUGHT

Every activity you choose and each encounter you have with another person has the potential to be a learning experience. As you are learning, however, do your best to avoid hurtful or dangerous situations. Friends, relatives, or *trusted* advisors can assist you with this. *Wisdom* and self-*respect* are good qualities to keep in mind for this section.

Sincere Interest

It was mentioned above to be *sincere* in your motives for doing community *service*. This same principle also applies for any activities you choose to do to meet someone or to do with a partner. Otherwise, you might give an inaccurate impression to a new acquaintance that you are *truly* interested in doing what they are doing. If your interest fades or is insincere, your partner will be disappointed, and there may be a negative effect on your friendship.

It will be important to *discern* your friend's motivations for participating in an activity as well. There will be dissension between the two of you if you discover the person was not *honest* with you.

Internet Connections

The Internet can be an effective means of meeting new people and following up with people you meet, because it connects you to others all over the world. **However, just as when you meet people in person, it is important that you practice *truthfulness* and *honesty*, and *encourage* these qualities in others when meeting online.** The Internet can make it easy for people to present a false image of their identity, character, age, experience, employment, or relationship status, which can result in poor experiences.

The Internet can also make it easy for someone to carry on multiple relationships at one time, or have a series of encounters that never deepen. At times, Internet "dating" can put you in the mindset of always seeking the next "right" person and never being satisfied. With so many people to choose from on-line, it can be difficult to know when to choose someone to build a relationship with and step out of the process of trying to find someone else.

Sometimes, a person you meet electronically, or want to follow-up with electronically in order to get to know better, is geographically far away from you. The two of you can then determine how you will effectively get to know each other under these circumstances. Various technical or electronic devices and methods can assist you in the process, and you can watch for new and innovative inventions that appear regularly.

As you choose how to communicate electronically, remember to maximize your effective communication. Consider trying possibilities that allow you regular, inexpensive connections, so that you can fully communicate with each other and see each other. You can also use these methods to get to know each other's family and friends. If you and someone else only communicate with written messages, you can miss many cues that come from seeing each other's body language and hearing each other's voices, such as emotions, emphasis on certain words, or tone. Therefore, it is a good idea to use whatever technologies expand your voice and visual contact.

As you connect with people, it is *wise* to consider what boundaries support your safety, wellbeing, and the *integrity* of the relationship. Unless you already know someone, be cautious about giving out your phone number or address to someone electronically. Guard your very personal information from people you do not really know. If you decide to meet someone in person that you have first encountered through the Internet, make sure that others know about it. Meet the person in a neutral, safe, public place or group setting. Especially avoid meeting or continuing communication with someone who sends you messages or says things that are disrespectful, abusive, violent, obscene, crude, sexually suggestive, or that make you feel uncomfortable in any way.

A pitfall with the Internet is that you and another person can have a "…false sense of closeness that develops after you've…instant-messaged them for hours. Because of the anonymity factor, you're more likely to share intimate details with this stranger than you would if you had just met…. This false sense of closeness makes you fall deeper and faster for a guy that you hardly know, and you develop unrealistic, high expectations…."[13] It will *help* you, therefore, to picture what you would be saying to someone if you were actually together face-to-face.

If you become serious about someone you meet or develop a relationship with online, spending time with them in person will be a very important part of determining whether the relationship should go forward further. This may involve rearranging your life to travel and spend adequate time together. When you are together, it will be *wise* to engage in activities that assist you in getting to know each other's characters. (See Chapter 9 for ideas.)

Being Friendly

In many places of the world, the cultural advice is that it is unwise or unsafe to be *friendly* to others outside of your family or close circle of friends. At times, this is a good caution for your own protection. Excessive concern about your safety, however, can make you cold and unfriendly. *Friendliness* is a positive quality when practiced *wisely* and with *moderation*, and it allows you to meet and build relationships with many people.

Over time, you will begin to develop the ability to tell early in a friendship whether it is one you want to keep. If you have serious doubts about the person's potential as an ongoing friend or as a partner, it is best to stop investing time in sustaining the connection between the two of you. In the following situation, Eduardo discovers Rosie's level of interest in their relationship through their interactions:

> Eduardo begins stopping at the corner convenience store most days on his way home from his shift at the factory to pick up snacks and something for dinner. He also wants to see Rosie, who is usually behind the counter. With each visit, he learns more about her and begins sharing brief comments about himself. He wants to ask Rosie to go out with him, but she seems very shy. So, he *patiently* lets her get used to seeing him.
>
> One day Eduardo suggests they see a movie together, but she says she is busy. Another time he invites her to join him for dinner at the restaurant next door, but again she declines. He decides to slow down again and continue being *patient*. After a few weeks like this, he is excited to learn he has received a promotion at the factory. However, he is disappointed that his hours will change, and he will no longer be stopping in at the store at the same time that Rosie is there working.
>
> Eduardo tells Rosie about the promotion, and she says she is happy for him. But, Rosie expresses no emotion about not seeing Eduardo regularly. It is clear she is not interested in developing their acquaintance further. He decides it is best to stop investing time and energy in his friendship with Rosie and moves on.

Sometimes you may mistake someone's *friendliness* for interest in a relationship. This can happen when you meet someone casually, and you take their polite interest to mean more than the person intended it to convey. It can also happen when you are interacting with someone in a *service* industry, such as a restaurant server or store clerk, who in part is being paid to be *friendly* to you or hoping for a larger tip.

Many acquaintances you meet have the potential to become friends without becoming relationship partners. As you interact with others, try to build friendships with them, without automatically eliminating them because you do not feel a romantic spark of attraction. The outcome could be unexpected. You could end up feeling attraction grow after some time of getting to know the person. Or, you could have a lifetime friend who simply does not become a partner.

Gatherings, Seminars, and Conferences

Large gatherings, seminars, or conferences, especially those attended by many people from your age group, can provide you with a good opportunity to meet new people. You can learn of others' interests based on particular courses or sessions they choose to attend. You can get to know someone in a low-risk group setting.

Because the encounters are short-term, however, they can tempt you into presenting an unrealistically "perfect" picture of yourself. Perhaps you justify the pretense since your interactions are just for a few days. But what if you then establish the beginning of a relationship with someone? If you start a relationship with someone on this basis, it may falter as you start to reveal your "*true* self."

When you meet people at national or international events, your initial attraction to someone might be difficult to sustain effectively long distance, and it may simply die a geographically challenged death. In an increasingly mobile and technologically connected society, however, geography is often not a limiting factor. [See Chapter 9 for more information on long-distance relationships.]

Dating

As you meet people and develop friendships, you may go out on dates with someone or with a variety of people. The intent of a date is generally to have a social opportunity to be with someone, allowing you to get to know them better. In many cultures, dating has become an accepted choice for recreation, companionship, fun, and finding a mate. However, in the words of author, Joanne Kimes, "Chances are if you've been dating for any length of time, you've experienced the rejection, heartache, and utter disgust that the entire dating process can bring. You hate the stupid rules and playing the silly games...."[14]

Copyright 2000 by Randy Glasbergen.

—GLASBERGEN

"I CAN'T GO TO THE MOVIES WITH YOU, ELENORE. I'M STILL GROUNDED FOR SOMETHING I DID IN 1937!"

Often these days, as quick decision-making becomes increasingly popular, a date can last only a few minutes. Dating expectations can include having casual sex after only a brief acquaintance, something that seriously interferes with character exploration and the development of your friendship (see Chapter 5). The games can include dishonesty, sending mixed signals about being available or not, or some of the romantic myths that were addressed in Chapter 6. Remember that the pop-culture fantasy of finding yourself in a magically romantic liaison makes for an entertaining movie premise, but it is unlikely to result in a lasting relationship in real life.

Okay, so dating is often not what you would want it to be. It is still an option, however, and one you will probably use at times. Chapter 9 will also give you some alternatives to consider.

~ *Questions for Reflection* ~
1. What experiences have you had with the issues in the "For Careful Thought" section, and how did your choices turn out?
2. In the future, how will any of these choices be different for you in terms of what you will do or not do?

BEGINNING TO SHARE

When you have found people who are potential friends and partners, you begin to get to know each other. In the initial stages of a friendship, *honest* inquiry about each other is an exciting and important task. Your interactions are often intensely bonding as you discover new information. This can be *true* whether you are sharing in person, by mail, over the telephone, via the Internet, or using some other method. Your *honesty* and *truthfulness* in this process will build *trust* between you and a partner. Here is a humorous proverb from Gambia to *help* you remember to be *truthful*: "You should not trust a man who says that the hippopotamus is not an ugly animal."[15]

Copyright 2004 by Randy Glasbergen.
www.glasbergen.com

"If I want to impress a woman online, what font
should I use? Aristocrat Bold so she'll think I'm rich
or Comic Sans so she'll think I'm funny?"

It takes time and effort to build the in-depth knowledge between two people that comes with lasting friendship. Many factors will affect how fast you engage in personal discussions with someone. These include your own personal boundaries and your response when others do not *respect them*, your personality, your culture, your communication skills, your need or desire for intimacy, and the situation. **You should not feel rushed in sharing with a new acquaintance the information and emotions that well-established friends share.** Remember, friendships grow through stages from being casual acquaintances to becoming close friends. Part of this comes as you build *trust* that a friend will keep your confidences private. There are aspects of yourself that you will want only your closest friends to know.

It is common for people who are still in the acquaintance stage to be uncertain how much they wish to tell about themselves. Much you will initially share is "public" information that many people know about you. If a topic or personal matter comes up that you think is too sensitive to discuss early in your friendship or relationship, then have self-*respect*, be *courteously assertive* and clear about your feelings on the matter, and postpone the discussion until you feel more comfortable. For example, sensitive information can include discussing why a previous relationship ended, or personal problems your family or children have.

When you begin to let someone know you, you may notice that culture affects the acceptable topics and boundaries around personal information you both share. For instance, depending upon someone's culture or the country you are in, a person can ask you questions to determine the following information as soon as you meet each other:

- Where you were born and where you are currently living
- Your parents names and location
- The well-being of your family
- What your employment is
- The date of your birth
- Your religious beliefs
- Your relationship status

Try to determine the relevant cultural norms before you decide to let someone's questions or comments bother you. In some cultures or faiths, an independent third party or relative can even be the one asking questions before a couple meets or as their relationship grows. However, even when someone assists you to find or develop a relationship, it is important and *wise* for you to become a full participant in directly ensuring you know the person well yourself.

There will be content in the remaining chapters that will assist you with how to share information that is more personal and that may be difficult or sensitive.

ACTIVITY

Make a list of what is important for you to know about someone (This may be what you wrote on Worksheets 7.1 and 7.3.). Then prepare a list of questions to ask that will *help* you to find out the answers. Prioritize the questions so that you identify which ones you will ask someone the first few times you meet them, and then which ones you will ask as you progress with deepening your friendship.

Topics to consider can include education, employment, religious or *spiritual* beliefs and practices, children, relationship status and experience, favorite activities, and more. If possible, try out the questions with one or more people. Then, edit the questions based on how well they worked or if they were not effective.

✧ *Encouragement* ✧

Establishing a friendship as the basis of a relationship may strongly appeal to you. However, it may also be a new concept and be difficult for you to do at times. Keep up this important work, and remember to have fun in the process.

Date: _____

Worksheet 8.1: Appreciating Friends

This worksheet will assist you to appreciate your friends and better understand the value of a friendship-based relationship.

Instructions:

A) Describe what you appreciate in two of your friends who are not partners or previous partners, and the friendship you have with each of them.

B) Share these lists with the two friends separately, and note their responses to your positive comments.

C) Note in the last question what from these and other friendships you want to have in a relationship.

1. Female Friend's Name: _____

   What I appreciate in her and about our friendship is:

   _____

   _____

   Response to sharing:

   _____

   _____

2. Male Friend's Name: _____

   What I appreciate in him and about our friendship is:

   _____

   _____

   Response to sharing:

   _____

   _____

3. How do I feel about their responses? What did I learn from this experience?

   _____

   _____

4. The aspects of these and other friendships that I have that I want to see within a relationship are:

   _____

   _____

   _____

Date: _____

Worksheet 8.2: Widening Your Circle of Friends

This worksheet will assist you to understand how you are currently spending your time. It will then assist you to determine what you could be doing differently with your time to increase the number of friends and potential partners you have.

Instructions:
A) Answer the questions that follow.
B) Set goals in question 4 to increase the number of friends you have.

1. What are the main activities that I generally spend my time doing?

_____

_____

_____

_____

_____

_____

_____

2. How do these activities help me to meet new people?

_____

_____

_____

_____

_____

_____

_____

3. What other activities can help me to meet someone who can be a partner?

_____

_____

_____

_____

_____

_____

4. What are a few new activities that I now choose to become involved in? By when? (Mark the goal dates in your calendar.)

    _____ Date:_____

    _____ Date:_____

    _____ Date:_____

    _____ Date:_____

    _____ Date:_____

5. How can these activities assist me to find a potential partner?

    _____

    _____

    _____

    _____

    _____

    _____

    _____

6. What can I do to overcome my fears about doing these activities and increase my courage?

    _____

    _____

    _____

    _____

    _____

    _____

    _____

7. After I have participated in these activities, what is my assessment of them? Do I want to continue doing them? Why or why not?

    _____

    _____

    _____

    _____

    _____

    _____

    _____

A Consistent Partner:
Shifting to a Serious Relationship

Angus and Lily have known each other for a few months. They serve together on a community relations board for their city, co-chair a monthly interfaith devotional service, and participate in a bi-weekly spiritual study session together. They have developed a good working relationship and a firm friendship founded on mutual respect. Angus, a postal worker, has been a widower for 5 years, and Lily, a floral designer, has never married. They are feeling love grow between them and both enjoy performing community service, watching old movies, and reading historical novels. They decide they are ready to be a couple.

After dancing with a few people, you may discover that you do not want to keep shifting from one dance partner to another. You are ready and want to *commit* to a regular partner, and discover if you can dance the same dances together. You want a deeper relationship with one person, with time to explore and discover more about each other.

As you and your friend transition to being a "couple," you shift in how you relate to each other and to each other's friends and family members. You will spend an increasing amount of time in communication and doing a variety of activities together. You will consider including family and friends in your activity choices, as well as choosing activities that give you opportunities to know each other well. If you are in a long-distance relationship, you will also work through when it is best to be together in person and how to spend your limited time together.

As you and your partner interact, feelings of *love* will grow between you. You will begin to discover whether you are temporarily "in love" or whether there is the possibility of a deep *committed love* between you. You will also learn to distinguish when it works to act individually from when it is more appropriate to act as a team. This includes exploring how to practice *respect* and *equality* with each other in your communications and activity choices.

The more you learn about each other, the more you will assess your ability to be *excellent* dance partners. When you move smoothly on the dance floor as a team, with *courtesy* toward other dancers, your *confidence* in a happy and successful future together increases. The more positive signs you see in your relationship, the more optimistic you can be about going forward. You can also feel free to make increasingly serious *commitments* to each other.

BECOMING A COUPLE

Sometimes you and a partner will flow naturally from friendship into a relationship. In other cases, however, you may have to intentionally raise the topic with a friend and discuss it together. If you agree to move forward as a couple, some of your interactions and activities will change, and you will draw on *confidence*, *creativity*, *flexibility*, *patience*, and more to work through the transition. In some cultures, a partner may expect that sexual intimacy will automatically be included in the relationship as it becomes more serious. Remember from Chapter 5, however, that this is a choice, and you can choose to wait until marriage.

Copyright © Randy Glasbergen.
www.glasbergen.com

"If the wax drips down MY side of the candle, we start dating seriously. If the wax drips down YOUR side of the candle, we never see each other again. Isn't that a lot simpler?"

When you and another person are in a relationship, your family and friends will speak of the two of you as a "couple." You will spend considerable time together on the telephone, connecting via the Internet, and in person. **Your goal at this stage is to deepen your friendship and your *trust* with your partner and begin to know each other well.** This includes increasing your knowledge of your partner's character, and communicating openly and appropriately about your lives, choices, and any character issues that arise. It also includes meeting each other's families, if this has not yet occurred.

Meeting Family

Sometimes it is easier for your partner and your parents (or those who raised you) to interact when you are still living at home. If this is your situation, then a partner will naturally spend time at your home with you and your family. If you no longer live with your family, but you are still in contact with your parents, you will then determine when it makes sense to introduce a partner to them and to other family members. The timing will vary depending upon your age and circumstances.

If your partner's parents live far away from you, you may only meet them if you are very serious about each other and willing to travel. If you and your partner also live at a distance from both each other and your parents, the challenge of meeting increases even further. **Until you meet each other's families, however, there will be important gaps in understanding your partner.** You can use other forms of communication to assist you, but at some point, being together in person is *wise*.

When you do plan to introduce a partner to your parents, it will be good to let them know that you have ended a previous relationship, if that is the case, and that you have a new partner. Also, share with them any requests or expectations you have about what they say or do not say about you. It is particularly important that you are clear with them about what you consider as confidential or personal information that you are not yet ready to address with your partner. [*Note:* If you are estranged from your parents, it is important to try to resolve the problems and build *unity* if possible.]

Here are many of the factors to keep in mind when you consider introducing a partner to your parents:

- Your parent's interest in meeting your partner
- What input or guidance you want from your parents about the person
- Whether it is wise to meet because you suspect your partner is only in your life temporarily
- What preparatory information will be *helpful* to your parents
- If your parents had a close relationship with any previous partner of yours, whether you have discussed the end of that relationship with them, so that they are prepared to meet a new partner
- What information your partner needs to know about your parents and about interacting with them
- What assumptions are likely to be made about you as a couple, and whether there will be interference or premature pressure to marry
- Whether to do activities with both your family and your partner's family together
- Whether gifts are appropriate or expected

- Whether you have young siblings who were attached to a previous partner, or who will become attached to your new partner, and how you can make the adjustment easier for them

Before you introduce a partner and your parents, think carefully about what information they both need from you to be prepared for the meeting. It is important not to prejudice your partner by setting up negative expectations for the interaction with your parents. For instance, it would be unwise to say that, "My mother is cold and will not accept you." Your partner may then defensively interact with her on that basis, rather than being prepared to act in a *loving* and *friendly* way.

Perhaps you can let your partner know if there is anything they should be aware of about your parents that may catch them off guard if they are not prepared, such as if your father has a disability that impairs him from speaking clearly, or something similar. Your partner will appreciate knowing ahead of time that the culture of your family is to bring a gift, or if there will be a young child there who will enjoy a book or a toy. *Note:* If you have children, introducing them to a partner is covered in Chapter 13.

Beyond your parents, you may have other immediate family members or close relatives who are important to you. Introducing and spending time with them will also be part of your relationship-building process.

ACTIVITIES AS A COUPLE

Obviously, how you communicate with each other and what you share is a significant part of your relationship. However, there is much more. **The more varied activities you do together, and the more people you interact with, the more you will gain valuable knowledge about each other.** Dates tend to be one-on-one activities, which may limit the amount of knowledge you can gain. Many character qualities and personality traits in others only become obvious when someone is interacting with other people besides just you.

You will learn much more about your partner's actual character qualities by observing their actions than you will by listening to them talk about their values and what they believe. Sometimes people act differently in situations depending on whether they are in a leadership or a participatory role, or whether they are among friends or strangers. Engaging in activities with friends, family, and others will also give you the opportunity to observe how everyone gets along. **You and your partner will explore what the two of you have in common, and whether as a couple you can handle the differences that are natural between two people. You can observe whether you**

bring out the best character qualities in each other. *Note:* Chapter 10 will *help* you to *strengthen* your observation skills.

Activity Ideas

This section includes some activity suggestions that can assist you in getting to know someone. You will probably think of many more to do as well. You can do most of the ones on the list together with a partner, or with family members, friends, or new acquaintances included. As you and your partner discuss which ones to do together, you will discover that some are mutual interests and some only one of you enjoys. If one of you enjoys an activity more that the other, you can still both choose to participate, or you can choose something different to do together. You may also try out activities that neither of you has done before to explore what is mutually enjoyable. Over time, it will be important to identify core activities that you both appreciate, and you will continue doing them together.

One activity idea is to become involved in a community *service* project together. The Bible says, "…[S]erve one another in love. … Love your neighbor as yourself…."[1] Time spent in *serving* others will *help* you to see how your partner interacts with others they do not know well.

As you discuss which activities to do, including which ones to do with family members and friends, be cautious that neither of you dominates the choices nor tries to force the other to do something they do not want to. You can learn a tremendous amount about your partner by observing their choice of entertainment and activities. Sometimes

couples can become caught in a cycle of one partner never being happy unless they choose the activity, and the other passively goes along to keep things calm. This unwise dynamic can negatively affect the two of you as you go forward and make increasingly significant decisions. It is a good practice at this stage to begin learning how to do mutual decision making, which is a vital skill to have throughout your relationship.

The suggested activities include ones such as watching television and movies, and these are occasionally enjoyable or relaxing to do. You might like to watch something together and then discuss it. Often, however, movies and television can fill your time but limit your conversation and connection with each other. As you and a partner choose activities, ensure you have a balance of ones that are fun and relaxing, as well as ones that give you direct opportunities to get to know each other. Chapter 10 will help you to understand how to observe your partner and learn important information as you engage in these activities.

Share Time

- Take nature or beachside walks
- Visit art galleries or museums
- Visit amusement parks
- Share photographs
- Throw a party
- Watch television or movies
- Go shopping
- Study and discuss religious or *spiritual* quotations
- Exercise at a fitness center
- Play board, card, or video games
- Listen to music
- Practice meditation or yoga
- Take an educational class
- Walk with or care for a pet
- Visit the library
- Pray together
- Spend time with friends
- Go dancing
- Spend time with family
- Attend a concert
- Attend religious conferences, workshops, summer schools
- Do home/yard work and repair
- Read a book aloud to each other
- Do homework or study together

Serve/Work

- *Help* with a home repair project
- Visit elders
- Plan a meeting or a conference
- Teach a children's class
- Care for children
- Handle taxes/finances
- Volunteer
- Join or start a committee
- Plan a devotional/prayer meeting
- Facilitate a *spiritual* study class for teens or adults

Be Creative

- Build or decorate
- *Create* an art project
- Share family recipes and learn to cook new ones
- Write an article, story, poem, song, or book
- Plant and tend a garden
- Do a jigsaw puzzle
- Make a movie
- Sing songs or play musical instruments
- Make clothing or jewelry
- Build sand or snow sculptures
- Write letters or emails to each other
- Learn and practice a new language
- Design a website with graphics

Enjoy Sports/Adventure

- Play cooperative games
- Ski cross-country or downhill
- Travel
- Play volleyball or other group sports
- Camp
- Explore caves
- Hike
- Go canoeing/rafting
- Climb hills or mountains
- Play tennis or other racquet sport
- Ride bikes
- Rollerblade or ice skate
- Bowl
- Swim
- Surf
- Ride horses
- Fly kites
- Drive in a road rally or race
- Play football/baseball/soccer
- Snorkel/scuba dive

As you and your partner do activities together, ensure that you discuss how to find a balance that works for each of you between quiet activities or occasions that are more social. The two of you will also learn to balance when you need time together and when you need time apart. As with dancing, when you and your partner participate in an activity in unison, you build teamwork and become more in tune with each other as a couple. You both also learn when you need to sit and rest. It is good to dance in different styles, varied locations, and along with many types of music to determine what you both enjoy the most. Consider how this couple is developing their relationship:

> One Saturday afternoon a month, Gina and Mike volunteer to repair and clean homes for the elderly in their city with a local *service* organization. Gina's brother, Mario, usually participates with them. The couple learns how they *cooperate* with others, whether they can be *patient* with each other, and how much they both value *helping* others. Mike and Mario get to know each other as well.

> During the week, Mike attends a night class working toward a computer certification, and he and Gina do not see each other often. They regularly plan activities for their weekends, however. One of the things they often do together is join Mike's parents and grandmother for Sunday dinner. The more his family gets to know Gina, the more they like her *courtesy* toward them, the *compassion* she shows toward his grandmother's ailments, and how *strong* she is in handling the difficulties that come up in her life.

Just as Gina and Mike learn more about each other in different settings, you and your partner will learn more about each other by doing the same.

ACTIVITIES

1. Make yourself comfortable, perhaps with music playing in the background, and visualize which of the activities from this section appeal to you. Reflect on which ones will *help* you and a partner get to know each other's characters. If you wish, illustrate your choices of activities by making a collage (a poster using pictures and words cut from magazines).

2. Create a one-month relationship calendar. Mark each day with a specific action you will take to develop your readiness to be in a relationship. If you already have a partner, then mark what activities you will do together to deepen your relationship.

3. Complete **Worksheet 9.1: Doing Service for Others** to choose what *service* activities you want to do with a partner. If you are in a relationship, you can use the worksheet to decide together with your partner.

┌───┐

~ Questions for Reflection ~

1. What types of activities do I want to participate in with a partner? Avoid? What types of activities will support me learning about the character of my partner?
2. Do I have beliefs that will prohibit or discourage drinking, drug use, smoking, premarital sex, or other actions that a partner might want me to do with them?
3. How and when will I choose to communicate my *commitment* to these standards to my partner? What are my expectations of their actions and standards?
4. What *spiritual* activities do I want to try together with my partner? How will I handle any unwillingness on their part? What is essential to me? When can I be *flexible*?
5. What are my needs for having time on my own and time together with my partner? How will I *respect* these and communicate them to a partner? When I have a partner, how will I *respect* their needs related to time together and apart if they are different from mine?

└───┘

BEING IN A LONG-DISTANCE RELATIONSHIP

In a society that is increasingly mobile and provides the technological means to connect with people globally, you and a partner may very well be in different places for a significant portion of a relationship. Remember, just as with a relationship when you are together in person more often, you will need to begin with knowing yourself. Then, *detachment* will *help* you to consider objectively whether you are a good match with your partner.

Mobile and Internet-based communications are reducing geographical barriers. However, there are some realistic expectations to consider. Remember that to sustain any relationship, it is essential to be *honest* about the "real" you rather than portray a "perfect" picture of yourself. As your exchanges continue, you will develop an understanding of your partner, the rationale behind their words, and aspects of their character. **Although getting to know a partner from a distance is not the same as being together in-person, you can thoroughly build a friendship and explore a potential future this way.**

Often long-distance methods of communication actually allow you and your partner to get to know each other in ways that you might not if the two of you were together in the same place regularly. There may be less nervousness with communications, which *helps* with getting to know each other well. You can learn about character qualities, choices, interests, previous experiences, what you are both involved in currently, and where you see yourselves in the future.

• You can ask each other focused questions, such as ones that will tell you if your partner matches your requirements on Worksheets 7.1 and 7.3. You can find it useful to study the same relationship book and discuss it to learn about each other's lives. You can use *Can We Dance?* in this way, with each of you reading the chapters and completing the worksheets separately, and then discussing them together.

When you and your partner are together in person, you can further deepen your relationship, assess the reality of each other, and learn more about each other's character. *Detachment* can assist you to stay in exploration mode and not be attached to the eventual outcome of your relationship.

There are some cautions that are *wise* to consider with a long-distance relationship. When you and your partner see each other infrequently, your times together can be very intense, romantic, and almost "magical." **You are each able to be your best selves for these brief periods, and you have no effective way of knowing about each other's behavior in between visits within a real-life context.** The two of you may view any problems that occur in your visits as stemming from the stress of being apart, and feel that always being together will prevent them. These assumptions can falsely lead you and your partner to believe that being together in a more serious relationship or marriage will be a wonderful experience. You can then end up together, only to find out that neither of you really knew each other.

To counteract the risks of a long-distance situation, it is best to spend visits doing activities that maximize getting to know each other. These can include participating in community *service*, spending time with family, attending a *spiritual* or religious event, and more. If you come from different cultures, then include experiences that expand your knowledge of whichever one you are visiting. Chapter 13 will give you more ideas about this. During your time together, continue to observe your partner's character qualities, and try to establish your actual compatibility. Consider this situation:

> Lena and Zelipe met a few months ago while attending a conference in the city where he lives. However, they live and work in adjoining countries. Once Lena is back home, they are only able to visit each other every few weeks. They find it difficult to be apart, and they express frustration during their telephone calls and in emails. Their communications are not going smoothly.
>
> However, on the positive side, Lena and Zelipe stay with each other's parents during their visits, which gives them the opportunity to get to know each other's families. One weekend, Lena invites Zelipe to attend a workshop about relationships with her. They learn new communication skills that *help* them to improve their long-distance interactions.

If you and your partner become serious about each other, it will be *wise* to live in the same area, or visit for extended periods, so that you can get to know each other in more detailed and practical ways. Lena and Zelipe can miss learning many significant aspects of each other without this opportunity. Remember that the goal in living closer is to ensure you know each other's character thoroughly. Until you are seriously considering marriage, traveling or moving to be near each other is not a firm *commitment* to be together in the future. The caution in this circumstance is that you might feel compelled to go forward unwisely with the relationship simply because one of you moved to be closer to the other.

Long-distance relationships give you the opportunity to experience diversity in ways that would not have been possible in the past. Global communications allow you to expand your access to potential partners in other countries and cultures. Long-distance relationships can be part of connecting people together as one human family. "In reality, we humans have far more in common than we do differences."[2]

~ Questions for Reflection ~

1. What methods of communication will I be comfortable using with a long-distance partner?
2. What will *help* me to be successful in a long-distance relationship?
3. How can I thoroughly get to know a partner, especially their character, in real-life situations when we are living in different places?

FEELINGS OF LOVE AND ATTRACTION

As you deepen your emotional connection to your partner, you will begin to feel *love* toward them. You may wonder if it is genuine and lasting *love*, and how and when to express it to your partner.

Feeling "In Love"

As your relationship deepens, you may feel as if you are "in love," and wonder what this means and how it affects the future. Being "in love" can feel as if you are in a very fast, twirling dance with someone, and it can be both wonderful and make you dizzy. It will be a necessary challenge to determine whether your feelings are temporary, or whether you are experiencing a *committed love* that is lasting.

When you are "in love," it can be difficult to think of anything besides your partner, and you want to be together as much as possible. Physically, you may experience an increase in heart rate, passion, and other physical sensations. These intense feelings will feel very real and may seem almost obsessive. You may invent fantasies around your partner that color your view of them, or daydream about each other. Consider this couple:

> Last night, Janice and Calvin went on their fifth date. Much to Janice's delight, they took swing dance lessons at a local studio. In the morning as she sits down to pay her bills, she stops paying attention to the numbers. Instead, she replays in her head each minute she spent with Calvin. "He was so romantic when he spun me around on the dance floor. I loved the way he smiled right before he dipped me! Every minute was magical. I just know that we will be together forever."
>
> Across town, Calvin pauses while he is washing and waxing his car in his driveway. "Janice felt so good in my arms and followed my lead so naturally. I cannot believe I am with someone so beautiful and sweet. This is one special relationship!"

Just as you may experience, Janice and Calvin feel very attracted to each other. **It actually takes little effort to "fall in love." If your relationship stays at the physical or lower nature level, it is hard to sustain. Being "in love" is often full of a great deal of fantasy and lust.**

You may experience an intensification of sexual thoughts and desires, but is important not to rush into hasty decisions about physical intimacy. You are caught up in intense emotions, and it is probably difficult to think clearly about your choices and their consequences (Chapter 5). It is difficult to sustain these sensations and emotions, especially as you get to know each other through real day-to-day experiences. **In fact, feeling "in love" may interfere with clear thinking and may make it difficult to see what a partner is really like. It is wise to practice some *detachment*, so you can still *care* about the person, but see them more clearly.** Consider this quotation:

> Today you will see two souls apparently in close friendship; tomorrow all this may be changed. Yesterday they were ready to die for one another, today they shun one another...! This is not love; it is the yielding of the hearts to the accidents of life. When that which has caused this "love" to exist passes, the love passes also; this is not in reality love.[3]

Couples typically interpret physical attraction and intimate physical pleasure as *love*. The feelings of being "in love" and experiencing sexual attraction can be components of your relationship. But, be cautious. **These emotions are not necessarily an accurate predictor of the future success and longevity of the relationship.** Calvin and Janice in the previous story have spent their time together in social situations, but they actually know very little about each other's character. They think their physical reactions to each other mean that they are "in love."

Being "in love" can be compared to how a torch works that welders use for cutting steel. When the torch is first lit, the nozzle has to be turned open to full blast in order to get it started. However, for it to be effective in cutting steel, the flame has to be adjusted downward and maintained for an extended period of time. When the flame is adjusted, sometimes the welder turns the flame down too much, and the flame abruptly stops with a loud pop. When you are in this stage of a relationship, in order for you to sustain it, the flame needs to be turned down…without turning it off.

~ Questions for Reflection ~

1. Have I ever felt as if I was "in love"? What did it feel like?
2. What is my view of the sustainability of being "in love"?

Committed Love

Love is a complex concept. People describe it in various ways, depending on their experiences and beliefs. It can be called a character quality, an emotion, an action, a magnetic attraction, a *spiritual* bond, the force that brings life into the world, the link between the Creator and humanity, a light that guides people through dark times, and dozens of more descriptors. These all relate to *love* as a quality and as an expression of your higher nature. *Love* can become a *pure* light that shines between you and a partner and brings *joy* to both of you.

As you build a friendship-based relationship with someone, it is likely that your feelings of genuine *love* for the person are also growing. The question is, what are you attracted to in the other person? The reality is that you connect with a partner on physical, mental, emotional, and *spiritual* levels. Your body responds to your partner's body if you are together in person, or perhaps visually to a photo.

You respond through your five senses—sight, sound, smell, touch, and perhaps taste. Mentally, there can be an intellectual attraction as you stimulate each other's thoughts and ideas and share insights. Emotionally, you can respond to each other's needs and feel *love* toward what you appreciate in your partner. Mentally, emotionally, and *spiritually* you are attracted toward the character qualities you see in them. *Spiritually*, you appreciate the *beauty* in your partner's soul. When someone pleases you and attracts you on all levels, you know that you *love* them.

Love grows and deepens gradually as you increase your knowledge and appreciation of your partner. Author Justice St. Rain speaks of *love* in this way:

> Contrary to popular opinion, love is rarely a thunderbolt out of the sky. It is, rather, a hundred thousand million tiny raindrops that fill us up and sweep us out to the ocean. It is the result of small, repeating positive interactions. It is knowledge born of consistent contact. It is a flame that must be fed tiny twigs before being given sturdy sticks or large logs.[4]

The choice of *committed love* toward your partner will be based upon your clear knowledge of their *strengths*, growth areas, and misuses. However, *loving* someone is a conscious and daily choice, and not one merely based upon emotions. Choosing to *love* is an important and more lasting concept than simply feeling "in love." Some days you will feel less attraction toward your partner because they are unhappy, annoying, or behaving poorly. In this situation, you can still choose to *love* them and *help* them through listening, showing *compassion*, and being *assertive* when they act hurtfully. Your assistance *helps* them to re-balance and move from a focus on their lower nature, so that they can reclaim being their best self. If you turn *love* off like a tap every time there is a difficulty, your partner will never believe you *love* them.

One of the questions that is likely to arise for you is when to tell your partner that you *love* them. The first time one of you expresses *love* will be a big moment for both of you. As your feelings for each other grow, you may naturally express what is in your heart. Remember, however, that your words carry with them the qualities of *responsibility* and *commitment*. You are expressing an emotion that the other person will expect to last, and if you withdraw that *love* or stop expressing it later in your relationship, the other's reaction will be very negative.

Consider whether you are expressing yourself *honestly* when you share a statement of *love*. Do not say it unless you really mean it or only because a partner said it first. Moreover, remember that most people prefer to be treated in a *kind* and *loving* way rather than simply hearing the words, "I *love* you," without action as well. Yet, saying "I *love* you" lets your partner know that you have a *strong* emotional attachment to them. **Both words and actions are essential to communicate *love* effectively.** Your partner then gives you feedback about what they appreciate.

Loving someone in a *committed* way is sustainable throughout a long-term relationship and marriage. Consider this perspective from author Joseph Sheppherd in *A Wayfarer's Guide to Bringing the Sacred Home*:

> Love is not romance, nor is it passion, though it can include both at times. Some people associate love with affection, sentiment, infatuation, devotion, rapture, ecstasy, and more. The fact that there are so many different words associated with the concept of love reveals that it is something more than the imagination can hold. Love is like electricity: It is familiar to everyone, but no one knows its true nature. Love is not merely one thing or another. It is inherent in all things, and it is that quality which holds things together.
>
> We often associate marriage with the romantic notion of love. We may believe in something called a "soul mate" and dream of finding that one special individual in all of the world who is right for us. This notion is a relatively recent Western invention[;]…the romantic notion of love is not a realistic foundation for a marriage. … Romantic love is like the sudden burst of light that flares up when you light a candle; yet the candle's longevity and usefulness are dependent on its ability to burn strongly, slowly, and consistently. In marriage it is better to base our expectations on the qualities of a person's character. Liking and respecting the person whom we are actually with will provide the greatest measure of satisfaction, as will liking who we are when we are with that person.
>
> Loving the soul and the character of our mate and being comforted by our mutual loving-kindness are enduring foundations for a marital relationship. They bring out the sacred qualities that lie hidden deep within us.[5]

This deep level of lasting *love* has considerable *respect* and *sincere caring* at its foundation. It requires many interactions and thorough knowledge of each other's mind, heart, soul, and character.

There is also a piece of *love* that cannot be analyzed and categorized. There is mystery in why two people feel *strongly* toward each other that defies logic. When you both feel that magic and see the sparkle in each other's eyes, it adds to all the other reasons for you to be together and *commit* your *love* to each other.

Note: A vital communication tool, "The Five Love Languages," is covered in Chapter 15.

ACTIVITIES

1. Complete **9.2: Discerning Love for Your Partner** to understand better your feelings of *love* for a partner. If you do not have a partner, you can complete part of the worksheet thinking of a close friend.
2. Create an object (examples: card, letter, trinket) that you can give a partner to show your affection. If you have a partner now, then create a personalized one.

~ *Questions for Reflection* ~

1. How do I view being "in love" compared to building a gradual *"committed love"* with a partner?
2. What is my view about the importance of letting a partner know that I *love* them? Will I use words? Or will I show it in some other way? Or use both?

PRACTICING EQUALITY

Currently throughout the world, there is a growing movement toward *equality* between women and men, and this is prompting one of the most significant paradigm shifts underway in couple relationships. Organizations such as the United Nations and the Council of Europe (COE) have championed human rights and gender equality. The COE defines it as "… an equal visibility, empowerment and participation of both sexes in all spheres of public and private life."[6] The United Nations is vigorously promoting the rights and freedom of women to live without being subjected to physical, sexual, and psychological abuse, and to have full access to education, all of which are components of *equality*.

Each generation explores the best ways for men and women to interact and shifts closer to fully practicing *equality*. However, many people have different understandings of what *equality* means, and mixed responses to it as a concept. What *equality* will generally look like in relationships over time is unknown, but there are some principles that can guide you to including it in your own relationship.

One of the prerequisites for achieving *equality* is deep *respect* between you and a partner. This means that neither you nor your partner is better than the other is, and you each have a body, mind, heart, and soul that are of high value. You also acknowledge the value of each other's thoughts, feelings, and contributions to your relationship. Neither you nor your partner has the right to dominate,

control, force, or dictate to the other. If you are having a discussion on any topic, you listen carefully and share your thoughts and feelings with each other. Your goal is to make decisions together that you both wholeheartedly support. For some matters, however, you may know more than your partner does, and your partner defers to you. Other times, it can go the other direction. Even when one of you occasionally defers, however, it is a mutual decision, and you must both *respect* it and follow it together.

Equality in discussions and making decisions applies as you consider each of the activity ideas from earlier in the chapter. You will both participate in sharing your views about each of them and decide which activities to do. Inequality will occur if one of you makes all the decisions, and the other simply goes along with them.

Money can be an issue that arises related to activity choices, and who pays for an activity can have layers of significance for both of you. Historically, the male always paid for activities. With *equality*, this can shift into you and your partner taking turns at paying. Sometimes you can also pool your resources and share the expense, or each of you can pay your own way.

Think about what significance you place on who pays and for what. Do you see it as your *responsibility* to pay all the time, or do you have to pay your "fair share"? Do you think poorly about yourself or the other person based on how you both handle paying? Are you making choices based on cultural practices? Are you looking at the finances of both you and your partner and making decisions based on facts? It is important that you think about the significance you place on "who pays," and do your best to avoid money being a source of disunity between you and your partner. Consider how this couple handles money in their situation:

> Early in their relationship, Soo and Amadi realize their perspectives on money are significantly different. As a medical technician at a small hospital, Soo earns only enough money to pay her bills each month and save a small amount for the future. She learned from her parents that if she socializes with friends or a partner, she should pay her fair portion. Amadi, on the other hand, owns his own business and is doing very well financially. His parents taught him that he should pay when he takes women out socially.
>
> As Amadi and Soo participate in activities together, he wants to pay for Soo, but she is uncomfortable with it, and she feels she should pay for her portion. As this continues and they further discuss topics concerning money, they realize that they need to agree, or it will be a source of difficulties for them. Amadi understands that Soo takes pride in and feels as if she actively contributes to the relationship if she does pay at times. Soo also understands, however, that Amadi is in better position to be *generous* and pay the expense of participating in activities together.

Soo and Amadi sit down with each other one evening and discuss different ideas about how they can *respect* each other's values and yet move forward. Soo indicates that she has been thinking about applying for a higher paying position at another hospital. Amadi *encourages* her to try this option. Soo and Amadi agree that for now, he will pay the majority of any expenses, but Soo will contribute a portion occasionally.

In the past, relationships have often been guided by the belief that the man is the "head" of a relationship or home, with the woman *responsible* for "submitting" to him. Amadi could have taken this position with Soo in the previous story. Roles and *responsibilities* had traditions and customs associated with them, with men in a dominant position, and couples rarely shifted away from these. Consider this alternative view of the "headship" concept from Dr. Les Parrott in *7 Secrets of a Healthy Dating Relationship*:

> Headship [of a partner/wife/home] is not being the first in line. It is not being the boss or ruler. It is being the first to honor, the first to nurture, the first to meet the other's needs. A true administrator is also a servant.
>
> A healthy relationship, whether in dating or marriage, is built on a mutual desire to submit one's needs to the other. Emptying ourselves of our self-centered desires is the bridge to a deeper and more meaningful relationship.[7]

An area that people have struggled with as they try to understand *equality* is how to interact with or treat a partner. At times, this has resulted in abandoning long-held customs, such as holding a door open for a partner. Your key to determining your actions is character not customs. If you and your partner perceive holding a door open as *courtesy*, then that is the standard to strive for, regardless of your gender. In the quotation above, the standard is that both partners should *serve* each other.

Another area that has caused some challenges for people is the false assumption that men and women should receive *equal* treatment in relation to physical achievement. While sometimes there can be *equality* in physical *strength*, this is often not the case, and the genders have different physical bodies regardless. In Kenya, they say, "It is not necessary for fingers to look alike, but is necessary for them to co-operate."[8] *Equality* has more to say about your minds, hearts, and souls than your bodies. Consider this view:

> The world of humanity has two wings—one is women and the other men. Not until both wings are equally developed can the bird fly. ... Not until the world of women becomes equal to the world of men in the acquisition of virtues and perfections, can success and prosperity be attained....[9]

You and a partner practice *equality* in a relationship when you interact as peers. This includes the two of you finding common interests and doing activities together. The more you see yourselves as being in a partnership, the *stronger* the bond between you will grow. Consider what therapist Agnes Ghaznavi, M.D., says in *Sexuality, Relationships and Spiritual Growth* about developing this bond of *equality*:

> It is…important, in a relationship of equality, to have certain common fields of interest, concern and endeavor, be it in the community, in the family and neighborhood, in art or science or business or any other field. But in the last resort even this is not sufficient. The partners have to lay a firm spiritual foundation."[10]

You and your partner can foster a *spiritual* bond between you in a number of ways. Consider doing some of these activities together:

- Explore each other's beliefs
- Do yoga, Tai Chi, or some other meditation practice
- Pray
- Spend time relaxing in nature and appreciating it as an awe-inspiring creation
- Attend worship or devotional services
- Read *spiritual* books and discuss them
- *Encourage* and develop character qualities

There will be more about *spiritual* bonding in Chapter 15.

Essentially, *equality* is something you will work out between the two of you. It may take *assertiveness* on your part at times and *flexibility* at others to achieve it *cooperatively*. Achieving *equality* is a *commitment* you both make together. It has its foundation in the recognition of all people as valuable. Here is this perspective from Don Coyhis of the Mohican Nation:

> We all come from one Great Spirit but we are all different and unique. Nothing in the Great Creation has a twin that is identical. Even children that are twins are different. Every single person is extremely special and unique. Each person has a purpose and reason why they are on the Earth. Just like every leaf on a tree is different, each one is needed to make the tree look like it does. No leaf is better or worse than the other—all leaves are of equal worth and belong on the tree. It is the same with human beings. We each belong here and do things that will affect the great whole.[11]

ACTIVITY

Choose a project to work on with a partner or other close friend that involves *cooperation*. This might include arranging books on a bookshelf, bringing order to CDs or DVDs, rearranging or redecorating a room, organizing a filing system, building something together, landscaping, cooking, or cleaning out cupboards or a closet. Assess how well you completed the task. How did you handle differences of opinion? Were you able to *respect* each other's input, complete it successfully, and end the project in *unity*?

POSITIVE RELATIONSHIP SIGNS

As a relationship develops, there are some indicators that you and your partner can use to determine if the two of you are dancing well together. You can tell that your relationship is progressing in a positive way when you and your partner are both:

- Maintaining your friendship and enjoying each other's company
- Listening to each other effectively and talking freely to each other as *equals* without holding back important information and feelings
- Giving and receiving positive suggestions from each other concerning character quality development and other life issues
- Demonstrating character qualities that the other appreciates and honors
- Learning together
- Making decisions together, and not dictating to each other
- Sharing tasks when you work on projects together
- *Respecting* each other
- Interacting with both sets of parents with *love*, *respect*, and with appropriate and agreed-upon boundaries
- Interacting in positive ways with your own and each other's friends
- Having fun together and enjoying a compatible sense of humor
- Beginning to understand and appreciate each other's culture
- Understanding and *respecting* what is important to each other
- *Encouraging* each other in your individual and mutual pursuits
- *Trusting* each other
- Giving each other private or quiet space when needed
- Meeting each other's agreed upon expectations, boundaries, and requests (See Chapter 6)
- Demonstrating effective conflict prevention and resolution skills

- Remaining even-tempered and level-headed during adversity, grief, fear, or danger
- Staying in friendship mode while handling disagreements
- Maintaining a high degree of *unity* and harmony between you

This is probably not a complete list, so make sure you take the time to see if you can think of any other measures that you consider positive ones. Be aware, however, that it will take time and relationship development to achieve a list like this. You should not realistically expect it all to happen quickly. The list gives you a way to measure the ongoing health of your relationship. If it becommes obvious that many of these items are not going to happen, you can then assess and reconsider your relationship.

ACTIVITY

If you are in a relationship, use the drawing tools in a computer software program, or pen and paper, and make cartoons with captions that reflect your positive experiences, questions, concerns, or assessment of various aspects of your relationship. Share these with your partner, and ask how they would have captioned the same cartoons. Or, ask your partner to create their own cartoons at the same time that you are completing yours. Together, then *create* new cartoons and captions together. If you are not in a relationship, then consider creating cartoons that depict aspects of friendship or relationships generally.

∾ *Encouragement* ๛

Making the choice to create a relationship with someone can be a difficult and exciting move. However, with the skills you have been learning so far in this book, you are well equipped to make this important choice. A relationship on a firm foundation will last. Enjoy the process of becoming closer to your partner!

Date: _____

Worksheet 9.1 Doing Service for Others

This worksheet will assist you to assess the types of service activities you would enjoy working on with a partner. If you are in a relationship, then you and your partner can use it to choose what service activities will help you both to grow as individuals and together, learn about each other, and make a difference for other people. Think about how you can still do service even if you are in a long-distance relationship.

Instructions:

A) Select or enter each activity you would like to participate in yourself. If you are with a partner, then they will also mark their preferences, and then together you will mark the ones you both feel strongly about working on as a couple.

B) Under the "Time Needed" column, consider the time it will take to accomplish each activity. Also, note the frequency, such as "daily," "weekly," or "monthly."

C) Write down specifically what you will do for each choice. If you are on your own, go ahead and become involved in the activity that appeals to you, as you may meet a partner in the process. If you are in a relationship, then proceed with taking the appropriate actions to carry out the service activities you both agree are important.

Possible Activities	She	He	Both	Time Needed	Specific Actions to Take
Care for children of family or friends					
Coach a children's or teen's sports team					
Organize or teach a class for children, teens, or adults					
Visit and help residents in a nursing home or people who need or appreciate home visits					
Assist at prayer or devotional meetings or worship services					
Participate on a civic or religious committee that plans an event to help others					

Possible Activities	She	He	Both	Time Needed	Specific Actions to Take
Perform a civic improvement activity, such as picking up trash or planting a garden					
Prepare a meal for a friend, a relative, or a person who is unable to leave their home					
Create a website for a non-profit organization, or consult with them via the Internet					
Facilitate a spiritual or religious study group					
Teach literacy or tutor students					
Mentor a child who does not have both parents involved in their life					
Raise funds for a worthy cause					
Help at a community food bank or food service					
Build or maintain a home or other structure for someone					
Set up a health or hygiene education program or facility					
Other:					
Other:					

Questions for Reflection: [Answer whichever ones are appropriate.]

1. What did I learn about myself in the process of choosing activities?

_____

_____

2. What did I learn about myself through participating in an activity?

_____

_____

3. What did I learn about my partner while choosing activities?

_____

_____

4. What did I learn about my partner through participating in an activity?

_____

_____

5. What difference did I make for those I served?

_____

_____

6. What motivates me and how do I feel about participating in service?

_____

_____

7. How do I feel about serving together with a partner?

_____

_____

8. Do I want service to be a regular part of a relationship? Why or why not?

_____

_____

9. Which service activities are most important to me?

_____

_____

10. Which service activities are most important to my partner?

_____

_____

Date: _____

Worksheet 9.2: Discerning Love for Your Partner

This worksheet will assist you to assess the love you feel for your partner. If you do not yet have a partner, then complete as much of this worksheet as possible about a close friend.

Instructions:

A) Determine the person toward whom you have loving feelings.

B) If the person is your partner, then complete the entire worksheet. If you are completing it about a close friend, then complete items 1, 2, and 3 only.

1. The person I feel love toward is: _____

2. What I love about them is:

   _____

   _____

   _____

   _____

3. I express love to them in the following ways:

   _____

   _____

   _____

4. My partner expresses love to me in the following ways:

   _____

   _____

   _____

5. I can tell that I am "in love" with my partner because:

   _____

   _____

   _____

6. I can tell that the love between us is committed love and will last because:

   _____

   _____

   _____

Dips and Twirls:
Observing Your Partner's Moves

Andy and Liz are working side-by-side in the community center, filling boxes with cans of food. Their team will later deliver the food to low-income families in the area. The couple is newly in a serious relationship, so they decide that a service activity like this will help them to get to know each other better. They commit to making positive comments about each other's character qualities throughout the day. They struggle at times with impatience and frustration as they experience dropped cans, fatigue, hard work, and a fellow worker's rudeness. However, they also notice and acknowledge in each other the qualities of courtesy, generosity, excellence, perseverance, and caring.

You have been regularly taking dance lessons, so you invite your partner to go to a dance with you. Hours spent practicing your steps, polishing your dancing shoes, and moving to music have you all ready to go. Now, you need to know if your partner can dip, twirl, and move in harmony with you. The experience of dancing with your partner will tell you whether it feels good to dance together, and whether your styles and techniques are compatible. Perhaps your partner is too rough, or their style is so self-centered, you feel as if you are dancing alone. You might appreciate or dislike how your partner handles the two of you bumping into another couple. It will be clear whether your partner is *courteous*, or instead hogs space or flings arms and feet without consideration for others on the dance floor.

Every time you are with your partner, or the two of you are with family or friends, you have the opportunity to learn. You are engaged in relationship exploration. As you observe your partner, you will see an array of details about their life and choices. Many of their actions will be positive, and you will appreciate them. At times, however, the way your partner acts around you may be difficult for you to *accept*. For instance, perhaps they get along well with your friends, but they keep offending your mother.

Just as with the challenge of learning to dance, it can take time to learn effective observation techniques. A delicate part of the process is learning to observe without offending your partner. *Respect* for your partner's body, mind, heart, and soul is important. Successful observation, including understanding and processing what you see and hear, is a practical and necessary skill to learn, however. This skill will assist you to keep "both eyes open" to clearly see your partner, and be sure you are choosing someone who is a good match for you. *Can We Dance?* is part of the Both Eyes Open™ series of books for this important reason. (See details about the series in Appendix D.)

UNDERSTANDING OBSERVATION

Observing is the process of becoming aware of information through *careful* and directed attention. The more attentive and systematic you are in your observations, the more knowledge and insights you will gain. In dancing, you watch how your partner's feet move or how your partner twirls you. In a friendship and relationship, you observe what the other person says and does—or does not say or do. Good observational skills allow you to perceive details about your partner's appearance, choices, character qualities, words, actions, and attitudes. Of course, your partner will be aware that you are learning about them, and they will be learning about you at the same time.

The intent of observing and assessing your partner is to *help* you avoid being blinded by being infatuated. As you learned in Chapter 9, infatuation, or being "in love," is usually an intense and short-lived passion for someone. **Practicing *detachment* and getting to know someone thoroughly instead, will *help* you to have a lasting relationship built on *committed love* for your partner.** Your intent is not to be judging your partner's behavior as right or wrong, but rather to determine whether the person has what is important to you. Your goal is to determine whether the two of you are a good match for each other.

Effective observation *helps* you to see a partner with "both eyes open™". Fully seeing what is important about someone requires more than a superficial understanding about them. You need more than an online profile or a brief resume of a person's life experiences. You will also miss key information about your partner if you close one eye in denial of problems, or take someone else's opinion about your partner as fact without checking it out. You are "...not intended to see through the eyes of another, hear through another's ears nor comprehend with another's brain. ... Therefore, depend upon your own reason and judgment and adhere to the outcome of your own investigation...."[1] **It is in the best interests of your relationship if you *encourage* your partner to observe and get to know you thoroughly as well.**

If you want to be a partner with someone who knows how to dance the waltz well, it will be a good idea if you first know what it looks like when someone is dancing the waltz. It is the same with observing other people. For instance, if it is important to you to have a partner who is well-skilled in the use of *honesty*, *courage*, or *kindness*, it will be a good idea for you to first have a picture in your mind of what it looks like for a person to be *honest*, *courageous*, or *kind*. This is part of why your work in Chapters 1-3 is so valuable. By knowing your own character, you will be very effective at observing the character of a partner. By also knowing what you are looking for in a partner from your work in chapters 6 and 7, you will be able to focus your observations on what is most important.

You will make some observations quickly and easily. However, other aspects about your partner will only become clear to you as you take time to participate in a variety of activities and have deep discussions together. **Observation will *help* you to know how you and your partner both handle your relationships with others, family obligations, education, work, community *service*, religious or *spiritual* activities, *commitments*, and *responsibilities*.** This observation is especially important when you and your partner come from different family, cultural, or religious backgrounds.

You may choose to be systematic in identifying what you want to learn about someone, and track the results of your information-gathering process, perhaps in a journal. Remember to use *wisdom* in how you handle your notes. It is a good idea to keep them in a private location, and at some point destroy them. After all, the notes you keep are to assist you—they are not for public display. Your partner will not appreciate you sharing your personal observations openly with others. Their embarrassment or anger at you, and the resulting distrust in you, could end your relationship. As your relationship progresses, however, and there is some stability and *commitment* between you and your partner, you will want to share and discuss your observations with them. *Encourage* them to discuss their observations with you as well.

Throughout the process of getting to know someone, you will learn information directly from your partner and from other people. **Be *discerning* and *carefully* assess the accuracy of any information you get from a third party that you do not directly observe or confirm yourself. This is *true* whether the person's statement to you is negative or positive.** If someone shares with you negative and untrue information about another, that is misleading; however, if one shares positive and untrue information, it is also misleading. [*Note:* There is information about backbiting, gossip, and slander in Chapter 12.]

Seeking knowledge about your partner is *wise*. "The mind of an intelligent man acquires knowledge; the ears of the wise seek out knowledge."[2] You will then use *wisdom* and *discernment* in assessing the knowledge that you gain. Be cautious about over-analyzing what you observe or prolonging the process unnecessarily as an excuse to avoid *commitment* to a partner.

An important reminder in the observation process is for you to practice *tactfulness*, *respect*, *courtesy*, and *moderation* as you gather information. **You are engaged in *loving* observation, rather than being a detective or spy on an intense case or secret mission.** If you are inappropriate by being sneaky, suspicious, or intrusive in your words or actions, you can alienate your partner. Your intention is really to carry out a systematic and impartial search for *truth*. You are engaged in a thorough, *detached*, and mutual process of understanding or "investigating" each other's character, in particular. Your goal is to be clear about your partner's character *strengths* and to minimize the possibility of encountering unpleasant surprises in their character later on.

As you observe your partner, you will have various thoughts and reactions. Both appreciation for your partner and concerns will arise. As you participate in the observation process, you will consider both the immediate and the long-term future of your relationship, and whether to stay together. As you observe issues, you will raise them with your partner. **Remember to make the *commitment* to work through concerns together, without abandoning the relationship over small and petty issues. These are often growth and learning opportunities.** If you think that you might be with someone long-term (or marry them), what you learn through resolving them together will be especially important.

You will not be perfect at this observation process—you will do your best. If you believe in prayer, you may wish to ask for *spiritual* assistance to guide you and *help* you to observe accurately. You can also ask for protection from making any major mistakes!

Sometimes you and your partner will find it easy and fun to observe each other. You will tease and joke as you learn new details. **Avoid being so serious about observing that you forget to enjoy learning about a relationship partner. The process is often fun, fascinating, and light-hearted. It is also an opportunity to learn about yourself.** Remember to relax and not be in serious observation mode all of the time.

ACTIVITY

Begin the process of learning and *strengthening* your observation skills by pretending that you are a reporter for a news organization. Choose a location to observe people. On a notebook or piece of paper, write down what and whom you are observing in your surroundings. Choose a length of time for your observations that makes sense for your life, whether it is 30 minutes, a day, or a week. You can notice what people look like, and such aspects about them as what they are wearing, doing, saying, and their tones of voice. Once you have completed your observations, write a story in which you include the scene and conversations.

Challenges in Observing Others

Do you remember the self-assessment process you went through in Chapter 2? You identified what gets in your way and what makes it difficult to be *honest* with yourself. Just as you sometimes resist observing and assessing yourself, you may have moments when you feel it is too difficult to stay focused on observing your partner. The same way your feet may get in the way when you are dancing together, barriers and problems can also occur when you attempt to observe and assess a partner. Your awareness of these barriers will *help* you to avoid them or push through them quickly and *persevere*. These interferences can include:

- Excessive focus on romance or projecting fantasy onto the relationship
- Lack of awareness of your partner's actions
- Snap judgments without clear facts
- Denial about what you are observing and its significance
- Being overly emotionally attached
- Intense sexual passion
- Fear of being alone
- Excessive concern about your partner's reaction if you raise an issue
- Setting your partner up on a pedestal and looking at them as nearly perfect
- Attachment to your partner's physical appearance, social position, or wealth as more important than their character, words, and actions

Effective observation requires that you be objective and *detached* enough from your feelings toward your partner that you can clearly assess the facts about their character. *Detachment* does not mean that you avoid or stay away from your partner or stop your relationship. You still care about them, and are attracted to them. It simply means

letting go of the intensity of some of your emotions, so that you can think more clearly and make more objective and fair-minded choices.

Keeping an open mind is also important for astute observation. Prejudices, biased opinions, quick interpretations, or judgments will interfere with you *discerning* the *truth* about your partner. *Discernment* empowers you to "…make distinctions between what is real and what is an illusion."[3] You can pause and realize that you are adding your own interpretation to someone's actions or words, and you can *accept* that you may not have the full picture. The qualities of *courtesy*, *patience*, and *perseverance* will support you in objectively obtaining all of the facts. You may also find it *helpful* to pray and/or meditate to *strengthen respect* and *detachment*, both of which will *help* you to slow down the speed of your conclusions and avoid false ones.

Sexual involvement or fantasizing about physical touch between you and your partner can cause physical and hormonal reactions that can interfere with your ability to make accurate observations. Your perceptions of your partner can be unrealistic as a result. If you base your choices about your partner upon sexual responses, you may project that a relationship situation is positive, when in fact it is not going well.

In trying to *discern* someone's character, it may be useful to gain observations and insights from parents, other relatives, and friends. When asking for the opinions of others, it is important to word your questions carefully. It is good to ask people to only share their positive comments or talk about general concerns. You are asking them to suggest areas that might cause unsolvable problems or conflict in a long-term relationship.

The questions that you ask people who know your partner can be similar to, "What do you think are our *strengths* as a couple, and what problems do you foresee in our relationship?" You are not asking them to list all the negative qualities of the other person. If everyone you ask struggles to say something positive, that by itself can indicate there is a problem. [There is information about backbiting, gossip, and slander in Chapter 12.]

~ Questions for Reflection ~

1. What *helps* me to observe someone effectively?
2. What interferes with my ability to observe a partner? How can I address this?
3. Am I remembering to observe myself, too?

OBSERVING BODY LANGUAGE AND CLOTHING

Everyone communicates in ways that do not involve using words. These include choice of clothing, using eyes or touch, facial expressions, body positions, hand gestures while speaking, and so on. How someone dresses and presents themselves in their interactions with you will draw you toward them, leave you feeling neutral, or push you away. These physical aspects of a partner may be the initial focus of your observations.

Below is a list of various types of body language or ways of dressing. Think about how you respond to these in others. They can invite you to talk to someone or discourage you, depending on your tastes, experience, culture, or judgments. Consider these:

- Giving flirtatious looks
- Raising eyebrows
- Winking
- Shuffling feet
- Staring
- Touching a shoulder
- Wearing baggy clothes
- Wearing tight clothes
- Frowning
- Hugging
- Wearing heavy makeup
- Wearing no makeup

- Smiling
- Wearing a low-cut top or open shirt
- Wearing short skirts or shorts
- Kissing (consider different types)
- Giving a shoulder or back massage
- Looking down or away
- Keeping eye contact
- Pointing a finger at others
- Showing your bare feet
- Wearing headphones
- Having a distracted or bored facial expression

Some of these, such as very revealing clothes, can prompt you to conclude that the person is inviting physical touch from you. This may or may not be *true*, as your interpretation of what is provocative may be different from theirs. Culture can be a factor in interpretations as well. For instance, looking down or away and avoiding someone's eyes may show *respect* in one culture and disrespect in another.

Flirting is a common practice in relationships. In its mildest form, it is unlikely to be harmful, but be observant and try to learn why someone is flirting with you. Someone may use it to indicate that they find you attractive. At times, however, someone may flirt with you to communicate sexual availability. Also, this could be an unwise attempt to make another person jealous. If you respond to someone's flirting either positively or negatively based on the assumption that they are available, and in fact they are not, you can end up embarrassed or in a difficult situation.

Skillful observation includes noticing a partner's body language and non-verbal signals. Perhaps they smile *compassionately* when someone is sad, frown after someone speaks to them rudely, squeeze your hand at an emotional or scary moment during a movie, or look at you in a puzzled way after you say something. Confucius says, "…to speak without observing the expression on his face is to be blind."[3]

These types of communications express your partner's attitudes and personality. They can also communicate meaning when they are used along with words. Therefore, you will observe whether your partner's words and gestures, together as a complete message, are attractive and appropriate, unpleasant, or perhaps hurtful. Does your partner smile while telling a story? Do they use gestures that make the message so intense that you are uncomfortable or anxious in response?

A Word of Caution: It takes highly skilled specialists to interpret body movements accurately, especially as their significance varies among different cultures. **As you observe someone else's clothing choices or gestures, you can easily misinterpret them entirely. So, although these observations will give you some clues about a person, be careful about making assumptions.** You can always use verbal communication to verify the accuracy of your conclusions.

ACTIVITY
Go with a friend or your partner to a store, college, city street, or some other location where you will see a variety of people wearing different outfits. Discuss your responses to what people are wearing and how they are behaving.
~ *Questions for Reflection* ~
1. What judgments do I tend to make about others based on their clothing and body language? 2. What messages about character can I gain from observing these? 3. When have I misinterpreted someone's body language or gestures? How did I handle the situation?

OBSERVING CHARACTER

By listening carefully to various input, and combining that information with your own observations, you will be able to *discern* much about your partner's qualities. Knowing their *strengths*, imperfections, and the degree to which your partner is working on them, will *help* you in making choices.

While growing up, you may have been taught to only say something good about other people or focus on their positive qualities. This is an *excellent* practice to keep throughout your life in maintaining relationships. However, it may trip you up a bit in a relationship exploration context. When you are choosing someone to be in a serious relationship with or potentially marry, it is vital to identify the person's character qualities and habitual behavior to obtain a complete picture of them. This will *help* you to assess the potential for the relationship to be lasting and successful.

On the other hand, you may habitually criticize others instead of speaking positively about them. You can achieve balance by now using *discernment* to observe when your partner uses character qualities effectively. The goal is to become able to understand how your partner's character affects their life and relationships and how you interact and affect each other. *Excellent* observation skills allow you to see which behaviors your partner repeats consistently, and whether they are beneficial or they can become an issue or conflict.

It can be easy to be infatuated or distracted by an attractive face or a charming personality without taking a closer look at your partner's character. Your objective observation skills will *help* you to avoid this pitfall. To get to know someone's character and behavior takes time, *patience*, experience, *trust* in your inner voice, reflection, prayer, common sense, and *perseverance*. It also takes teamwork and openness between you and your partner, and your own willingness to learn and grow. Consider this perspective from author and relationship educator Charlie Michaels:

> Although you may not consciously be aware of it, most people have created a mental picture of an ideal partner—and you probably have as well. While

this is good from a character quality standpoint, it can be a hindrance if your vision includes specific physical traits as most images do. Whether you favor a dark-eyed, brunette with a strong profile and a dimple, or a green-eyed, redhead with freckles and an impish grin, there will be a tendency to assign all the positive qualities of your ideal partner to anyone who matches the physical traits that appeal to you. It is crucial to separate physical attributes from character, personality, and behaviors. It is vital to hold all prospective partners to the same standards in your heart and mind. Just because someone looks the part does not mean they are the real thing.

You may have heard the saying, "appearances can be deceiving." It's true. Just because someone looks like a younger version of your beloved grandmother does not mean they have anything more than an outer shell in common. Resist the temptation to assume a new acquaintance has the interests, abilities, character qualities, or love for you that your grandmother had. Show your fairness, kindness, and maturity by eliminating the unfair expectations you have placed on this person just because he or she looks like someone with whom you had a real or imagined relationship. Save yourself from the inevitable disappointment that will come if you fool yourself into seeing attributes that are not there. Keep your eyes open and see the person before you, not the memory in your mind or the hope in your heart.[5]

As any good researcher will tell you, you must start by having well-defined categories for what you will be researching. In terms of character qualities, this means paying close attention to what they look like when your partner is in action. Remember, Part 3 is there to *help*.

Often you can get clues to someone's character quickly. For instance, you can walk down the street, and someone greets you in a *friendly* manner. You watch a mother be *responsible* by giving her child healthy food. You notice a couple getting off a bus, and see how one waits *courteously* for the other on the sidewalk before they enter a building. You may see a person in the laundry room of your apartment building folding their clothes in a neat and *careful* way. These are all indications of their character qualities.

Even in new friendships and relationships, you can begin to gain some knowledge of your partner's character. Consider the couple in this story:

> Charlene and Patrick are good friends and new partners. He invites her to meet his parents and sister, who are visiting from Ireland. During his family's visit, she enjoys watching him talk and laugh with them and learning more about his character. She observes him *thoughtfully* meeting his family at the airport, *flexibly*

handling changes in plans, and *moderately* suggesting activities without trying to fill every minute. The *love* and *caring* Patrick feels for his family are evident to her.

Charlene notices, however, that Patrick assumes his mother and sister will prepare each meal for them. He goes into the living room with his father while the women cook and then do the dishes after the meal. He bluntly states with a chuckle that the kitchen is women's work. He has shown her many great qualities, but she has questions about his *helpfulness* and willingness to practice *equality*.

It is important to remember that one of the best tools that you have in your toolbox for building a relationship is positive acknowledgement of a partner's behavior and effective use of character qualities yourself. **The more you can focus your attention on your partner's positive behavior and acknowledge it, and the less you focus on the negative, the better. This *encourages* your partner's heart and spirit.** Charlene will be *wise* to acknowledge Patrick's positive behavior.

Charlene will also determine through further observation and discussion with Patrick whether he is inclined to change his assumption about women's *responsibilities* and, therefore, change his behavior. Together they will examine what *helpfulness* and *equality* look like for both of them within their relationship. After she learns his attitudes, and whether he is likely to change, she can then decide whether Patrick's behavior is a minor or major problem for her. Remember, she can *encourage* Patrick to change, but she cannot expect it to happen in order to make her happy. The choice is his.

ACTIVITY

Go to places such as a shopping center, workplace, or school, and watch people you do not know interact with others. What character qualities do you observe? Which behaviors do you consider positive and which ones negative? If you were friends with the person, how would you *encourage* the positive and discuss the negative?

~ Questions for Reflection ~

1. How do I know that I am beginning to understand someone's character?
2. How might discovering something I perceive as negative behavior affect my relationship and interactions with my partner?
3. What weak character qualities or shortcomings in someone might make it difficult or impossible for me to be friends or in a serious relationship with them?
4. What are the consequences of ineffectively assessing the character of someone I am in a relationship with? What surprises could be significant problems?

Clarity and Consistency

People often initially have a tendency to hold parts of themselves back, or to be on their best behavior, in order to make a good first impression. Behaving well is a good idea, but it will take time for you and your partner to relax with each other enough to see the main facets of each other. Confucius says, "Look at the means a man employs, observe the path he takes and examine where he feels at home. In what way is a man's true character hidden from view?"[6] He also says, "I used to take on trust a man's deeds after having listened to his words. Now having listened to a man's words I go on to observe his deeds."[7]

Remember, for most of your observations to be useful, you will have to know how your partner consistently uses or misuses character qualities. **Consistency is an indication that the behavior is deeply ingrained in your partner's character and is likely to be present throughout your relationship.** You will observe whether your partner is usually *loving* and *courteous* to everyone, or are they are polite to you, but rude to others. Is your partner *joyful* and *enthusiastic* regularly and appropriately? Are they often discourteously late to pick you up, or not ready when you arrive to pick them up? How do they usually speak to their parents or to any children that they or you have? Do the words your partner says match their actions? Do they keep or break promises made to you or others?

Consistency does not mean your partner will be perfect. Remember that everyone has times when they falter or do not behave as well as they want to. However, if your partner has a quality as a *strength*, they will resume practicing it effectively both quickly and easily.

In this story below, notice how Bakari observes Kadence, and assesses aspects of the consistency of the quality of *purity* in her, which include cleanliness and orderliness, and what he observes about himself:

> Kadence and Bakari are developing a mutual friendship as they work part-time together at the library in their town. They also see each other at times outside of work. One day at the library, Bakari searches his desktop frantically. He is looking for a book his manager asked him to put away in the fiction department. He knows it is there, and he is *confident* he will find it quickly. As he sorts through the papers, books, and containers from his lunch, he looks up and notices his friend Kadence alphabetizing her cart of books by author and then by title.
>
> Bakari sighs and thinks about how organized Kadence is. Her clothes are neat, her car is clean, and she puts her paper clips and pens away in their containers instead of leaving them scattered on the desk as he does. Bakari knows he has

many great qualities, but maintaining his work environment in an orderly way is not one of them. He knows this difference between them can present a problem if he and Kadence become more serious about each other.

Through his observations, Bakari can tell Kadence is a clean and orderly person. If someone asks him to describe Kadence, Bakari can objectively give this positive information about her.

You can tell if you know the character of someone by how you respond when someone asks you to describe them. Perhaps your parents or a friend says, "Tell me about him," or asks, "What is she like?" As you try to answer, all you can come up with is, "Oh, he is so nice!" or "She is wonderful!" This is an indication that it would be *wise* for you to spend additional time together with your partner and improve your observation skills. You can also benefit from learning more about how to describe someone's character.

Another sign that you can benefit from *strengthening* your character observation skills occurs when you can only describe your partner in relation to you. For instance, when asked to tell what the person is like, you might say, "He's so good <u>to me</u>," or "She is always doing things <u>for me</u>."

The goal is for you to be able to say that your partner is *generous*, *friendly*, or *courageous* generally, not just what their words or actions are toward you. The former is a self-centered perspective, and it will be better if you can see what the person's qualities are no matter with whom they are interacting.

As you make your observations of your partner, remember to be watching for the 10 important character qualities that you identified in Worksheet 7.1. If they are present in your partner, it is a positive sign that you are in a good relationship. If your partner lacks or regularly misuses these ones instead, it makes sense to reevaluate your involvement with them. This is particularly *true* if the person is not interested in or engaged in developing their character qualities.

If you find that you are struggling to observe someone's character effectively, you will find it useful to study the qualities in Part 3 or read other material about character.

ACTIVITY

Develop specific observation questions about each of the 10 character qualities you identified as desirable in your partner on Worksheet 7.1. An example for the quality of *perseverance* is this: Does my partner finish projects once they start working, or do they procrastinate or perpetually leave the project only partially done?

┌───┐
│ **~ *Questions for Reflection* ~** │
├───┤
│ 1. Am I generally an accurate observer of others' characters? If not, what will I do to improve my skills? │
│ 2. How do I tend to describe others? │
│ 3. Do I or others perceive me as being overly judgmental in my attitude, critical with my words, or having unrealistically high standards? Am I the opposite, rarely noticing obvious character weaknesses in others? How might either of these approaches affect my assessment of a partner's character? │
└───┘

Handling Challenges

Good character clues come from seeing how your partner handles disagreements, illness, dissension, difficulties, or when a situation is not going well. What character *strengths* do you typically see them practice when things are not going smoothly? Do character *strengths* such as *compassion, courage,* or *flexibility* come to the forefront? Does your partner instead retreat into destructive anger, frustration, depression, denial, or inappropriate actions? How do they behave when they feel sad or disappointed?

Difficulties are often great opportunities for your own personal development, and you will be able to observe if this is how your partner chooses to respond to problems. **Both you and your partner will be more successful in the relationship if you learn and grow from responding well to difficulties and issues.** No, this does not mean that you should find a difficult relationship to be in to aid your personal development! **Be assured that every relationship and marriage has plenty of challenges that arise naturally. You do not need to make life more difficult by being in a relationship filled with constant behavior and character problems.** If you are both struggling to maintain harmony, you will spend all of your energy trying to keep the relationship going, with little focus on anything else. This can cause you to neglect your family, friends, work, or community *service.*

You may find it challenging to find opportunities to observe how your partner handles problems, but this is a vital piece of your learning process. It can be particularly difficult if you simply go on social dates, or if you and your partner are in a long-distance relationship. Usually this type of observation only occurs when you spend a significant amount of time with your partner in real-life situations.

If your relationship is becoming serious, you will want to know how your partner responds when they are in a bad mood, short-tempered, tired, or frustrated. What character qualities do they draw on to stay calm and keep their responses appropriate? What qualities do they tend to misuse at this time? It is also good for you to know how you respond to their anger or upset feelings. How do the two of you resolve any hurt feelings or misunderstandings that happen between you? [See Chapter 3 for information about forgiveness and amends.]

However, a current lack of opportunity does not mean that you should devise difficulties intentionally to see how the other reacts!

If the opportunity to observe how your partner handles challenges does not arise naturally, then it will be best to try alternatives. You can ask key questions that *help* you to *discern* how your partner will act when they are tired or short of temper, after a long day, or their expectations are not met in the way they would like. Or, you can find challenging activities to participate in that will give you deeper experiences together. This might include such ideas as *helping* after a disaster in your area, traveling and working in another country, teaching children, and more. You can learn how you handle problems together, and you may discover that many problems are easier to handle with teamwork.

ACTIVITY

If you are in a relationship, choose three different challenging activities to expand your opportunities to observe your partner's words, actions, and character. This can include such options as working with or teaching children together, doing a *creative* project together, attending a large social occasion as partners, or asking your partner to assist you with managing a financial problem. If you are not in a relationship, then ask a friend to participate with you, so you can develop your observation skills.

```
┌─────────────────────────────────────────────────────────────┐
│                  ~ Questions for Reflection ~                 │
├─────────────────────────────────────────────────────────────┤
│                                                               │
│  1. What problems are difficult for me to respond to          │
│     effectively?                                              │
│  2. How could a partner assist me with handling these         │
│     problems differently?                                     │
│  3. What could strengthen my ability to be effective in       │
│     responding to challenging circumstances?                  │
│                                                               │
└─────────────────────────────────────────────────────────────┘
```

OBSERVING INTERACTIONS WITH FAMILY

Every family situation and dynamic is unique, so you will determine the best ways to accomplish effective observations. **Whenever possible, it is very important for you to observe how you and your partner interact with both sets of parents. This is also good for relationship building and family harmony.**

Family observation includes learning how your partner treats their parents, and how your partner's parents treat them. **It is particularly *wise* to observe your partner's interaction with their parent who is the same gender as you.** This will *help* you to learn how your partner will treat you throughout your relationship, and how your partner will expect you to treat them. Try to discover what type of dissension, conflicts, or disunity your partner has had with their parents in the past, how your partner acted at the time, and what they have learned from their mistakes.

You may be tempted to assume that because your partner *cares* so much for you, they will never treat you as poorly as you see them treat others. This is a risky assumption. Alternatively, if your partner treats their parents with *respect* and *courtesy*, it is likely this behavior will appear in your relationship.

Some specific aspects to consider in your family observations are:

- Do you see *love* and support among family members?
- Do they have a sense of humor about their differences?
- Do you see a struggle for control, or unhealthy competition?
- Do they fight and put each other down?
- Do you see them treating each other with *respect* and *equality*?

Depending on your own family experiences, you will likely add many more questions to this list. Keep in mind that if you are observing a family from another culture, or one that speaks a different language than you do, the process will be more complicated.

You may need some translation assistance. See Chapter 13 for some ideas for being in a multicultural situation.

Of course, you will also observe the interactions between your partner and your own family. If you *trust* your parents' ability to *discern* character in others, observing how they speak to and respond to your partner will be particularly important.

You can also learn from how both sets of parents act toward you and your partner as a couple, and what *wisdom* or guidance they offer. Your parents often know you and your partner better than anyone else does, so asking for their input and guidance may be valuable. Be sensitive to whether it is better to be more *detached*, because a parent is inappropriately controlling and attempting to interfere in your relationship instead. Your age and maturity will likely be factors in their level of involvement as well.

In some religions or cultures, parents may be very involved in the process of getting to know a partner and their character. All the parents and the couple meet and *respectfully* discuss the viability of the relationship from the beginning, as they assume that if the relationship is a good one, it will end in marriage. In the process, parents often provide guidance to the couple about how to maintain their relationship. If you are in this situation, you will benefit from listening to the *wisdom* of your families. **However, it is also important that you make a free choice of a partner and not let your parents or other relatives coerce the two of you to be together.** If either of you are unwilling, the relationship will be unhappy, or it will not last.

As you, your partner, and your families interact with each other, you will notice that you are also examining your own family experiences. You will think about the relationship your parents had with each other while you were growing up, and how that may have influenced you. It is also important to understand your relationship with each of them now. Your parent-child interactions have resulted in many of your beliefs, fears, and expectations about having a relationship with a partner. How are any unresolved issues with parents affecting you and your partner now? **The more resolution and *peacefulness* the two of you have with all the parents, the better it will be for you as a couple.** Otherwise, you and your partner may both tend to project unresolved resentments or unmet expectations with parents onto each other.

You can take many steps to address outstanding family issues. These steps include *spiritual* or therapeutic counseling, *forgiveness*, making amends, seminars, books, and more. Your partner may also *help* you to identify patterns between you and your parents that you were not previously aware of having, and you may do the same for them. If you are estranged from your parents, no healing can occur in the relationship if you are no longer in communication or contact. Perhaps making a plan that includes contacting them will be a good step to open the door of communication. If your goal is to begin to resolve the problems that led to your estrangement from your parents, tell them that you have a willing heart to do that very thing.

You may have missed an experience with your parents' relationship, or there was negative role modeling with them. **If you did not learn what was necessary from your parents, it is possible that together with your partner you can identify and learn the appropriate couple behavior.** For instance, you can learn to give positive acknowledgement to each other, even if the experience with a parent was full of criticism. Skill building is possible at any age or stage of life. [Remember to use the self-assessment and problem resolution sections from Chapters 2 and 3 as resources.]

Note: You may have stepparents, foster parents, or others who fulfilled parental roles for you. The information from this section also applies to those relationships.

~ Questions for Reflection ~

1. What roles do parents play in my assessment of a partner?
2. What dynamics are interesting or unique in my family?
3. What type of relationship do I want to have with a partner's family?
4. What interactions between family members in a partner's family would be concerns for me?

ACTIVITIES

1. Cook a meal and invite your partner and their parents to come. Do your best to be welcoming, *courteous*, and hospitable. After everyone leaves, assess what you observed about the interactions among the attendees.

2. Complete **Worksheet 10.1: Learning from Your Parents' Relationship** to assess what you have learned from observing your parents. You will then *discern* what aspects of their relationship you do or do not want to have in a relationship with a partner. When you have a partner, you can use this worksheet to observe your partner's parents as well.

OBSERVING INTERACTIONS WITH FRIENDS AND OTHERS

A primary resource for observing your partner with their friends will actually be Chapter 8. It gives you a good overview of the qualities to look for in friends. You can discern whether your partner chooses people with those qualities. As you observe how your partner interacts with their friends, consider:

- Do they stay in touch with friends, or regularly ignore them?
- How do they speak about friends when the friends are not present?
- Do they let their friends talk them into unwise activities?
- Do they let friends boss them around and make decisions for them?
- Do they have long-term, healthy friendships that they enjoy?

Being in various situations will allow you to observe the way your partner practices character qualities with many different types of people. Does your partner:

- Adapt to different social situations appropriately for the occasion and culture?
- Change temporarily and insincerely simply to please people?
- Begin conversations and/or participate in them easily, or is it difficult for them to be with or communicate with others?
- Interact well and show *courtesy*, *confidence*, and *respect* with:
  o Both genders, all ages, friends, professional associates, and new acquaintances?
  o People of a lower socio-economic level than they are?
  o People who are being of *service* to them? This can include such people as restaurant servers, hotel cleaning staff, bus drivers, store clerks, trash collectors, administrative clerks, or store employees.
  o People of a higher socio-economic level than they are?
  o People from different cultures or races?
  o People with different *spiritual* or religious beliefs?
  o People with physical, mental, or emotional disabilities or limitations?
  o Anyone smaller or weaker than they are, such as children or pets?

If your partner does not treat others well, there is a good chance that one day you will be on the receiving end of similar behavior. The same is *true* of *loving* behavior that demonstrates your partner's character *strengths*.

ACTIVITY

Arrange an activity with your partner and one of their friends. Carefully observe the interactions between them. If you do not have a partner, then do an activity with two of your friends and observe their interactions.

~ *Questions for Reflection* ~

1. How do I interact with my friends?
2. How do I interact with the various types of people that are listed in this section?

OBSERVING YOUR INTERACTIONS AS A COUPLE

As you interact with a new partner, you are naturally curious about each other's lives. You both ask questions and share increasingly detailed information as *trust* grows between you. **Observing how you and your partner communicate with each other is vital.**

© 1998 Randy Glasbergen. www.glasbergen.com

GLASBERGEN

"He's my new boyfriend. I know he's cold and unemotional, but on the other hand, he never criticizes me, he doesn't complain about my friends, and if things don't work out, he'll be gone in the Spring!"

Here are some thoughts about what you can observe and learn from your interactions together with your partner:

- What questions does your partner ask or not ask you?
- Do they keep turning the conversation back to their own life?
- Do they ask so few questions that you wonder if they have any interest in you?
- Do they ask so many questions that you feel pushed too fast in the relationship?
- Do they talk about themselves too much and overwhelm you?
- Do they say so little that you feel as if you are pulling every piece of information from them against their will?
- Are there important subjects they refuse to discuss?
- Are they positive and *respectful* or negative and hurtful?

- Do their eyes regularly wander to other people or parts of the room while you are talking with them?
- Do they ignore or discount what you say?
- Do they show genuine interest in your opinions and stories?

Note: The remaining chapters of Part 2 will guide you through learning a variety of communication skills. As you learn to use the skills with others, and particularly with a partner, you will have many opportunities to observe interactions.

When you are with a partner as a couple, you begin to develop a "couple personality." Who you are together as "we" or "us" is a different entity from who you are individually. The more time you spend with each other and develop shared practices and memories, the more you will have an identity as a couple. The question to ask yourself is, "Do I like the couple that we have become?" Some aspects for you to observe about yourselves as a couple are:

- Are you better together, or do you regularly bring out the worst in each other?
- Are you able to be *honest* and your *true* self around your partner, or do you pretend to be someone you are not or hide key aspects of yourself?
- Are you happy or unhappy when you are together?
- Do you feel positively energized, or very drained and discouraged after spending time together?
- Do you feel safe and comfortable with your partner in public, and when the two of you are together in private?
- How do others around you act? Do others like to be around the two of you?
- Are your friends and family positive and *encouraging* of your relationship, or are they expressing reservations and concerns? What are they saying?
- What concerns do you have about the relationship? Are the concerns valid?

Some character qualities and behaviors are most effective when you and your partner practice them together as a couple. *Cooperation* is one of these. Can the two of you work on something together, or do you both become frustrated and get in each other's way? Dancing is an example of a *cooperative* activity that can demonstrate underlying challenges in your relationship. Couples who struggle with being *cooperative* can experience a power struggle on the dance floor. Each partner thinks they know the steps and direction better than the other does, and perhaps tries to force the other. The couple argues about which way is correct or best. One tells the other they are not doing the dance correctly. They believe the dance itself or being right is more important than maintaining the relationship.

Pause and listen to your instincts and feelings about your relationship as you engage in activities together. If you are feeling unsafe, overly criticized, or very anxious, it is important to pay attention and not make excuses or justifications for your partner's poor behavior. Are there behavior patterns that the two of you can discuss and change? Do you need outside assistance? Or, is the behavior an entrenched pattern, and therefore, change is unlikely? Then you will need to consider ending the relationship.

On the other hand, if you are picking up consistently positive signals, and you are feeling *loving, confident,* and *unified* with your partner, then those feelings affirm your positive choice to be together.

It is also a great idea to get some outside observations and feedback from close and *trusted* family, friends, or advisors about their view of you as a couple. It will be difficult for you to be totally objective about how you and your partner are acting together.

ACTIVITIES

1. If you are in a relationship, ask a friend to make a movie, slide show, or photo album of you and your partner as a couple. This can be when you are with family members, doing community *service*, at a social occasion, or engaged in other activities.

   As you look at the pictures, what do you observe? Are either of you practicing identifiable character qualities? Are you happy with how the two of you are interacting together and with other people, both individually and as a couple? If you do not have a partner, then do the activity focused on the interactions between you and your friends. What do you observe?

2. If you are in a relationship, identify a skill that you have and your partner does not, and one that your partner has and you do not. Consider activities such as cooking, gardening, using a particular tool, or whatever fits for the two of you. Teach each other the skills, and then discuss the experiences. Alternatively, you can do this activity with a friend.

~ *Question for Reflection* ~

1. What activities are particularly important for a couple to do together to have observation opportunities?

OBSERVING LIFE MANAGEMENT SKILLS

Part of your observation and assessment process will be determining if your partner (and you) can function independently and *responsibly*, managing the details of everyday life maturely. When someone can take care of themselves, there is greater likelihood that the person can be a full partner in a relationship and spend appropriate time sustaining it. You may have a number of thoughts about what qualifies as a mature individual. Consider whether some of the possibilities below are important to you in a partner.

<u>**Physical and Life Maturity**</u>

- Eating balanced and nutritious meals
- Handling personal physical well-being, including exercise, cleanliness, and dental/medical care
- Obtaining and maintaining appropriate clothing
- Handling the cleaning and maintenance of a vehicle and home
- Going to work and/or school as appropriate, and completing the associated tasks
- Earning a living or be gaining the education needed to do so
- Keeping debt low and paying bills on time

<u>**Mental Maturity**</u>

- Reading books and participating in ongoing learning
- Staying informed about current events
- Engaging in problem-solving discussions when needed
- Having self-*respect* and *respect* for others, not trying to control or dominate them
- Expressing one's *true* self openly and *honestly,* and demonstrating a willingness to *accept* another person's *true* self as their *equal* partner

<u>**Emotional Maturity**</u>

- Recognizing feelings
- Not being overwhelmed by feelings
- Effectively expressing feelings
- Being happy, even when life has difficulties
- Handling challenges effectively and in *cooperation* with others
- Taking personal *responsibility* and not blaming others or making excuses when something does not go smoothly
- Relating well and solving problems *peacefully* with parents, family members, friends, neighbors, and co-workers
- Regarding a partner as a teammate and not as a parent-substitute

Spiritual Maturity

- Having faith in a greater *spiritual* Power
- Being willing to turn to *spiritual* sources for insight and *help*
- Praying regularly as well as during difficulties
- Meditating or reflecting
- Reading scripture or other books with *spiritual* content
- Participating in spiritually-centered activities
- Recognizing the need to make a contribution to others in the world and *joyfully* taking action

Achieving maturity is a lifetime process, so some aspects of maturity may not be present in a partner when you enter a relationship. The two of you can then discuss how you will approach any areas that either of you still need to develop. Do not assume someone is aware of the need to mature and is willing to do so without discussion with them. You may have differing perspectives on the matter. **However, be sure that any very important aspect is clearly present in a partner before you *commit* to being in a serious relationship.**

Consider Rachel's actions in the following story, and see if you think that she is mature enough to be in a serious relationship:

> Rachel enjoys working with children of all ages. She baby-sits regularly and teaches children's classes for her faith community. She tried college, but she thought it was too much work, and she dropped out. Many of her friends *encourage* her to become a teacher. However, she has some fears and doubts about going back to school, and she is working occasionally as a clerk in a store. She gets along well with her family, and she generally has an optimistic attitude about life. When

she is not working, she often ends up at local bars or clubs—wherever her friends want to go. Sometimes she drinks with them, even though she believes drinking is a bad idea, and she knows it is against the teachings of her faith.

As you look at this story, what expectations do you have about Rachel being in a relationship? What are her *strengths*? Does she simply lack *confidence*? Is she practicing *friendliness* appropriately? If you were Rachel, what actions would you change to reflect greater maturity?

How mature you are may be connected to how old you are, but not necessarily. Maturity does not always match the number of years someone has lived. Immature behaviors can be part of anyone's life at any point. It is wise, therefore, for maturity to be a key focus area for you when using your observation skills, rather than making assumptions based on someone's age.

~ *Questions for Reflection* ~

1. What do I consider mature behavior in myself? In others?
2. How do I handle my *responsibilities*? Which ones do I particularly struggle with fulfilling?
3. If I have a partner, how do they handle their *responsibilities*?

ACTIVITIES

1. Identify three areas where you want your behavior to be more mature, set development goals, and begin taking action. Reflect on your progress periodically, and make adjustments in your methods and actions as needed to ensure results.

2. Play an electronic or video game with a friend or partner, and pay attention to how they respond to the content and the competition. What kind of game do they choose? How violent or vulgar is it, and how do they respond to any violence or vulgarity that is in it? Do they become aggressive during the play, or treat it as light fun? How do they handle losing? How do they act when they win? What else do you observe that might indicate the person's level of maturity?

RESPONDING TO NEGATIVE OBSERVATIONS

Anything from a toothache to a problem at work can occasionally affect someone's mood, tone of voice, or behavior. When your partner is acting in a negative way, it is important to *discern* its source. You must also discover whether this is an isolated event, or whether it is repetitive behavior that will be a fundamental problem consistently over time. Can you avoid minimizing problems, but also be *merciful* and *accepting* of occasional incidents?

Understanding what is happening in your partner's life *helps* you to *moderate* any emotional reaction you have to a partner's misbehavior. This knowledge also assists the two of you to discuss how to handle what happened or to prevent it from happening again. Your observations aid you to *discern* whether your partner's actions were serious enough to address or better to *forgive* and let go.

Bringing up anything to do with someone's character requires *tact*, *sincerity*, and sensitivity. You are *responsible* for the words you speak. Especially with casual acquaintances, a new friend, or a new partner, it is best to keep your observations to yourself, and not raise concerns about their words and actions. If you do not yet have a foundation of *trust* and *unity* between you, the person may feel your comments are an invasion of their privacy.

As you get to know a partner better, you will be in a better position to raise an issue *tactfully* without offending them. You can discuss together how the behavior is affecting you and explore ways to address it. **One way to measure whether a relationship is ready to become more serious is if the two of you are willing to engage in the serious discussion of life issues that relate to character and behavior.** These can include struggles to be *patient* or *loving*, concerns about parenting, or differing priorities. If you and your partner are open and *honest* about concerns, and you welcome *gentle* input, influence, and guidance from each other, this is a positive relationship indicator. If every discussion the two of you have about serious topics results in an explosive problem or one of you attempting to dominate the other, then your relationship is in difficulty.

As you learn about your partner and communicate with them about your observations, avoid justifying intrusive questions or critical feedback comments. This includes saying to your partner that you are just trying to *help* them. Using observation solely to find data to use for criticizing your partner will be a misuse of *discernment* and destructive to your relationship.

Over time, relationships flourish when there is both willingness and openness to influence each other in positive ways. However, premature or critical comments will cause someone to feel as though they are under a microscope, and perhaps that you are manipulating or trying to force them to change. [You may find it *helpful* to re-read the sections in Chapter 7 about expecting a partner to change.]

If you are addressing serious issues involving character and behavior, and if those discussions are creating disunity, it will be *wise*

to stop. Either you or your partner may need to apologize or make amends. Do not restart the discussion about the topic until the two of you make a *strong* effort to understand what is happening, why it is happening, and what you can do to stop escalating the discussion into a conflict. Are you demanding or expecting change from your partner? Are you requesting your partner consider changing? Is your partner being overly sensitive about you raising any concern? Is the problem one you can work on together? Are you both willing and able to take the necessary time to work on it? Do you need assistance from someone else to see the situation clearly? Two willing hearts can calmly navigate together as friends and begin to understand what is happening.

When a conflict occurs, both of you are doing at least something that is causing it. However, it is important for you to focus on what you can change in yourself rather than pointing a blaming finger at your partner.

First, find out what you are doing and *accept responsibility* for your actions. Make a plan for yourself for how you will act differently next time, regardless of whether or not your partner will act differently. Then, once your partner is willing to continue the discussion, you can offer them calm reassurance that you have changed your attitude and are ready to proceed (with no expectation of a change in them). This demonstrates that you are *sincere* and *pure*-hearted. Finally, you can calmly listen to your partner to understand what is happening, and hear what they think they are *responsible* for in the situation.

If you are aware that your partner is actively engaged in improving a behavior or addressing a character issue, then your observation and responses will determine:

- How serious the issue is to your relationship
- Whether the person is *committed* to and serious about changing
- Whether there are signs of long-term success
- How much change will have to happen for you to be able to sustain a relationship together, and how quickly you want it to happen
- How many opportunities or chances you are willing to give the person to change
- What you are willing and able to do to assist your partner
- Whether this is an opportunity for you to be *flexible* and *accepting*
- What your boundaries, needs, and expectations are, and whether you have clearly communicated them
- Whether it will be *wise* to just wait and not push a resolution to the issue, giving your partner the time and space they need to work through it on their own

Responding to negative behavior is one of the most difficult areas of relationships, so you may struggle with what to do at times. The chapters that follow, all of which address aspects of communication, will assist you.

REFLECTING AND PROCESSING OBSERVATIONS

As you reflect on what you are observing in a partner and begin to understand the dynamics of your relationship, it may *help* you to answer the following questions:

- What do you like about your partner?
- What seems to be working well in their life?
- What does not seem to be going well in their life?
- What annoys you about them?
- What is positive in your interactions when you are together?
- Is your partner supportive as a friend, even when there are minor disagreements between you?
- How does your partner respond when faced with difficulties?

You may not see answers to these questions immediately, and they may change over time. The key is to stay aware.

If you are mindful and consciously observing your partner, you will begin to understand whether:

- They accomplish their *responsibilities* with *integrity* and fulfill their *commitments*
- Their behavior is *wise* and appropriate in most situations
- They are *sincere* and consistent in practicing their character qualities

Ensure you are thoroughly observing these areas about your partner:

- How they act in a group of people
- How they handle money and financial decisions
- How they raise issues for discussion
- How well their communications of all kinds meet your needs or expectations
- Their personal habits of cleanliness and eating
- Their ability to apply *equality*
- How they handle their personal belongings and maintain their home
- Their level of *patience* and *detachment* during stressful events
- Their level of *acceptance* and *forgiveness* toward others with whom they disagree or who have hurt them
- Their consistency of work history
- Whether they associate with different people or ones who are all similar

Be fair-minded with yourself and your partner. Seek to be comprehensive in understanding your relationship. Know your character and their character well enough to make intelligent choices about what to do with your observations and relationship choices. Observing constructive behavior in your partner supports you in going forward. It gives you a firm, legitimate foundation on which to build a *strong* friendship-based relationship.

As you dance together, you might discover that you and your partner are at different skill levels, however. You can see a partner's character (and your own) in how they handle this disparity. Sometimes the more skilled dance partner is impatient with the less skilled partner, and becomes visibly irritated. Alternatively, the skilled partner can be very *patient* and *encouraging* toward their less-skilled partner. If the less skilled of the two of you is mature, *confident*, and has a good sense of humor, then it will be possible to *accept* any shortcomings and handle them appropriately. Whichever of you is in this situation will keep trying to improve, but will not be overly stressed. A less mature, less *confident* partner might blame the other for their mistakes, and perhaps give up and refuse to continue. Of course, these dynamics can also occur in relationships.

As you process your observations, you will assess the viability of the relationship. Do you keep dancing? What dance will you do? You have a number of choices. For instance, you can:

- Participate in relationship education or coaching, professional counseling, or seek *spiritual* or religious guidance to gain assistance or build skills
- End the relationship and stop seeing each other or spending time together
- Spend more time with mutual friends instead of being alone together
- Shift to being casual friends
- Deepen your friendship
- *Commit* to deepening the relationship with each other, and begin to discuss the possibility of marriage

How much time will you need to spend in this process of observation? It varies. You will need enough time to know if the relationship should continue or must end. For some, the length of time will be short; for others, the length of time will be longer. Your mutual *honesty*, your availability to be together as a couple, and your choice of activities will all be factors.

By keeping "both eyes open"™ to observe your partner fully, you will gain the necessary information to make informed choices. You

264 • *Can We Dance? Learning the Steps for a Fulfilling Relationship*

can then choose to *accept* whatever imperfections you are seeing in your partner as a tolerable risk to your happiness, and embrace the person as they are. Alternatively, you can decide there is an unacceptable risk, and you will choose to end your association with your partner [Remember that Chapter 4 has insights about ending a relationship]. Once you have chosen to *accept* your partner's imperfections, you will not be surprised when they surface later on in the relationship. You can even decide in advance how you will deal with them through your own good character choices, perhaps with *gentleness*, *compassion*, or *forgiveness*.

ACTIVITY

Select someone to observe, such as a partner or another person you will see regularly for a few days. Then complete **Worksheet 10.2: Practicing Observation Skills**.

❧ *Encouragement* ☙

Effectively observing a partner is a vital but sometimes difficult new skill. You now have a far greater understanding of both its importance and how to use this new tool. Be *kind* to yourself as you practice it, because it will take time to be good at it. *Perseverance* will benefit you and a partner over time. You will grow to appreciate how *helpful* and enjoyable effective observation is for you, as it enhances your ability to know your partner well.

Date: _____

Worksheet 10.1 Learning from Your Parents' Relationship

This worksheet will assist you to observe your own parents and learn more about how they and their relationship affect your attitudes and actions within a relationship. If you are in a relationship, you can use this worksheet as a discussion guide to learn about your partner's parents as well.

Instructions:

A) Answer the questions that follow about your parents' relationship. If you did not see them, answer the questions according to the primary marriage or relationship that you grew up seeing. If you grew up with more than one parental-type relationship, then use a separate piece of paper or your journal to complete the worksheet content for each.

B) If you are not in a relationship, skip the questions that relate to that, and come back to them when you are in one.

1. What words to I use to describe my parents' relationship?

   a. _____   d. _____
   b. _____   e. _____
   c. _____   f. _____

   Other comment: _____

2. What have I observed in my parents' relationship that I want to see in mine?

   a. _____   d. _____
   b. _____   e. _____
   c. _____   f. _____

   Other comment: _____

3. What have I observed in my parents' relationship that I do *not* want to see in mine?

   a. _____   d. _____
   b. _____   e. _____
   c. _____   f. _____

   Other comment: _____

4. What positive aspects of my parents' behavior toward each other am I repeating with friends and a partner?

   a. _____   d. _____
   b. _____   e. _____
   c. _____   f. _____

   Other comment: _____

5. What negative aspects of my parents' behavior toward each other am I repeating with friends and a partner?

a. _____   d. _____

b. _____   e. _____

c. _____   f. _____

Other comment: _____

6. What have I observed about the interactions between my friends and partners and my parents?

_____

_____

_____

_____

7. What other observations about my parents do I have that would be useful for me to consider for a relationship?

_____

_____

_____

_____

_____

_____

_____

_____

_____

_____

_____

Date: _____

Worksheet 10.2: Practicing Observation Skills

This worksheet will assist you to improve your ability to observe others effectively. Choose your partner, if you have one, or someone else, to observe for a few days. It would be best to let the person know you are observing them and obtain their permission. When you have a partner, you may wish to repeat this activity.

Instructions:

A) Make specific notes of your observations in the table below. In the first column, note the person's words, gestures, attitudes, or actions.

B) In the second column, note any character qualities you saw the person practice at the same time.

C) In the third column, note your appreciation, concerns, or interpretations about what you observed. This can include noting whether the person's practice of a character quality was effective, weak, or misused.

Words, Gestures, Attitudes, or Actions	Character Qualities	Observation Notes

Words, Gestures, Attitudes, or Actions	Character Qualities	Observation Notes

Questions for Reflection:

1. What was the observation experience like for me?

_____

_____

_____

2. What did I learn about the other person?

_____

_____

_____

3. What did I learn about myself?

_____

_____

_____

4. In what ways did this experience strengthen my observation skills?

_____

_____

_____

Advanced Practice: Gaining Communication Skills

Dakota and Ivan meet in an evening woodworking course at a local community center. They go out for coffee after a few of the sessions and start to get to know each other. When the course ends, they work on a project making a table for Dakota's home. Throughout the project, they listen carefully to each other's ideas. Ivan occasionally becomes frustrated when the project runs into challenges, but he practices self-discipline and stays focused. Dakota encourages him to respect himself and take a break when he needs to. Ivan is enthusiastic about Dakota's creative ideas for adding an intricate design to the table legs. As they work cooperatively together, they also start to share personal thoughts and stories about their lives.

Once you have a dance partner, your goal is to learn to dance smoothly together. This requires establishing a firm foundation of friendship and *trust* through *truthful* and *honest* communication with each other. The better you are at communicating, the more you and your partner will learn about each other. Without this sharing and openness, it is difficult to dance in *unity*, and your movements can feel awkward and uncomfortable. If you were uncertain of the dance steps, would you rather dance with a complete stranger or a *trusted* friend?

Being in a relationship is not like freestyle dancing. In that type of dance, you do not connect or touch your partner, your styles of movement and interpretations of the music can be very different, and you act independently without adversely affecting each other. With formal dancing, instead, when you touch hands or your bodies are in a dance position, then controlling your balance, knowing the steps and patterns, and using leading and following skills become very important. Everything you say and do affects your partner in either a positive or a negative way. This is the same in relationships.

Communication is exciting, fun, exasperating, challenging, wonderful, scary, messy, risky, intimate, and much more. Whether verbal or non-verbal, it has physical, mental, emotional, and *spiritual* components. The goal in your communications is to develop a friend and partner who knows you almost as well as you know yourself—your character, your fears, your goals, your beliefs, and even your incredibly stupid mistakes. As you and your partner begin to know each other well, you can then *encourage* each other to be your best selves. Neither of you will stay the same as you are today.

The quality of your mutual communications will *help* your friendship and relationship to last over time. This chapter focuses your attention on learning communication skills that will assist you throughout your relationship. The remaining chapters will then include how to share experiences, explore sensitive matters, understand and prevent communication challenges, and build *love* and *unity* through your communications.

ACTIVE AND CONSCIOUS LISTENING

Effective communication occurs when two people exchange messages, and they both listen and understand the intended meaning of the message. **Communication works best in a relationship when you express yourself from your higher nature using the character qualities** (Chapter 1). This chapter will give you tools to assist you in doing this. Chapter 14 will assist you when you seem to keep stepping on each other's toes and speaking from your lower nature instead.

A key aspect of effective mutual communication is listening to each other. Have you ever noticed that if you rearrange the letters of LISTEN they form the word SILENT? **Silence makes it possible to listen fully to your partner with your ears, mind, eyes, and heart, which can include seeing a subject from your partner's perspective.** "…Everyone should be quick to listen, slow to speak and slow to become angry…."[1] Listening fully to your partner can *help* them to feel *respected, loved,* validated, and appreciated. Their *confidence* can increase, and they will feel more *loving* toward you. When you give this gift to your partner, it *encourages* them to listen well to you in return. Poet and author Oliver Wendell Holmes once wrote, "It is the province of knowledge to speak and it is the privilege of wisdom to listen."[2]

Listening to and understanding each other contribute to effective problem-solving discussions. When you are successful at resolving issues, you reduce or prevent dissension or disunity between you. **Conscious listening enhances *trust, love,* and *unity* between you and your partner.** According to Kathlyn Hendricks, Ph.D., and Gay Hendricks, Ph.D, conscious listening includes three levels of skill and depth:

Level One: Listen for the words—Give a simple, concise, and accurate summary of what you have heard the speaker say.

Level Two: Listen for the emotions—Hear from your heart the emotions under the words of the speaker.

Level Three: Listen for the wants and needs—Hear beneath the words and the emotions for what the speaker is really asking for and needing.[3]

Your openness and empathy can *help* you to *encourage* your partner to express what they want or need to share, and sense the emotions behind your partner's words. Sometimes when you are open and *loving* with your partner, you can sense what is going on in them even before they fully realize what their thoughts and emotions are. Gently sharing what you are sensing and hearing from them can then assist your partner in clarifying what they are feeling. [*Note: Excellent* information on this process is available in "Habit 5: Seek First to Understand…Then to Be Understood" in Stephen Covey's *7 Habits* publications.]

It can be easy to spend your time planning your response to your partner, which interferes with your ability to listen completely. When you plan, it is usually with the intent to:

- Judge or evaluate
- Criticize
- Influence or control
- Compare
- Fix[4]

In addition, you may focus on defending yourself or your opinion.

At the beginning of a conversation, your partner can let you know their expectations, or you can ask them what works for them. Should you simply listen to them and understand what they are saying? Is your input welcome? Do they want suggested solutions? Perhaps they are simply hoping for some validation of their point of view, sympathy, or a hug. Maybe they want an opportunity to offer an apology or straighten out a misunderstanding. **This practice can seem a bit awkward or strange initially, but you will find it tends to reduce misunderstandings and problems between you and your partner.** Having some understanding about where the conversation is going, and your role in it, can *help* you to listen well, and both of you will be less anxious.

When you listen, postpone your natural desire to be a problem-solver, unless your partner requests it or that is the goal of the discussion. Sometimes your partner will just need to understand their own thoughts and emotions by sharing them openly and freely. They may not be looking for a solution at all, but they simply want to have you with them as an empathetic companion.

Listening in the way that your partner needs shows them that you truly *care* about their feelings and their point of view. If you are distracted and not completely listening, your partner is likely to feel ignored or belittled.

When you are doing all three levels of listening, give feedback to your partner to verify that you are clearly receiving and understanding their communication. This can include nodding your head, making a sympathetic sound or gesture, or asking a clarifying question. It is important to stay focused and not do other tasks, such as answer the telephone, while your partner is talking. **As you are learning to listen, there may be times when your mind wanders. In this case, simply acknowledge that you are not sure you heard everything, and ask your partner to repeat what they said.**

Particularly if the topic is upsetting or very serious, it can *help* your partner when they know you understand the specific details they are sharing. You can do this by summarizing what they have said. You can phrase this, "Let me make sure that I understand what you are saying. I understood you to say…." or "So, you are saying…." If you have missed a key point, your partner can then add to or clarify the communication. Summarizing works best if you do it after every after each key point your partner makes; otherwise, it will be difficult for you to remember all the key points. Your partner can then do the same for you when it is your turn to speak. Summarizing is not simply repeating the exact words, which is disrespectful. It provides the additional purpose of slowing down your interaction when emotions are intense. Consider how this communication tool works for this couple:

Aliz and Ervin have been in a relationship for about 4 months. Together, they enjoy *helping* as volunteers at their library, watching old movies, and playing computer games.

One afternoon as they rollerblade through their neighborhood park, Ervin stops to chat with three long-time friends. Aliz waits *patiently* for him to introduce her to his friends, but it does not happen. Soon, the friends depart, and Aliz is upset. She becomes quiet and withdrawn from Ervin.

"Aliz, is something bothering you?" Ervin asks after a few minutes of silence.

"Yes, there is something I want to talk to you about. When you stopped to talk with your friends earlier, it upset me that you chatted with them for several minutes, but you did not introduce me to them," she says. "I felt really left out of the conversation."

"You think I did not treat you with *respect* by introducing you, and that left you feeling upset," summarizes Ervin.

"Yes, that's exactly how I felt! Can we please agree that you will include me the next time?"

"I'm sorry, Aliz. I was not paying attention. It won't happen again."

Ervin was able to summarize Aliz's concerns successfully because he was listening *carefully*. He did not become defensive, which would have shifted the focus to him. **When your partner is speaking, remember to stay focused on their words and not twist the conversation around to make it about you.** Even if what they are saying is about you, it does not mean you have to immediately jump in and defend yourself. Give your partner time to communicate fully what they want to share from their point of view, so you are sure you understand it. If you speak prematurely, it can interfere with your partner fully expressing what is on their mind. Your goal is to understand their point of view, not correct it, or manipulate it to agree with your own. When your partner is finished speaking, you can then request that your partner listen to your thoughts and feelings, or ask if they want input or feedback on the topic. Together, you can then work through the issue and resolve it.

Your attitude of *respect*, commitment to being *equal* partners, and your practice of character qualities such as *patience* will enhance how well you listen. If you are feeling *loving, caring, friendly*, and *compassionate* toward your partner (higher nature), you will listen differently than if you are feeling angry or resentful (lower nature). You are allies, not adversaries. It is important to remember that you are *responsible* for your mental attitude as you listen. If you are not ready to be a good listener, due to hunger, fatigue, distraction, a bad mood, or stress, say so. Suggest a delay in the communication until you are ready to handle it better. Agree on when and where the discussion will happen instead, so you will not be tempted to avoid it altogether. This will *help* you to maintain *unity* between you. At times, however, a problem may be so urgent that your partner cannot wait. In that case, proceed and try your best.

As your relationship grows, you and your partner will develop the practice of turning to each other to share, listen, and problem-solve. It may take *self-discipline* to do this, rather than slipping into the unwise habit of just turning to friends and family when you need to talk about important subjects and resolve relationship difficulties. It is very important to learn the skill of resolving problems together if you want your relationship to have a viable future. Of course, this does not mean that you should not also turn to friends and family under appropriate circumstances.

ACTIVITY

Ask a friend or partner to practice the three levels of conscious listening with you. Whoever initially speaks can choose whatever topic is important to them. Switch roles so that you each practice speaking and listening. You can then both discuss the "Questions for Reflection" that are in the box below.

~ Questions for Reflection ~

1. How do I feel when someone listens well to me?
2. Which of my actions, gestures, or responses lets others know that I am listening to them? Which new ones will I now try?
3. Can I focus and understand most or all of what others say to me? What *helps* me to focus?
4. Can I accurately sense the emotions of someone behind their words? If not, am I able to ask the person or my partner to verbalize how they are feeling?
5. Can I hear the wants and needs of a speaker beyond just what they are saying?

THE MEANING OF WORDS

One of the many adventures with communication is that new words are created all the time, and words can often have multiple meanings. People from various countries and cultures can also use words to mean different concepts than you might understand them to mean. Therefore, as you speak to and listen to a partner (and their family members), there is the additional *responsibility* of ensuring you are both interpreting words in the same way.

Words also communicate your attitudes, thoughts, views, and beliefs. If you say to your partner that their clothes are "filthy," your words can be interpreted two very different ways:

- "You work hard, and I appreciate that about you."
- "You are very messy, and you do not care about yourself or how you look."

If your partner says to you that you are "thrifty," they can mean:

- "You know how to manage money well."
- "You never share your money with others."

If you are uncertain about the meaning of a word your partner says, or the intent of it, speak up and ask. Do not jump to conclusions about what they are saying, but wait until you have all the facts necessary to form an appropriate opinion or response. Your *patience* in this process will prevent confusion or disunity between you.

At times, you will find it difficult or painful to hear what your partner says. They may give you feedback about something you have done that they do not like. Their words may be sharp or hurtful, either carelessly or deliberately. Sometimes when people are upset, they also say words that they really do not mean. Of course, your partner will need to be *responsible* for their words and any negative consequences. However, you are *responsible* for your response to what your partner says.

You may need to wait a few minutes before responding, to avoid reacting harshly, which will escalate the hurt feelings or disunity between the two of you. You may also need to ask clarifying questions and practice your character qualities. Maintaining *patience* and staying calm, as well as practicing *tactfulness*, *courtesy*, and *forgiveness*, will all make it possible for you to respond in a way that keeps your relationship and *unity* intact.

ACTIVITY

Complete **Worksheet 11.1: Understanding Your Communication Patterns** to improve your understanding of how you communicate and your communication needs when you have a partner. If you are in a relationship, you may wish to invite your partner to complete the worksheet as well. In this case, then use your journal or a separate book or piece of paper, so your partner can also answer the questions without seeing your responses until you are both ready to share and discuss them.

THE WAY YOU SPEAK TO YOUR PARTNER

When you speak to your partner, they will hear more than just your words. Your tone of voice also reflects your thoughts and feelings and powerfully indicates what is happening behind your words. You will notice that others believe what you say with your tone of voice more than with your actual words, and they can react to it.

As you speak, you also place emphasis on various syllables or words. Your tone and emphasis convey your emotions and signal to your partner the significance you place on what you are saying.

Before you say something, it is a good idea to pause and attempt to *discern* what feelings may influence your tone of voice or how you are speaking. If you are angry, but you attempt to be "nice," the other person will get the mixed message and be confused. If you ask "why?" in a judgmental tone, your partner may hear that you are blaming them and become defensive. If you say aloud what you are feeling and what is on your mind, you can hear how it sounds before you say it to your partner. You can also record your voice and replay it, or say the words to someone who is not involved in the issue for their feedback. If you involve another person who is not a professional counselor, ensure that you keep your comments vague, so that you are not sharing personal information that can hurt your partner.

As you listen to your tone of voice, you can begin to conclude that you have an inner problem to resolve, or some calming action to take before having the conversation with your partner. It is often *wise* for you to diffuse the potency of very intense feelings before you speak up. Otherwise, there is a chance that you can damage your relationship by communicating them. However, it is a good idea to identify any feelings you want to communicate clearly and directly along with your message. You then avoid sending mixed messages in which your words and tone do not agree.

Unless an issue is minor and you can simply *detach* from it, it is best to raise it directly in a *purposeful* attempt to resolve it, rather than keeping it suppressed. Avoiding direct communication can cause your feelings or concerns to come out through your attitude and tone of voice instead, and you can confuse and hurt your partner.

Once you have communicated what you think the problem is and the related feelings, then you can ask your partner to summarize what you said. Summarizing makes it clear that they understood your feelings and not just your words. You and your partner can then effectively address and resolve the problem.

Your tone of voice and the emphasis you place on words can also indicate information about your character. If you are demonstrating *patience*, your tone might be calmer than if you are practicing *assertiveness*. If you are practicing *friendliness*, your tone will be warm and welcoming. The emphasis you put on certain words and the volume of your voice also communicate how much importance you place on what you are communicating. Perhaps your forceful expression says that you care about *justice* in a situation. As you listen to your partner's tone and emphasis, then, you learn about their character as well.

ACTIVITY

If you are in a relationship, do the following activity with your partner. Otherwise, choose a close friend or relative. If no one is available, you may be able to learn from doing this practice by recording your voice and listening to the recording, or by saying each phrase aloud to yourself in front of a mirror and imagining your image is the person you are speaking to. Say a few of the phrases below in a variety of different tones of voice and with varied ways of speaking and expressions on your face. Say each one twice, once with a positive emphasis, and once with a negative emphasis. Watch the listener's reactions to these different expressions. Take turns so that each of you has the opportunity to both speak and listen.

- Excuse me
- Fine
- How are you
- Thanks
- Will you call me
- Whatever you want
- Sit down
- I don't want to talk now
- Sorry
- Can you help me

- Come with me
- Stop it
- Don't touch me
- What do you want
- Why did you do that
- All right, I'll do it
- Hello
- Leave it alone
- No problem
- Good morning

Reflect or Discuss: Which expressions did you like? Which ones will you prefer *not* to have in your communications, whether you are on the delivering or receiving end? Were any phrases difficult to say in a positive tone? Were there any phrases that you wanted to add "please" to automatically to make them sound more positive? Did any accent in your speech affect how your listener interpreted whether the statement was positive or negative? How did you feel when you spoke in different tones of voice or varied how you expressed yourself? What did you learn about your own style of communicating and the communication between the two of you?

~ *Questions for Reflection* ~

1. Do I ever use a tone of voice that bothers others?
2. What can I do to remind myself to avoid using it?
3. What tones from others do I especially appreciate receiving? Dislike receiving?
4. Do others tend to misinterpret what I say because of my tone or how I say it? How can I handle this?

CULTURAL AND LANGUAGE INFLUENCES

As you may have experienced in the previous activity, a partner's accent from the original language they learned can be one of the factors that affects the tone of a person's voice or how they say their words. People of the same culture often have a similar rhythm to their speech, place stress on the same syllables, and use similar voice inflections to convey "meaning" to others. **If you are not familiar with how your partner's culture influences their way of speaking, you may misunderstand what they are saying. If you and your partner are misunderstanding each other, then using tools such as summarizing can ensure you are communicating clearly.**

Such factors as your culture, your education level, and the communication habits of your family and friends, also affect your communications with your partner. You may have also learned to speak differently because of your gender. Sometimes men are taught to be more forceful, and women are taught to speak softly. You and your partner may be dancing very different dances. Some examples include whether either of you:

- Are direct or indirect in your approach
- Talk loudly or softly
- Share your life openly with others, or regard everything as personal and private
- Include *spiritual* quotations or words of *spiritual* praise throughout your everyday conversations
- Apologize constantly
- Use phrases or words that are only understandable to people who share your ethnicity
- Say "no" to whatever is offered to you, so as not to impose, even if you want to say "yes"
- Speak with a possessive tone of voice
- Use thoughtful silence
- Limit verbal conversation
- Use gestures or reach out to touch a hand or shoulder to emphasize words

Remember in Chapter 6, where you learned about how your culture can change the expectations you have for how you behave with a partner, depending on the stage of your relationship? It can also affect how, where, when, and why you communicate with your partner. For instance, in some cultures, your partner can *accept* you having friends of both genders when the two of you are in the early stages of friendship. Once you are in a serious relationship, however, your partner may have more difficulty in sharing your time with others, and express this concern through their words and actions.

You will learn more about exploring differences between you and your partner in Chapter 13.

ACTIVITY

Ask a friend who is of another culture to listen to you speak. Then have them explain what they hear you saying, how your tone of voice sounds to them, and anything that they do not understand. This will *help* you to see how your culture, ethnicity, gender, or the language(s) you speak affect how you communicate with others, and you will learn how others see you. This activity will be especially *helpful* if you are of the majority culture in the country you live in.

~ *Questions for Reflection* ~

1. When have I been aware that my culture has influenced my words, and someone has misunderstood me?
2. How does my culture affect my gestures?
3. How does culture affect the other ways that I communicate?

POSITIVE WORDS AND PRACTICES

Obviously, what comes out of your mouth can have a powerful effect on your partner and on your relationship. If you spend your time being constantly critical of your partner, it will erode the bond between you and shut down communications. If you use positive comments and *encouragement* instead, your relationship is more likely to be healthy and thriving.

The more you learn to speak to your partner with phrases that assist them to be their best, and the more your partner learns to do the same with you, the *stronger* your relationship will be. Then, the more positive and effective the words and actions you each demonstrate, the more you both influence each other in positive directions by example.

Acknowledge and Encourage

If you use acknowledging and *encouraging* words that speak specifically about your partner's *strengths* or efforts, it will *help* to *create* a solid foundation of *friendship, love,* and *confidence* in each other and in your relationship. *Sincere* and positive comments are rooted in the practicing of *acceptance* and *generosity*. These type of comments are like a gift to your partner to validate the things they say or do. Your *encouragement helps* your partner to make good choices. It often inspires them to be involved in activities and achieve greater accomplishments in life. They will feel more willing to adjust an attitude, practice a new behavior, or apply a character quality more effectively.

At times when a relationship is struggling, it can be difficult to find positive comments to make. Then it takes effort to look for even the smallest acknowledgment you can make of your partner's efforts.

"You don't appreciate the nice things I do. Yesterday I burped 'I love you' in Morse Code and you didn't even thank me!"

Dr. Gary Chapman talks about the importance of *encouragement* and the power it has to release potential in another:

> Giving verbal compliments ["You look great today!"] is only one way to express words of affirmation…. Another…is encouraging words ["I have confidence you will do very well and achieve your goal. Keep going *strong*!"]. The word *encourage* means "to inspire courage." All of us have areas in which we feel insecure. We lack courage, and that lack of courage often hinders us from accomplishing the positive things that we would like to do. … Encouragement requires empathy and seeing the world from [the other's] perspective. … With verbal encouragement, we are trying to communicate, "I know. I care. I am with you. How can I help?"[5]

Note how Hailey *encourages* Aaron in this scenario:

> Aaron is having difficulty deciding whether to go back to school or continue working full-time. He wants to work part time while pursuing a new career in engineering. However, he also values the stability of continuing to work in the

technical support department at the company where he has been for a few years. Over dinner one evening, he shares his dilemma with Hailey, his close friend and partner:

"You're getting good evaluations at work, which is important," says Hailey.

"But I'm not feeling fulfilled there," Aaron responds. "I'm just wondering whether I can actually be successful as an engineer."

"I know changing careers will take *courage*, which is one of your *strengths*," says Hailey. "I have *confidence* in you that you can be successful and *persevere* through the financial challenges of working only part time. What can I do to *help* you?"

Hailey uses three *encouragement* tools in her response to Aaron:

1. She acknowledges one of his character *strengths* (*courage*) that will *help* him to be successful, and she states another quality (*perseverance*) that will assist him.
2. She expresses *confidence* in his success.
3. She offers to *help* him.

Encouragement is not just verbal. It can take the form of supportive actions, such as *helping* with a task or sharing an inspirational quotation.

Remember that your praise of your partner or your *encouragement* to them will lose their effectiveness if you use it as a comparison that says, "You are better than someone else." Comparing requires that you both hold a negative view of the other person. Your tone of voice and phrasing are also important, so that there is no implied criticism underneath the praise, perhaps relating to how your partner previously performed an action. You can hear it happening in this example: "It was thoughtful of you to FINALLY pick me up on time!". To be most effective, praise and *encouragement* are unconditional and freely given. "…[P]eople form much more positive emotional connections when they encourage one another's dreams and aspirations." [6]

Complaints Instead of Criticisms

The overall goal for you throughout your relationship is to keep the level of positive comments high, which contributes to the *strength* of your friendship. Also, it is very important to keep the amount of negative comments low. If you do decide it is necessary to voice a complaint, however, the following method can prevent hurt feelings:

- Ensure that you include an acknowledgement of your partner's character *strengths*
- Direct the complaint toward your partner's actions (or non-actions) and what you perceive happened or did not happen, not as a personal attack at your partner

- Communicate *respectfully* about what did not work well in the situation from your perspective
- Concisely state your view and then *detach* and step back; do not repeatedly hammer your partner with your concern
- Give your partner time to think about what you said and consider a response
- Be ready to offer suggestions to improve the situation when your partner is ready to hear them
- Resolve the issue, or the way to approach it, through discussion

Personal criticism, rather than voicing a legitimate complaint as outlined above, is often highly destructive. It can quickly become an attack on a person's character qualities. It would be difficult, if not impossible, to come up with enough positive words to eliminate the negative effect of your telling a partner that they are lazy and irresponsible (*responsibility*) or an untrustworthy jerk (*trustworthiness*). In Liberia, they say, "Kind words do not wear out the tongue."[7] [You will learn more about character attacks in Chapter 14.]

~ Questions for Reflection ~

1. When was a time that I *sincerely encouraged* someone? How did it feel? Was it easy or difficult?
2. When did someone *encourage* me? How did it feel? How did I respond?
3. When did I criticize someone? Did it include a character attack? What was the outcome?
4. When has someone criticized me? How did it feel? Did it include a character attack? What was the outcome?
5. Are positive or are negative comments the regular pattern in my interactions with others? How do they respond? Are there any changes I want to make in this pattern?

ACTIVITIES

1. Practice *encouragement* with a friend or partner by inviting them to take dance lessons or some other class with you that they have wanted to do, but have been afraid to try. Use the activity as an opportunity to also observe and acknowledge their character qualities.
2. *Create* a greeting or note card, poster, screensaver, poem, song, or some other artistic expression for a friend, relative, or partner who needs *encouragement*.

Character Quality Language

As touched on in the previous section on *encouragement*, a vital communication skill for you to practice is recognizing your partner's effective use of character qualities. One way to incorporate this practice into your communications is by learning a skill called Character Quality Language.[8] Using this language is a key way to act *loving* toward your partner and communicate your *love* and appreciation for them. You can also use this skill to *help* you retrain your thinking if you tend to use your inner voice to deliver negative or harsh comments to yourself (Chapter 2).

Below are two examples of statements that you can say to a partner. The first is a positive statement that is similar to what you may already be comfortable making. The one that follows uses Character Quality Language instead.

Good Statement:
I am happy that you want to try some new activities with me!

Better Statement Using Character Quality Language:
I really appreciate how *enthusiastic* and *courageous* you are being about going water skiing with me this weekend. I know you have not had much experience with being out on the lake in a boat, and I am happy that you are going with me.

The first statement is positive, and your partner will likely feel appreciated. However, the second is more specific and acknowledges the character qualities your partner is using at that moment.

Here is another pair of statements as a further example:

Good Statement:
Thanks for looking after my daughter when she fell.

Better Statement Using Character Quality Language:
I appreciate how *caring* and *helpful* you were to Becky when she fell off her bicycle. She was so upset, and your attention and concern *helped* her to calm down.

You may experience that it is often easier to be critical than to recognize and appreciate when someone does something well. It takes practice to look consciously for someone's positive actions and speak specifically about them, but it is worth the effort. It is very affirming for everyone involved when you do. This skill is also useful for other relationships, especially in parenting, as this language is very effective with building character in children.

Using Character Quality Language may feel unnatural at first, because it is not how you are used to speaking or hearing others talk. You often speak and hear more negative words than positive ones. However, if you are *sincere* in using this language, you will find that it becomes comfortable and easy and can transform your relationships. Acknowledging your partner's positive attributes *encourages* them to practice the qualities effectively.

It is difficult to discuss and understand thoughts and experiences for which you and your partner have no common vocabulary. Character Quality Language gives you just that, because both of you can learn how to look for and acknowledge the qualities in each other. Remember that philosophers, religious leaders, relationship experts, and more, all *encourage* the practice of these qualities. [See Part 3 for details about the qualities you can *creatively* use in acknowledging your partner or others.]

Sincere Character Quality Language builds your partner's *confidence* and self-*respect*, as well as your own. It also creates a foundation of positive interactions between the two of you. These positive interactions then assist you both to act in ways that include the character qualities. This *helps* you and your partner to become powerful examples for each other and everyone around you.

ACTIVITIES

1. Begin with reviewing the four qualities that you chose in Worksheet 3.1 to develop and *strengthen*. Watch for when a partner, friends, or family members practice them. Use Character Quality Language to acknowledge when these people practice these qualities, and assess how they respond. Start with acknowledging even the smallest display of a quality. Your positive words will likely bring the qualities out even more.

   Continue to use Character Quality Language in your everyday life with other people and qualities, and assess how they respond. At the same time, begin using Character Quality Language in your inner dialogue with yourself when you notice that you are practicing a quality well in your own life.

2. Send a greeting card or *create* a visual or artistic acknowledgement of someone's *excellent* practice of a character quality that you appreciate.

3. When you have a partner, complete **Worksheet 11.2: Character Strengths in Your Relationship Partner**, to assess your partner's quality *strengths*. Make sure you compare your answers with Worksheet 7.1 to assess whether your partner has the quality *strengths* that you consider most important. Once you have identified your partner's *strengths*, then use Character Quality Language to acknowledge them. If you do not yet have a partner, then you can practice with a close friend or relative.

~ *Questions for Reflection* ~

1. How do I respond when someone acknowledges one of my character qualities?
2. Do I ever discount or reject this kind of positive comment? Why or why not? Do I accept it graciously, instead? Why or why not?
3. How do people respond when I acknowledge their character qualities?
4. What effect might it have on a relationship if my partner and I use Character Quality Language consistently with each other? With any children that we each have?

✍ *Encouragement* ❧

Communication is a foundational skill in relationships, so it is *excellent* that you are strengthening your skills. With each successful effort, you are seeing your interactions with others become smoother. This is a great time to practice Character Quality Language on yourself and acknowledge your progress.

Date: _____

Worksheet 11.1: Understanding Your Communication Patterns

This worksheet will assist you to assess your communications with others. If you have a partner, then you may wish to each complete this worksheet separately and then discuss your answers.

Instructions:

A) Complete the sentences that follow. If you have difficulty with any question, then observe your interactions for a few days and come back to it.

B) You will be most effective at completing this worksheet if you review the explanations of "encouragement," "equality," and "respect" in Part 3 first.

1. When someone listens to me respectfully, I feel _____ and I am likely to respond in this way:

   _____

   _____

2. When I do not think that someone is listening to me respectfully, or they interrupt me, I feel _____ and I am likely to respond in this way:

   _____

   _____

3. When I slip into thinking that I am right and someone else is wrong, these thoughts and actions help me to shift into openly listening to them and respecting their point of view: _____

   _____

   _____

4. When someone says these phrases to me, I feel discouraged:

   a. _____

   b. _____

   When someone discourages me, I feel _____

   and I am likely to respond this way: _____

5. When someone says these phrases to me, I feel encouraged:

   a. _____

   b. _____

   When someone encourages me, I feel _____

   and I am likely to respond this way: _____

6. When I am tempted to speak to someone in anger, or in some way that causes disunity, I take these actions to calm myself down and ensure that my communication is honest, respectful, and maintains unity:

   _____

   _____

7. When someone speaks to me in anger or yells at me, I feel _____

   and I am likely to respond this way: _____

   _____

   _____

8. When someone criticizes me, I feel _____

   and I am likely to respond this way: _____

   _____

   _____

   Criticism toward me is especially hurtful when it is about these topic areas:

   _____

   _____

9. When someone speaks to me with respect and equality, I feel _____

   and I am likely to respond this way: _____

   _____

10. I like to prepare for a serious discussion by carrying out these actions:

    _____

    _____

    When there is a need for a serious discussion with someone, such as a partner, and there are decisions to make, I prefer to be in the following places:

    _____

    _____

    It does not work for me to try to have a serious discussion if I am in the middle of these activities:

    _____

    _____

11. I communicate more effectively when these circumstances exist: [examples: I am not hungry, I am rested, I am not feeling pressured...]

    _____

    _____

Date: _____

Worksheet 11.2: Character Strengths
in Your Relationship Partner

This worksheet will assist you to identify your partner's character qualities. It will also help you in learning how to use Character Quality Language. If you do not yet have a partner, then you can use this to practice on a close friend or relative, and return to it when you do have a partner.

Instructions:

A) Review the list of character qualities below, and circle the qualities that demonstrate your partner's strengths.

B) Choose 3 of the qualities and write down the words below that you can say to acknowledge your partner for these qualities. Consider using Character Quality Language. Follow through and communicate these to your partner.

C) Compare your answers with Worksheet 7.1 to assess whether your partner has the qualities that you consider to be the most important ones for you.

Acceptance	Discernment	Idealism	Respect
Assertiveness	Encouragement	Integrity	Responsibility
Beauty	Enthusiasm	Joyfulness	Self-Discipline
Caring	Equality	Justice	Service
Chastity	Excellence	Kindness	Sincerity
Commitment	Faithfulness	Love	Spirituality
Compassion	Flexibility	Loyalty	Strength
Confidence	Forgiveness	Mercy	Tactfulness
Contentment	Friendliness	Moderation	Thankfulness
Cooperation	Generosity	Patience	Thoughtfulness
Courage	Gentleness	Peacefulness	Trustworthiness
Courtesy	Helpfulness	Perseverance	Truthfulness
Creativity	Honesty	Purity	Unity
Detachment	Humility	Purposefulness	Wisdom

Quality 1: _____ Acknowledgement: _____

_____

Quality 2: _____ Acknowledgement: _____

_____

Quality 3: _____ Acknowledgement: _____

_____

Intricate Steps:
Sharing and Resolving Sensitive Matters

Leesa and Rafe are new residents in a neighborhood where there are regular social events at a central building. They meet one evening at a potluck dinner, where they discover they have brought similar vegetarian food to share. While they do mingle with others, they keep coming back to each other. He enthusiastically tells her about his latest project as an architect, and she talks about her challenges in the courtroom as a lawyer. They discover a mutual appreciation for jazz music and going to air shows to see unique planes. They see each other regularly for a few weeks and enjoy being together very much. They begin to share about their lives at a deeper level. Leesa talks about the struggle she had with confidence after being engaged to a man who verbally abused her, and Rafe talks about the effects on him from his parents' divorce when he was 13. They now try to understand how these experiences and other issues have affected them individually, and how what has happened in their lives may affect them as a couple.

In Chapter 11 you learned essential communication skills. These will *help* you as you now go deeper into learning about the person you are dancing with and spend more time dancing together. The more you dance with one person exclusively, the more you will get to know each other's dance steps and subtle movements. In the same way, you and your partner will deepen your relationship by sharing previous experiences, working through relationship difficulties and other challenges, and exploring and agreeing on how to approach sensitive matters. Through all of this, your friendship will *strengthen* and your emotional intimacy will increase.

Sharing sensitive information about yourself and your past requires a high degree of *trust* and *honesty* between you and your partner. It takes time and experience with each other for there to be enough safety and security in your relationship for sharing to occur smoothly. This is especially *true* if what you have to share is very personal or quite negative. However, if your previous experiences are still affecting your thoughts, attitudes, words, or actions, and they will influence the interactions you have with your partner, it is vital that you find a way to share them. Your sharing will be very general at times to effectively gauge how ready your partner is to respond to certain topics, and to do your best to avoid backbiting and gossip about others.

Imagine for a moment that your previous dance partner caused some troubles for you. Now you have a new dance partner, and you fear that some of the previous problems will affect how you relate to and dance with your partner in the present. Perhaps you danced with a rough partner who stepped on your toes, led you into collisions, squeezed your fingers, or twisted your wrist. Maybe you were with someone who did not know how to dance at all, was unwilling to learn, and yet made it all seem like it was your fault.

You will not want your past to hinder your ability to be in a great relationship in the present. You will not want events from your past that your partner knows nothing about silently influencing your current actions and reactions. Your partner cannot attempt to meet your needs when they do not know about nor understand them.

When you share your experiences and needs, your current partner will then have the opportunity to practice qualities with you such as *gentleness* or *compassion*. The more you feel understood and the more positive experiences you have with your new partner, the more *encouraged* you will feel to continue together.

DEEPENING THE RELATIONSHIP

In your initial conversations with your partner, you cover the general topics of each other's educational background, work, and hobbies. If you have not already done so, you will begin to interact with each other's relatives and children from previous relationships. You will probably meet friends and coworkers as well. These interactions will raise topics to discuss. As your relationship progresses and *trust* builds, you share family histories, beliefs, expectations, and outlooks on life.

The topics become progressively more sensitive, and this chapter and the remaining ones will assist you with them. As you go through these chapters, you will have specific discussions about topics of importance to both you and your partner, including how you view sex and intimacy before marriage. You will discover how you are similar and how you are different, particularly related to culture. You will gain insights into when you are *enthusiastic* about your differences as a couple, or when they are a source of problems or conflict instead. It is important to know how to approach the deeper discussions about specific topics or types of issues that will naturally occur in a growing relationship.

Throughout all your interactions, you will also learn more about your partner's character. You will have many opportunities to use all the character qualities yourself as you handle complex discussions, difficult interactions, and issues that arise. Remember to focus on having your communications come from your higher nature (Chapter 1). If you slip and speak from your lower nature, you can apologize and start over in a more positive way.

As your friendship and relationship grow, it is essential that you share your *true* self. When getting to know each other, questions will arise about how you have handled or are handling your relationships with siblings, parents, friends, previous partners, or former spouses. You will explore how you communicated and acted with all these people and what it was like growing up in your home, neighborhood, schools, faith community, and much more. Often your stories will be full of laughter as you share amusing or strange things that happened in your life. You may also have difficult or painful stories to share.

You may be concerned that revealing sensitive information will disrupt your relationship before you have developed a *strong* bond. You may question what information is important to share and what is best kept private for the moment, or even for the long-term. This is important self-questioning, because *discernment* and *wisdom* about what and when to share is important.

To find answers, *honestly* put yourself in your partner's place and determine how the information will affect them, and what they will consider necessary to know. Are there things in your past that affect the way you communicate, or the way you need your partner to communicate with you? If you do not share the sensitive information, what could be the effect on your relationship? If you share it later rather than earlier in your relationship, what could be the result? Once you share the information, you cannot take it back nor change how you said it, so having a well-thought-out plan is *wise*.

There is a difference between postponing a discussion and hiding key information about yourself to pretend to be someone you are not. You cannot avoid postponing a discussion indefinitely. Remember about the importance of not wearing masks (Chapter 2)? If you lie about or hide an issue to cover up something significant about you or your life, it will weaken the foundation of your relationship. You are in effect hiding behind a mask and keeping secrets that will likely emerge later. When your partner learns the *truth*, the bond of *trust* you have will be shaken or broken.

Consider the difficulties this couple is having:

> Roya and Derrick meet through a social gathering at a mutual friend's home. They enjoy the time together discussing their jobs and activities. At the end of the evening, they exchange contact information and agree to stay in touch. A couple of weeks later, they go to a concert and have a picnic together while listening to great music. Derrick asks Roya if she has ever been engaged or married before, and she sidesteps the question and says she does not really want to talk about her previous relationships.
>
> Derrick decides to give Roya some time and drops the topic. They continue to see each other, sometimes along with other friends, and they get together as a couple a few times for a meal or a movie. She continues to act as if everything in her life is fine and avoids talking about any previous relationship experiences.
>
> Roya signs up for a 5-mile walk event to raise money for a children's charity. She invites Derrick to participate. As they walk, Roya gets quiet, and Derrick asks what is on her mind. She pauses and then shares that this walk is always somewhat emotional for her, as she once had a child who died of a serious condition. Derrick expresses sympathy, but Roya still will not talk about the circumstances.
>
> Roya's comment, however, raises thoughts of his past for Derrick as well. He wonders whether he should admit that he had a child with a girlfriend. He lost touch with his son years ago, but he does not want to look bad by admitting this to Roya. She notices a strange expression on his face, and wonders if he is holding something important back. When she asks what he is thinking, he quickly changes the subject and suggests that they walk faster.

Roya and Derrick deliberately avoid sharing important information that will *help* them to build a closer friendship and relationship. Their confused hearts and minds seem to be going in different directions. They are not being *honest*, *courageous*, or *generous* with each other in ways that will move them into being serious partners. They need to build more *trust* in each other so that they can share what is on their minds and hearts, or let the relationship go. Each has a *responsibility* to ensure their own behavior is effective in maintaining their relationship. Drs. Les and Leslie Parrott put it this way: "…if you fail to cultivate these qualities—loyalty, forgiveness, honesty, and dedication—you can't expect to keep true friends."[1]

Sharing Previous Experiences

It is natural that being in a relationship will trigger emotions and memories from the past, whether positive or negative. Your experiences all color how you respond to a partner. As author and Spiritual Life Counselor Iyanla Vanzant writes:

> Relationships bring up your stuff, and feelings are the stuff we are made of. ... Very important love rule: You must learn to be as honest as possible about what you feel. A simple mental sentence should do the trick: "Right now I am feeling ___." Once you acknowledge what you feel, you have a choice whether or not to express it.[2]

Before you choose to share something from the past and your current feelings about it, become clear in your own mind what your expectations are from sharing. Do you want your partner to:

- Share their experiences and feelings in return?
- Validate or recognize how well you handled a difficult situation?
- Hold your hand while you cry, grieve, and heal?
- Listen and learn?
- Be *accepting* of your past?
- *Encourage* and *help* you in overcoming current difficulties?

Once you know what your expectations or hopes are, discuss them with your partner, and determine whether they agree to fulfill them willingly.

The goal of sharing is not to gossip or tear down someone else or yourself, and it is definitely not a time for criticism, argument, or hostility toward each other. It is a time for *compassion*, *love*, and the empathetic listening skills you learned in Chapter 11. *Honest* sharing is not a confession of sins. However, the most difficult things to share may be in direct proportion to the size of your individual mistakes. You may feel a compelling need to be *honest* about a particular mistake to *discern* whether your partner can and will continue to *accept* you for who you are. At the same time, it will be *wise* to communicate your *commitment* to avoiding a repeat of what happened. **This sharing is about being *caring* and *responsible* for your actions and communicating anything that might affect your partner.** [*Note:* Backbiting, gossip, and slander are covered later in this chapter.]

You will determine for yourself what level of detail is appropriate to share *honestly*, while holding on to self-*respect* in the process. You may be able to talk generally about an incident without giving specifics. For instance, you might talk about learning to be *assertive* with a relationship partner instead of accepting verbal abuse, without sharing

294 • *Can We Dance? Learning the Steps for a Fulfilling Relationship*

who said what specifically, under what circumstances they said it, or describing the entire situation in detail. Ask yourself what was important about the situation to share without having to tell all of the details.

You need to find the balance between sharing your *true* self and sharing every mistake or incident that has happened in your life. This is particularly the case if an incident from the past is completely over and has no possibility of affecting the present or the future. What you share needs to move your relationship forward, or be so important that you know it will affect your behavior or reactions in the relationship. If it will affect the other person, it is fair that they know what is on your mind, how it could affect them, and why. It will take *care* and *wisdom* to talk both clearly and sensitively about very difficult or important aspects of your life.

Some issues that may affect a partner, and are therefore important to share, include:

- Having an incident or pattern of unfaithfulness in relationships
- Being abused or experiencing some other traumatic event
- Having or previously having a sexually-transmitted infection/disease (STI/STD)
- Having a child or children
- Having a serious medical condition or disability
- Being previously (or currently!) married or cohabiting with someone
- Questioning your religious beliefs
- Having *strong* convictions or beliefs about something most people do not
- Having a pattern of mismanaging money

You know yourself and your life the best, so there may be other issues as well. Use your best judgment to *discern* what to share. It is also important to use *wisdom* in *discerning* when you need the assistance of a professional in choosing what to share. They can also assist you to resolve any problems that arise from your communications with your partner.

~ *Questions for Reflection* ~

1. What do I consider the most important topics to discuss thoroughly with a partner? When will I share this information?
2. What *helps* me to share personal information with someone?
3. Are there things about myself that I do not intend to share with a partner? Why or why not?
4. What information do I think is essential for a partner to share with me? How can I *encourage* a partner to share with me? What if they refuse?
5. What information is *acceptable* for a partner not to share?

ACTIVITY

Re-visit the list that you made in Chapter 8 of what you consider most important to know about a new friend or partner. If you have someone new in your life, assess how well you know them. What further questions or topics do you want to bring up for discussion?

Sharing to Heal from the Past

Emotional healing often can and does occur in a friendship-based relationship where there is *honest* and *compassionate* communication. Consider this quotation from Susan Page, author of *The 8 Essential Traits of Couples Who Thrive*:

> In our deepest inner selves, we all long for wholeness, for all our wounds to be healed, for the purpose of life to be clear, and to see our role in that purpose. We want to be forgiven for our failures and loved for who we are. We long for a connection to the earth and the heavens, to feel a part of the natural cycle of life. We want to feel at peace with ourselves, and we want to feel unconditional love from some completely trustworthy source.[3]

There is a caution, however. **When sharing your history, you may be tempted to look to your partner to take over the *responsibility* from you to heal, solve, or fix damage from past relationships. But, this is still essentially your own work to do.**

If any issues are deep and serious, you will be *wise* to obtain some personal counseling to assist you with being a whole and healthy partner. It is not a sign of weakness to seek guidance from knowledgeable people. Be *kind* to yourself, and if you feel

Copyright 2006 by Randy Glasbergen.
www.glasbergen.com

"**I need you, darling. You complete me.**"

you are struggling with unresolved issues, seek *help*. This way you will be able to build your relationship on solid ground, rather than upon the shifting sand of emotional uncertainty. (See Chapters 3 and 4 for further assistance.)

You may also sense that your partner's reactions and behavior toward you stem from unresolved issues in their past. You can ask them some specific questions to *encourage* them to share, such as:

- "Is there anything in your past that you feel is important to address before we continue in this relationship?"
- "Is there anything about me or our relationship that troubles you or reminds you of a parent, previous partner, or difficult situation?"
- "Do you have concerns about our future?"
- "Is there anything important in your past that are not yet ready to speak with me about, but you will benefit from sharing it with some other person, such as a *trusted* advisor, parent, or counselor?" [Assess if that will *help* them then be able to share the matter with you, and whether the other person should be present.]

Roger and Penny experience the process of sharing a difficult topic:

> Roger and Penny find each other initially through a dating *service* on the Internet. They spend time getting to know each other through email, and they realize they live in the same city. They first meet each other in person at a local Mongolian restaurant, and they spend the evening talking about a wide range of subjects. The evening is a positive experience for both of them, and they decide to continue seeing each other. They go to movies, eat out with friends, and spend time involved in a cleanup effort at the city park, all of which *help* their friendship to grow.

> One day, Roger notices Penny looking longingly at two nearby teenagers. He asks her what she is thinking, and she admits that she was previously married. She shares that her two teenage children are now choosing to live with her ex-husband. Roger sits down with Penny on a park bench and, in a *compassionate* and *caring* manner, asks if she wants to share her feelings about this situation. She shrugs her shoulders, smiles slightly, and changes the subject to what they plan to do later that evening.

> Time after time, Penny avoids talking about her children. Roger is concerned about how she is handling her estrangement from them. He wonders if she will hold inside any other emotions or refuse to deal with issues that come up in their relationship. He raises these concerns with Penny. She decides to get some counseling to work through her issues with her children and improve her ability to share her feelings with Roger. They slow down their relationship for a while, so that Penny can concentrate on handling this matter effectively.

> Roger stays in close touch with Penny to assure her that he is a supportive friend. Penny begins to feel in her heart that Roger *truly* is a safe person that

she can *trust*. Little by little, she opens up to him, and their relationship resumes. Roger's *trustworthiness*, *compassion*, and *patience*, and Penny's *honesty* and willingness to face her past and her current situation, *help* Penny in her healing process. Their use of these qualities contributes to their relationship developing in a healthy way.

As new issues arise in your relationship, it is best to handle any concerns appropriately and promptly, rather than avoiding a discussion out of fear of disrupting the relationship. If necessary, you may need to give yourself some time to calm down or reflect on your thoughts and emotions before you talk to your partner about them. However, it is unwise to leave things unsaid for long, or they begin to fester. Usually, when you postpone raising an issue, it becomes more of a problem, and dealing with it later becomes more difficult. Your partner may resent the fact that you delayed sharing, or they may hear about the issue from someone else and question your *love* or *trustworthiness*. It is also important for you to learn how you and your partner will handle difficult communications together, and whether you require skill-building practice in this area.

Note: If you have a partner, and you have not already done so, it will be *helpful* for you to go through the communications worksheets in Chapter 11 together, or review them before discussing sensitive topics. It is also useful to choose a character quality you and your partner will both practice during the discussion.

ACTIVITY

Complete **Worksheet 12.1 Assessing the Current Effect of Previous Relationships** to be clear about how the past may affect a new relationship.

TRUST AND HONESTY

It takes time and *trust* to *create* a friendship-based relationship and effective communication between you and your partner. Your *trust* in each other will grow or change as you share experiences together and what is on your mind and in your heart. The *trust* then solidifies as you keep the sharing confidential. When you dance with someone for the first time, you may feel awkward and not sure of how you will move together. You may have taken lessons at different places and from various teachers. You will begin with the basic steps and patterns. As you continue dancing, you develop a feel for your partner's abilities and style of movement. You gradually take small chances, trying different step variations and patterns. If it goes well, you continue; otherwise, you go back to the basic dance steps with this person or someone new.

Technique is the key to dancing together smoothly and in harmony. This includes proper dance position, connection, paying attention, and reading the movement signals. Dancing, like communication, is not something you do <u>to</u> a partner or they do <u>to</u> you, it is something you do <u>with</u> a partner. Dance partners need to pay attention to each other, communicate and listen with their senses and bodies, and have control of their own balance. When you violate the principles of movement and partnering, the dancing will be rough, uncoordinated, uncomfortable, and unfulfilling. **To build *trust* through communication in a relationship, partners need to pay attention, speak *truthfully*, listen attentively, *cooperate*, and exercise *self-discipline* with their responses.**

Feeling Safe to Share

The degree to which you and your partner *trust* each other affects the ability you each have to risk being vulnerable and sharing important aspects of yourselves. Getting to know and *trust* someone is particularly essential for there to be intimate and safe communication about personal issues between the two of you. **For *trust* to grow between you and someone special, it requires that you both *create* a feeling of safety and security for each other.** The following actions can assist you to do this:

- Keep promises and *commitments*
- Demonstrate the ability to keep what others and your partner shares as confidential (no gossip)
- Share personal information gradually, and discover whether your partner's response is *respectful*, positive, *accepting*, and non-judgmental
- Avoid using sensitive information to tease or harm your partner, or to manipulate them to do something that you want them to do

As *trust* builds, both you and your partner can increase it by communicating your thoughts and feelings with each other mutually and freely. It *helps* if you use *care*, *tact*, and *wisdom*, but without unduly censoring what you say. Consider this scenario:

Cherise and Jackson begin discussing more sensitive and personal topics. While they are each nervous about sharing with the other, they know from experience that they can *trust* the other to have a *respectful* response. Cherise shares that she is hesitant about *committing* to a deeper relationship with him because she struggles with *trusting* men generally. Her father was regularly in jail, changing jobs, or moving in and out of the house. She and her mother could rarely count on him to be around. She wonders now if any man she *cares* for will act the same way. However, she is able to make many other *commitments* in her life, such as to her faith community, her employer, and to her friends and family. These successes give her hope that she can do the same in a relationship.

Jackson, in turn, talks about how difficult it has been for him since breaking up with his previous girlfriend. He was ready for marriage and proposed to her. However, she was unwilling to take on the *responsibility* of marriage. Jackson shares his frustration with how that situation turned out, and his concern about being with someone new and having the same thing happen again. Cherise and Jackson's conversation *helps* them both to understand each other better.

Jackson knows that he wants the relationship with Cherise to grow. For that to happen, Cherise will need to see him as unlike her father before she will be able to *trust* him. This may take some counseling work with a professional or simply more time together. With more involvement with Jackson, she will see that he has a high level of *integrity* with his personal *responsibilities*, work, and relationships. He is very unlikely to abandon her. Cherise, in turn, is insightful enough to know that Jackson will need to see her as an individual and unlike the woman who hurt him. This will *help* him to *trust* her with his feelings and become close to her.

Jackson agrees to focus on seeing the qualities in Cherise that make her a mature and *committed* friend who will be with him for the long-term. Together they agree to spend more time doing activities together, believing that this will *help* them gradually build their *trust* in each other.

As your relationship develops, you will share information about yourself and *encourage* your partner to do the same, just as Cherise and Jackson did. Throughout this process, you can provide the essential feedback to your partner to assure them that you are listening and understanding what they are communicating. You will then build *trust* with each other gradually.

It will *help create trust* if you and your partner discuss the importance of *respecting* each other's private sharing, which will include agreeing on boundaries around confidentiality. *Trust* is an integral part of being friends. For *trust* to occur in a friendship-based relationship, it requires that you be *honest* with each other. This includes being able to express what is on your mind and receive *respect* from your partner in return. It is essential that neither you nor your partner regard this intimacy lightly.

If you do not like choices that your partner made, or you are angry about how others treated your partner, you may need to practice *self-discipline* so you *moderate* any negative emotional reactions that you have when your partner shares. Otherwise, your reactions can lead you to treat your partner or others poorly.

ACTIVITY

Play a game with someone—cards, board game, or sports—and notice whether the person is *honest* and fair in the game, or if they have a tendency to cheat or show poor sportsmanship. Notice how you respond as you discover whether the person is *honest* and *trustworthy*.

~ Questions for Reflection ~

1. How do I show *trust* in a partner (or a friend)? What can I do to increase their *trust* in me?
2. How will I know if I can *trust* a partner and that it is safe to share something?
3. What will I share about me that I will consider betrayal if a partner (or a friend) breaks confidentiality?
4. What does breaking *trust* look like to me? When have I thought a partner (or a friend) violated my *trust*? How did I respond?
5. If a partner (or a friend) breaks my *trust*, will I be willing to *forgive* them and offer them a second chance? Under what circumstances?
6. How can I re-build *trust* with a partner (or a friend) if it has been broken?
7. What are the signs that it is *wise* to end a relationship (or friendship) and no longer give another chance to someone who keeps behaving poorly?

BACKBITING, GOSSIP, AND SLANDER

As you and your partner share with each other, there are some boundaries for you to consider that will assist both you and your partner to be *respectful* to each other and to others in your lives. These include not backbiting, participating in gossip, or slandering another person. These are generally lower nature communications, which can harm you and others (Chapter 1). Staying away from these negative actions builds *trust* between you and your partner.

Negative words about others and spreading information about others through gossip have been mentioned throughout the book as communication practices that tend to harm a relationship. **Backbiting occurs when someone speaks in a negative, spiteful, derogatory, or defamatory way about another person who is not present.** The words may actually be *truthful*, but the intent and effect are destructive. It creates disunity between people, whether or not the person spoken of finds out what was said. The Qur'án says, "Woe to the backbiter, even if his tale is true, for the taint is in his motive."[4]

Gossip is spreading personal or sensational information that is sometimes *true*, but often inaccurate or incomplete, and the intent or outcome are harmful. When you know something interesting about another person, it is very tempting to share it with others. Often doing this draws attention to you from the people listening, and this can make gossip seem more positive than it is.

Slander occurs when you spread information that is clearly false, and it is also known as calumny. This action, in particular, can damage *trust* very severely, and it can cause irreparable harm to a relationship.

When you and your partner share about your pasts, it is important to do your best to avoid backbiting, gossip, or slander about others, including previous partners. It is especially important to be cautious about unreasonably prejudicing your partner against people in your life that they may encounter.

Backbiting and gossip can happen in relationships when either you or your partner discusses private details about each other with friends, family members, neighbors, or coworkers. When your partner shares with you or you with them, this is generally confidential, unless you agree otherwise. You can also communicate a complaint to someone about your partner with the intent that the person listening to you feels sorry for you or thinks negatively about your partner.

If you talk poorly about your partner's behavior or character even in a casual way, consider that this may be backbiting. If the people you speak to then spread what you said to others, it can then be gossip. As this happens, the information is often distorted and embellished, which may cause harm or embarrassment to you, your partner, or both of you. Bahá'u'lláh says that backbiting "…quencheth the light of the heart, and extinguisheth the life of the soul."[5] It negatively affects both the speaker and the listener. It also often affects the person who is talked about.

At times, a friend may think they know something potentially negative about your partner. If they share it with you, consider whether it is backbiting about your partner. In Ghana, they share this wisdom: "Those who speak to you about others will speak to others about you."[6]

If a friend wants to raise a concern, it is best if you either stop them or *encourage* them to speak in generalities and not in specifics. For instance, perhaps your friend hears that your partner was unfaithful to a girlfriend. Instead of sharing this information, your friend can simply urge you to ask your partner about their relationship history. **Being general in this way gives your partner the opportunity to share**

information directly with you. [*Note:* If the concern someone wants to raise with you is about something that may affect your safety or well-being, then see the next section.]

Copyright 2004 by Randy Glasbergen.
www.glasbergen.com

"WE WERE GOING TO GET SURROUND-SOUND,
BUT MY SISTER GETS UPSET WHEN PEOPLE
TALK BEHIND HER BACK."

Avoiding backbiting can be difficult, since you may be used to talking through issues and expressing frustrations with close friends and family members. **Before you speak, ask yourself whether the person you are speaking about will be diminished, essentially made "smaller," in the view of the person to whom you are talking.** If so, then consider whether it is better to stay quiet. It is better to communicate about issues directly with your partner rather than to speak about your partner to other people.

You may want some input on your relationship from those close to you, however, and this can involve sharing private information. For this to have a fruitful outcome rather than a harmful one, it is vital that you choose advisors who are *trustworthy*, *wise*, **and who have a well-developed character. It is especially important to keep the discussion centered in the higher nature rather than the lower one.** This person will easily agree to keep your discussion confidential. Your goal from the discussion must clearly be to gain perspectives on how to handle a situation more effectively, improve your relationship, or change your words or actions so that they are more effective. **The goal is constructive action, not idle talk.** Whether your discussion is with a professional counselor, religious leader, family, friends, or parents, the goal is to actively communicate from your higher nature and not engage in idle or destructive talk from your lower nature (Chapter 1).

~ *Questions for Reflection* ~
1. When have I seen backbiting, gossip, or slander cause harm? 2. What might happen in a relationship if I backbite or gossip about my partner? 3. Whom will I go to if I need *wise* and *trustworthy* guidance about a relationship?
ACTIVITY
Visualize a clean bowl of water becoming murky through dumping backbiting comments into it. See it being stirred with gossip. Then, visualize a clean bowl of water and imagine someone's character qualities floating in it, perhaps as flower petals or attractive and beautiful confetti. See the qualities being stirred with *encouragement*. Meditate on which bowl of water represents what you want in your life. You may find it *helpful* to physically carry out this activity rather than doing it as a visualization, and do it either by yourself or with a small group of friends.

Backbiting and an Abusive Partner

An exception to the indirect approach in the previous section occurs when someone who cares about you is aware that your partner could endanger your safety or health. Perhaps your partner has a history of abuse or violence, for example. Then, it is wise for someone to be direct in raising their concerns with you, so you can determine the facts and protect yourself. Your partner will be one source of information, but be cautious. Someone with a serious problem may minimize or deny it. They may also lie or make false promises about never repeating the behavior. You may need to look for additional sources, such as police reports if your partner has been in legal trouble for their behavior, or from family members aware of the situation.

Upon learning the facts and circumstances, you will then be in a better position to assess whether your partner is likely to repeat their abusive actions, or whether they have successfully dealt with their problems. Warning signs of a violent or abusive partner are when they:

- Embarrass, belittle, and make you feel unworthy
- Isolate you from friends and family
- Tell you that you are crazy or stupid
- Use intimidation to control you
- Control your finances

- Make you feel trapped
- Physically harm you by slapping, pushing, grabbing, punching, choking or kicking you
- Threaten you verbally or with a weapon
- Get angry or lose control when drunk [on alcohol] or high [on drugs]
- Force you to have sex
- Stalk you or harass you at home or work[7]

If any of these are occurring, then you will need to seek assistance to protect yourself and any children that you have as well. Domestic violence centers, doctors, social workers, or law enforcement officers may be good sources of assistance.

JEALOUSY AND MISTRUST

Jealousy is a destructive problem in a relationship, and it comes from being fearful that someone will take your place with your partner. You are suspicious that you have a rival, and you begin to feel threatened and then guard what you see as your territory. Jealousy can result in frustration, sadness, threats, clinging dependency, rage, self-criticism, hurt, anxiety, loneliness, resentment, embarrassment, and more. It is a very negative and destructive emotion that is centered in your lower nature (Chapter 1).

When taken to its extreme, jealousy can cause you to demand exclusivity and then work to cut your partner off from anyone else. Some people can react to jealous feelings by becoming extremely angry or violent. This reaction can only result in greater harm to everyone. If you or your partner struggles with this type of response, then professional counseling is indicated. **Jealousy is internally destructive to your mind, heart, and soul. It can make it difficult for you to think clearly and accurately about your partner, and it can cause disruption or loss of the relationship.** This loss can occur, even when everything else in the relationship is going well. Jealousy is a very important issue to handle effectively.

There are a number of causes for jealousy. They can include:

- Fear that your partner will find someone they like or *love* more than you
- Insecurity and fear of abandonment
- Fear of loss of affection
- Low self-*respect* and poor self-worth
- Lack of *confidence* that your partner really *cares* about you
- Tendency to assume the worst of others' behavior
- Inappropriate or unfaithful behavior in a partner

All of these points may relate to your past. Friends' or family members' experiences and the media may also be influencing your concerns about your relationship.

Jealousy can arise more frequently when you know that your partner has had many previous partners, especially when those relationships included cohabitation or sexual intimacy. Concerns about your partner's ability to be *faithful* in your current relationship can then arise. You may have even more difficulty with *acceptance* if your partner is still friends and in regular contact with someone with whom they were previously sexually intimate. Remaining friends with a former partner may be a healthy choice for some people, but then it is wise for a person to think through *honestly* about why they want to maintain the relationship.

If your partner maintains an ongoing connection to a former partner, how does it affect you? You may feel discomfort, jealousy, or insecurity, or instead you could be very *confident* in your current relationship and the *unity* between the two of you. Will you ask your partner to make adjustments in how much time they spend with a former partner? What can you do to determine the *truth* of the situation and determine that they are now genuinely only friends?

As you observe your partner interacting with a previous partner, you may see some warning signs. Examples of inappropriate behavior with a previous partner can include taking care of their emotional or physical needs, holding on to a key to their home, or turning to that person to work through issues instead of to you. Some questions to consider are:

- What emotional communications are still actively occurring between the previous partners?
- Is your partner willing and capable of *detaching* from the previous partner?
- What is your partner emotionally gaining from keeping the relationship with the previous partner?
- What is unresolved or incomplete from the previous relationship? Is your partner feeling guilty for anything from the previous relationship?
- What is your partner afraid of happening if they let the relationship go?
- Is your partner holding onto the previous relationship as a safety net in case the relationship with you does not work out?

In addition to actual contact with a previous partner, even the memories of previous relationships may provoke you or your partner to make assumptions or comparisons that may become an obstacle. You may project what worked with a previous partner onto your current partner, who actually has different needs and wants. Your current partner may become jealous as a result. Looking to the future, comparisons are especially damaging within a marriage if you were to compare your spouse unfavorably to a previous sexual partner. Your spouse may feel insecure, always wondering if they are as "good" as your previous partner(s). It can be very hurtful if you communicate that you find your spouse lacking in some area that a previous partner satisfied.

Sorting out the causes and solutions for jealousy and mistrust in your relationship will require various actions on your part. These can include conversations with your family, discussions with others who know you well, meditation, prayer, or counseling. You may find it useful to return to Chapters 2, 3, or 4 to assess yourself and determine whether there are any lingering, unresolved issues from previous relationships. You can then take the appropriate action.

One way to address jealousy is to focus on your character quality practice and character development. The better you are able to develop your qualities, the more *confident* and secure you will feel in your own self-worth. This will improve interactions with your partner and increase your ability to be *trusting*.

Sometimes, however, placing *trust* in someone is unwise. Jealousy can be an important indication of a problem you and your partner may need to address. You may choose not to continue in a relationship if your partner is being unfaithful or behaving inappropriately with others. If your partner flirts with or touches someone in an intimate or sexual way, your *trust* in them is likely decreased or broken. You can then work to either rebuild *trust*, or stop seeing each other.

~ Questions for Reflection ~

1. Do I ever feel jealous of a partner or a friend? Under what circumstances? How does this affect my relationships with them?
2. Do I *trust* a partner to be *faithful* to me? Why or why not? What increases *trust*?

Agreements with a Partner

Whether jealously is based on facts or is ill-founded, and whatever the circumstances and issues are that are causing it, you and your partner will need to objectively discuss the situation. Do either you or your partner have emotional issues from previous relationships or your pasts that are affecting the views you both hold of the current situation? What will maximize *unity* and healthy relationships for everyone involved?

The goal in the discussion will be for you and your partner to resolve and end both the jealousy and, if applicable, any unwise actions that are contributing to it or coming from it. You will also find it useful to agree on the behaviors, communications, and boundaries that are important and *respectful* to both of you. You and your partner will then have to do your best to follow through with any agreements you reach in order for the situation to calm down emotionally.

Tina Tessina, a psychotherapist and author, suggests using the following guidelines to overcome jealousy:

> Make sure you and your partner feel comfortable with your agreements. Discuss the possibility that one or both of you might be jealous. Make some agreements about how you'll behave, and make sure you'll be willing to keep them. Don't frighten yourself or your partner by testing too hard, demanding the impossible, or risking too much. Keep in mind that jealousy breaks down trust. If you begin to be upset, talk about it and encourage your partner to do the same.
>
> Keep each other informed. Lying to your partner about whether you have broken an agreement does more damage than breaking the agreement. If you slip up, tell the truth. If it's your partner who has slipped, be open to listening to him or her without blaming or getting upset, so the two of you can negotiate a solution to the problem. If you or your partner continually create situations that aggravate jealousy, you may need to find a counselor to help you solve the problem.
>
> Give yourselves time. Patience and communication are your best allies. As you learn and grow together, trust gradually builds. As trust grows stronger, you can begin to relax the rules and allow yourselves more flexibility and freedom.
>
> Remember to be gentle with yourself and each other. Don't be angry with yourself or your partner for being jealous. You'll have much better luck if you just see jealousy as a normal, human problem and work it out together.[8]

The more you and your partner use *excellent* communication skills and effectively practice your character qualities, the greater your opportunity will be to avoid, resolve, or dissolve any jealousy between you.

It can seriously disrupt your relationship and erode its foundations if you are repeatedly jealous even though your partner has not betrayed your *trust* and is being *faithful*. It is important that both you and your partner treat each other as *trustworthy*, which will *help* to keep *trust* and *love* intact.

~ Questions for Reflection ~

1. Am I still in contact with a previous sexual partner? What is the nature of my relationship with them?
2. How does my new partner (if I have one) feel about the relationship? What is the relationship between the two of them?
3. How will I respond if a partner initiates contact with a previous sexual partner after we agreed it would not happen?
4. If your partner chooses to look after the needs of a previous partner, how will you respond?

DISCUSSING SEXUAL EXPERIENCES

One of the sensitive topics for you and a partner to discuss is sex. **When you have had sexual experiences with previous partners, there comes a time when it is necessary to be *honest* with your current partner.** You may not need to be specific, but you will at least share the generalities of what happened.

As part of this discussion, you will probably also share what led up to the circumstances, or why you made the choices that you did. Previous sexual experiences can be an embarrassing topic, but it is an important one if you and your partner are becoming serious about each other. Sensitivity is especially important if either you or your partner experienced sexual abuse. Explore with your partner what will *help* create a safe, *trusting* environment for your sharing, and what will assist you in being open and *honest*.

If you want to verbally share about your sexual experiences without being physically aroused or initiating intimate touch with each other, you might find it *helpful* to set up a supportive structure. This can include praying together first, holding the conversation over the telephone, or choosing an appropriate location. You can consider whether the location gives you privacy, but others are close enough so that you will not be tempted into sexual touch, such as meeting at a park. Be aware of whether you are both focused and willing to participate in the discussion. If you have concerns about your partner's reaction, or you wish to raise a very difficult topic, you may choose to have the conversation together with a therapist, *spiritual* counselor, or *trusted* third person.

As you think about what to share with your partner, avoid giving unnecessary details that will simply burden your partner or that may be unnecessarily negative about someone. There are aspects of your life that may not be *wise* to divulge. Sharing your experiences is not "confession"; it is simply communicating information about your life that can affect the quality and course of your relationship with your partner in the future. If your experiences affect how you behave with your partner in the present, or if they can negatively affect your partner's well-being (such as when an infection or disease is present), then share whatever is necessary. Otherwise, consider keeping it private, brief, or general rather than specific.

Be aware that some questions your partner asks you about your experiences (or you ask them) may be embarrassing or difficult to answer. If you feel very uncomfortable about a question, it is *wise* to postpone answering it until you have thought through how to give an answer or whether to answer it at all. If you choose to answer it, be as forthright as possible. Request that your partner be *tactful, compassionate,* and sensitive toward you as you share.

There may be some emotional and vulnerable moments as you communicate your experiences. Before you share, consider what personal preparation, such as meditation or prayer, might assist you to stay focused and calm in the discussion. If you or your partner becomes very upset or angry in the discussion, you may choose to postpone it. If you do this, then remember to set a time when you will resume the discussion, or set it as soon as you are both calmer.

As the two of you share intimate details about yourselves, pay attention to your thoughts, judgments, and emotional responses. Do you expect your partner to share the same level of detail that you are doing? How do you feel about what you are sharing or hearing? Can you fully and appropriately express your feelings and thoughts to your partner? Do you shut down your emotional responses and try not to think about something your partner shares? Give yourself time to process your feelings, and seek assistance if you need to before speaking, acting, or responding in any way. You may want to wait to respond until you have some time to think it through *carefully*. This will give you the time needed to make a *careful, tactful*, and appropriate response.

Your previous experiences may have been positive, which will assist you to have similar experiences in the future. Many people, however, have had difficult or abusive sexual experiences. In this case, consider whether you need professional assistance, such as counseling, to assist you with understanding and resolving any feelings or issues that can affect your partner or relationship. [*Note:* Refer back to Chapter 4, page 85, for the behaviors related to sex that can be warning signs in a relationship.]

ACTIVITY

Complete **Worksheet 12.2 Discussing Your Sexual Experiences** to explore what experiences and situations you and a partner will share with each other.

> ### ~ Questions for Reflection ~
>
> 1. What aspects of my sexual history are important to share with my partner? Can I share them? Why or why not?
> 2. What aspects of my history of sexual experience with others are important to keep private and not share with my partner? Why or why not?
> 3. How do I feel about my own sexual history? How much do I want to know about a partner's history?

SEXUAL INVOLVEMENT

You and your partner may be on the same page with whether to have sex with each other before marriage or not. However, you could also be approaching it from very different vantage points. You and your partner will then need to discuss the values, beliefs, and boundaries you each have. The goal is to agree on a mutual choice on this topic. Chapter 5 gave you some foundational information for this discussion.

Agreeing on Your Choices

To maintain harmony as you participate in the relationship dance, you and your partner need to be dancing the same dance. It will not work if you are trying to waltz, and your partner is dancing tango. In the same way, it will be important for you and your partner to agree on how you will handle sex and physical intimacy in your relationship. Without agreement, there will be uncomfortably awkward and difficult moments between the two of you as you each make choices and pull different directions.

You and your partner need to be compatible in your attitudes toward your dance partnership. Otherwise, you will be stepping on each other's toes or invading each other's space. Good dancing requires sensitivity toward your partner's needs and *respect* for your partner's choices, boundaries, and limitations. When you try to get your partner to dance various moves, and they are uncomfortable with them, you will feel off-balance and uncoordinated together. If your partner does not want to dip, drop, or do aerial stunts, these will not work smoothly if you try to insist. Together, you decide on the dance and steps you will or will not do.

The same guidelines apply to physical intimacy in a relationship. **As with any other major relationship topic, your ideas and attitudes about sex and physical touch need to be compatible for the two of you to be in harmony. This requires giving each other the freedom to make individual choices without pressure, and includes making a mutual**

decision that will be the best one for both of you. *Respect, caring*, and *acceptance* will guide you in this process.

Few topics raise as many opinions and feelings as the topic of sex. Therefore, it makes sense for you and your partner to think *carefully* about how your choices will affect your lives. You may think that having sex is fine as long as it is between consenting adults, or you may have *strong* convictions about not having sex before marriage. Your sexual history can be complete innocence, and you are choosing to be a virgin. You can have some experience and wonder why you should not gain more. You may have had multiple partners and are now wondering whether that was a *wise* choice. Your views and choices may or may not be supported by your family, culture, or *spiritual* community. Whatever choices you have made have brought you to where you are today.

As discussed in Chapter 5, one choice you can make alone or as a couple, is abstinence. This is essentially saying no to sex before marriage. Another choice is *chastity*, which goes beyond abstinence to include such aspects of your life as your thoughts, activity, entertainment, and clothing choices. Along with making these choices, you would also look at your purposes in life and see what activities to fill your life with, so that sex is not the dominant focus in your relationship. Consider how this couple handles their situation:

> Bernie and Hilda belong to different faiths and meet at an interfaith benefit concert. They enjoy the music together and agree to see each other again. After a few months of building a friendship, they decide to make their relationship exclusive. Hilda knows Bernie finds her attractive, and she feels the same way about him, but they are *committed* to building their relationship and waiting for marriage to have sex.
>
> To *help* them resist being physically intimate, Hilda and Bernie talk to close friends of theirs and decide to spend more time going out in a group. This *helps* them to avoid the temptation of becoming too intimate physically, and allows them the freedom to enjoy being together and still honor their convictions.

Whatever your beliefs and history about sexual relations are, there are many reasons to wait until the wedding night. If you have already willingly had sex with a previous or current partner, however, then you can consider choosing a new approach now.

Note: You may find it *helpful* to refer back to Chapter 5 to review what it says about committing to abstinence and *chastity* before marriage, and about the consequence of any choices that you make.

~ *Questions for Reflection* ~

1. What do I see as possible difficulties in discussing the topics of sex, abstinence, and *chastity* with a partner?
2. What kind of setting will be *wise* for this discussion?

ACTIVITY

Choose a few songs that reflect sexual choices or that reflect your attitude about sex. Share and discuss these with your partner, if you have one, or with a friend.

Maintaining the Choice to Wait

When there is intense sexual attraction between you and your partner, it can interrupt or stop the flow of ideas, emotions, and relationship exploration between you. **You have a choice of acting on the feelings or *detaching* yourself from them.** Perhaps you need some physical distance from each other for a while, or it may be useful to be sure that you are usually in groups or with family members rather than being alone together.

Some cultures, faiths, or families regard it as improper or unwise for unmarried couples to spend time alone with someone of the opposite sex. This can be *true*, even when the couple is in a *committed* relationship and talking about marriage. You and your partner will determine together whether any guidelines or practices apply to you, and how they can support you.

It can *help* you to prevent the opportunity and temptation to have sex, and serve your best interests as a couple, if you reduce or eliminate private situations. This is how one couple handles this:

> Kim and Dylan meet in high school and decide to attend the same college together so that they can continue their relationship. They have decided to have a *chaste* relationship and practice abstinence, so they decide on a number of practices to *help* them *respect* this choice. When they study together, they do it in public areas on campus, not in each other's rooms. They make sure to pray together and study *spiritual* subjects at least once a week. The campus has a small interfaith chapel, and they visit it whenever they can. They participate in a psychology campus club together, which matches their majors, and they play volleyball for fun in the campus league.

Kim and Dylan agree to limit their touch to occasional hugs and kisses. If either of them is tempted to go beyond this, they agree to be *honest* with each other and spend some time apart to reassess their actions and motives. Keeping their *commitment* is not easy, but they are determined to be successful.

If you are struggling to keep your *commitment* to abstinence or *chastity*, it can be a good idea to add new activities to your life, or to release energy through healthy methods such as exercise. You may find it *helpful* to pray or meditate to increase your inner *strength* and to focus on your higher nature (Chapter 1). *Self-discipline helps* you to control your emotions and not act on hormonal urges or allow sexual desire to overwhelm you. With careful thought and control, these feelings will lessen, and you can once again focus on getting to know your partner. **Your power of choice is *stronger* than your passions, although it will not be easy, and it will take effort and *perseverance*.** Redirecting your focus away from sex and physical attraction will *help* you to make better decisions about a partner. "…[P]assion will not break through a well-reflecting mind."[9]

If you choose to practice abstinence or *chastity* as a couple, then one way to support your choice is to agree on the boundaries about touching you will follow. Relationship experts Drs. Les and Leslie Parrott suggest that there is a practical way to approach a portion of this topic. They say:

> The secret to saving sex for marriage is found in a single word: boundaries. Couples who abstain from sex without shutting off their sexuality have learned to set specific boundaries and stick to them. They have made intentional, deliberate, and conscious choices about how far [in physical touch] they will go.[10]

Setting boundaries means that you have a clear list of behaviors that can lead to intimate touch or sexual intercourse, such as holding hands, kissing, removing clothes, or touching specific parts of each other's bodies, and which ones, if any, you will or will not do. It will be useful to discuss how physically close you will be with each other in a variety of circumstances. This discussion *helps* you to determine for yourself and together with your partner what your limits and boundaries are as a couple, before the two of you are in a situation that can lead to sexual touch or a struggle to keep your *commitment* to *chastity*.

When you and your partner agree on boundaries and choices, there is greater *respect* between you. Agnes Ghaznavi, M.D., in *Sexuality, Relationships and Spiritual Growth* says:

> When mutual respect is growing in the hearts and minds of partners, their relationship is permeated by a realization of freedom and love, and this

forms a firm bond. This freedom, of course, is not freedom in the sense of infidelity, but freedom of the spirit and the mind.[11]

Besides practicing personal *self-discipline* and *responsibility*, maintaining abstinence and *chastity* can benefit from some external assistance. This might include asking for guidance from parents, or you can spend time with a peer group or faith group where everyone is *committed* to waiting for marriage to have sex. Consider, "We may drink water and eat food at any restaurant…, but having sex whenever, wherever, and with whomever does not meet the deep longing of the human soul for an exclusive sexual relationship."[12]

~ *Questions for Reflection* ~

1. What is my commitment about *chastity* or abstinence?
2. What will *help* me to maintain *chastity* and abstinence if these are my choices?
3. How will I handle a difference of opinion between a partner and myself on this topic?

꧁ *Encouragement* ꧂

There were many difficult topics in this chapter. Some may have triggered a variety of thoughts and emotions in you. It is very important to find healthy and productive ways to process your thoughts and release your emotions. It might also be a good idea to take a break from discussion and do a fun or entertaining activity together with a friend or partner.

Date: _____

Worksheet 12.1 Assessing the Current Effect of Previous Relationships

This worksheet will assist you to understand how previous relationships may affect a current or future relationship. If you have a partner, then it would be good for both of you to answer these questions separately and then discuss them together.

Instructions:

A) Answer each of the questions. If you find it difficult to answer one, then consider talking it through with a close friend, family member, or trusted advisor.

B) If you have a partner, determine their perspective on each of the questions. Consider how your handling of the matter affects your partner.

1. What role do previous partners or spouses have in my life now? In the lives of my family members or friends?

   _____

   _____

2. Will there be a reason for new and previous partners to meet each other, such as when children are involved? How can this go smoothly?

   _____

   _____

3. Will there be a reason for new and previous partners to build a civil or positive relationship? How can this occur?

   _____

   _____

4. How will I handle jewelry, photos, gifts, household furnishings, and other items that are associated with former involvements? Can I detach and not project emotions and memories onto these? Will I need to dispose of some or all of them? Which ones?

   _____

   _____

5. What nicknames or terms of endearment (Honey, Sweetie, Baby, Darling…) are off-limits for a new partner to use because they were common in a previous relationship?

   _____

   _____

6. How will I respond if I accidentally call a new partner by a previous partner's name? How will I respond if a new partner does this to me?

_____

_____

7. How am I handling any feelings and reactions toward previous partners?

_____

_____

8. Do I need to communicate directly to a previous partner that their communications or in-person contact are not welcome, or that the communications must change in nature if they are to continue? What character qualities will help me to do this in an assertive, self-respecting, and confident way?

_____

_____

9. How will I handle a current friendship with a previous partner?

_____

_____

10. If there is an ongoing friendship between me and a previous partner, what are the boundaries that need to be in place regarding where meetings occur and what topics are appropriate to discuss? What protects the integrity and unity of my new relationship?

_____

_____

11. Will any contact or friendship my partner has with previous partners be an ongoing point of dissension between us? How can I minimize this? Can I find any positive aspects in the situation? If my partner is still in contact with a previous partner by choice or legal requirements can I accept this? Can I identify any positive character qualities in their previous partner to help me with accepting the person in my partner's life?

_____

_____

12. Is there any need for professional coaching or counseling to assist me with previous relationship issues? What is my goal?

_____

_____

Date: _____

Worksheet 12.2 Discussing Your Sexual Experiences

This worksheet will assist you to determine what sexual history you have that is important to share with a partner, and what you will want to know about a partner's history. You will then consider how to respond to the information. *Note:* Some of these issues are very sensitive, and you may need the assistance of trusted advisors or professionals to assist you with them.

Instructions:

A) Answer the questions by yourself, taking time to think carefully about each one. Do your best to discern the emotions that accompany each topic and record those as well.

B) If you have a partner, ask your partner to answer these questions separately. If you do not have a partner, then make notes about what information you will consider vitally important that a partner share with you.

C) Discuss your responses with your partner, if you have one, or with a trusted advisor, family member, or friend, while avoiding backbiting or gossip.

1. What positive sexual experiences have I had? How will these affect me in future sexual experiences? What are my expectations about sex with someone else?

   _____

   _____

2. What uncomfortable or unsatisfactory sexual experiences have I had with others? With my current partner? How did I handle the situations? How are these experiences affecting me now?

   _____

   _____

3. Have I been sexually abused, including such actions as incest, rape, sex in response to threats, or forced touch? How did I respond? What help have I received? How is this affecting me now?

   _____

   _____

4. Have I participated in sexually risky behavior, or acted contrary to my beliefs or those of my family? Are any of these predictors of my ability to remain faithful to my partner and respect their needs or beliefs?

   _____

   _____

5. Have I ever been sexually abusive to someone? What help have I received? How is this affecting me now?

   _____

   _____

6. Have alcohol or drugs contributed to me being involved in sexual activities? How committed am I to abstaining from using them now and in the future?

   _____

   _____

7. Have I ever been exposed to a sexually transmitted infection or disease (STI/STD)? Have I been tested appropriately for them? Are there any conditions undergoing or needing treatment? If I am not seeking testing or treatment, why not? Can the conditions still be transmitted to a partner? How are they affecting my ability to conceive a child?

   _____

   _____

8. What type of relationship do I currently have with previous sexual partners? Does my partner know about these relationships? Does my partner have any concerns about them? How will I resolve these concerns?

   _____

   _____

9. Have I ever willingly had sex as a brief encounter with someone I just met or did not know well? Why? What was the outcome?

   _____

   _____

10. What, if any, tendencies do I have toward an excessive attachment, dependency upon, or addiction to sexual experiences, either alone or with a partner, such as: reading or viewing pornography, masturbation, watching television shows or movies with sex scenes, reading sexually explicit novels, viewing the sexual acts of others, sexual experiences that harm myself or others, or having constant or violent sexual fantasies that lead to sexual arousal?

    _____

    _____

11. Are there aspects of my previous choices that I feel a need to hide because I fear what my partner's response might be? What are these? What are my concerns? How will this information harm my partner or disrupt the relationship? What could help me to be honest?_____

    _____

12. Have I made a significant change in behavior or lifestyle, such as ceasing to have sexually-based relationships or ceasing to have multiple sexual partners? Is this a sincere and lasting change? Am I afraid that I may easily resume old habits, or that underlying issues were not fully resolved? Am I confident of ongoing success instead?

_____

_____

13. Have I ever been pregnant or fathered a child inside or outside of a marriage? How did my previous partner or spouse and I handle this situation? How will it affect my current relationship?

_____

_____

Questions for Reflection:

1. What concerns do I have about my own experiences affecting a current or future relationship?

_____

_____

_____

_____

_____

_____

_____

2. When you have a partner: What concerns do I have about my partner's experiences affecting our relationship?

_____

_____

_____

_____

_____

_____

New Dances:
Exploring Some Differences

While working for international companies, Cara and Beck meet during brief assignments in England. They discover they enjoy reading the same books and seeing the same films, even though she is from Viet Nam, and he is from Sweden. Quickly they strike up a friendship and agree to stay in touch when they return to their countries. Once home, they both use their computer webcams to enjoy weekly conversations via the Internet, and they stay in daily contact through email. After a few weeks of building their relationship, they begin to realize how important their families and cultures are. They decide that they will have difficulty continuing with their relationship without exploring these more deeply first. Beck travels to Viet Nam to meet Cara's family, and a few weeks later, Cara goes to Sweden and meets Beck's. They realize from these trips just how different the food, music, and customs are in each of their countries. However, they connect strongly with each other's families, and they are confident that they have enough in common to go forward further with their relationship.

In the previous chapter, you explored some sensitive topics, and you continue the process in this one as you explore your differences. Perhaps your partner specializes in a particular ethnic dance that you are unfamiliar with doing. Maybe your partner dances and prays at the same time, while you are used to sitting quietly. Possibly your partner enjoys less lively dances because they are older than you are. If either of your parents are involved, they may like or dislike your dance altogether. If you or your partner has children, they may want to join the dance too. The two of you may then find it difficult to dance together as a result.

It can feel exciting to try out new steps, stretch your skills into new movements, and expand your experience in new directions. It is also a discovery process as you assess just how challenging dancing together might be at times. Is the dance exciting only because it is new and different, or is it really one that you can see yourself doing over a long period of time? Will you dance your partner's favorite style at times, and on other occasions will your partner dance yours? Will you and your partner develop your own unique dance to blend the dances you both know how to do so well?

The shifting of people and the sharing of cultures across an increasingly shrinking planet makes it highly likely that you can be exploring what it is like to be in an intercultural relationship. The cultural diversity between the two of you can provide you with delightful variety and learning, which *help* you to learn how to find points of unity and harmony. You and your partner may need to immerse yourselves in each other's culture to determine exactly how to achieve a harmonious relationship.

As you and your partner strive toward understanding each other, either or both of you may struggle with prejudice, both your own and that of family members and friends. Your character qualities of *patience*, *acceptance*, *respect*, and more will influence your ability to handle the situation constructively.

Other areas than culture may challenge your expectations of a relationship and cause you to assess your assumptions, lifestyle, and beliefs, and how they will affect a relationship. One sensitive area you will explore is your *spiritual* or religious beliefs and practices, if any, and the role they play in your relationship. Whether your relationship is interfaith, same faith, or no faith, *spiritual* questions arise between you and from relatives and friends. You will also consider if there is an impact on your relationship from factors relating to your ages or to any age differences between you. Whether you are younger, older, or one of each, the ages you and your partner are now also affect your present and future choices in a relationship.

Family is also a factor for you to consider. Part of learning about each other will include interacting with parents and determining their role in your relationship. If there are children involved in your relationship, then there are bonds to build with them and concerns about the role of your partner in their lives. The family dance can become very complex.

Working through all of the variety and differences between you and a partner will take *acceptance*, *creativity*, *flexibility*, *tactfulness*, *respect*, and *wisdom*. *Unity* is very possible, if you make that your focus, and strive to find what you have in common and build on it.

UNDERSTANDING DIFFERENCES

Effective practice of character qualities, as you are discovering, is the foundation of a relationship. However, many other aspects about you and your partner can enhance your relationship, or negatively affect its viability. You explored many of these aspects in Chapter 6 when you clarified your expectations, and in Chapter 7 when you identified what is going to be important to you in a partner. **When you have a partner, it is important for you to explore the commonalities and differences between the two of you, and how they affect your relationship.**

It can be a source of *strength* for you and your partner if you have similar values, beliefs, and purposes in life. It does not work if the two of you have your arms in dance position, and then one partner starts dancing the swing, and the other the foxtrot. Very

322 • *Can We Dance? Learning the Steps for a Fulfilling Relationship*

often you can do swing or foxtrot to the same music, but both partners need to be doing the same dance at the same time, if you are dancing together.

Differences between you and your partner may enrich your relationship, if you are willing to learn about them and adapt to them. **Some amount of differences between you and your partner are natural and can work very well. Often they provide excitement, balance, and learning experiences for each other. Understanding the different aspects of each other can be fun, challenging, and complex. At times, however, your differences will cause challenges. Any unexplored and unaccepted differences can be grounds for discord between you and your partner. The more you understand, appreciate, and *accept* each other, the fewer misunderstandings will occur based on your differences.**

When two people from different cultures come together, the relationship may start out as intriguing and fun. You may respond positively to the differences in your partner because they are new and interesting. As time goes on, however, the differences you found fascinating at the beginning of a relationship can cause problems. After a while the novelty wears off, and you or your partner may want to have things a certain way. Will you continue to find a difference just as exciting after you have experienced it over time? Will it continue to be positive, or will it frustrate, annoy, or discourage you? You will be *wise* to be aware that there is a difference between visiting and experiencing a culture on a limited basis rather than connecting to it more regularly.

Even when you and your partner come from the same country or from similar cultures, there can be other differences between you. For instance, if the two of you come from or live at very different socioeconomic levels, or still live with parents, you may approach daily living differently. Perhaps one of you has independent living skills, such as doing laundry, shopping for groceries, cooking, paying bills, and so on, and the other has had someone else look after these responsibilities. One of you might have skills in living on a small amount of money without going into debt, and the other is accustomed to having, spending, and borrowing significant amounts. If you are both open to the possibility, you can learn from each other. As you and your partner learn and gain experience, you will both expand your skills.

Your exploration of each other's lives includes your families, which have their own internal cultures and expectations for behavior. They may have their own ethnic cultures as well. Any time there are two families interacting with each other, there is potential for either clashes or harmony. It will *help* your learning process if you are open and *respectful* when participating in activities with your partner's family. If you and your family are lively and talkative, while your partner's family is cool and reserved, you may choose to modify your words and actions around their family somewhat. However, as you get to know them and they get to know you, your differences can become a source of enrichment, endearment, and amusement.

As you increase your understanding of the differences between you and your partner, your goal is to understand whether they are important factors for your relationship. The question to ask yourself is whether you can maintain *unity* in your relationship with the differences present, and whether you can avoid disunity and avert problems that the two of you cannot resolve. It is unwise to have a significant amount of the time and energy of your relationship focused on communication conflicts that arise from an inability to resolve how the two of you will manage your differences.

You will be happier as a couple with a high level of harmony between the two of you. The skill and effectiveness of the communication between you and your partner will affect your mutual understanding and harmony as a couple and your ability to sustain your relationship. If communication skill building or other supportive efforts do not work, and if your relationship is filled with conflict over your differences, then it is best to assess whether you should be together as a couple.

Note: Be aware that this chapter is only a brief introduction to how to understand and work with differences between you and a partner. If you have a high level of complex differences between the two of you, it is best to explore and learn what else you need to know to support your relationship effectively.

~ Questions for Reflection ~

1. What is my general attitude toward differences between other people and me?
2. What are my perspectives on differences between a partner and me?

ACTIVITY

Spend some time with your family members and determine how you would describe your family to a partner. Consider aspects about them such as their habits, regular activities, ways of communicating, expressions of affection, attitudes toward children, *spiritual* practices, ways of preparing and serving food, and entertainment choices. Be *creative* and develop a way to share your family with a partner. This could include writing a story about them or preparing a photo album with specific photos that reflect the aspects you want to communicate.

CULTURE, ETHNICITY, AND RACE

If your partner is of a different race, nationality, ethnicity, social and economic class, or from a different part of the same country, their culture will be different from yours. **A person's culture determines both their worldview and how they act and react in it.**

According to Joel Crohn, Ph.D., in *Mixed Matches*, differences in culture between you and your partner will affect you and your partner's attitudes toward use of time, family relationships, sex, food, monogamy and faithfulness, how to express anger and affection, ways of disciplining and rewarding children, interactions with strangers and friends, and the roles of men and women, among other things.[1] In addition, people from various cultures or upbringing may communicate differently. For instance, the use of silence may vary, as one person may use silence to express anger, and the other may use it at any time they need to think deeply about a subject.

Being in a relationship with someone of a different culture from yours can be very exciting and interesting. You and your partner each expand your worldviews by learning about each other's culture and thinking more about how your own culture looks at the world. It can be *humbling* to see that you may have picked up an attitude from your culture that it is the best one in the world, and you actually look down on other cultures. **Diverse relationships require their own unique type of preparation for you to create a lasting friendship-based relationship.**

Learning About Your Partner's Culture

You will be *wise* to learn as much as you can about your partner and your partner's culture. You may find it *helps* you to gain increased understanding and appreciation of your partner if you put yourself deliberately into experiences similar to what is familiar to them. You can do this a number of ways. For instance, you can travel to where your partner grew up, or spend time with their family or friends. You can also visit an area where your partner's culture is very clear and *strong*, such as an area of a city where people of the same culture live and gather. If your partner commonly speaks a different language with their family, you may need to learn their original language to understand their communications and take part in them. Reading books, taking courses in intercultural communication, watching movies, or eating at ethnic restaurants that share the culture can also increase your understanding.

As you gain an understanding of the culture of your partner, also keep in mind that more than one culture may have influenced your partner's life. For instance, if your partner's early childhood was in Japan, but they have lived in the United States since, then both cultures will have significant influence in their life. Their own personal culture will be a blend of their Japanese family, as well as the culture of their new neighborhood and the people they became friends with at school growing up. You will need to explore with your partner which culture dominates various aspects of their life. They may not immediately know, since they are accustomed to their own cultural mixture. As you ask your partner questions, however, they will reflect and discuss the topic with their family and friends and respond to you. You will also observe your partner in various circumstances, which will *help* you to understand them better.

As you and your partner spend time together, you will also share your own culture with them in the same ways that you learned about theirs. This may be a difficult task if you happen to be of the majority culture in the country in which you live. Because most people in your surroundings share your culture, you may not know or have ever explained why you do the things you do or think of the world in the way that you do. This will give you an opportunity to examine the things that you feel are truly meaningful to you about your own culture and upbringing.

Culture can be thought of as the glasses through which you view the world. As people who wear glasses can tell you, since they always wear them, sometimes they do not even realize they have them on. You may not actually realize the dramatic influence that your culture has upon how you see the world. "Culture comprises what we feel; what we learn; what we do; who we spend our time with; memories of and preferences for smells, tastes, sounds, and feelings; images and stories we cherish. It is the resource we all draw on when we problem solve, interpret information, plan for the future, assess ourselves and others, and locate ourselves within time and space."[2] For all these reasons you will want to understand your own culture and that of your partner, and see how the two cultures affect the ways you and your partner view the world and respond to it.

It will be *helpful* to you and your partner to discuss in detail what each of you thinks, feels, and believes about the following aspects of your lives as part of your cultures:

- Attitude toward family
- Relationships with parents
- Relationships with children
- Roles of women and men
- Socio-economic status
- Fundamental communication skills
- Physical hygiene/body fitness
- Your own and other people's race, ethnicity, or culture
- Role of religion
- Physical ability
- Importance of education
- Importance of employment/career
- Money/finances
- Political convictions
- Clothing/manner of dress
- People at different ages, such as teens and elders

You will discuss both your differences and commonalities in your responses to each of these, and you will likely discover other aspects to explore as well. As you examine the commonalities between the two of you, which ones *encourage* you to feel hopeful about the future of your relationship? Which differences raise concerns? How will you address them? What opportunities are there for practicing *acceptance*?

Consider how this couple is doing their cultural exploration:

Shane, a tall, slim man with blonde hair and blue eyes, grew up in Ireland with his parents, who moved to Canada when he was 16 years old. While attending college in Canada, he meets Kessie, a wonderful dark-skinned woman from Ghana attending school on an international scholarship. Both are active in student government and *service* activities on campus, and they become close friends. Because they are becoming serious about each other, they decide to use their summer break to travel to Ireland and Ghana to learn about each other's culture and meet family members.

Throughout their experiences on the trip, they learn how completely different their lives have been, something that was quite masked because they met in a different country. Kessie grew up in a tiny village and knew everyone there, while Shane spent his childhood in the city of Dublin. Kessie was home-schooled with her brother and sister, while Shane attended a Catholic school with other children of factory workers. Kessie's family practices a mixture of native beliefs and Christianity taught to them by missionaries. Shane's family is actively Catholic. After seeing their differences, they both realize that they need more time to understand each other and *discern* how their backgrounds can affect their relationship in the future.

If you and your partner were raised in very different ways, it will take *courtesy, flexibility*, and *patience* to understand each other, and learn of your commonalities as fellow human beings. It may require *perseverance* to *discern* whether the differences you find will divide you, or whether your commonalities will be *strong* enough so that you can stay together in *unity* and harmony.

Other Factors for Success

The same process of learning, appreciation, and *acceptance* will occur with the friends and relatives you and your partner have, who may initially express discomfort or prejudice. They may or may not adjust and *accept* you and your partner over time. **If those around you are experiencing mixed reactions to you as a couple, it may be a good time to remind others to focus on character as a more important element in your relationship than your races or cultures.** "Our differences are the source of learning and creativity in all of our important relationships, and learning to recognize, appreciate, and use these differences are the keys to enriching family life."[3]

Discussing how you each view humanity as a whole will *help* you and your partner to put the cultural differences in your relationship in perspective. You can also discuss how your cultures or races fit into this global view. If you regard humanity as one family, you will see that "...the various races of human kind lend a composite harmony and beauty of color to the whole."[4] If either of you do not have this viewpoint, you are more likely to see cultural or racial differences as a significant problem between you. The same dynamic applies to your families, who could be *accepting* or prejudiced about differences between the two of you.

A number of factors can support the success of an intercultural or interracial relationship. These are:

1. Commitment to the relationship
2. Ability to communicate
3. Sensitivity to each other's needs
4. A liking for the other's culture
5. Flexibility
6. Solid, positive self-image
7. Love as the main [relationship] motive
8. Common goals
9. Spirit of adventure
10. Sense of humor[5]

~ *Questions for Reflection* ~

1. What do I consider unique about my own culture?
2. What are my thoughts and emotions when I think about having a partner who was raised in a culture different from my own?
3. What will I be willing to do to learn about a partner's culture?

Understanding Prejudice

One area for you and your partner to explore is any history of feeling prejudice or experiencing it from others. "…[P]rejudice…is an unquestioned emotional attachment to a falsehood that is assumed to be the truth. In other words, it is an emotional commitment to ignorance."[6] It can cause subtle negative actions and reactions to occur between you and your partner.

Even if you believe that everyone around the planet is a human being worthy of *respect*, you may have picked up subtle negative attitudes from people around you who are prejudiced, or who are angry that others have discriminated against them. You must be vigilant in eliminating these attitudes, and even the momentary thoughts of prejudice or superiority that cross your mind. If you do not, you may prevent yourself from initiating or sustaining an interracial or intercultural relationship.

Honestly examine whether you have a partner of another race or culture just to prove that you are not prejudiced. Are you responding positively to your partner because you believe they fit a cultural stereotype, and you have not verified its accuracy with your partner? For example, you can be assuming that all people of a certain race are hard workers, financially responsible, very sexual, or fun loving. Your relationship will be difficult if you have a bias and see your partner as a representative of their race, rather than as an *equal* and unique human being.

It will also be useful for you to understand the potential for prejudiced responses that others may have toward both you and your partner, and agree between you how you will both handle them. Either you or your partner may be more sensitive to others' prejudiced words or actions and *help* the other to see and understand them. If you are clear that you and your partner are receiving prejudiced reactions from people, then agree on the character qualities you will use in responding. These can include *kindness, courage, forgiveness, love,* or *justice,* depending on the circumstances. *Honest* and *loving* discussions between you and your partner will assist the two of you to understand the complexities of interactions that are occurring.

ACTIVITIES

1. Complete **Worksheet 13.1: Exploring Culture, Ethnicity, and Race in Your Relationship**. You can complete the whole worksheet with a partner, or only complete part of it and then finish it when you do have a partner.

2. Go to an area with couples and families from different cultures and races. Bring a camera to take photos of the variety of people you see (with their permission). Then, *create* a display, slide show, or collage with the photos. Reflect on your responses to the images. Share them with a partner or your friends and family and observe their responses. Do they say anything that seems like prejudice? When you look at the photos, what do you notice someone doing that is different from the way you would do it? What do you appreciate about the people you are observing? What draws you toward or closer to them? What causes you to want to move away?

3. Visit an area near you where the residents and business owners are from a race or country other than your own. If you have a partner of a different race or culture, then choose an area that will *help* you to learn about them. Assess what you experienced and learned from a brief visit. What would you need to do to learn more about a culture?

SPIRITUAL HARMONY

There are many *spiritual* and religious beliefs and practices in the world. You or your partner may be following one or more of them, or this may not be a significant part of your life. **It is important for the two of you to discuss your views about *spirituality* and its role in your lives and relationship. If you hold different beliefs, then it is also *wise* to assess whether you can be in a harmonious relationship together and not have problems with each other's *spiritual* beliefs or practices.**

Spiritual bonding can be a *unifying* factor in your relationship, whether it is a common belief in a Higher Power, a particular faith, or some shared *spiritual* practice. Defining and growing that bond together, and agreeing upon its level of importance in your lives, is an important aspect of building relationship intimacy.

You may discover that it is difficult, if not impossible, to maintain an interfaith relationship, if your individual beliefs seem too different. This is especially the case if you slip into thinking that you believe what is best or right, and that your partner is inappropriate or wrong (or your partner does the same to you). **However, different beliefs are not necessarily a barrier to a**

relationship, if you and your partner are committed to finding points of *unity* together. If you can both focus on a common guiding force and source of inspiration, this can hold you together in *unity*. You may be able to pray together, attend each other's worship services, attend interfaith gatherings, and *respectfully* discuss your *spiritual* perspectives. As your relationship develops, you will need to determine if you can build a relationship around common beliefs or a *spiritual* focus.

Various *spiritual* or religious practices can also be factors in your relationship exploration. As you assess how your individual practices affect you and your partner now, also think ahead to the possibility of marriage. Practices can include dietary restrictions, days of worship, ways of dressing, views on contraception, expectations of raising and educating children, parental consent for marriage, and more. Think about the beliefs and practices in each of your families as well, and understand the impact of these on your relationship.

Even if you seem to have similar beliefs and practices, you will still be *wise* to explore thoroughly the many aspects of *spirituality* and religion and their impact on your relationship. If you are members of the same faith or congregation, it is a pitfall to make assumptions about each other's beliefs or *spiritual* practices. For instance, you might assume that because you are of the same faith, you will pray together every day. "Who believe in the Unseen, are steadfast in prayer…."[7] Your partner, however, may prefer to pray alone. And this is just one detail. Within one religion, you can have different denominations or sects and wide-ranging philosophies and interpretations of scripture, as well as differing religious practices. Once you then understand each other's perspectives, you can look for what you have in common and assess the *strength* these have in supporting your *unity* as a couple.

You or your partner could be uncertain about what to believe. Perhaps, the two of you do not belong to a religion, but you still have personal *spiritual* practices. Maybe you are investigating different options. One or both of you may regard yourselves as members of a religion, but struggle with practicing all of its beliefs. Often people have *spiritual* or religious beliefs and practices they follow out of habit or custom. It is better to know in your heart for yourself why you believe what you do because you searched for and discovered it for yourself. Likewise, you can *encourage* your partner to find their own answers, so that they know why they believe what they do. This process of discovery can become an exciting journey to travel together as a couple.

As you share what you each believe and listen to each other, it is *wise* to maintain your openness and minimize any prejudiced responses, so you can *carefully* listen to your partner's viewpoints. You will practice *acceptance*, *courtesy*, and *respect* in this process. You may even find that this discussion allows you to clarify your own beliefs.

Whatever your beliefs, you may regard your use of character qualities as a *spiritual* practice, because the world's religious scriptures all *encourage* character development. **However, do not assume that simply because someone is or claims to be *spiritual* or religious that they have a good character.** You still have to be thorough in observing and understanding a partner's character qualities.

ACTIVITIES

1. **Worksheet 13.2: Spiritual Exploration** gives you an opportunity to explore your beliefs and practices and how they might affect a relationship. This worksheet is primarily for you and a partner to complete and discuss. If you do not have a partner, simply read it so that you know what topic areas to consider when you are in a relationship, and complete it at that time. Some of your beliefs may not match the questions. If not, then simply answer those that apply to you.

2. If you want to explore *spiritual* practices that are different from your own, then attend a meeting or services of your partner's religious or *spiritual* community, or invite your partner to attend yours. You can also attend a different meeting or worship service with a friend or relative. Reflect on your responses to the experience. What new perspectives did you gain?

3. Plan and carry out a devotional/prayer gathering for friends and family, or spontaneously pray with another (willing) person. This can be very easy and simple. Perhaps you and friends can gather and pray for a sick friend or relative, you can pray with someone going through a difficult experience, or you and your partner can pray to express *thankfulness* for a blessing.

4. Practice accurately explaining to a partner or friend your understanding of their beliefs. Pause so they can share any corrections or new information with you.

~ *Questions for Reflection* ~

1. How can a partner and I maintain harmony in our discussions about differing beliefs?
2. What role do religion and *spiritual* philosophies have in my life? What role do I want them to have in a partner's life? In our interactions as a couple?
3. What *spiritual* practices do I want to have in common with a partner?

AGE AS A RELATIONSHIP FACTOR

You may meet and feel attracted to people of many different ages. You may consider age as completely irrelevant, and you believe that if your partner is older or younger than you are, it makes no difference. On the other hand, you might consider that when you were born and the years you have lived through have shaped you in significant ways. As a result, you may want a partner who has lived through the same decades and similar experiences as you. People often tend to react judgmentally toward couples where there is a large age gap, but the decision on this is ultimately up to you and your partner. **Time likely affects your bodies more than your hearts and souls.** How important is your partner's age to you?

If there are decades, rather than years, between you and your partner, and you choose to be together a long time or marry, eventually you will have challenges with one of you aging, having serious physical illness, or dying earlier than the other. You will want to consider the impact of this on you and on any children you have together. If the older partner already has children from a previous relationship, those children may be close in age to the younger partner. This closeness may work well, or it could be awkward or contentious.

Older Couples

With or without an age gap, if you are in a serious relationship at an older age, you and your partner have a number of issues to assess for their potential impact. Evaluate the importance of the following factors considering their impact on both of you at all relationship stages, including looking forward to the possibility of marriage:

- Involvement with families from previous relationships
- Financial support going to a former spouse or to support a child
- Ability to have sex
- Ability to conceive a child
- Expectations from the partner or relationship
- Time priorities that direct focus on career, family, and/or time together
- Unresolved emotional issues from the past
- Fears about failing at new relationships
- The response of previous children
- The stage of your grieving process from a previous relationship
- Effect of aging bodies and minds
- Sharing long-held possessions and money
- Caretaking or involvement with older parents
- Rigid habits and behavior patterns that are less likely to change

No person or relationship is perfect, however, and it may be worth going through some challenges to have a great companion.

"WHEN I WAS 15, MY PARENTS SAID I COULD DATE WHEN I'M 16.
WHEN I WAS 16, MY PARENTS SAID I COULD DATE WHEN I'M 17.
TO MAKE A LONG STORY SHORT, JIM, CALL BACK NEXT YEAR."

Encouraging each other and *accepting* each other's imperfections while you learn and grow together, can make it possible for you and your partner to engage in a variety of activities and *service* to others, whatever your age.

Younger Couples

On the other hand, if you are still a teenager, the amount of involvement you have with someone, the wishes of your parents, and your maturity in being able to handle all aspects of relationships are factors to consider. **This is a great time to develop your friendships and learn relationship and observation skills.** Through school and social activities, you will meet new people and have the opportunity to develop *strong* and lasting friendships with many of them. It is best to avoid being in an exclusive relationship at this stage, especially as a younger teen. It is also wise to avoid being in a close relationship with someone who is significantly older than you are. You will have years of maturing to do to catch up to them mentally, emotionally, and physically.

When you are a teenager there are a number of important factors to consider. Your hormones, reasoning abilities, knowledge, experiences, and maturity are changing rapidly, and these can affect how dramatically you respond to someone. You may observe that your emotions are very intense toward a potential partner or partner one day, and cool toward them the next. Intense feelings may also increase your desire to be physically or sexually intimate with a partner. You may believe that the relationship will be lasting because of these feelings, only to discover it is brief. Remember that sexual intimacy will change your relationship, and change the way you view each other. It can interfere with the development of a friendship, the ability to see a partner's character clearly, and put you at risk for pregnancy, infections, or diseases. While you might think sex will draw you closer to a partner, it will more likely introduce you to issues that you are not prepared to handle (Chapter 5).

During your teen years, it is *wise* to avoid putting your energy into the development of a relationship, but instead focus on group activities, such as athletics, clubs, religious youth groups, Scouts, community *service*, or whatever is available in your area. If you do not have appropriate activities available, then you can take individual initiative and begin something for you and your friends, probably with the assistance of a *helpful* adult, teacher, or parent. Group activities will give you many opportunities to build friendship, communication, observation, and relationship skills.

~ Questions for Reflection ~

1. What are the benefits and problems of a significant age difference between a partner and me?
2. What are the benefits and problems with having a relationship in one's teens? Over age 20? Over age 30? 40? 50? 60? 70? 80? Higher?
3. What are the advantages of having a relationship at the age I am at now?

ROLE OF PARENTS

Every person, family, culture, and faith has a different view about how involved parents can and should be in the relationships of their children. Parental involvement also varies according to your age, the laws of the country where you live, the teachings of any religion you or your parents are members of, and your experience with relationships.

Some parents, faiths, and cultures favor complete parental control over the choice of a partner and all the couple's activities prior to marriage. Others leave the choice of a partner and the development of the relationship completely in the couple's hands. You may wish to consider a *moderate* balance between these two perspectives.

Parental Guidance and Boundaries

Parental input can be valuable at any age. However, it is especially important for young people in their teens and twenties, who are still forming their characters and their views on the world. If you are at this age, you and your partner can benefit from seeking guidance from your parents and other mature people in your life, particularly if you are considering marriage. Research shows that your brain does not fully develop until age

25, especially the frontal lobe that affects the ability to develop strategies, plan for the future, regulate emotions, and look at situations from others' perspectives.[8] This does not mean that you have to be 25 to choose a partner. It does mean, however, that if you are under this age, it is even more important that you involve your parents and learn key relationship-building and communication skills.

Being successful in a relationship requires that you use your knowledge, best judgment, character qualities, and follow your beliefs about what is right. You will be *wise* to consider any *thoughtful* advice that your parents wish to give in this process. *Ideally*, they know you well, have your best interests in mind, and are part of your support system. The more harmony you can maintain with your parents, the better it will be for you and your partner as a couple over time. This is especially *true* if you or your partner have children, and your parents wish to have a positive relationship with their grandchildren. Often the roots of family disunity can stem from a lack of understanding and compatibility between a partner and your parents.

When you do seek your parent's assistance or guidance in finding a partner, or ask them to give you input about a relationship, it will be useful for you to establish a set of fair boundaries with them. For instance, it may not be reasonable to give your parents the right to interfere or pressure you with your choices, especially when you are simply exploring a friendship or relationship with someone.

Parental pressure on you to move toward or away from someone can cause problems between you and your parents, and possibly urge you to make hasty or unwise decisions about a partner. You certainly do not want to jump forward into a serious relationship with someone before you are ready. Nor will you want to end a relationship prematurely that is starting on a positive foundation.

Parental guidance and involvement can be very necessary, however, in certain circumstances. These can include you being under your parents' legal guardianship, and you are engaged in risky or illegal behavior, such as underage drinking or sex. Parents will be involved if you are living with them, or if your wellbeing and safety are at risk.

Even when it is *wise* and *helpful* to consider your parents' opinions and *accept* guidance that they offer you, it will take *courteous* and *respectful* negotiation with them to determine how much authority they will have over your choice of a partner. If their will is very *strong* in wanting you to end a relationship when they disapprove, you will want to consider their feelings and understand their concerns.

Whatever your circumstances, how you interact with your parents and concerned family and friends will give you opportunities to call upon the best use of all your communication skills and character qualities, especially *love* and *respect*.

Challenges to Address

You and your parents may have to agree on specific issues for you and your partner to address in your lives before your parents will *encourage* you to go forward as a couple. For instance, perhaps they want you to finish college before being in a serious relationship or considering marriage. Maybe they have concerns about your partner's ability to hold a job, be faithful, or be a good parent. In extreme instances, you may have to decide between *loyalty* to your parent's authority and *loyalty* to the relationship. Are you willing to risk the relationship with your parents if it comes to that? Are they being unreasonable, or are you being unreasonable? What will be the consequences of each choice? Perhaps *respectful* discussion can keep *peace* in your family.

Depending on their culture and beliefs, your parents may consider their relationship with you as very personal and private. Alternatively, they could be open to considering a discussion involving you, your partner, and your partner's parents about what is best for your relationship. Because your relationship does not exist in isolation, consider that what you do affects your parents, and the same in reverse. An important part of *creating* relationships that succeed, therefore, is including parents in your relationship process wherever appropriate. Consider how it could work:

Talia grew up in Israel, and Len grew up in Norway. In their late teens, both of their families moved to a large city in Australia. They meet at school, and as new students in an unfamiliar place, they form a bond. As they get to know each other in their classes and in the breaks, they become close friends and want to date each other. Talia's parents are protective of their daughter, however. They have definite ideas of who she should have relationships with, and Len does not match them.

The couple considers rebelling and sneaking around behind her parents' backs. Instead, they decide to discuss the situation with Len's parents, as they are supportive of the relationship. They ask his parents for assistance in talking to Talia's parents. Their four parents meet with Talia and Len for dinner at her parent's home.

It is awkward at first, as none of them have ever been in this situation before. After awhile, however, they warm up to each other and begin to talk about Talia and Len. They each share what they see as good points about the friendship between the couple, and they discuss their concerns. Talia's parents have the opportunity to express their fears about their daughter—will she focus too much on the relationship and fail at school, and will she convert to Len's religion and abandon her own.

Len's parents explain to Talia's parents that they have raised their son to *love* and *respect* all faiths, and Len assures them that he will never pressure Talia to convert. After the evening of getting to know each other, her parents' attitudes soften. They agree to her involvement with Len with clear boundaries that balance their relationship and *responsibilities*. Talia *commits* to raising her grades as part of the discussion. Talia and Len both assure their parents that they *love* and *respect* them.

Family Interactions

As you and your partner interact with your parents, it is important to look at the bigger picture of your lifetime goals. If you someday marry this person, then giving your parents the opportunity to know your partner's character and build their own relationship with them will support you in the long term. If you give your family the opportunity to be involved early on, it will be much easier for them to continue to provide family support when you may really need it during the normal challenges that arise in life and relationships.

As you, your partner, and your families spend time together, you can observe:

- Which character qualities you and your partner use effectively in your interactions with your families
- Which character qualities you see your parents and your partner's parents using effectively with the two of you and each other
- How your partner resembles their parents in behavior and attitudes
- How your partner resembles your own parents in behavior and attitudes
- Whether you are drawn to positive or negative aspects of your partner because they remind you of familiar aspects in either of your parents
- How the parents handle differences of opinion and decision-making
- Your level of affinity for people who could be your in-laws in the future
- Your partner's expectations about your relationships with both your parents and theirs, and your expectations about these as well

As you make these observations, discuss them with your partner. If you have any concerns to share, remember to be sensitive and *tactful*. It may be difficult for your partner to see and understand your concerns, and they could become defensive about their family. The same could happen if your partner raises with you a concern that they have about your family interactions. **Remember that you have two goals while spending time with parents and other relatives. One is thorough exploration of your viability as a couple, and the other is building family unity wherever possible.**

ACTIVITY

Have a meal with your parents or plan some other activity that will build harmony between you and them. If you have a partner, invite them to come. If you have a partner who has parents, invite them to come, or have a separate meal with them. Set a personal goal for the occasion to ask for guidance on a particular topic or issue. You can also take the opportunity to practice your observation skills by identifying key character qualities in your parents, your partner, or the parents of your partner. Some likely ones for you to spot are *helpfulness*, *courtesy*, or *cooperation*.

~ Questions for Reflection ~

1. What role do my parents play in my friendships and relationships? Am I in agreement with their approach? Can I influence it to improve?
2. What input and guidance do I need and/or want from my parents?
3. What boundaries do I need or want to set with my parents to prevent inappropriate interference?

WHEN THERE ARE CHILDREN

If you are a young couple with no children, the subject of having children can probably wait until you know each other very well, and you are beginning to discuss a future together. However, if you already have children, or if you are older and want to have children before it is unlikely to happen smoothly, it makes sense to talk about the subject of children earlier in your relationship. You and your partner may be in different frames of mind on the subject of children or in different life situations. Either or both of you may have children already. One of you may want more children, and the other does not. One of you may see stepparenting as a possibility in the future, and the other is uncertain. All of these are vital to clarify and eventually come to agreement about.

If you already have children, when appropriate, you will introduce them to your partner. It will be a problem if you become involved with someone and then discover that your partner and your children cannot get along at all. It will also be difficult if you find out after you have invested a lot of time in a relationship that your partner has no interest in becoming a stepparent to your children in the future. **It is important to make certain that you share the information about your role as a parent and your expectations for your children's interactions with your partner as soon as possible.** It will not take long to determine if parenthood is an unmovable obstacle in your relationship. In this case, do not hesitate to end it.

It is essential to take your children's feelings, needs, and concerns *respectfully* into consideration when you are going out socially. If they are young, you will arrange for a *responsible* caregiver for them. Deciding what you will say to your children about your social life away from the house is something that will take empathy, *compassion*, fairness, and sensitivity to their needs.

Children raised in a single parent household can respond to you having a partner in a number of ways. They can quickly become attached to any friend or partner that you bring into their lives. Alternatively, they may withhold their involvement until they see if the person will stay around, and therefore may *strongly* resist building any kind of rapport with your partner. They may see having positive interactions with your partner as disloyalty to their other parent.

If your children become attached to your partner, and your relationship does not work out, they will be hurt. It may be difficult for them to become close to a future partner as a result. You may inadvertently teach them that relationships do not last. A relationship ending can especially reinforce this view if they have already experienced a divorce, the death of a parent, or a parent leaving them.

Because of the complexity of this situation, it is a difficult judgment call whether to find out quickly if everyone gets along, as mentioned above, or choose to be sure your relationship is going well before you introduce your children to your partner. Even though you are not married, you and your partner may find it useful to obtain counseling or information about getting along in stepfamilies. [An excellent source of information is www.saafamilies.org.]

It will make sense that part of the character exploration you do with your partner includes identifying the qualities that you will want in a potential stepparent for your children. You will also notice the effect your new partner has upon your children and the same in reverse. Does your partner bring out your children's best character qualities? What character qualities do your children bring out in your partner? If you ask them, your children will more than likely be a great source of feedback to you about whether they approve or disapprove of this new person in your life and why.

Interactions between children and partners can be difficult, depending on the attitude of everyone involved. If you have given your children a good reason to feel jealous or abandoned by your new relationship, they may automatically disapprove of it. However, if you have given them reason to feel *accepted* and included in it, you will find that they are usually *faithful* observers and supporters of their parent's happiness over time. *Courage, courtesy, respect, patience,* and *love* will all aid the process.

If your children are adults, they will be less directly involved in any relationships you have, yet they may be better prepared to offer you feedback than if they were young children. Moreover, it makes sense and is *courteous* to introduce them to your partner if your relationship becomes serious. Any possible expansion to the family has an emotional impact on all its members, regardless of whether you still live with them or their ages.

~ Questions for Reflection ~

1. What are the needs of my children as I participate in a relationship? How can I be sure those needs are met? How will I set priorities if my children's needs seem to conflict with my needs?
2. What considerations do I need to have for a partner's children?
3. What relationship am I willing and able to build with a partner's children?
4. What do I visualize as the relationship a partner will have with my children? How might that relationship be affected by the children's other parent(s)?

ACTIVITY

If you have a partner, plan and carry out an activity that builds *unity* between you, your partner, and any children you both have. Refer back to Chapter 9 for some ideas if needed. If you do not yet have a partner, choose a good friend who is a parent, and do the activity with them. Use the opportunity to observe character qualities and practice building *unity* among those participating.

✎ Encouragement ✍

Relationships focus on togetherness and unity, so it may have been challenging to explore differences in this chapter. You are courageous to engage in this effort. You are doing a great job of keeping "both eyes open™" and building your knowledge and skills. This is a good time to do something to celebrate diversity.

Date: _____

Worksheet 13.1: Exploring Culture, Ethnicity, and Race in Your Relationship

This worksheet will assist you to describe your experiences and perceptions about cultural, ethnic, and racial diversity. If you have a partner, then you can invite them to answer these questions separately from you. Then you can discuss both sets of answers together.

Instructions:

A) Complete the sentences below.

B) Share your answers with others who have culture, ethnicity, or race in common with you, and discuss them to verify their accuracy. Then share the answers with someone who is from a different culture, ethnicity, and race, and encourage them to ask questions. Include any additional insights or notes on your worksheet.

1. I describe my family's culture, race, and ethnicity as:

   _____

   _____

   _____

2. I describe the culture of my society or the area where I live or come from as:

   _____

   _____

   _____

3. Some unique features, beliefs, behaviors, or expectations of my culture, ethnicity, and race are:

   _____

   _____

   _____

4. I most appreciate these aspects of my culture, ethnicity, and race:

   _____

   _____

   _____

5. My culture, ethnicity, and race are likely to affect my partner in this way:

   _____

   _____

   _____

6. My experiences with expressions of prejudice toward me, reacting in a prejudiced way to others, or observing expressions of prejudice are:

_____

_____

_____

_____

7. Prejudice has affected me in this way:

_____

_____

_____

_____

8. If my partner is of a different culture, ethnicity, or race from my own, this is how I will learn about it:

_____

_____

_____

_____

9. I appreciate cultural, ethnic, or racial diversity for these reasons:

_____

_____

_____

_____

10. If my partner or I experience prejudice because of our relationship, I will respond in the following ways:

_____

_____

_____

_____

11. If my partner or I experience prejudice because of our relationship, I would want my partner to respond in the following ways:

_____

_____

_____

_____

Date: _____

Worksheet 13.2: Spiritual Exploration

This worksheet will assist you to explore your views of and experiences with spirituality and religion, as well as how any beliefs you hold and practices that you do can affect a relationship. If you have a partner, then discuss your answers with them. If your partner is willing, have them answer the questions separately, and then you can discuss your answers together. Even if you have little or no experience with spirituality or religion, it is wise to complete this worksheet, as these topics will likely come up with a partner and their family at some point.

Instructions:

A) Answer the questions in sections 1 and 2 if you do not have a partner, and answer all three sections if you do have one.

B) If you do not yet have a partner, then return to section 3 when you do.

Section 1: Beliefs and Practices

1. Do I consider spirituality or religion a high, medium, or low priority in my life? How does the priority differ from what it was as I was growing up? If I have a partner, what priority do they give spirituality or religion in their life?

   _____

   _____

2. What, if any, are my primary spiritual or religious beliefs?

   _____

   _____

3. What, if any, are my regular spiritual or religious practices, responsibilities, and involvement? (Consider prayer, meditation, reading, worship, teaching others...)

   _____

   _____

4. Do I believe in God or some kind of Supreme Being? Why or why not?

   _____

   _____

5. What is my family's attitude toward my beliefs and practices?

   _____

   _____

6. What is my attitude toward others' religious or spiritual beliefs?

   _____

   _____

Section 2: Spiritual Challenges

1. What shows that I am being faithful to my beliefs? What helps me to stay faithful to what I believe?

    _____

    _____

2. Have I ever felt estranged from God, my religion, or my spiritual faith? Why? Did I resolve this? If so, how? How do I feel about it now? If I have a partner, what does my partner think and feel about my struggles?

    _____

    _____

3. Are there any teachings of my own belief system or religious faith that I struggle with or have difficulty understanding, accepting, or following? What are these, and what are the issues?

    _____

    _____

4. Are there any religious laws or teachings that are part of my partner's belief system or religion that I seriously struggle to accept? What are these, and what are the issues?

    _____

    _____

5. Am I angry at a Supreme Being or a spiritual or religious leader? Why? If I am, do I use that as a reason to turn away from having spirituality as part of my life? How will I resolve this issue?

    _____

    _____

Section 3: Beliefs and Practices with a Partner

Answer these questions if you currently have a partner; otherwise, return to this section of the worksheet when you do.

1. What beliefs and practices do my partner and I have in common?

    _____

    _____

2. What are our differences in beliefs? Do any of these differences present a problem to me? To my partner? How will we handle these differences?

    _____

    _____

3. If my partner and I are following different religions or sets of beliefs, what are they? What are the implications of this for our relationship? How do I feel about not being able to share the same faith practices?

   _____

   _____

4. What are my attitudes toward my partner's spiritual life? How do I view their commitment to their beliefs? Their commitment to being involved in serving their faith community, if they have one? To sharing or teaching others about their beliefs?

   _____

   _____

5. How do my partner's family and friends view my religion, spiritual beliefs, or lack of either of these? Am I happy with their attitude? Is their attitude causing a problem for me? If so, in what way?

   _____

   _____

6. What activities have my partner and I engaged in to get to know each other in a spiritual setting? Outside of one? Do we need to do more in either category to reach a balance? What will we do?

   _____

   _____

7. Will my partner likely include or exclude me with their activities? How do I feel about this? Would my partner and I attend each other's religious or spiritual events or services? Why or why not? Which ones?

   _____

   _____

8. If my partner chooses to change their beliefs, what character qualities and attitudes will assist me to accept this change?

   _____

   _____

9. What other spiritual or religious issues are on our minds?

   _____

   _____

   _____

   _____

Unified Movement: Preventing Communication Missteps

Talisha and Drew have been getting to know each other for the last few months after meeting through a matchmaking website. Lately, however, they keep having serious arguments. Drew makes commitments that have him spending less time with Talisha, and he does not discuss these with her beforehand. Talisha makes negative comments about Drew's job taking up too much of his time, his involvement in too many activities, and him not looking after his yard and home adequately. Drew yells at Talisha for trying to manage his life. They are both frustrated and unhappy with what is happening, but they are not sure how to change it. They still value the reasons they had for starting the relationship, and they do not want to lose it. They decide to seek help from a relationship coach. One of his recommendations is for them to reconnect to their memories of happier times when their relationship worked well and repeat their positive behavior from that time. With his help, they also learn some new communication skills.

You and your partner may need to remind each other occasionally, and even more on bad days, that you are partners and not opponents, friends and allies and not enemies and adversaries. Partnership is a personal choice you and your partner make so that you both build your relationship upon *unity, friendliness, cooperation*, and mutual reassurance. Your lives and attitude toward each other will then be happier and more *peaceful*.

Self-discipline and sensitivity *help* you to dance well with each other as a team. Together you must move to changes in the tempo and rhythm of the music. If you are off balance, it will have an effect upon your partner. Learning to dance requires controlling your own movements, as well as the ability to be sensitive to your partner's changes in direction, position, balance, and length of steps. Of course, there will be slips, stumbling, or getting off the rhythm at times. However, when you are skilled dancers who know how to maintain *unity*, you can gracefully recover as partners. Then you can both make the transition from missteps to smooth dancing. Others watching you may hardly know you stumbled. You quickly find your balance and footing again and continue dancing.

The same themes hold *true* in your communications with your partner. You need to know some of the basic techniques, and you learned many of them in Chapters 11-13. In this chapter, you will gain greater insights into how you can prevent or minimize relationship missteps or dissension. An important part of this prevention is ensuring that you avoid misusing character qualities. Therefore, you will learn more about how these happen and why. You will also identify and address a number of unwise communication habits that you may have developed that can disrupt a relationship.

Ideally, you and your partner will practice and develop communication skills together. However, your partner may be reluctant to participate for a variety of reasons. Perhaps they feel as if you are forcing the matter, or it does not fit with their cultural upbringing. Someone may have criticized their ability to communicate, or they feel unsure about their communication skills. But, remember, the more you learn on your own, the better you can support and model the techniques and *encourage* or influence your partner to use similar skills. Do you remember the butterfly effect discussed in Chapter 3? Every change you make, no matter how small, will affect your partner.

COMMUNICATION CHALLENGES

It is unlikely that you will enter a relationship expecting it to be full of problems. In fact, you probably hope that it is filled with *joy*, companionship, and excitement. However, you may instead discover that you and your partner argue or disagree about many aspects of life and your relationship. Perhaps you do not understand why this is happening, or what is causing it to happen. This section outlines some of the common communication problems that couples have. It also presents some ways for addressing those problems skillfully and to keep your relationship intact.

Patterns and Methods

Throughout your respective lives, both you and your partner learned and practiced many ways of communicating. Your communications reflect either your higher or your lower nature (Chapter 1). You can be positive or negative, praising or attacking, agreeable or argumentative. Your methods can be loud, soft, dramatically expressive, or calm. You communicate in ways that you observed in parents, siblings, friends, teachers, coworkers, partners, and others. Some of these methods are probably healthy and constructive, while others may be poor habits. If you continue learning and practicing, your communication skills will increase and improve.

If you expect your partner to communicate in the same way that you learned to do while you were growing up, it will lead to misunderstandings and problems. For instance, one of you may fear that your relationship will fall apart if the two of you seriously disagree about something. The other might feel that the relationship is not healthy or interesting if there is not an occasional loud disagreement. One may see arguing as healthy debate, and the other may see arguing as what caused the breakup of a parent's marriage. It is important for you to share and discuss your communication expectations with your partner. Doing so will provide an opportunity to determine what your mutual styles are, and what will be realistic in your interactions.

Sensitivity

Communication in a close relationship can be emotionally challenging at times. You will soon discover what topics are sensitive ones. If you do not *carefully* pay attention to what each other says, you may unintentionally hurt each other's feelings. This communication mishap is like stepping on your dance partner's toes. You may use harmful words that accidentally—or intentionally—make your partner upset. If this occurs, you can assess your motives and use of character qualities. Remember that you do not want to hurt someone you *love*. It will be appropriate to apologize as well.

While much of what your partner says will be positive, sometimes what they say can prompt you to feel sad, angry, or frustrated. All this can make you occasionally wonder whether it is easier to just stay silent. However, it is better to say what is on your mind with *tact* and *wisdom* and continue developing your communication skills, character qualities, and sensitivity to your partner's needs. The *Tanakh* says, "A gentle response allays wrath; a harsh word provokes anger. … A healing tongue is a tree of life…."[1]

Sharing and Sabotaging

If you regularly suppress your thoughts and emotions, and do not share them with your partner, both of you will likely become very unhappy and frustrated. You can then begin behaving negatively toward each other. If you do not speak up, your partner will have no idea what is wrong. At times, a buildup of suppressed thoughts and emotions can explode as excessive anger and damage your relationship. Whenever you or your partner seem to stop sharing, *gentle* and *loving encouragement* can *help* it to resume.

John M. Gottman, Ph.D., and his team at the Relationship Research Institute in Seattle, Washington (USA), have discovered a number of indicators that warn of a relationship beginning to deteriorate. The research

Leo, are you suppressing your emotions again?

focuses on married couples, but the findings are also valuable for unmarried couples to be aware of, especially as they relate to communication. Your communication patterns as a couple begin to form as soon as your relationship begins.

The warning signs are:

1. Starting interactions negatively and harshly
2. Being critical of your partner's character (character attack)
3. Showing contempt for your partner
4. Being defensive with each other (a form of blame)
5. Withdrawal to avoid communication, thereby shutting your partner out (stonewalling)
6. Strong and overwhelming physical responses to negativity (flooding), such as increased heart rate, blood pressure, or sweating
7. Many attempts at repairing the relationship have failed
8. You have only bad memories in your relationship and no good ones[2]

You can prevent most of problems on the list above if you use the communication practices in Chapter 11, such as careful listening, watching your tone of voice, using Character Quality Language, and offering *encouragement*.

~ Questions for Reflection ~

1. What are some of the negative ways that I communicate? How do people respond to these?
2. What was the communication style like in my home growing up? Did I learn any good communication habits there? Poor habits? What am I doing or going to do to change the poor ones?

CHARACTER AND COMMUNICATION

If you think about what you have been learning about character throughout the book, you can begin to see just how destructive a character attack on your partner can be. Look at these examples:

"You should have paid your bills. You are so **irresponsible**!"

"Where were you? You were late picking me up! I can't **trust** you to do anything right!"

These examples are attacks on your partner's *responsibility* and *trustworthiness* using statements that inflame the situation through harsh criticism. **Character attacks criticize someone for misusing or lacking qualities.** It is also very damaging to your partner when you call them names, such as "jerk" or "stupid." These types of communications cause estrangement between the two of you and reduce *trust*. They make it difficult to share openly and *honestly* or feel comfortable around each other.

You can also harm your relationship if you think critical thoughts about your partner without actually saying anything. Your thoughts will influence your attitude and the tone of voice you use with your partner. This, in turn, affects your actions toward them.

Using Character Quality Language is your first best plan of action to prevent and avoid damaging communications related to character (Chapter 11). The more you use it in your mind and speech, and acknowledge your partner's character qualities, the fewer communication problems will happen in your relationship. Speaking this language keeps you centered in your higher nature (Chapter 1).

The more you focus on your *strengths* and practice them effectively, and the more skilled you become at acknowledging your partner's *strengths* and development efforts, the greater will be the level of *unity* between you. Revisiting Chapters 2 and 3 will also assist you with ongoing character assessment and resolving issues, so that lack of *forgiveness* or feelings such as anger do not linger and affect you in the present.

Instead of doing a character attack, you can make a fair-minded complaint to your partner based upon *justice,* or simply raise a concern. Showing appreciation to your partner and using Character Quality Language can change the previous examples from above into problem-solving situations, or opportunities for your partner to apologize or make amends. *Thoughtfully* consider these two examples:

> "Honey, I am concerned that you do not seem to be paying your bills. I know you are trying hard to be *responsible*. Is there a problem we can talk through together? Maybe I can *help*."

> "I am tired and upset that I had to wait a long time for you to pick me up. You are a *thoughtful* person, so I know that you wanted to be here on time. What happened?"

These responses open an opportunity for your partner to share, and for both of you together to determine how to prevent a similar situation from arising again. Responding appropriately also requires you to be *patient* and *self-disciplined* so that you do not automatically react and defensively attack your partner's character. The goal is harmony and *unity*.

ACTIVITIES

1. Spend time with a friend or acquaintance who has been difficult to communicate with at times, and focus on using new skills and improving communications with them. Pay attention to your words and actions, and notice the results from your efforts. What are you learning that you can apply to communication with a partner?

2. Think about a time when you got angry with someone, or someone got angry with you. Analyze the character qualities that you were using well, and then look at those qualities you were not using effectively. Do the same for the other person. Are you now more clear about what caused the problem?

~ Questions for Reflection ~

1. Do I ever attack others' characters? What words do I tend to use? How do people respond?
2. When has someone attacked my character? How did I respond?

MISUSING CHARACTER QUALITIES WITH A PARTNER

In Chapter 1, you began to learn about misusing character qualities. Throughout the book, you have then been learning about effectively practicing character qualities, and you have gained some insights into what misusing them looks like. Now it is time to go deeper into understanding how you are misusing qualities, and gain insights into the negative effect that misuses have on a partner and a relationship. This understanding will empower you to avoid misusing qualities, which will contribute to harmony between you and a partner.

Do you remember the definition of misuse from Chapter 1? It said that a character quality misuse occurs when you are *strong* and effective at practicing a character quality, but at times you ineffectively practice it in one or both of the following ways:

- To excess, and/or
- At the wrong time or place

You also learned that in both cases, the outcome is that your words or actions cause varying degrees of harm to others or yourself and often result in some level of disunity or dissension. When you misuse a character quality, the result is either interpersonal or internal conflict. When you feel a lack of harmony within yourself, your inner voice will be sending you messages to pay attention (Chapter 2).

Additionally, if you experience disunity with a partner, it is a signal to look at how you are practicing your qualities. As you expand your understanding of misuses, you greatly increase your ability to identify what is going wrong, either before or when a conflict occurs. You then have the opportunity to take corrective measures to practice your qualities more effectively and rebuild *unity*. Psychotherapist Erik Blumenthal says, "...nothing can be achieved through conflict and quarrel. Conflict begets further conflict...."[3]

You also learned that the way to resolve misuses is to use a "*helper* quality" to assist you with adjusting your practice of the quality so that it becomes beneficial rather than harmful. You will find it consistently useful to look at the quality of *moderation* as the first *helper* quality you turn to, so that excessive practice of the quality lessens. You can apply *moderation* to take a step back and pause to see if you are using a quality at the wrong time or place, as well. You will find that it is useful to think through other qualities that can be particularly good *helper* qualities for you. When you are choosing a *helper* quality, look for ones that you practice effectively or that you rarely misuse. If *respect* is one that is an effective *strength* for you, it is often a good choice.

How Misuses Happen

As discussed in Chapter 1 and summarized above, there are two main ways that a character quality can be misused. A quality can be used to excess; for example, if you are *generous* with buying presents for your partner, even though you have no money to spare. You can also practice a quality the wrong time or place; for example, if you practice *acceptance* when someone is being abusive toward you.

Sometimes misuses stem from being too self-centered or from attempting to control or dominate a partner. Perhaps you are practicing your *strength* of *friendliness* by being *friendly* only to those who can *help* you get ahead in your career. However, your partner is concerned that you are not being *friendly* to any of your mutual friends. The resulting dissension causes tension, hurt feelings, or estrangement between you and your partner.

Lower nature feelings, such as pride, anger, insecurity, fear, anxiety, or hate can also lead you to misuse a quality and cause a disruption in your relationship. These negative feelings block you from *wisdom* (Chapter 1). Perhaps feeling insecure about your partner's affection can cause you to be too *accepting* when they repeatedly criticize you. Anger or hate can have you misuse *purposefulness* and plan revenge against someone. Both of these situations will result in harm and disunity.

Another example of a misuse is a reaction to something negative that happened in the past. You are afraid that the past will repeat itself, and you hope that *strongly* practicing a certain quality with a great deal of focused attention will prevent the negative event or something similar to it from occurring again. You might behave—often unconsciously—as if practicing the quality will produce an automatically positive result for you. Consider how this happens for Patricia:

> A year after her divorce, Patricia is still angry with her ex-husband for being unfaithful to her. She *purposefully* goes on with her life, not realizing that this emotion causes her to misuse *discernment*.
>
> Patricia attends an evening college class with other men and women her age. She hopes to meet new friends and maybe even develop a new relationship. After class, many of the attendees go to a nearby restaurant for something to eat and conversation. Each time Patricia participates, she is *friendly* to the women in the group, but she struggles with interacting with the men. She smiles at them, but underneath her polite words, her tone of voice is angry and judgmental as she asks the men questions. She is determined to *discern* whether they will be the type of men who will cheat on a wife. Instead of *helping* her to find men who might be potential partners for her, this behavior causes the men to avoid her.
>
> The outcome of Patricia's misuse of *discernment* is alienation from others. Her anger contributes to the misuse, and she prevents herself from developing friendships or relationships with men.

Discernment is an important quality for Patricia to practice as she goes forward. However, her unresolved emotions from the previous relationship cause her to use the quality unwisely. Applying *moderation* will assist her to be more consistent in her interactions with both women and men. Practicing *justice* as a *helper* quality will also assist her to be fair and not critical of people without any cause.

Conflict as an Indicator of Misuse

A useful indicator that you are misusing a quality is that some type of conflict has arisen with your partner. In dance class, when you are practicing steps with a partner, you move one way, and they sometimes move with you. Other times, you might lead, and your partner struggles to follow the steps. You may flow smoothly together with your partner at times, and at other times you jerk, twist, and do not look like you have any idea of how to dance. In the same way, when either of you are misusing your qualities, your interactions may be poor, and your relationship becomes troubled with disunity.

354 • Can We Dance? Learning the Steps for a Fulfilling Relationship

To *help* you begin to assess and understand why a problem is happening between you and a partner, you can *thoughtfully* ask yourself the following questions:

- What is occurring when you feel angry, hurt, or frustrated with each other? Under what circumstances does your partner express these feelings to you?
- What problems or conflicts arise with people other than your partner? Do the same issues arise each time there are disagreements or misunderstandings? If so, do you know why? What can you learn from these interactions with others to *help* you with your partner?
- When an action that you intended to be positive instead has a negative result, what quality were you trying to practice?

For example, you may effectively practice *courage* when facing challenges. However, perhaps you have turned this positive quality into harmful, reckless, and risky behavior like skydiving over treacherous mountainous areas. Your partner is very upset about the risks you are taking with your life and sees your behavior as a misuse of *courage*. As you reflect on their concerns, you begin to understand that this is *true*.

To resolve the problem, you can then practice *moderation*, which will guide you to change to a safer landing location than the mountains. You can also turn to *helper* qualities to assist you. This can include adding *care* and *respect* for your partner as well as for others who will be upset if you are badly injured or who will miss you if you die. You can also practice *respect* both for the people who *love* you and for your physical well-being. It takes *courage* to jump from an airplane with a parachute, and these efforts to stop misusing it will *help* you to change the recklessness back into genuine *courage*. Confucius says, "Virtue never stands alone. It is bound to have neighbors."[4]

Resolving Misuses with a Partner

To prevent problems in your relationship, you will need to be sensitive to your partner's perspectives. You will also need the ability to be *flexible*—without sacrificing your *integrity*. *Discernment* is also required to see how the dynamics of your character quality *strengths* tend to interact with your partner's. Sensitivity and *discernment* will *help* you to gain *wisdom*, which is necessary to identify and resolve misuses.

Once you have identified that you are misusing a quality, you will want to look to other *helper* qualities to assist. As mentioned above, the first quality you should look to is that of *moderation*. This quality *helps* you to use all the other qualities effectively so that you do not hurt others or yourself. Think of a dial that has three positions, left, center, and right. "Left" means you get hurt, "right" means your partner gets hurt, and "center" means you are practicing a quality in the appropriate balance with *moderation*. This means that you and your partner both benefit. If you aspire to keep each quality that you practice in the center position, you will be practicing *moderation*. If you see conflict, disunity, or harmful behavior happening, then picture this dial, and assess which quality is off-center. This will *help* you to make certain that neither you nor others are hurt.

Your choices will shift depending on the needs of your situation. What might appear to be an effective application of *moderation* at one time, may not be *moderate* the next time. *Discernment* and *flexibility* will *help* you to change your actions according to your current interactions and circumstances. "Once you make a decision, you are committed to it. Yet, be flexible. Monitor progress, make adjustments along the way when necessary to achieve your goal."[5] However, do not change your beliefs or principles in the process, however. Consider this example where the couple finds it challenging to determine the appropriate use of various qualities:

> Mei Lu and Shen have been good friends and partners for a few months. Shen recently injured his arm in an accident at work. He is on medical leave for a few weeks while it heals. Mei Lu *cares* for him by bringing over food and *helping* him with some of the household tasks he finds difficult, such as cooking, washing the dishes, and doing laundry.
>
> After the cast comes off of Shen's arm, Mei Lu visits him, continues taking *care* of him, insists that she lift and carry things for him, and does the housework. He does not want to hurt her feelings, so even though the doctor wants him to resume some activities, he *tactfully* lets her keep *helping*. However, this prevents Shen from rebuilding the muscles in his arm appropriately and regaining full use of it. Shen's *tactfulness* is a problem, and Mei Lu's *caring* is no longer beneficial. His physical therapist tells Shen he is progressing too slowly. He is frustrated about his progress, and so he finally raises the issue with Mei Lu.

In this scenario, it would have been *wise* for Mei Lu to be *sensitive* and *discern* that it was not appropriate for her to *care* and *help* in the same way throughout Shen's recovery. It would be more *caring* after the cast comes off to stop doing tasks for him gradually. Shen also misuses *tactfulness* by keeping silent instead of *assertively* expressing what he needs to say in a *kind* way. As with dancing, you and your partner both have to do your own parts, *moderating* your movements so you flow smoothly together.

In applying *moderation* to various qualities, there are some considerations to keep in mind. **Remember that applying *moderation* to *truthfulness*, for**

instance, does not mean that lying is acceptable. It does not support your relationship to lie, tell half-truths, or withhold important information. 'Abdu'l-Bahá says, "Truthfulness is the foundation of all human virtues. … When this holy attribute is established in man, all the divine qualities will also be acquired."[6] Adding *moderation* to this quality means that you *discern* when it is appropriate to tell all of the details about the *truth* that you know, and when it is not *tactful*, timely, or *wise*. Consider in this scenario below how Selim struggles with *truthfulness* and ends up misusing *creativity*:

> Peri and Selim have been in a relationship for a few weeks. They agree to save their money so that they can attend a special concert together. Every week, Peri shares what amount she has saved, and she asks Selim how much money he has set aside. He tells her an amount each time. However, he is not really saving the money, because he decides after their agreement begins that he will be able to make money quickly by participating in a *creative* idea a friend has proposed.
>
> Selim does not want Peri to be concerned about how he is actually using the money, so he keeps pretending that he is saving it. However, when it comes time to buy the tickets, his friend's idea has ended badly, and there is no money. Selim admits to Peri that he did not save the money. In his mind, Selim had justified *creating* a story about saving money and telling it to Peri, because he thought there would be no harm, and that his *creative* idea to make money would work out fine. Peri is angry and disappointed, and she is not sure whether to *trust* Selim again.

In this scenario, Selim misused his *creativity* by hatching a crafty plan that would both allow him to spend his money and get the tickets without Peri finding out about it. In this situation, Selim is practicing his *creativity* unwisely, and his relationship would have benefited from *truthfulness*, as well as *love* and *respect* toward his partner.

When Peri discovers what Selim has done, she can launch a character attack and accuse Selim of being an untrustworthy liar. If, instead, Peri values her relationship with Selim, and she wants to minimize their conflict as well as benefit his character growth, she can address the misuse by speaking to him about his *strength*. She could say, "I see how you were trying to be *creative* by finding a way to spend your money and get the tickets at the same time. However, I am very disappointed about not being able to buy the tickets. Can we discuss better ways to use your *creativity*?" Selim would be less likely to become defensive, and their relationship may be able to move forward.

Shortcoming or Misused Strength?

Sometimes when you assess your words and actions, you can appear to have a shortcoming or be missing a quality altogether. This is a common and incorrect assumption that people typically make. However, in *truth*, you are actually misusing a quality strength, and you are not missing a quality at all.

This means that whenever you or others are unhappy with your words or actions, it makes sense to *discern* the true cause of your behavior. Is it caused by a quality you are missing or by one that you are misusing? It would take determined effort to develop a missing quality, if that is the cause.

If instead the root of your behavior is a quality you are misusing, you simply need to find the quality strength that you already have. You then *moderate* it or use *helper* qualities to make it effective for your life and in your relationship with your partner. Understanding the difference between these two will affect the choices you make to address the issue.

If you look closely at the quality of *discernment*, for example, you can see that it empowers you to see clearly and deeply into all matters and make *wise* decisions based on what you discover. However, if you tend to be critical, you take what you *discern* and make negative comments about it instead. You may be misusing a quality like *discernment*, and you fail to see how you can be using it effectively instead. When used appropriately, *discernment* is a powerful force for the good of a relationship, since you can use it to determine and understand the needs of your partner.

Consider this story:

> Eliska is working on her third project of the day one Saturday afternoon at her home. Her partner Ryan has come over to *help* her move some furniture, but she comments incessantly that he never seems to get the table or couch in just the right place. He is beginning to get annoyed at her attitude and criticisms. Eliska's negativity and faultfinding is causing him to wish he had stayed at his own house, or gone to the park to play baseball with some friends instead.
>
> Ryan *assertively* speaks up and requests that she stop making negative comments. Eliska responds that she is just trying to have her home look nice by *discerning* and pointing out where improvements could happen. She agrees to think about her actions, however, and how she is actually practicing *discernment*. Through this reflection, she realizes that she is always looking for what is not going well around her, and she becomes critical about what she sees. It is also unusual for her to say anything positive when she *discerns* something going smoothly. She is rarely *encouraging* to others or *courteous* about appreciating others *helping* her.
>
> When Eliska sees Ryan the following weekend, she apologizes for how she treated him. She asks for his *help* again the next day, and she promises to behave differently. As he frowns and considers declining her request, she responds with *encouraging* words that assure him she is *sincere* in her desire to change, and she will

not be critical of his efforts. Eliska knows it will be difficult to rebuild a *trusting* relationship with Ryan, but she is willing to *persevere*.

It is comforting to realize that even when you or a partner are misusing a quality, whether it is from not understanding the quality or from good intentions that do not work out well, you are still building your capacity to use the quality correctly as a *strength*. In other words, you are exercising the right muscles, but in the wrong way.

As you learn to identify which qualities you tend to consistently misuse, you will be able to accomplish one or more of these worthwhile objectives:

- Empower yourself to transform how you use a character quality so that it becomes beneficial to you and to others by practicing *moderation* along with it
- Determine which character qualities to call on as *helper* qualities to assist you to stop misusing a *strength*
- Discover new character *strengths* in yourself that can only become clear once you stop misusing them

The more you understand and observe character qualities in yourself and others, the more nuances and layers you will observe. The dance can be easy at times when you naturally practice a quality beautifully. However, at other times, the steps and moves may dazzle or challenge you with their complexity and difficulty. This is the dance of life.

~ Questions for Reflection ~

1. When have I misused a quality, and my words or actions have harmed a partner or others?
2. How do I feel when I misuse one of my character qualities and cause harm, conflict, or disunity? How do I resolve the situations when this occurs?
3. What specific times have I struggled to act with *moderation*? In what ways would applying *moderation* in these situations have benefited my words, actions, and a partner?
4. If I have a partner, does my partner appear to be misusing any character qualities in ways that affect our relationship? Which ones? How can I influence a shift in my partner's behavior? Is my partner willing to work on practicing qualities in better ways?
5. If I identify that I am misusing a quality and causing myself personal harm, but I think that I am not harming others, is this a reason to not make a change? Is it possible to only harm myself without harming anyone else?

ACTIVITIES

1. Think of recent situations that resulted in disunity or dissension between you and a partner or another person. Identify what quality you misused, and then what qualities you could have practiced along with it that could have *helped* you to prevent the problem.

2. Complete **Worksheet 14.1: Assessing Your Misuse of Character Qualities**. This worksheet will give you experience in both identifying qualities that you tend to misuse, as well as what will assist you to improve your words and actions.

3. When you have a partner, complete **Worksheet 14.2: Character Challenges in Your Relationship Partner**, to assess your partner's weak qualities and those that they are misusing.

IMPROVING COMMUNICATION PATTERNS

When you and a partner communicate well, it *encourages* further communication. **However, at times you may challenge a partner by using a communication method that is, consciously or unconsciously, an attempt to control them or to manipulate the situation.** You can tell this is going on when you notice that you are trying to get your own way without being fully *honest* with a partner. If this is the case, then working *purposefully* to eliminate this behavior will *help* you to sustain a relationship. Communication is not a game for you to win at the expense of your partner.

If the poor communication behaviors are coming from your partner rather than you, and no changes are happening, then it is your *responsibility* to bring the issue up for discussion between you. If the communications become destructive or hurtful, and your partner chooses not to control or change their words or actions, then you will assess whether to stay in the relationship. Communication is an essential aspect of all relationships. If both of you engage in poor behavior, then you and your partner can consider whether either of you are ready to be in a *committed* relationship.

Eliminating Unwise Communication Behaviors

As you look at the (long!) list below, assess your communication and decision-making patterns, and see if you are using any of these unwise communication behaviors. Most of them are actually manipulative techniques to get your own way about something or prove that you are right. It is likely that *honesty* and *respect* are both missing from the interactions. Consider whether you ever or often use these strategies:

- Pouting
- Complaining
- Teasing hurtfully (not playfully)
- Strategizing to get your way
- Exaggerating your speech, body language, and movements to convey negative emotions
- Faking crying
- Whining
- Giving excessive and insincere compliments
- Having a hidden agenda/unspoken boundaries or expectations
- Distracting inappropriately
- Using other people to communicate for you
- Speaking or acting with uncontrolled anger
- Criticizing
- Manipulating
- Refusing to share your opinions, and then blaming your partner for how a situation turns out
- Acting like a victim to gain sympathy
- Giving solely in order to get something in return
- Justifying negative behavior
- Interrupting
- Stubbornly insisting on or forcing your viewpoint on your partner
- Taking an extreme position and blaming your partner using words such as "you always" or "you never"
- Deliberately bringing up your partner's "hot button" issues to get them upset
- Implying or stating that you are right and that your partner is wrong
- Having a competitive "win-lose" attitude
- Insulting, using sarcasm, or using profanity
- Concealing important information
- Being forceful or dominating in words, tone, or physical movements
- Walking away while the other is speaking (unless there is danger of violence, in which case you certainly should leave)
- Answering the telephone and carrying out a conversation with the caller while your partner is trying to speak with you
- Refusing to validate or respond to your partner's point of view or feelings

- Pointing a finger or using other aggressive gestures, postures, or actions (examples: fist waving, foot stomping, door slamming)
- Dictating by saying, "you should," "you must," "you have to," or "you cannot"
- Threatening anyone verbally, emotionally, physically, or sexually
- Threatening to leave the relationship
- Turning every conversation around so that it is about you

Repeatedly using these unwise habits may be an indication of emotional immaturity or insecurity. If your partner knew your motives for communicating in one of these ways, would they think you were being *honest* with them? **Eliminating these behaviors from your life and interactions with a partner will increase your ability to have a happy, lasting relationship. Having a mature discussion that leads you and your partner to reach a mutual decision about a course of action will be a better choice and be more likely to maintain harmony with your partner.**

If you notice a significant number of unwise communication patterns in your relationship, it is practical to ask for some outside assistance with building skills, and to learn new and different strategies that will prevent and resolve conflicts.

Note: If either you or your partner has a mental illness or a combination of mental and physical illnesses, or if you are concerned that this might be a factor in your relationship, you will be *wise* to seek professional counseling and medical assistance individually or together. Indicators of a problem can include depression, excessive emotional withdrawal, compulsive lying, excessive and unreasonable anger, paranoia or unreasonable suspicions, very high levels of anxiety, eating disorders, unexplained constant or rapid shifts in emotional expressions, unreasonable reactions to normal stress, abuse of or addiction to alcohol or drugs, suicide threats, or repeated abusive and damaging comments or behavior. Obviously, all of these can negatively affect communications between you and your partner.

~ *Questions for Reflection* ~

1. Do I do any of the unwise communication behaviors in this section? Why?
2. Do I see the harm that I cause when I communicate in any of these ways?
3. Which behaviors am I willing to eliminate? Am I willing to *persevere* until I successfully stop doing them?
4. What can be the effect on a relationship if I make these changes?

ACTIVITY

Choose one or two of the unwise communication behaviors from this section that you do. For a few days, make concentrated efforts to stop using them. Pause and reflect on the difference it makes in your life and relationships by avoiding these behaviors. Then, choose one or two other negative communication behaviors to work on, and repeat the process.

Building Harmony Instead of Being "Right"

Few dynamics are as destructive to the vitality of a relationship as one partner insisting on being "right" about a topic, and interacting as if their partner is "wrong" in their thoughts, actions, or beliefs. It is a very common human desire to be right, and you may be so under some circumstances, but taking this position causes you to hold stubbornly onto your own opinion or complaint. When this occurs, you and your partner take opposite ends of an issue, with no possibility of understanding, compromising, or agreeing. Consider how this right-wrong dynamic affects this couple:

> While Shirlee and Asher have attended the same school together for a couple of years, they recently became close friends during their summer break. Now they are in the same high school Literature class. The teacher instructs their class to divide into study groups, and Shirlee and Asher naturally join the same one.
>
> The assignment for each group is to read and discuss the themes and characters in a set of short stories. However, Shirlee interrupts the other participants, constantly says negative comments about others' answers, and insists her interpretation is the only correct one. After she does this several times, even to Asher, he becomes frustrated and angry with her.
>
> The following Friday, Shirlee invites Asher to attend the football game with her, but he is very hesitant. He dislikes the way she is acting in the class, and it is beginning to affect his feelings about their friendship. The more she insists that her way is correct, the less he feels like being around her.

If you take *strong* positions, as Shirlee is doing, your partner may feel as if you are trying to be in charge of them and that you are trying to dominate them. **You likely use overly *strong* or pride-filled words that clearly tell your partner that you think they are wrong. This approach does not allow room for new facts, other perspectives, or creative alternatives.** There is disunity and dissension between you and your partner. Consider what therapist Mehri Sefidvash says about communication:

> If we wish truly to communicate with our partner about a problem, we must share our own point of view with him. To do this, we must accept that our partner, too, will have a point of view about the subject and this may well be different from ours.[7]

While there are obviously certain circumstances in which "right" and "wrong" are clearly defined by laws, civil authorities, or religious scriptures, that is not what this section is referring to. The mindset to avoid is thinking that you know better than anyone else does. When this is your attitude or position, your words and tone of voice can easily reflect disrespect, criticism, or anger toward your partner. In this way, you end up discounting your partner's input and harming your relationship. [See Chapter 11 for more about tone of voice.]

There is a significant negative impact on your relationship if you always have to be "right." The *love* and vitality in your relationship certainly suffers. You can spot this pattern by asking yourself these questions:

- Are you *loving* and connected with your partner, or are you disconnected from each other and experiencing disunity?
- Are you moving forward, or are you stuck in a viewpoint or position?
- Are you open to new possibilities and ideas, or discounting ones your partner suggests?
- Can you *compassionately* understand your partner's viewpoint, or are you treating it as unimportant?
- Are you listening to your partner, or are you tuning them out?
- Are you maintaining *unity* and harmony, or are you argumentative and hostile?
- Are you *accepting* what your partner says, or are you correcting every little detail they express?
- Are you providing your partner with accurate feedback on what you think they are trying to say, or are you interrupting them and refusing to let them finish speaking?

If you answered yes to the second half of any of the questions above, you may be focused on being right and harming your relationship as a result. **_Humility_ assists you to see that you can be mistaken or not have all the facts, and to shift your position to allow for your partner's input. Another quality that can *help* you to alter this dynamic between you and a partner is practicing *equality*. If you truly act as *equal* partners who *respect***

and value each other, then the views both you and your partner hold are important and valued. You can then focus your energy on the situation and on *creating* the best solution together.

Using *respectful* words in your communications with your partner is vitally important and builds your relationship. When *respect* is your focus, you are in "friendship mode," not adversaries, and regard each other as members of the same team.

ACTIVITY

Pick a topic to communicate about with your partner, a close friend, or a relative. Practice taking turns being the speaker and the listener. Assess together when either of you used words, phrases, or a tone of voice that communicated one person was right and the other wrong. Identify words or phrases that either of you used that showed an attitude of openness, invitation to share, and *acceptance* instead.

~ Questions for Reflection ~

1. When am I most likely to decide that I am right and someone else is wrong?
2. What *helps* me to shift into being more open and *accepting* of others' ideas?

Reducing Mind Reading

Being sensitive and aware of what is happening with a partner is important in a relationship. Sometimes when you are attempting to be sensitive, however, you can end up believing that you are accurately reading your partner's mind. In fact, you are actually making assumptions. **It is a romantic myth that couples should always be able to "read each other's minds" and know what the other means, thinks, and needs. Making assumptions can cause misunderstandings and problems between you and your partner instead.** In dancing, this is called anticipating your partner's moves. However, when you do this, you can guess wrong and mess up the pattern that the leader has in mind. This throws off the timing and balance of the dance.

Alternatively, you could assume that your partner should be able to read your mind. You then do not directly communicate your needs and wants with your partner. You might instead say to yourself, "If they really *love* me, they will know what I want and need!" However, this often leads to hurt feelings and breakdowns in communication, and you do not end up with your needs met. Do not expect your partner (or anyone else) to know what you want if you have not told them. Maybe you think that you have given sufficient clues or hints, but they may not be obvious to your partner, even though you think they should be. Consider how this couple handles this type of situation instead:

> Colin and Katie have been close friends and partners for a number of months. Katie's birthday is approaching. She knows, however, that Colin may not realize that this month is her birthday or that she loves surprises. As Katie and Colin walk through a park one afternoon, Katie begins to share with Colin how much she enjoyed her birthdays growing up. Each year, her family made the day exciting in many ways, and they made cookies so that she could share them with her friends at school. She enjoyed playing games with her friends, and the great presents she received with colorful wrapping paper. It was special for her to both receive gifts and give the treats to others.

> Katie mentions to Colin that her birthday is coming up, and asks him if he would be willing to *help* make that day special for her. She shares some specific ways he can do this for her. He is *thankful* that she shares her wishes with him, because he wants her to be happy with the day.

When you have firmly established *trust*, and you and your partner are getting to know each other well, sharing what is in your heart, soul, and mind can be a source of *joyfulness*. There can be a real spark of connection between you and your partner and a feeling of communicating "on the same wavelength." At times, you may accurately guess what is on your partner's mind before they speak, or you finish each other's sentences. Your increased sensitivity to each other may make you accurately aware on occasion of each other's moods and emotions. **While being in tune with each other can be great when it works well, it is not *wise* to place *strong* significance or importance on this happening. Just because you are accurate at times does not make mind reading a *wise* communication method, nor does it indicate you are "perfect partners."**

It is unwise to make assumptions about what your partner thinks, feels, wants, or needs. You may have already guessed that if Katie in the previous story had left it to Colin to read her mind, she would have had a disappointing birthday. If you expect your partner to read your mind, you will become upset when they do not do it consistently or accurately. At times, you may even feel that your partner's assumptions invalidate what you are really thinking and feeling. You could also feel disappointed that your partner does not know you as well as you thought they did. A practical alternative would be to communicate your expectations, wishes, or needs in specific detail to your partner. Your partner then has the opportunity to agree, decline, or suggest an alternative.

Some individuals may have more of a tendency to mind-read than others may. They are aware of and analyze possible dangers or concerns in their environment, and they are watchful for things that may require attention. This can include everything from vigilance crossing the street to staying near a cooking pot to ensure it does not boil over.

When focused appropriately, this personal vigilance is a great benefit to the teamwork of a relationship. This type of person can be *excellent* at watching out for and acting to prevent circumstances that cause conflict or disunity. These same individuals, however, may also have a *strong* tendency to try to predict prematurely what a partner is going to say or do. If this pattern is one that applies to you, practicing *patience* and *self-discipline* will *help* you to give your partner *encouragement* to express their own thoughts freely. Then, once you have heard their thoughts, you can respond.

~ Questions for Reflection ~

1. Do I ever make assumptions about what my partner or others are thinking or feeling?
2. How do I resolve any negative situations that result from inaccurate mind reading?
3. What direct communications or requests are important for me to make with a partner?

ACTIVITY

Play a guessing game about what you are each thinking with a partner or a friend. Devise a minor consequence for every time either of you is wrong.

FACTS OR INTERPRETATIONS

Sometimes when you are doing the relationship dance, you may notice that your head is spinning with thoughts and questions: "Will he call me? Does she like me? Was I crazy to say that to him? Did she think what I was wearing was okay, or was she really just laughing at me? What did he mean when he said that? What was the significance of taking me there? Why did she say that? Was he mad at me?"

When something happens or does not happen in a relationship, you may immediately try to make sense of it, imagine its significance, and try to sort out its effects on you and others. This can be positive at times if it *helps* you to understand and *accept* your partner. It

becomes a problem, however, when you carry it to excess. You might notice how you start imagining all kinds of things when your partner does not respond to you, looks at you strangely, says something you do not understand, does not call or stop by, and so on. Often, then, you are likely to have a cautious or negative interaction with them the next time you have contact. It is important to be aware that your interaction may be largely based on your interpretation (which could just be your imagination), and not on reality. Notice how this dynamic happens for these two people:

> Janette and Max meet at a social event for singles at a local community center. They sit down to eat with a group, and Janette notices that Max has a number of stains on his shirt. She starts picturing him at his home—putting on wrinkled pants and a shirt that has a stain from the previous night's dinner. She looks at his current stains and interprets that he obviously does not care about cleanliness or appropriate dress. She wants to be with someone who not only *cares* for her, but also *cares* for himself. She cannot imagine herself walking down the street and holding hands with Max as people stare at him.

> After several days, Max calls Janette and invites her to dinner. She is still thinking about her concerns, and she thanks him but firmly declines. Several days later, Janette talks to Max's good friend Davis, who she also met at the social, and he asks how she liked Max. He shares how embarrassed Max was that evening by having stains on his shirt. He came early to *help* with preparations, and someone accidentally spilled food on him while setting up the dishes for the dinner. There was no time for him to go home and change shirts.

> Janette regrets that she misjudged Max based on her interpretations. She decides to contact him, apologize, and ask that they go out after all. He agrees, and she finds that Max is a great person to be with, and they have much in common.

Janette's thoughts and judgments, based on what she imagined and assumed, initially interfered with her ability to begin a relationship with Max. Remember the discussion about expectations in Chapter 6? The root of your assumptions or interpretations can be an unfulfilled expectation. Janette has an expectation about a partner's appearance and cleanliness. This influences the interpretations and choices that she makes. Her experiences have left her with certain standards of cleanliness and dress she expects to see in a partner.

Another kind of interpretation or assumption about a situation or a person occurs because you make a connection to a previous experience—one that has little or no applicability or relevance to the current situation. This causes your past to affect what happens in the present,

368 • *Can We Dance? Learning the Steps for a Fulfilling Relationship*

and prevents your future from shifting into a different, and hopefully more positive, direction. You continue reliving the past and imagining that it is impossible to change. Notice how this happens for Kevin:

> Acadia and Kevin see each other regularly at the fitness center. Acadia enjoys exercising when she has time to do it. She joined the fitness center to take off weight gained from dining out with customers during frequent business trips. She is naturally slim, and she simply wants to maintain a healthy lifestyle.
>
> Kevin also enjoys working out, but he is very sensitive about women and weight loss. His wife, Maryann, had regular challenges with her weight. Maryann ended up thin and sick from anorexia, refused treatment, and she died from the condition.
>
> Now, Kevin becomes concerned as Acadia begins to lose weight. He starts imagining and projecting that she is anorexic like Maryann. He becomes more distant and less talkative with Acadia, based on his assumption that the past will repeat itself. Acadia is confused by his change in behavior, which had been positive and *friendly*.

Acadia and Kevin can likely resolve this situation by having an *honest* discussion about what is happening. In other words, they need to determine the facts. However, Kevin's fear, which is based on his previous experiences, might prevent such a discussion from happening. Even if the discussion occurs, it still may be difficult for him to stop imagining that something bad will happen. If he is unable to *detach* from his concerns and stop his negative imagination, he is unlikely to be able to have a relationship with Acadia.

It is a common occurrence to react to someone's words or to what a person does or does not do. Instead, try this process:

- Listen to your inner voice, and identify how it is prompting your lower nature to come up with automatic questions and hasty and usually negative interpretations, assumptions, judgments, or imagined scenarios (Chapters 1 and 2)
- Pause; recognize that this type of thinking will cause you to be angry or upset and have a negative interaction with your partner
- Consciously choose to stop your mind from going in this negative direction
- Investigate the *true* circumstances or determine the facts
- Base your next choice on these facts
- Make a deliberate choice in what you think and how you respond that will likely produce a positive result
- Listen to and *creatively* problem-solve with your partner

Consider a situation where someone walks past you and does not say anything to you. Immediately, you begin making judgments about the person and interpret their action in a negative way. The next time you see them, you are likely not to speak to them. The fact of the situation is that someone walked past you and did not greet you. You have no way of knowing why. Perhaps they just received bad news, and they were preoccupied. Maybe they were writing a story in their head. Maybe they are shy. Anything is possible. You can recognize that you do not know what is *true*, and choose to have a positive interaction with the person instead. Perhaps you even say, "I saw you yesterday, but you seemed a bit distracted. Is anything wrong?"

When something happens, and you begin to make quick interpretations, it may *help* you to try a number of activities to head yourself in a more positive direction. You might find it *helps* you to calm yourself down and think more clearly if you do such activities as meditation, music, prayer, sports, exercise, working with your hands, or cleaning. The character qualities of *patience, thoughtfulness*, and *discernment* will also *help* you to work through your automatic reactions and determine what is *true*. Remember to "…look into all things with a searching eye."[8] The more self-aware you are, the greater will be your opportunity to choose a *thoughtful* and planned response. These types of *self-disciplined* responses are the key to stopping negative reactions that damage your relationship.

It is essential to remember, especially when tempers are short, that your partner cannot "make" you angry nor "make" you act or say anything that you do not choose of your own free will. What you say and how you act is totally your *responsibility*. Above all, do not lose your necessary focus on *respect* for your partner and yourself.

The following reminders can expand your ability to handle situations effectively:

- Focus on your own and your partner's character qualities
- Practice *self-discipline*
- Give your partner the benefit of the doubt, and assume that they have good intentions
- *Respect* your partner
- Acknowledge that everyone makes mistakes
- Think positively (higher nature)
- Avoid negative outcome thinking (lower nature)
- Be open-minded
- Try to put yourself in your partner's place, and look at the situation from their perspective
- Imagine a positive scenario or interpretation that is more empowering
- Realize that there is more than one possible explanation for every situation

You will protect your relationship if you wait to raise your concerns with your partner until you are in a better state of mind. Try to connect

to *joyfulness* and also to *thankfulness* about the positive aspects of your life. This will uplift you and *help* you to think more clearly. You can then more easily practice character qualities, acknowledge your feelings, and share them without being destructive and blaming. In the scenario with Max, Janette could have been more *accepting, friendly,* and *kind.* In the next example, Kevin could have drawn on *confidence, courage,* and *flexibility* with Acadia.

As you determine the facts of a situation, it is possible that you will actually discover that something negative happened or is occurring. However, any choices you then make will be based upon reality, not on hasty interpretations, false assumptions, or wild imagination.

ACTIVITY

Complete **Worksheet 14.3: Acting on Facts, Not Interpretations** to increase your skill in identifying how you can improve your response to situations. You may find it useful to have a partner or a friend work with you on completing this activity.

~ Questions for Reflection ~

1. How have I caused harm through my imagination and reactions?
2. How can I stop my imagination from leading me into negative, unproductive, or destructive words or actions?
3. In thinking of a specific situation, what character quality might have been missing? How could practicing it have *helped* me to *create* an improved outcome?

MAINTAINING WELL-BEING

A key way to prevent miscommunications, character quality misuses, and conflict between you and a partner is to be mindful of your own well-being. If you attempt to communicate when you feel stressed or in danger of losing your temper, you are unlikely to do it well.

Trouble can occur if you are overcommitted and trying to do too much; in emotional or physical pain; affected by hormones, such as during premenstrual or menopausal periods for females; overly hungry or tired; angry, or upset about something; or feeling lonely or sad. **You may be so involved in a relationship that you forget to practice responsible self-*care.***

Here are some possible actions you can take to look after your well-being:

- Breathe slowly and deeply
- Rest
- Exercise (remember dancing is an option!)
- Build, construct, clean, or repair something that uses your hands and muscles
- Maintain a healthy and balanced diet
- Keep in close contact with uplifting friends and family members
- Confide in a close and *trusted* friend or family member
- Ask someone to listen to your feelings
- Pause and take time to calm down before reacting to something or someone
- Pray
- Meditate
- Take a walk in nature
- Create something artistic
- Do something physical like chopping wood, shredding old documents, or tearing down an old building (Make sure no one needs it, and that no one is inside!)
- Read a positive book
- Get a sufficient amount of sleep
- Have a hobby or learn a new skill
- Slow down a bit and live life at a more moderate pace [*Note:* There is an excellent book we recommend entitled *A Pace of Grace* by Linda Kavelin Popov.]

You can also find it *helpful* to explore your behavior in a journal, or with a close friend, parent, counselor, or relationship coach. Often someone else can objectively analyze what is going on in your life better than you can. They can also *help* you to make a plan for exactly which character quality or qualities you will use the next time you are tired, stressed-out, or in danger of losing your temper.

Some days, due to fatigue or stress, it may be very difficult for you to use a quality effectively. But, when you have to dig deep for a quality, you develop

Nicolas, I'm hungry, I'm sleepy, I have a cold, my car got towed away, I lost my purse and my glasses, and I have a nasty papercut. I think I need to rest a bit before I spend the evening with you.

your *spiritual* and higher nature muscles (Chapter 1). The same occurs when you have to work hard to master a dance step—your leg muscles *strengthen* through practice. Being tired or even ill is not an excuse to skip using a quality or to use it poorly. It is an opportunity to develop character *strength* through self-awareness and finding the quality that you need, in spite of the situation you are in or how you are feeling. It may assist you to choose a particular quality that usually works well for you in difficult circumstances. For instance, *patience*, *self-discipline*, or *peacefulness* could be useful.

When you are having problems, however, you can communicate with your partner, family, or friends that it will assist you to receive their *compassion*, *caring*, or *helpfulness*. **It may be difficult for you to ask for *help*, but it allows others the opportunity to be *generous* with their time, and it assists you with *strengthening humility*.** If *help* comes to you from a partner, you will gain insights about their ability to respond to you when you need them.

Courteously calling for a "time-out" or pause for a break in a discussion is a particularly *helpful* tool when the emotional temperature begins to rise, and you and your partner both stop being your best selves. You may think that you are required to keep hammering away at an issue until you solve it. In fact, this can be counter-productive. Often, if you notice that one or both of you are starting to get upset, agreeing to have some time apart to calm down can provide you with time to think more clearly and see new perspectives. This break can be a brief few minutes or it can last for days, depending on the circumstances. Just make sure that you are in agreement about when and how to resume the discussion, and who will initiate it. Then, be *trustworthy* and follow through.

ACTIVITIES

1. Choose one or two of the well-being strategies from this section and try them for a few days. How did they work? Are there others that you now want to try?

2. Plan which character quality or qualities you will use the next time you are tired, stressed-out, or in danger of losing your temper.

❧ *Encouragement* ❧

You are doing vital personal growth and development as you learn constructive ways to communicate. We have every *confidence* in your ability to transform your unwise communication patterns. Your progress is exciting, and we *encourage* you to reward yourself for your worthwhile efforts.

Date: _____

Worksheet 14.1: Assessing Your Misuse of Character Qualities

This worksheet will assist you to clarify the qualities you misuse, and identify strategies to practice them effectively instead.

Instructions:

A) Review the character qualities in Part 3 or refer back to your Worksheet 2.1, and identify three qualities that you misuse at times, thereby hurting another person and causing dissension or disunity. If you have a partner, then focus on your interactions with them.

B) Identify the helper qualities for you to practice, and determine how these will affect your words and actions.

1. First quality that I sometimes misuse: _____
   Helper qualities that can assist this quality to be an effective strength instead:

   _____ Moderation _____   _____

   _____   _____

   What new ways can I speak and act using these helper qualities?

   _____

   _____

2. Second quality that I sometimes misuse: _____
   Helper qualities that can assist this quality to be an effective strength instead:

   _____ Moderation _____   _____

   _____   _____

   What new ways can I speak and act using these helper qualities?

   _____

   _____

3. Third quality that I sometimes misuse: _____
   Helper qualities that can assist this quality to be an effective strength instead:

   _____ Moderation _____   _____

   _____   _____

   What new ways can I speak and act using these helper qualities?

   _____

   _____

Date: _____

Worksheet 14.2: Character Challenges in Your Relationship Partner

When you have a partner, this worksheet will assist you to assess their character misuses and weaknesses. If you do not have a partner, then you can come back to this worksheet when you do.

Instructions:

A) On the list below, put an "M" next to the qualities that you observe your partner has as strengths but is frequently misusing. Use the detailed descriptions about character in Part 3 to assist you.

B) On the list below, put a "W" next to the qualities in your partner that you observe to be weak, or that your partner rarely practices.

M or W?	Character Quality	M or W?	Character Quality	M or W?	Character Quality
	Acceptance		Faithfulness		Peacefulness
	Assertiveness		Flexibility		Perseverance
	Beauty		Forgiveness		Purity
	Caring		Friendliness		Purposefulness
	Chastity		Generosity		Respect
	Commitment		Gentleness		Responsibility
	Compassion		Helpfulness		Self-Discipline
	Confidence		Honesty		Service
	Contentment		Humility		Sincerity
	Cooperation		Idealism		Spirituality
	Courage		Integrity		Strength
	Courtesy		Joyfulness		Tactfulness
	Creativity		Justice		Thankfulness
	Detachment		Kindness		Thoughtfulness
	Discernment		Love		Trustworthiness
	Encouragement		Loyalty		Truthfulness
	Enthusiasm		Mercy		Unity
	Equality		Moderation		Wisdom
	Excellence		Patience		

Questions for Reflection:

1. When I compare this list to Worksheet 7.1, where I chose the qualities that would be most important for me in a partner, what do I notice?

   _____

   _____

   _____

   _____

   _____

2. Are there inconsistencies in my partner's practice of character qualities that concern me? How will I handle them?

   _____

   _____

   _____

   _____

3. Are there qualities my partner is misusing? What seems to trigger these misuses? How can I encourage my partner to practice helper qualities and shift their misuses to strengths instead?

   _____

   _____

   _____

   _____

   _____

   _____

4. Are there qualities that I think my partner needs to strengthen? How can I encourage this to happen?

   _____

   _____

   _____

   _____

   _____

Date: _____

Worksheet 14.3: Acting on Facts, Not Interpretations

This worksheet will assist you to practice identifying the facts in various scenarios, the possible negative interpretations or assumptions that you make and then react to, and when and how it would be wiser to respond. You can complete this worksheet on your own, or invite a partner or friend to role-play or work through each scenario with you.

Instructions:

With each scenario below, identify the following aspects of the situation:

- **Facts:** What you know for sure, and what is actually happening

- **Quick Interpretation of the Facts:** Your judgments and conclusions about your partner's words or actions

- **Likely Reaction with Partner:** The words you say and the actions you do with your partner based on your negative interpretation. These often result in conflict or miscommunication.

- **Re-look at the Facts:** See if you can now separate the facts from your interpretation. What different or more positive interpretation of the facts would empower you to have an improved interaction with your partner?

- **Positive Interpretation of the Facts:** What your interpretation could be if you think positively about your partner, or you take actions to stay calm and centered instead of being judgmental and upset.

- **Improved Interaction with Partner:** The words and actions you do based on your positive interpretation. These often result in further discussion, determining new facts, and more effective communication.

Example:

Facts: My partner promises to call me at 5:30 p.m. after work and does not do so. It is now 8:30 p.m. They are not answering their telephone.

Quick Interpretation of Facts: My partner does not care about me, cannot keep commitments, and is discourteous.

Likely Reaction with Partner: Critical; attack character; angry; upset.

Re-look at the facts.

Positive Interpretation of Facts: My partner has been delayed. I hope they are okay. I'm sure I will hear from them as soon as they can call or get here.

Improved Interaction with Partner: Willing to listen and express concern; allow partner to tell what happened; calm; caring.

Scenarios:

1. **Facts:** I ask my partner to stop at the grocery store on the way to my home to buy a can of icing for my child's birthday cake. My partner arrives without it.

   Quick Interpretation of Facts: _____

   _____

   Likely Reaction with Partner: _____

   _____

   Re-look at the facts.

   Positive Interpretation of Facts: _____

   _____

   Improved Interaction with Partner: _____

   _____

2. **Facts:** I pick up a credit card receipt for a $200 item that my partner accidentally drops. I know that my partner is short of money.

   Quick Interpretation of Facts: _____

   _____

   Likely Reaction with Partner: _____

   _____

   Re-look at the facts.

   Positive Interpretation of Facts: _____

   _____

   Improved Interaction with Partner: _____

   _____

3. **Facts:** My partner is having a medical test. They are scared about the outcome.

   Quick Interpretation of Facts: _____

   _____

   Likely Reaction with Partner: _____

   _____

   Re-look at the facts.

   Positive Interpretation of Facts: _____

   _____

   Improved Interaction with Partner: _____

   _____

4. **Facts:** My partner agrees to lend me their car. When I arrive to pick it up, they appear reluctant to give me the keys.

   Quick Interpretation of Facts: _____

   _____

   Likely Reaction with Partner: _____

   _____

Re-look at the facts.

   Positive Interpretation of Facts: _____

   _____

   Improved Interaction with Partner: _____

   _____

Questions for Reflection:

Think of a time when you made a false interpretation of a situation and then reacted based on your conclusions. Then answer these questions:

1. What happened (the facts)?

   _____

   _____

2. What was my quick (likely negative) interpretation?

   _____

   _____

3. How did I react? What was the outcome?

   _____

   _____

4. What positive way could I have interpreted the situation instead?

   _____

   _____

5. What can I now do differently to respond to similar situations?

   _____

   _____

   _____

   _____

   _____

Smooth Dancing:
Strengthening Unity and Love

Gabrielle and Samien meet each morning on the train platform and have many discussions as they travel to work. They usually have a seat to themselves and talk through a variety of topics together. It works well for them to have serious discussions in this setting. Early in their relationship, they both realized they have a tendency to get too loud and forceful when disagreeing on an important topic. It helps them to speak more respectfully to each other if they have discussions where others can overhear them if they begin arguing loudly. In addition to this practice, they have agreed to wait a day to discuss something that upsets one of them. They find that having time to calm down and reflect before talking helps them to have more unified and productive discussions.

You are beginning to see clearly just how many factors contribute to your skillful partnership and the smooth flow of your dancing. In dance, you sense and respond appropriately to each other's movements, as you work with the energy that flows between the two of you. It is all about connection and communication. As partners, you are "tuned-in" to each other. When you dance, you build on each other's actions. Whatever you do and whatever your partner does becomes a part of the overall pattern. You dance the same dance as a team. If you both want to change the type of dance you are doing as a pair, you will do so in a unified manner.

Much of the *loving* and *creative* energy that can flow between you and a partner depends upon the *unity* and good communications in your relationship. *Unity* may be an unfamiliar concept to you, as it is not usually a hot topic on the nightly news, Internet headlines, or front page of the newspaper. This chapter will *strengthen* your understanding about how vital it is for your relationship success that you and your partner achieve a high level of *unity* between the two of you.

Many tools will *help* you and your partner to keep your relationship *unified* and *strong*. From your work in previous chapters, you have many of them now in your relationship toolbox. This chapter adds the "Love Languages," because the better you are at letting your partner know you *love* them, the happier your partner will be, and the more *loving* you will feel. You will also gain understanding and skill with repeating what works and humor and laughter. In addition you will reaffirm the importance of *spirituality* as a practice, and learn how to set guidelines for maintaining *peaceful* and *unified* communications with your partner. While there are times when you and a partner will step on each other's toes, your *commitment* to *unity* will hold the two of you together.

THE IMPORTANCE OF UNITY

Think about how you feel when you are not getting along with someone, especially when it is a partner. Your stomach hurts, your head aches, you might be angry. **Disagreements, arguments, contention, strife, or fights going on, whatever the topic, cause disunity. The very survival of your relationship depends upon maintaining a high level of *unity*.** When you think of *unity*, think of words like affinity, attraction, unison, affection, togetherness, reconciliation, and oneness. What would a relationship be like if those were your primary focus?

With *unity*, you find points of harmony with each other. This does not mean that you do not have different opinions, viewpoints, or aspects of your personality or lives. Think of a garden of flowers, where each one can be different in color or fragrance, but they blend into a harmonious whole. Consider a choir, where different voices are required to achieve a beautiful song. **The goal is for you to share your thoughts and feelings in a *respectful* way that does not harm your partner, and for the two of you to work together to come to a *peaceful* agreement. You are friends, and your bond it vital to the two of you. Sharp words and cutting actions can fray and sever that bond over time.**

Biologically, *union* between two entities creates life and growth. *Unified* married couples are the foundation for *unified* families, communities, and a global society. For this reason, disharmony among family members, or arguments about your family, are extremely harmful. When there is *unity*, instead, families experience prosperity, emotional comfort, security, tranquility, and happiness. ***Unity* has enormous power. It calls on you to reconcile your differences, not magnify them.** "Set your faces towards unity, and let the radiance of its light shine upon you. Gather ye together, and…resolve to root out whatever is the source of contention amongst you."[1] Consider how this couple works out a family challenge:

> While Gregor and Chantal take a break from doing their homework, they discuss their plans for the weekend. Gregor's family wants them to attend both a birthday party and a family dinner on Sunday. Chantal is upset, however, as she knows these will tie up a large portion of the day, and she has papers to write for her class and a test to prepare for. She loves Gregor's family, but it will be very difficult to give up

a whole day to spend with them. Gregor's family is very important to him too, and although he has a lot of homework as well, he does not want to make his family upset by not going. Gregor and Chantal begin to argue, but decide they are just too tired to resolve the problem properly. They agree Gregor should talk to his mother about the issue, and they can discuss it again the next day.

Gregor talks to his mother the next day about family, Chantal's concerns, and college all being important. His mother agrees to *help*, and talks to the family. They all decide that having the couple attend the family dinner is enough. Chantal and Gregor are able to do their homework during the day and spend the evening with the family, so they both end up happy with the outcome.

Part of what maintains *unity* between you and your partner is fairness, an aspect of *justice*. If either of you feel a regular sense of injustice at what is happening in your relationship, then resentment will begin to simmer. You are both partners in the relationship. Losing that feeling is a clear indication that you have some re-balancing to do to maintain *unity*. In the story above, Gregor will also need to make adjustments to spend time with Chantal's family, or Chantal will become resentful. Remember when you discuss situations, part of what *helps* you to build *unity* is involving all those affected by a decision in the discussion leading up to it.

***Unity* occurs when diverse people, with their individual talents, abilities, and *strengths*, come together and build something greater than what can happen separately.** It flourishes when there is *encouragement*, support, togetherness, and *courtesy*. It includes both you and your partner striving to *create* situations in your relationship where you are both successful.

***Unity* does not mean that you cannot take individual initiative. Yet, acting on your own must not cause problems for each other.** This means that the two of you agree on when it is appropriate to act alone and when it is best to work *cooperatively*. When you are successful at this effort, the result is comfort, security, tranquility, and *joy*.

ACTIVITY

Complete **Worksheet 15.1: Building Unity Effectively** to assess what words, actions, and activities build *unity* between people, and practice these with a partner or a friend.

BEING A COUPLE

As you and your partner develop your relationship, you will increasingly *discern* what changes to make as individuals to support smoothly functioning as a couple. Being a couple also requires determining together when it is appropriate for you to act as individuals and when to act together. Acting as a couple may be uncomfortable at times, but it is vital for your success as partners. **Your choices will now affect your partner, and your partner's choices will now affect you. This makes it very important to practice *courtesy* and *respect* and communicate with each other before you take actions or make significant decisions.**

The more serious you are as a couple, particularly if you choose to marry, the more important it becomes to have an identity as a couple. Then, you as a couple can make *unified* choices for how to maintain your relationship and how to function together with others.

Balance and Unity as a Couple

Great dance experiences and relationships require balance. When you are a couple, and one of you moves very independently in a direction without considering the other, the balance between the two of you is disturbed. The other partner then has to choose whether to stumble or fall, move to maintain the balance, or stop the movement and request some discussion. Achieving and maintaining balance as a couple is not instantaneous, and being consistent in taking each other into consideration and discussing key topics together will require time and practice. It also takes time to learn each other's values and most likely actions and responses.

Experience and *discernment* will assist with determining what decisions the two of you can make independently without disrupting your *unity*, and which ones are vital to discuss. Two minds, hearts, and souls willingly working together can usually *create* better solutions, and it *strengthens* your relationship to work through a problem together. Discussing choices *helps* to ensure that you find the best outcomes for both of you and for your relationship. **You move forward from making solitary decisions into the blessings that come from joint discussions and *unified* choices.**

However, even when you are familiar with each other's moves on the dance floor, there will be surprises along the way. Other dancers on the floor may bump into you and present challenges that need a response from both of you. When you support each other through all the varied moves of the dances you choose to do, and respond to the challenges, it will build *trust* and *confidence* between you.

Together you and your partner will work to find balance and *equality* in each situation, so that neither of you are overly nor unwisely dependent on the other. It is difficult to say what this looks like, as it will have variations connected to both the circumstances and to the personalities and needs of you and your partner. However, it is possible to say that for you to be most effective at *serving* the needs of each other, both you and your partner also need to know how to take care of your own selves in a mature way (see Chapter 10, page 257 about life management skills and maturity). Self-care includes recognizing your own needs and being personally *responsible* for meeting them or asking your partner to *help*.

You will not be able to *serve* all of each other's needs, nor should you expect to. However, both of you will grow in your ability and willingness to meet each other's needs over time. This is especially *true* as personal and mutual goals become clear to each other, making it easier for you and your partner to *encourage* each other and move forward in life to achieve them. It is certainly important to a relationship that you meet as many of each other's needs as possible.

There may occasionally be an imbalance in the lives of both you and your partner, or unexpected situations. Perhaps one of you has an accident or injury, or the other feels overloaded with project deadlines. These circumstances may require one partner giving an unusual amount of time and effort to the other, as well as some compromise between the two of you. However, if these incidents happen regularly, and the same partner is always the one to give assistance, you may need to examine the levels of *equality* and *respect* in your relationship. Be *discerning* and notice if at any time there is such an imbalance that one of you consistently expects the other to rush to the rescue, or is desperate to have the other solve his or her problems.

Unity and balance do not mean that you and your partner must both be the same. Nor do the two of you need to keep a ledger of who does what. Both of you will no doubt have your own unique skills and abilities to offer to the well-being of each other. Nevertheless, you do need to be *responsible* for keeping your relationship fair. Maintaining *justice* and *equality* requires that your joint efforts stay balanced over time. One of you may do more than your fair share one time, and the next time the other does more. This keeps vital balance in maintaining your relationship.

Being a *united* couple includes maintaining your individual identities and also creating your couple identity and building your relationship together. You and your partner both contribute to the wellbeing of your mutual relationship. You believe in each other, and you champion and support each other's personal development, work, activities, or lives in general. This *strengthens* the relationship and makes you feel close and *united* as a couple. You both offer to each other a mutual *respect* for the work or *service* you do, together or separately. Approaching your relationship in this way prevents you from clinging to each other's life, living vicariously through each other's successes, and deriving your self-worth solely through your partner.

Character growth and development accelerates in you and your partner, as you both "…strive together…towards all that is good."[2] As a couple, you are regularly of *service* to each other with effective character quality use—for instance, you or your partner may be *thoughtful*, *responsible*, or *helpful*. Through teamwork, both of you will become more effective at practicing character qualities together.

It is an indication that you have a *strong* and healthy relationship when you are both replacing poor behavior with better behavior and actively developing your character qualities. You and your partner are both engaging in growth that *strengthens* your higher natures and assists each other in the relationship (Chapter 1). **One outcome from these efforts is that you are improving all the relationships in your lives.**

~ Questions for Reflection ~

1. What does balance look like between being an individual and being part of a couple?
2. What do I appreciate the most about being part of a couple?
3. What is my view of offering *service* to a partner?

ACTIVITY

Discuss with your partner or a close friend how to do a home construction or maintenance project and carry it out together. Discuss how to handle any differences that might arise in the ways you both approach the task. Observe how well you are able to *cooperate* with each other, build *unity* between you, and what other character qualities you both use during the experience.

Balancing Time and Activity

You and your partner will give up time alone and other aspects of living a single life. The two of you will begin to *serve* each other's needs on an *equal* basis. Your friendship with each other will deepen, and your relationship will *strengthen*. Your choices are relationship-building blocks that inspire teamwork and *cooperation*. Having a genuine friend and partner brings you a sense of security and *caring*. Over time, you can share and work through most issues together. Supporting each other in this process will *serve* and *help* each other. Your dancing will flow smoothly with grace and harmony, and a minimum of stumbles.

Often you may experience wanting or needing to give up your own routines and activities and try new ones that your partner is involved in. This is part of contributing to the growth of the relationship and mutually moving in the same direction in your dance together. The rhythms of your lives begin functioning in synchronization and harmony. You and your partner want your lives on the same schedule or with enough free time in both of your lives so that you can maximize your time together. You may notice that you stretch your internal clocks in unfamiliar directions. You may sacrifice sleep or other routines in order to provide time to talk or be together. If you are in a long-distance relationship, you might change your schedule and activities so that you are both free to be on the telephone at the same time across time zones.

There is a need for some restraint with this, however. You may not be able to sustain an unnatural pattern like changing your sleeping times to spend more time with your partner. Make the important changes that you can, but *accept* when you have different needs or patterns than your partner does. Make sure that you do not abandon a part of your regular routine that is a fundamental part of your health and sound living habits. For instance, do not give up a vital exercise program to spend idle time with your partner. You must assess which activities and lifestyle choices you wish to adjust, and which ones to leave behind temporarily or permanently. You will determine which new activities you want to do with your partner, and which ones are new to you both.

Remember to *honestly* share your thoughts and feelings about any new activities the two of you do, but do not judge them until you fully try them. It will harm your relationship if you pretend to like an activity and mislead your partner into believing that it is mutually enjoyable. On the other hand, it is good to participate in things that you may not particularly enjoy on your own, but will enjoy because your partner enjoys it. Consider that you a re giving your partner a gift of your time, *respect*, and fellowship. However, make certain that you can do it with *pure* motives and without resentment. Do not view it as "doing a favor" for them or with the expectation of receiving a favor back. Neither one of you should feel dragged uncomfortably around the dance floor. As you practice and gain *confidence* in the relationship dance, you will find that your skill at maintaining a mutually supportive rhythm, balance, and flow will naturally increase.

~ Questions for Reflection ~

1. What aspects of my single life will I leave behind by being part of a couple?
2. What will I have to change about myself or give up doing to be in a relationship? Will it be worth it?

When you have a partner:

1. What changes am I making to be with my partner or to develop our relationship? Are they healthy, *wise*, sustainable, and realistic?
2. What changes is my partner making so we can be together? Are they healthy, *wise*, sustainable, and realistic?
3. Are we both making changes freely and willingly, or are we actually resentful? Are we expecting a reward for our efforts, or are our motives *pure*?
4. What acts of *service* are we doing for each other? Are they healthy, *wise*, sustainable, and realistic? How are they affecting our relationship?

FIVE "LOVE LANGUAGES"

Part of maintaining a friendship-based relationship includes ensuring that you know how to express *love* for each other well. If you are uncertain whether your partner really *loves* you, or your partner is uncertain about your feelings, your relationship begins to feel very insecure. The more you use *loving* words and practice *loving* actions toward each other, the more your feelings of *love* will grow.

Copyright 2004 by Randy Glasbergen.
www.glasbergen.com

"This is a special night and we'd like everything to be as romantic as possible. On our pizza, could you group the anchovies into couples?"

Expressing *love* is much more than just saying a certain phrase, such as "I *love* you," even though this is part of it. **People actually express and understand *love* in a variety of ways, which are all part of the bonding process between you.** Author and relationship expert Gary Chapman speaks of this topic in his Five Love Languages books.

Chapman says that each person has a symbolic "love tank" inside of them that fills up when they receive *love* from another person. However, the best way to fill each other's tank is for the two of you to express *love* to each other in specific ways. You and your partner need to feel *loved*. For instance, if receiving a gift makes you feel *loved* and your partner gives you one, then you will feel affirmed that your partner *loves* you, and your "love tank" level will go up.

If your partner views time spent together as an expression of *love* and you rarely spend time with them, and perhaps only give gifts to them instead, they may begin to doubt that you really do *love* them. If someone's "love language"—the way they feel *loved*—is through receiving acts of *service*, then they will feel this way: "…let us not love with words or tongue but with actions and in truth."[3] **If you consistently do not receive *love* in the way that is most important to you, then you may begin to question whether your partner truly *loves* you. This can cause gradual erosion in how bonded and *unified* you feel in your relationship.**

Listed below are the five languages summarized from Chapman's *The Five Love Languages for Singles*. Each language is followed by some types of actions that can effectively express *love* to your partner—or others, such as relatives or friends—and meet their needs. **The goal in a relationship is to learn to practice all five of the languages, because they can all enhance your relationship. However, it is especially important to use in a consistent way the primary one your partner most appreciates.**

As with any interaction between you and a partner, *moderation* applies, and communication *helps*. Together you can both discuss how often and to what extent you each will appreciate receiving *love* in these ways:

1. **Give Words of Affirmation:** verbal compliments; words of appreciation; praise, and encouragement; kind words; noticing and appreciating the other's positive actions and qualities

2. **Give Gifts:** tangible objects freely offered; symbols that you were thought about; gifts of any size, shape, color, or price; visual symbol of love with no strings attached or to cover up a failure; given anytime, not just on special occasions

3. **Give Acts of Service:** willingly (not forcibly) do things for the other; welcome helpfulness; timely and positive response to requests (not demands) of the other; acts of kindness; done with loving attitude (not fear, guilt, or resentment); acts that reflect equality and partnership

4. **Give Quality Time:** being available; doing something enjoyable and interactive together; giving uninterrupted, undivided, and focused attention; quality conversation in which both talk and listen; creating memorable moments; self-revealing intimacy

5. **Give Physical Touch:** loving (never abusive) physical contact at appropriate times and places; tender hugs, touches, or pats on the arm, shoulder, or back; back or foot rubs or massages; kissing; holding hands; holding while crying and comforting; sex within the covenant of marriage with your marriage partner[4]

See if you can spot the "love languages" this couple expresses with each other:

> After meeting in college, Jacinta and Roberto have been partners for the last year. They are beginning to discuss the possibility of marriage. When it fits with their work schedules, they meet for dinner and spend time talking together before going to their homes.
>
> Jacinta works as a customer *service* manager for a busy high-tech company. All day long, she deals with customer complaints and problems. At the end of the day, sharing the high and low points of her work experiences allows her to calm down and feel better. Roberto is able to listen to her and express understanding about her problems.
>
> Roberto works as a supervisor on a construction crew that has challenges all day long. As he talks about his day, Jacinta reaches out often and holds Roberto's hand across the table. Feeling Jacinta's touch is important to Roberto, and it reminds him of how much she *loves* him.

Jacinta and Roberto are successfully expressing their *love* to each other, Roberto in giving quality time to Jacinta, and Jacinta in giving Roberto physical touch.

You may immediately identify your primary "love language," or you may struggle with identifying it. The degree to which you have experienced "love languages" in your life affects and limits your initial ability to give and receive them. For instance, if you needed quality time from your father and never received it, you may notice that you *strongly* need it in a relationship. However, you can also not be sure what it looks or feels like.

The good news is that the past does not have to determine the future when it comes to expressing *love*. Even when the love languages seem like foreign languages, you can learn them. Just as with the character qualities, it takes consistent practice and learning from feedback about what works. You can become "love languages" multilingual!

Chapman indicates that in some cases, when you find it difficult to express *love* in the way a relationship partner needs, you may have a block that originates with a parent. It is possible that your partner's need is the same as one of your parents, and you never learned how to practice it effectively with them as you grew up. Identifying the "love languages" that are most important to your parents now, and practicing with them if possible, can *help* you to release your self-expression with your partner, as well as improve your relationship with your parents. If you can learn and practice a "love language" with a parent, you can then express *love* to your partner more freely and effectively.

Chapman says that having a healthy and *loving* relationship with your parents is important for singles who want to be successful in a relationship. He says:

> …many single adults have fractured or broken relationships with parents.
> The lack of feeling parental love leaves them with an emptiness that cannot
> be filled by academic or vocational success. The message…is that no matter
> what has happened between you and your parents, if you will take the initiative
> to discover their primary love language and begin to speak it, the potential
> for healing and reconciliation are real. … On the other hand, you may have
> a strong, loving relationship with your parents. If so, then discovering their
> primary love language will simply enhance that relationship.[5]

If it is impossible to practice giving *love* with your parents, such as if one or both of them have died or there is some other serious barrier, you can still improve your skills. By practicing the "love languages" with close friends or other family members, you will increase your ability to express *love* to your partner. You can also share with your partner that you are *committed* to learning their language, and ask for their support. For instance, if your partner's language is physical touch, and you do not naturally use this language, your partner can touch your shoulder, hold your hand, or lightly hug you and *encourage* you to do the same in return. If, over time, your partner is unable to express *love* to you effectively, it will be a signal to reconsider the relationship.

Note that, according to Chapman, some of the expressions of physical touch, such as sexual intercourse, are most appropriate within marriage, not at this stage of your relationship. This concept was covered in Chapter 5.

How to Identify Your Love Language

You will find it *helpful* to identify the primary "love languages" that work best for both you and your partner—although as mentioned above, it is great if you use them all! You can then discuss ways to keep each other's "love tank" full. Imagine, not just hearing your partner say the words, "I love you," but also experiencing their *commitment* and *love* through actions that you find the most meaningful. Then, imagine how good your partner will feel when you do the same for them.

If your primary "love language" is not clear to you, however, then here are some ways Chapman says you can determine what it is:

- Observe your own behavior so you notice how you typically express *love* and appreciation to others; a large percent of people express in words or actions what they most want to receive
- Observe what you request of others and what you wish they would do, which will indicate your emotional needs
- Make note of your own internal or verbal complaints about what you do not receive
- Ask yourself key questions about your partner, relatives, and friends and what they say and do that you have a positive response to

The method is similar for determining the "love language" of someone else:

- Observe their expressions, complaints, and requests
- Ask questions
- Experiment with offering each "love language" to a partner, relative, or friend and observe their responses

While you are going through this process, you may also begin to identify a secondary "love language" that you *strongly* appreciate.

Alex and Leola tried out all of the "love languages" with each other to determine their primary needs. Here is how they now keep filling each other's "love tanks":

> Teaching at the same university allows Alex and Leola to spend time together to nurture their relationship. In the last few weeks, Leola learned she especially values the "acts of service" "love language." She has chosen to save her money toward buying a house and not to buy a car right now. She feels the most special when Alex picks her up on rainy days so she does not have to take the bus to work. It is also great when he brings lunch to her desk when she has an overloaded schedule and cannot take a break. Sometimes it is difficult for Alex to take the time to do this, but he knows it is important, and he appreciates spending time with her.
>
> While Leola appreciates when others do *service* for her, Alex needs quality time from Leola. He teaches sociology and urban studies courses to graduate students, and he often needs to talk through his frustrations with students and his ideas

about the courses with her. Alex's mother is also very sick, and he finds it *helpful* to talk to Leola about his mother's healthcare options.

Two categories of people may struggle more than others when they attempt to identify their primary "love language":

1. Those who always felt *loved* and who received all five languages from their parents, and who, therefore, may find that they desire a mixture of all five languages from their partner.

2. Those who grew up in very dysfunctional families and who never felt secure in their parents' *love*, and who may, therefore, have to seek professional *help* in order to gain the *confidence* needed to receive and give genuine expressions of *love*. Both partners in the relationship may want to work together with someone they *trust* who can *help* them as they develop "love language" skills.[6]

It is worth repeating that it will enhance your relationship if you practice all five "love languages" with your partner. Time and energy may be an issue occasionally, however. So, if you have to choose one to give your partner, make sure you choose the one that is most important to them.

~ *Questions for Reflection* ~

Note: If you do not have a partner, then answer these questions with a close friend or relative in mind.
1. Which love language most makes me feel *loved*? Which is second?
2. How do I feel when someone regularly does one of the other languages with me and rarely does the one that means the most?
3. What is my partner's primary "love language"?
4. What can I do or say that will fill my partner's "love tank"?
5. Is my partner willing to learn to express *love* to me in my preferred "love language"? Why or why not?

ACTIVITY

Choose one action that you want to receive that matches your primary "love language," and *courteously* request it from your partner or someone else close to you. If you have a partner, identify your partner's primary "love language" and do at least one action that fills their "love tank" per week. If you do not have a partner, then do this practice with a close friend or family member.

IDENTIFY AND REPEAT WHAT WORKS

Sometimes, in spite of all your efforts to be *unified* and *loving*, you and your partner may become stuck in a negative cycle of interactions. Relationship therapist Michele Weiner-Davis suggests a simple, but *helpful* practice to try for couples who wish to turn around a conflict-filled relationship. She recommends that you stop doing what is not working—instead of doing the same thing and unreasonably expecting a different outcome. **Observe what you are both doing when the relationship is calm and harmonious and do more of it. If you have difficulty identifying anything positive in the present, then she encourages you to look back to a previous time in the relationship for answers.**[7]

Relationship researcher Dr. Gottman also advises you to stay in touch with positive relationship memories as a bonding tool. You and your partner can actually pull yourselves out of conflict and back into harmony if you recapture early positive memories of your relationship, and re-discover the feelings and behavior you had at the time. Sharing those memories with each other can rekindle affectionate feelings toward each other and put you back into friendship mode. Of course, you have to stay aware of whether the only thing you still have in common is positive memories of the past!

ACTIVITY

Identify a partner, friend, or relative where there has been some conflict in the relationship. On your own, think through your experiences with the person and identify any that were positive. If possible, share the memories directly with the person. If it is not possible, then reflect or write in your journal about whether you feel an increase in *unity* with the person by doing this activity.

PRAYER AND SPIRITUAL READING

As mentioned throughout the book, *spirituality* can be an area of important bonding for you and your partner. It also supports you as you develop your higher natures and character qualities (Chapter 1). Praying together is a key action that can support your *unity* and *strengthen* your bonds together. You will discover as you use whatever method is most comfortable for the two of you that prayer is a form of *loving* communication.

Prayer will increase your connection with a Higher Power and provide you with a way to request assistance for yourself and for others. It is also a means of expressing *thankfulness* for the blessings in your lives. As was mentioned in Chapter 2, prayer comes in many forms, and it varies by person, religion, culture, and more. In some cultures, movement accompanies prayer. Don Coyhis of the Mohican Nation describes this practice in this way:

> When we dance to the drum we pray to the Creator and attract the heartbeat of the earth. We never dance without reason; every dance has a purpose. We dance for rain; we dance for healing; we dance for seasons; we dance for joy; we dance for our children; we dance for the people; we dance for courage. The drum plays to the beat of the heart, to the beat of the Earth. The drum connects us to the Earth while we dance our prayers.[8]

Some people are comfortable with praying with someone else, while using their own words, scripture, or a combination. Others find praying with another person uncomfortable and too intimate, or they find the prayer practices of a partner too different. It is a good idea to try it a few times, however, to see if you and your partner can make it work. **Prayer provides a *spiritual* connection between the two of you. It is intended to be a positive experience that can assist you both in being happier together.** If you and your partner find that praying together is not creating a positive experience for the two of you, then pray separately and continue to explore other ways of building a *spiritual* bond.

You and your partner might become closer by reading *spiritual* quotations or books together, or read the same book with a *spiritual* theme and discuss it. You may choose to participate in such activities as an organized study of your faith's scripture together, a meditation group, or worship or devotional services. You can try praying over the telephone or for each other, or send inspirational email quotations to each other.

Author Honoré De Balzac wrote:

> Prayer is the fair and radiant daughter of all the human virtues [character qualities], the arch connecting heaven and earth, the sweet companion that is alike the lion and the dove; and prayer will give you the key of heaven."[9]

~ *Questions for Reflection* ~

1. What does prayer look like for me?
2. Am I comfortable praying with a partner?
3. What increases my comfort level in praying with someone else?
4. What *spiritual* practices are important to me as part of a relationship?

<table>
<tr><td>ACTIVITY</td></tr>
</table>

Pray with your partner, a close friend, or a relative about something that is important to one or both of you. Assess the experience and your feelings about it. What do you want to do differently another time?

HUMOR AND LAUGHTER

Joking, teasing in a positive way, laughing, or playing and having fun, are also *loving* and *unifying* communication practices and experiences in a relationship. Having a compatible sense of humor in your communication is especially important. You will probably feel drawn toward someone who can make you laugh. **Laughter lifts your hearts and builds the *loving* feelings you have toward your partner.**

Drs. Les and Leslie Parrott say that "…laughter is the shortest distance between two people…" and that it "…bonds people."[10] They go on to say that humor is good for physical health, *helps* couples cope with stress, and builds *love*. University of Denver, Colorado (USA), researchers Howard Markman and Scott Stanley are also proving that couples that have fun together, stay together.[11]

You can tell a great deal about your partner's character by what they find amusing or laugh aloud at. If they laugh at the misfortunes of others, they probably have a lot of growth to do regarding *compassion*. On the other hand, if your partner laughs along with a giggly child, then this may indicate they have the ability to be *joyful*.

It is important to remember that humor is not always appropriate, and you will observe if your partner has good judgment in this area. When used constructively, humor can lighten up difficult situations. However, a partner might do or say something that on the surface seems related to humor, but is instead destructive. This includes making sarcastic or derogatory comments or delivering insulting insinuations with a smile. These will tear the fabric of your relationship, and it can be difficult to mend.

It will take varied experiences together to determine if you are compatible with humor. As you assess your interactions consider these questions about your relationship:

- Do we find many of the same things funny?
- Are we both able to use humor to lighten difficult situations or heavy moods?
- Do we understand each other's jokes?
- Do we appreciate each other's sense of humor? Are there times when we do, and times when we do not? What distinguishes those?
- Do we know how to make each other laugh?
- How do other people *help* us to laugh and have fun?

The more time you spend with your partner sharing happy moments, the more the bond between you will grow. Identifying what circumstances and behavior *create* this mood will support you in continuing to do what brings you together in *unity*.

~ *Questions for Reflection* ~

1. How do I joke and tease? How do others seem to respond or feel about it?
2. How do I communicate or react when I do not appreciate when a person does something to me that they think is funny, such as tickling or teasing?
3. What makes me laugh?
4. How do I make others laugh? How do others *help* me to laugh and have fun?

ACTIVITY

Go to a funny movie or watch a funny television show together with a partner, close friend, or relative. You may also try spending time looking at cartoon books together in a bookstore. Do you find the same things funny?

STAYING CONNECTED DURING DISCUSSIONS

Every discussion you have with your partner can turn out either positively or negatively. A good outcome depends on your *flexibility* and your ability to agree as partners on what contributes to maintaining *love* and *unity* between the two of you.

The list below suggests some actions and practices that will support the goal of staying *loving* and *unified*. You will develop other techniques as you practice joint decision-making and learn what works and what does not. Some of these actions will become part of your couple communications guidelines that you will work on in the next section. Consider these ways to stay connected during discussions:

- Be *courageous*
- Sit and face each other; perhaps hold hands
- Pause to pray
- Choose a character quality for both of you to practice that will *help* the discussion
- Set the topic; stay on topic; agree when to change the topic
- Discuss any principles or character qualities that apply to the topic
- Maintain an openness to listen and learn from each other

- Be determined to look for *truth* together
- Share feelings calmly, openly, and *honestly*; listen *respectfully* to each other's feelings
- Share perceptions and offer feedback, and be willing to change your thoughts, feelings, and opinions as your partner offers clarifications of their perspectives
- Focus on the topic under discussion, and *carefully* avoid bringing up previous issues, particularly if your motive is to upset your partner
- Take turns being the speaker and the listener
- Allow each other to finish sharing a thought or explaining an idea
- Summarize what the other says to ensure understanding as needed
- Be empathetic (put yourself in your partner's position) and *compassionate*; try to understand each other's perspective by *patiently* allowing each to share their view of the situation without viewing the other as an opponent
- Validate each other's points of view and opinions
- Recognize when emotions are escalating, take a break, and agree to continue the discussion at another time; resume at the agreed time
- Take time to breathe deeply and calm down
- Say "ouch" if something is said that hurts
- Note when there is regret for something said, and stop to apologize
- Strive to come to a mutual and *peaceful* agreement
- Affirm the relationship and acknowledge each other for the willingness to work through the issue

Some of these methods may be comfortable for you and your partner to use, and some may never be. However, if the two of you experiment and practice together, the ones that work well will become clear.

Your *wisdom* will increase if, during and after a difficult communication or any decision-making session, you and your partner pause and look at the dynamics that happened. Take the time to reflect, discuss, and identify the lessons you both learned and ways to do better next time. Identify the specific examples that showed you were able to support each other, and evaluate any missteps that occurred.

Through these assessments, you will learn when you both listened well, where there is need for improvements, and when you *respected* or disrespected each other's thoughts and emotions. For example, did either of you raise something from the past that made the other upset or angry? Was it intentional? Did either of you interrupt when it was not your turn to talk? On the positive side, were you *respectful* of each other's opinions? Did you *encourage* each other to express yourselves fully? Did the process increase the *love* you feel for each other? Did your level of *unity* increase?

Discussions and decision-making sessions take skill and can be smooth or difficult depending upon many factors. However, your commitment to *love* and *unity* will guide you throughout. Consider this perspective from author Linda Kavelin Popov in *A Pace of Grace*:

> At any point in time, we have a way to bridge the distance [to someone we love]. It is something that not only revives intimacy, but also sustains it. Although it is very simple, at times it eludes our awareness. Our capacity to be fully present to each other in the moment is the single most powerful way to sustain love and to show that we cherish one another. It is the greatest gift we have to give anyone. When we are present, we engage in each other's lives, take each other seriously, and meet one another with full, focused attention, with discernment and understanding.[12]

ACTIVITY

In your next discussion with your partner or with a close friend or relative, attempt to implement as many of the suggestions in this section for staying connected as you can. Afterward, think about what went well and what you want to do differently another time. *Commit* to continuing the positive practices that worked well, and to finding ways to improve so your words and actions do not cause communication challenges with a partner or others.

~ Questions for Reflection ~

1. What *helps* me to have calm and constructive discussions with others instead of ones filled with dissension, conflict, and disunity?
2. What *helps* me to reach effective decisions with a partner? With others?

COMMUNICATION GUIDELINES

When you watch a graceful couple dance, you are amazed at how well they move together and weave amongst the other couples on the dance floor. Their *strong* communication skills *help* them to keep touching and moving together smoothly. **In your relationship, it will *help* you and your partner to work out a set of fair and equitable communication guidelines that address what works best to maintain your *love* and *unity*. They will *serve* as a support structure to keep you communicating from within your higher natures** (Chapter 1). If disunity threatens, you can turn to your guidelines and remember what you are *committed* to in your interactions.

You and your partner may not develop these guidelines until after you have spent considerable time with each other. Experiences will *help* you to see what is important to have on the list. However, it can also be a useful practice for a couple to start developing guidelines very early in a relationship and add to it over time. **By establishing agreed guidelines at the beginning of a relationship, you may actually prevent problems as your relationship grows.**

These guidelines will address how you and your partner want to communicate with each other, and also how to resolve issues that arise. There may be unique agreements that are only meaningful to you as a couple, such as "We will rub our left elbows when in public as a reminder to keep something private." Other guidelines might be common for all couples, such as "We will pause and resume later if we begin to be nasty, be very angry, attack each other, or feel disunited." You might also consider this one: "We agree to communicate *honestly*, directly, and as promptly as possible to minimize misunderstandings."

One area for you and your partner to discuss is how you each express anger. This includes what means of communicating it work well in your relationship, and what methods do not. You may discover that you can agree to express anger calmly and directly rather than yelling. For instance, you can say, "I am angry about [specifically state what the issue is] and here is why [state a specific reason]." Alternatively, you can both be comfortable expressing your anger loudly and passionately. As you discuss how to handle anger in your relationship, the key point to consider is how to express it without attacking each other's character and without harming your relationship. Remember that the *Tanakh* says, "Wounds by a loved one are long lasting...."[13] What can you include in your guidelines to address this topic?

Your guidelines also need to address how you will keep your relationship "cleaned up" when you make mistakes. What will *help* to keep you both free of grudges, resentments, and nagging doubts?

Maintaining harmony between you includes being very quick to *forgive*, asking for *forgiveness*, sincerely apologizing, making amends, and *detaching* from issues. Holding onto what happened and bringing it up repeatedly is like leaving a splinter in a finger for too long—it festers and becomes infected and painful. In extreme cases, the finger will need to be removed. In the same way, not practicing *forgiveness* will harm or destroy your relationship over time. Remember that Chapters 2 and 3 have details about character growth, *forgiveness*, and making amends. Consider how this couple establishes guidelines in their relationship:

> Emma's five-year marriage ended, and she has been involved in one relationship since, which is also now over. In both relationships, neither her spouse nor her partner *respected* her opinions, and she developed the habit of keeping her thoughts to herself. Now, she is developing a relationship with Tim, and he often *helps* her to clean her apartment, goes to the store with her, and asks for her advice with his finances. However, she is hesitant to share her *true* feelings with him or to express appreciation for his *kindness*, because she is unsure how Tim will respond if she says what she is thinking and feeling.
>
> One day, Tim directly asks Emma why she does not share her thoughts and feelings with him. When she *courageously* expresses her concerns openly to him, he is relieved to hear why she has been so reserved. Once Tim understands Emma's fears, and what happened to her in previous relationships, he assures her that he will *respect* her in all ways.
>
> Together, Tim and Emma list their promises to each other in their relationship. He writes down that he will invite her to share her ideas and thoughts in each of their conversations, and that he will listen to her with *courtesy*. Emma promises that when Tim invites her to share her thoughts and feelings, she will *trust* him and openly share them.

When you or your partner withdraws or has difficulty sharing thoughts or feelings—possibly due to upbringing, culture, or previous experiences—the other can be supportive, just as Tim was with Emma. This might include asking gentle and open-ended questions and *encouraging* your partner to share, while being cautious not to nag or pressure. Often problems seem much larger when you suppress your feelings and keep them inside.

Just as you and your partner sometimes step on each other's toes while dancing, the two of you can accidentally hurt each other's feelings while attempting to communicate. When you and your partner do experience problems with communications, then it is important, of course, for the two of you to do what you can to restore balance and *unity*.

It is best to practice *mercy* and believe the other had good intentions. This *helps* you both to stay focused on maintaining the positive spirit in the interaction. You can pause, and then when you come back together after a break, adjust what you are saying and how you are saying it. Sharing with your partner what is on your mind and in your heart then builds understanding and agreement. In this process, it *helps* to validate each other's feelings and not belittle them.

When things become tense between you and your partner, therapist Mehri Sefidvash suggests following this advice:

> Nearly all of us have had the experience of a situation in which there was a lot of tension or people's nerves were frayed and a shared laugh was enough to make the atmosphere warm and joyful again. All too often we underestimate the importance of a smile, an embrace, a kind word, a sincere compliment, or the giving of one's attention. It is precisely the small things that can change difficult moments into special ones.[14]

When there has been an imbalance in your relationship, restoring it can take time, discussion, identification of the *helpful* character qualities for the situation, or *spiritual* assistance, such as through prayer or meditation. Your goal is to restore or *create* a powerful sense of *unity* between the two of you. What can you include in your guidelines to reflect these actions?

As you *create* your guidelines, remember to include your new character and *love* skills:

- Use Character Quality Language
- Use the "Love Languages"
- Identify and acknowledge each other's character *strengths*
- Support each other's character development through *encouragement* and *gentle* feedback

Remember that communication between you and your partner is not about power, control, being right, or winning. It is full and *honest* expression between the two of you, using all the appropriate character qualities. It has the intention of building *love* and *unity* as a couple that is committed to a friendship-based relationship.

ACTIVITY

Complete **Worksheet 15.2: Communication Guidelines** in discussion together with your partner. If you are not yet in a relationship, write down a few of the guidelines that will be important for you in a relationship. Remember to look back over the entire book for ideas, especially Part 2. Then, when you have a partner, return to this worksheet and complete it together.

❧ *Encouragement* ☙

You have now done extraordinary foundational work for *creating* a happy and lasting friendship-based relationship. We know that this process has not always been easy, but we *trust* that your personal *confidence* in your relationship success has significantly increased. You are on a lifelong journey of personal growth that will assist you with having an *excellent* relationship. Our positive thoughts, hopes, and prayers are with you as you go forward!

Note: Be sure to turn to page 464 after Part 3 and read **The Next Step:** *A Harmonious Dance*—**Considering Compatibility**.

Date: _____

Worksheet 15.1: Building Unity Effectively

This worksheet will assist you to identify specific words, actions, and activities that can build unity in a relationship.

Instructions:
A) Complete items 1, 2, and 3.
B) Complete item 4, and then practice the unity-building items you have identified in it with a partner, a friend, or a relative.

1. Spend time reflecting on a time when you felt unified with another person. Describe how it felt, what you said to each other, and what you did with each other:

    _____

    _____

    _____

    _____

2. Spend time reflecting on the examples of people you have seen who are excellent at building unity with others. Choose one of them and complete the following:

    a. The person whom I have identified as building unity is:

        _____

    b. To build unity with others they have done the following actions:

        _____

        _____

    c. To build unity with others they have said the following things:

        _____

        _____

    d. This person has the following character qualities that assist them to build unity with others:

        _____

        _____

    e. The effect of this person's unity-building on others is the following:

        _____

        _____

3. Think of the times when you have successfully said something or taken an action that had a unity-building effect. Complete the items on the next page.

a. Describe an example of when you built unity and what you said and did:

_____

_____

b. What character qualities did you draw on to help build unity in this situation?

_____

_____

c. What was the effect of the unity you created on the other people involved?

_____

_____

4. Think about how you can build unity with a partner based on what you have learned from completing the above:
   a. The following words and phrases would encourage unity between a partner and me:

   _____

   _____

   _____

   b. The following actions that I perform for or with a partner would build unity between a partner and me:

   _____

   _____

   _____

   c. The following activities would build unity between a partner and me if we participate in them together:

   _____

   _____

   _____

Questions for Reflection:

1. When am I particularly effective at practicing unity? ?

_____

_____

2. When I did number 4 with someone, did I successfully build unity with them? What could I have done differently or better?

_____

_____

Date: _____

Worksheet 15.2: Communication Guidelines

This worksheet will assist you to create guidelines for effective communication in a relationship. If you are not yet in a relationship, then write down the ones that are important to you, and finish this worksheet when you do have a partner.

Instructions:

A) Consider all that you have learned about communication in Chapters 11-14. Spend some time reflecting about the practices that would help you to accomplish the goal of establishing excellent and peaceful communication patterns with a partner.

B) Then, write down in the table below the guidelines that would help you to achieve this goal. If you have a partner, then discuss and agree on the guidelines that work for both of you.

Examples:

a. We will let each other finish talking without interrupting.

b. We will honor and accept each other's feelings as valid.

c. We will take a break if our discussion is escalating into conflict, or we feel disunity between us.

Note: If you and a partner complete this together, it will be useful to create an attractive copy for both of you to have as a reminder.

OUR AGREED GUIDELINES FOR COMMUNICATION
1.
2.
3.
4.
5.
6.
7.
8.
9.
10.
11.
12.
13.
14.
15.

Part 3

The Best Dance: Exploring Powerful Character Qualities

Introduction and Instructions

Part 3 contains descriptions of 56 character qualities. Out of hundreds of possible qualities, these are very applicable to relationships. Each quality explanation includes:

- A brief definition
- Ways to tell that you are effectively practicing the quality
- Ways to tell that the quality is weak or ineffective, and you need to take steps to move it towards being a strength
- Ways to tell that you are misusing the quality that you actually have as a strength so that you can moderate your use of it and reduce conflicts with a partner or others
- A spiritual reflection quotation about an aspect of the quality

Remember that your character qualities are on a path of growth toward strength--the ability to practice them ever more consistently and effectively. You are highly unlikely to be at either extreme of the range of how to practice a quality, either totally strong or totally ineffective. Part 3 is a tool for you to begin to associate specific words and actions with a quality, not to begin thinking that you are either strong or weak (opposites) in practicing any of them. The goal is to build your self-awareness and empower yourself to practice the qualities effectively.

As you grow in your understanding of character, you will discover that there are more ways to apply the qualities than are listed. However, what is here will give you a good start, both for your individual growth, and for developing a strong friendship-based relationship.

Choose How You Use Part 3

It is wise to spend time reading all the way through this section to become familiar with the qualities. You can then easily refer back to helpful ones as you experience challenges in your life and look for solutions. You can also:

- Read a quality each day as a focus for practice
- Discuss one quality at a time in depth with a partner or friend
- Study qualities together with a group of friends

Activity Possibility: Ask yourself specific questions about each of the character qualities listed in Part 3. An example for *creativity* is this: Do I approach problems and challenges the same way each time, or do I search out alternate solutions?

Use *Can We Dance?* as your easy reference guide to assess your behavior and choices regularly. You will discover that it is a valuable tool to keep handy everywhere you go. You will learn to understand yourself, a partner, and others better than you ever thought was possible.

Character Qualities

Acceptance	Idealism
Assertiveness	Integrity
Beauty	Joyfulness
Caring	Justice
Chastity	Kindness
Commitment	Love
Compassion	Loyalty
Confidence	Mercy
Contentment	Moderation
Cooperation	Patience
Courage	Peacefulness
Courtesy	Perseverance
Creativity	Purity
Detachment	Purposefulness
Discernment	Respect
Encouragement	Responsibility
Enthusiasm	Self-Discipline
Equality	Service
Excellence	Sincerity
Faithfulness	Spirituality
Flexibility	Strength
Forgiveness	Tactfulness
Friendliness	Thankfulness
Generosity	Thoughtfulness
Gentleness	Trustworthiness
Helpfulness	Truthfulness
Honesty	Unity
Humility	Wisdom

ᲖᲐ *Acceptance* ᲖᲐ

Acceptance is acknowledging people as they are and not trying to change people or stop events from happening when there is no room for influence or control.

I am practicing Acceptance effectively when I:

- Acknowledge and show respect for others' thoughts, opinions, or actions
- Am calm and composed when people or circumstances cause me to alter my plans
- Build friendships with people who are different from me in many ways, such as personality, culture, or religion
- Do not try to change what I cannot about a partner, other people, or circumstances
- View and respond to reality as it is, even when I do not like it
- See and appreciate a partner just as they are

I need to strengthen Acceptance when I:

- Am easily agitated, critical, or lose my composure when people or events do not meet my expectations and there is nothing I can do to stop or alter a situation
- Try to change people
- Criticize others for not doing things my way
- Criticize myself and see aspects of myself as unworthy
- Resist or complain about the direction and circumstances of my life, daydreaming and wishing they were different
- Avoid following appropriate guidance from respected sources

I misuse the strength of Acceptance when I:

- Go along with negative situations inappropriately or let others treat me poorly or abuse me
- Remain silent inappropriately and therefore enable others to behave irresponsibly or harmfully toward themselves or others
- Do not responsibly exert influence or control to prevent or improve a negative situation

Spiritual Reflection: If it is possible, as far as it depends on you, live at peace with everyone.[1]

⸙ *Assertiveness* ⸙

Assertiveness is exerting personal effort to decisively speak up or act to improve a situation in a way that benefits others and oneself.

I am practicing Assertiveness effectively when I:
- Think and act for myself
- Step forward into appropriate leadership or involvement
- Believe I am a worthy person and take action to make my true self known, including my thoughts, ideas, opinions, feelings, boundaries, limitations, intentions, plans, or beliefs
- Request that someone meet a need that others or I have
- Act to resolve a problem
- Request respectful treatment from a partner

I need to strengthen Assertiveness when I:
- Allow others to treat me with disrespect, or to act on my behalf without my agreement or input
- Sit quietly instead of speaking up or taking action to share my thoughts, or to defend a just cause that I believe in
- Have no personal standards or boundaries for appropriate behavior for myself or others

I misuse the strength of Assertiveness when I:
- Behave in aggressive or pushy ways without considering the rights or viewpoints of others
- Use offensive words or an overly directive tone of voice in order to dominate others or to get my own way

Spiritual Reflection: Man is not intended to see through the eyes of another, hear through another's ears nor comprehend with another's brain. ... Therefore, depend upon your own reason and judgment and adhere to the outcome of your own investigation....[2]

❧ *Beauty* ❧

Beauty is outwardly expressing one's inner spirit and seeing natural and positive attractiveness wherever possible.

I am practicing Beauty effectively when I:
- See all that is wonderful and awe-inspiring in the world and in myself
- Groom and dress myself in an attractive way
- Take care of my home and property, keeping it clean and orderly, and adding to it in harmonious ways
- Have a sincere, smiling, or radiant expression on my face
- Recognize and encourage inner mental, spiritual, and physical growth and well-being in myself, a partner, and in others
- Develop or create what is pleasing to the body, mind, heart, and soul
- Enrich my life with music, art, literature, dance, science, nature, and spiritual quotations and activities
- Express appreciation for the attractive attributes and qualities of others, including kindness, gentleness, and respect

I need to strengthen Beauty when I:
- Neglect or disrespect my own appearance and well-being
- Allow my home or environment to deteriorate
- Frown upon or look at others with hostility or disrespect
- Disconnect from spiritual or inspirational sources
- Behave in ways that make me ugly, such as shouting, swearing, or acting under the influence of alcohol or drugs

I misuse the strength of Beauty when I:
- Act vain and superior about my appearance
- Am intolerant of mental, spiritual, and physical imperfections in myself or others
- Idolize people who look a certain way
- Wear extreme or provocative clothing or excessive jewelry; excessively decorate my body
- Treat someone as a sex object, or view and value pornography

Spiritual Reflection: ...By giving away our food, we get more strength, by bestowing clothing on others, we gain more beauty; by donating abodes of purity and truth, we acquire great treasures.[3]

↬ *Caring* ↫

Caring is giving sincere love, attention, consideration, and assistance to others in timely and appropriate ways.

I am practicing Caring effectively when I:
- Meet the various needs of others with consideration and empathy to provide them with relief and comfort
- Listen attentively and compassionately
- Give my best effort to complete tasks with consistent and thorough attention to the details
- Share my time with others to show that I am interested in them
- Look after my own well-being, that of a partner, and that of others in moderate and appropriate ways
- Maintain wise restraint and caution in potentially unsafe circumstances

I need to strengthen Caring when I:
- Callously ignore the needs and wishes of others
- Mistreat others or their possessions
- Respond negatively or harshly to others when they share their needs or concerns
- Make choices to be with people who are hurtful, or in circumstances that are harmful

I misuse the strength of Caring when I:
- Meddle in or manage others' lives without their need or invitation, become over-protective, or allow others to become unnecessarily or unhealthily dependent upon me
- Overly attempt to meet the perceived needs of others, communicating to them that they are less capable than I am

Spiritual Reflection: ...do good—to parents, kinsfolk, orphans, those in need, neighbors who are near, neighbors who are strangers....[4]

◈ *Chastity* ◈

Chastity is maintaining sexual purity in order to share it as a respectful and special gift with a marriage partner.

I am practicing Chastity effectively when I:
- Abstain from sexual touch and acts before marriage, and then stay faithful to a marriage partner
- Am moderate and modest in my use of words, clothing, and movements to avoid inviting inappropriate attention, touch, and untimely sexual attraction
- Strive to keep my mind free from focus on sexual thoughts, which helps me to control my sexual desires and impulses
- Avoid substances such as alcohol or drugs that reduce or diminish my inhibitions
- Make entertainment and activity choices that are respectful of others and myself
- Have strong friendships with both men and women without sex as a factor
- Interact with a partner with equality, respect, and gentleness
- Fill my life with purposes and service, placing less importance on sex

I need to strengthen Chastity when I:
- See sex as the only way to achieve happiness or have a relationship
- Act sexually seductive, touch someone intimately, or invite the same from them
- Place highest importance on a partner's physical attributes while ignoring their mental abilities and spirituality; view someone as an object instead of as a whole person
- View sex as a game, spectator sport, opportunity for conquest or bragging, method of becoming acquainted, or means of diversion or relaxation
- Pursue pleasure through excessive trivial activities that waste time, or entertainment or activities that are sexually stimulating
- Fantasize, view or participate in pornography, masturbate, or become attached to regular sexual pleasure
- Am sexually abusive, such as by being forceful, threatening, or violent

I misuse the strength of Chastity when I:
- Reject or disdain my own sexuality and sensuality, or act as if sex is dirty or wrong rather than it being a spiritual gift and part of the unique and priceless bond that unites a married couple
- Am unable to communicate affectionate feelings to a partner
- Judge, condemn, gossip, or backbite about the sexual actions of others [See chapter 12 for explanations of gossip and backbiting.]

Spiritual Reflection: One speck of chastity is greater than a hundred thousand years of worship and a sea of knowledge.[5]

ᜅ *Commitment* ᜆ

Commitment is making a reasonable promise or binding agreement to oneself, a partner, or to others that includes meeting certain goals or expectations and carrying out specific actions.

I am practicing Commitment effectively when I:
- Keep my word and promises, following through with actions to fulfill what I say I will do
- Accept and fulfill the responsibilities that go along with an agreement or decision
- Stay firm on an agreed course of action, even when it becomes difficult, and take action to improve the situation
- Act according to my firm beliefs
- Move forward in a relationship even when I feel some fear or anxiety based on previous experiences

I need to strengthen Commitment when I:
- Regard relationships as a short-term series of conquests
- Persist in breaking promises
- Fail to fulfill my agreements or resolutions
- Disrespect the value of my word or my stated intentions
- Ignore the responsibilities that are necessary for me to fulfill to maintain the integrity of an agreement

I misuse the strength of Commitment when I:
- Am inflexible, rigid, close-minded, or stubborn
- Unreasonably refuse to renegotiate promises
- Keep commitments even though clear evidence indicates they are unwise or dangerous, with a high cost to health, safety, or relationships

Spiritual Reflection: And being not weak in faith…what he had promised, he was able also to perform.[6]

❦ *Compassion* ❧

Compassion is having a genuine concern for others, a partner, and oneself, sensing the pain in difficult experiences, and wanting to take action to relieve it.

I am practicing Compassion effectively when I:
- Actively listen for the burden and pain others are carrying in their hearts, minds, and souls
- Support and comfort others when they are in trouble, injured, ill, or have made a mistake
- Hold someone's hand while they are grieving
- Strengthen or empower others to relieve their own suffering
- Pay attention to my own inner pain and struggles and gently give myself time to heal

I need to strengthen Compassion when I:
- Keep a cold or uncaring distance between a partner and myself or with others
- Ignore others' problems, feelings, or issues
- Judge others as weak or incompetent to handle their lives and problems
- Prevent others or myself from grieving or taking time to adjust to illness, deaths, failures, or traumas, and see grieving or the need for healing time as signs of weakness

I misuse the strength of Compassion when I:
- Overly involve myself in relieving the pain or responding to the needs of others and thereby neglect my own important responsibilities
- React to reduce someone's pain too quickly without knowing all the facts and therefore cause more harm
- Quickly defend someone against a perceived oppressor without considering the whole picture

Spiritual Reflection: A man should not hate any living creature. Let him be friendly and compassionate to all.[7]

⊰ *Confidence* ⊱

Confidence is trusting one's own and others' inner value and worthy intentions, and having the capacity to think and act effectively and accomplish stated goals.

I am practicing Confidence effectively when I:

- Believe in myself, the worth of my actions, and that I can handle whatever problems or circumstances arise; communicate that a partner or others are capable of the same
- Use my talents and abilities to benefit a partner, my family, others, and myself
- Assertively take appropriate initiative
- Pursue worthy goals individually and with others
- Try something new, knowing that I will be successful
- Use body language to convey inner self-respect, such as sitting or standing straight and tall or walking with dignity

I need to strengthen Confidence when I:

- Overwhelm myself with doubts and fears
- Waste energy thinking about why I cannot do something instead of using my resources to actually accomplish it
- Criticize myself and withdraw from others or activities
- Believe or act as if I am less capable or competent than a partner or others
- Participate only in easy activities or only set unchallenging goals

I misuse the strength of Confidence when I:

- Act self-centered or conceited about myself
- Brag about my accomplishments
- Am overbearing and bossy toward others
- Insist my ways and plans are best and those of others are wrong

Spiritual Reflection: ...the righteous are as confident as a lion.[8]

✌ *Contentment* ✌

Contentment is having a tranquil body, mind, heart, and soul and calm, accepting feelings toward relationships, employment, surroundings, and life in general.

I am practicing Contentment effectively when I:

- Calmly accept the natural flow of changes in my body and my life
- Spend my time wisely for pursuing purposes and professions that make the best use of my talents and abilities
- Enjoy the people and blessings in my life
- Peacefully seek to overcome challenges
- Pause to breathe, slow down, and enjoy the moment
- Accept the outcome of an activity, event, project, or goal
- Let go of trying to fix something or of making something turn out the way that I think it should
- Appreciate what I have and do not scramble and try to acquire more

I need to strengthen Contentment when I:

- Compare my life to others' lives
- Push, whine, or agitate the people in my life to change themselves or what is making me unhappy
- Am unsettled, anxious, or fearful about the future
- Want what others have that I do not, or idealize the relationship that others have

I misuse the strength of Contentment when I:

- Accept the inappropriate actions of others or do not remove myself from harmful situations
- Avoid solving pressing problems and rely on others to do the work for me
- Passively let my life and mind become stagnant or decline
- Proudly resist fresh ideas, the influence of others, and change
- Am determined to remain the same without improving myself or my life

Spiritual Reflection: Let your conversation be without covetousness; and be content with such things as ye have....[9]

Ꮳ *Cooperation* Ꮳ

Cooperation is working together in harmony to create or accomplish something that would be more difficult or impossible to accomplish alone.

I am practicing Cooperation effectively when I:
- Share thoughts, ideas, and time while working in partnership with others to accomplish worthwhile tasks, goals, and objectives
- Adjust my ideas, wishes, and expectations while building consensus with a partner or others
- Support the decisions we make as a couple or that are made by a majority vote of a group
- Plan activities or events with others
- Practice teamwork and good sportsmanship
- Accept assistance from others toward achieving goals

I need to strengthen Cooperation when I:
- Resist assistance from others and do too much on my own
- Refuse to participate in couple or group activities, act as a team member, or interact as a peer with my partner
- Regard others as incapable of participating in an activity
- Undermine or refuse to follow couples or group decisions

I misuse the strength of Cooperation when I:
- Sacrifice my values or principles to work with someone or to do things with others in unwise or harmful situations
- Keep silent about unwise partner or group decisions or actions to avoid making people upset or drawing attention to myself
- Work with others only to gain something from them

Spiritual Reflection: As long as the various members and parts…are coordinated and cooperating in harmony, we have as a result the expression of life in its fullest degree.[10]

418 • Can We Dance? Learning the Steps for a Fulfilling Relationship

❧ *Courage* ❧

Courage is taking brave and bold action, defending what is right, or completing a worthwhile challenge, even when there is fear, resistance, opposition, hardship, or danger.

I am practicing Courage effectively when I:
- Face and take effective action with a difficult challenge or risky situation in spite of feeling fearful
- Am self-possessed, confident, resolute, and brave when facing difficult situations or vital tasks that need to be done
- Try new activities, build friendships, and initiate a relationship without holding back important parts of myself
- Powerfully resume life after a difficult loss or error
- Speak what is on my mind and heart, even when it is difficult for a partner or others to hear what I need to say
- Make necessary changes in myself or my life, even when they are unpopular with a partner or others

I need to strengthen Courage when I:
- Give priority to my doubts and fears of failure and avoid acting or taking necessary risks
- Avoid sharing my thoughts and feelings appropriately with a partner, close friends, or relatives
- Allow others to dominate, use, or abuse me in any way
- Ignore or deny my own values and allow the unwise actions of others to continue unstopped

I misuse the strength of Courage when I:
- Speak brazenly or act recklessly without regard for others' feelings or welfare
- Behave boldly but in ways that create negative consequences or conflict

Spiritual Reflection: He gives courage to the weak when they would...give up self-reliance and hope.[11]

৯ৎ *Courtesy* ৯৯

Courtesy is showing gracious and loving consideration for others, putting their needs first, and using polite manners, respectful gestures, and kind language in speaking to others.

I am practicing Courtesy effectively when I:
- Notice others and interact with them with gentle sensitivity
- Show consistent love, caring, and helpfulness through my words and actions
- Politely assist others as a respectful gesture, even when they can do an action for themselves, such as opening a door or carrying something
- Make respectful requests of others instead of demands
- Use manners, such as saying "please" and "thank you"
- Provide gracious hospitality to others

I need to strengthen Courtesy when I:
- Selfishly put myself first, acting as though I am more important than others
- Behave abruptly or rudely, or am short-tempered with others
- Give orders to others inappropriately for the roles and circumstances

I misuse the strength of Courtesy when I:
- Am self-conscious and uneasy about how others think I am acting, or am too concerned with my formal manners and become stiff socially
- Behave insincerely without really being concerned about the true needs of a partner or others, typically to manipulate them or have my own way

Spiritual Reflection: When a…greeting is offered you, meet it with a greeting still more courteous….[12]

❧ *Creativity* ❧

Creativity is drawing on ideas and inspiration and producing or developing something new that has never existed before through artistic or imaginative effort.

I am practicing Creativity effectively when I:
- Develop and try new friendship-building and character exploration activities with a partner and discover new adventures, possibilities, and experiences
- Discover and develop my talents and engage in artistic activities like painting, poetry, writing, drawing, or playing a musical instrument, and encourage a partner and others to do the same
- Conduct experiments with science
- Use prayer and meditation to receive inspiration for artistic expression or to develop something new
- Use words and actions to develop new approaches and solutions to problems that produce positive outcomes in my life, relationships, community service projects, and employment
- Make uplifting and beautiful changes in my home or office
- Cook new and interesting food and combinations of foods

I need to strengthen Creativity when I:
- Narrowly focus on the presumed facts of a situation and close myself off from new possibilities
- Do something repetitively even when it does not work well, such as behaving in the same way in a new relationship as I have in the past
- Block, withhold, or lack confidence in my capacity for personal expression of all kinds
- Stay stuck in boring routines

I misuse the strength of Creativity when I:
- Mischievously devise plans that manipulate, hurt, injure, or insult others
- Desire something so strongly that I find dishonest ways to achieve it
- Daydream or make up stories that conceal, justify, or exaggerate my behavior
- Make interesting but disruptive changes for no good reason

Spiritual Reflection: It behoveth the craftsmen of the world...to exert their highest endeavor and diligently pursue their professions so that their efforts may produce that which will manifest the greatest beauty and perfection before the eyes of all men.[13]

✎ *Detachment* ✎

Detachment is stepping back from letting one's feelings and attachments be in control and gaining a greater perspective of what is happening.

I am practicing Detachment effectively when I:

- Empathize with others without making their feelings my own
- Think rationally and clearly, and my responses are based upon the known facts without personal bias, strong emotions, or imagined situations
- Gather and examine the facts of a project, situation, or person, and seek input from others
- Accept not being somewhere or with someone that I love
- Let go of overly strong fears of losing something or someone based on previous experiences
- Understand a partner's limitations and stop holding unreasonable expectations
- Throw or give away unnecessary items in my home or office

I need to strengthen Detachment when I:

- React emotionally rather than pausing to determine the facts of the matter
- Attach myself emotionally to someone or something so strongly that I abandon my own good judgment
- Depend excessively upon others, in such manner as to negatively affect my well-being or theirs
- Hold onto clutter even when it interferes with functioning effectively

I misuse the strength of Detachment when I:

- Insensitively fail to consider the well-being of others
- Isolate myself from others or treat them in a cool, distant, and unloving way
- Dispose of belongings without regard for value, sentiment, or usefulness

Spiritual Reflection: A serene spirit accepts pleasure and pain with an even mind, and is unmoved by either.[14]

∽ *Discernment* ∾

Discernment is clearly seeing a situation and another's character and motives without prejudice or bias, and determining what is beneficial and what is harmful.

I am practicing Discernment effectively when I:
- Carefully observe character qualities in a partner
- See a range of perspectives and facts, and respond appropriately and fairly to what is true
- Make effective choices between right and wrong, and understand the factors that influence the choices
- Understand my motives, intentions, expectations, and reactions and those of others
- Observe and analyze the needs in various areas of my life, relationships, home, and community
- Base my choices and my beliefs upon the best and most factual input, while still respecting my intuition and inspiration

I need to strengthen Discernment when I:
- Jump to conclusions
- Fail to listen carefully to others
- Am easily fooled into accepting false information
- Carelessly make choices without considering my morals, values, or principles
- Neglect to weigh the consequences of my words and actions ahead of time
- Miss or avoid seeing important aspects of a person or situation

I misuse the strength of Discernment when I:
- Pry into the private concerns or lives of others
- Forget to look for the positive qualities of others and look only critically and judgmentally for their flaws

Spiritual Reflection: …make your ear attentive to wisdom and your mind open to discernment…. You will then understand what is right, just, and equitable—every good course.[15]

❦ *Encouragement* ❧

Encouragement is offering sincere, uplifting acknowledgment of someone's character qualities, effective actions, or good intentions to inspire or assist them to continue or to foster their personal growth and development.

I am practicing Encouragement effectively when I:

- Assist people who are discouraged, especially when they try hard or are trying something new
- Show confidence in the ability of others to succeed
- Inspire someone to be courageous when they are struggling with fear
- Notice the choices and plans someone is making or wants to make and offer my sincere support to them
- Acknowledge the best in others

I need to strengthen Encouragement when I:

- Criticize, ridicule, belittle, or devalue the attempts, abilities, or character of others
- Ignore what is important to the people in my life
- Take for granted the efforts of a partner or other people close to me

I misuse the strength of Encouragement when I:

- Push or manipulate others to do something
- Try to get someone to do something that is harmful, unwise, or that they do not want to do
- Use insincere praise or flattery to get my own way with others

Spiritual Reflection: ...love each other, constantly encourage each other, work together, be as one soul in one body, and in so doing become a true, organic, healthy body animated and illumined by the spirit.[16]

◈ *Enthusiasm* ◈

Enthusiasm is externally expressing an inner genuine and joyful feeling about an important, wonderful, or extraordinary activity or goal in a high-spirited way.

I am practicing Enthusiasm effectively when I:
- Am happy and excited about something that is happening or could happen
- Look for the best in people and situations and share what I see with others
- Approach tasks or adventures wholeheartedly
- Appreciate the positive aspects of a task that could otherwise be seen as tedious, boring, or difficult
- Enjoy what I am doing
- Am filled with excitement about the Creator and participating in spiritual practices

I need to strengthen Enthusiasm when I:
- Regard everything as the same and nothing as great, extraordinary, or inspiring
- Am negative, discouraged, resigned, bored, or cynical
- Speak critically about the ideas of others
- Do not look forward to experiences

I misuse the strength of Enthusiasm when I:
- Impulsively jump into a belief, project, or idea without adequately assessing its substance or value
- Rave excessively about something and insist that others should be as excited as I am

Spiritual Reflection: ...the heart that has good soil and with a full spirit is strong....[17]

❧ *Equality* ❧

Equality is maintaining a balanced and respectful partnership between two people in a relationship that honors the minds, hearts, and souls of each and includes working together as a team.

I am practicing Equality effectively when I:

- Communicate my thoughts and feelings, and encourage a partner to do the same
- Listen carefully to a partner
- Honor the participation of a partner in our relationship
- Regard both a partner and myself as valuable human beings
- Am fair-minded and equitable in determining with a partner how each of us handles responsibilities that affect us both
- Have discussions and make decisions with a partner as appropriate
- Learn a new skill to create greater balance between a partner and me

I need to strengthen Equality when I:

- Give orders or make demands on a partner, or attempt to dominate or control them
- Act superior or inferior to a partner
- Expect a partner to do my fair share of tasks
- Insist that our roles and responsibilities be identical
- Hold back sharing important information or feelings that contribute to a discussion or decision, thinking they are less valuable or not legitimate

I misuse the strength of Equality when I:

- Am inconsistent in my expectations or constantly change my mind about what our roles or responsibilities should be
- Ignore, belittle, devalue, or am reluctant to point out our authentic differences

Spiritual Reflection: Divine Justice demands that the rights of both sexes should be equally respected since neither is superior to the other…. Dignity before God depends, not on sex, but on purity and luminosity of heart. Human virtues belong equally to all![18]

❧ Excellence ❧

Excellence is striving to achieve high standards and a superior quality of work that includes fulfilling one's capacity for character growth and development.

I am practicing Excellence effectively when I:

- Learn how to achieve the best outcome in situations, and strive selflessly to give my best in every endeavor
- Practice tasks, skills, talents, character qualities, and positive behaviors until I can do them consistently and effectively
- Create outcomes that endure or that others can sustain
- Achieve success through working with others cooperatively
- Approach my tasks in an orderly, neat, precise, and clear way
- Develop and act to fulfill my purposes in life

I need to strengthen Excellence when I:

- Treat my responsibilities carelessly
- Perform my work in a sloppy way
- Neglect my relationship with a partner and others
- Avoid developing my character qualities
- Settle for mediocrity, adopt society's standards, or set such low standards of achievement for myself that I do not fulfill my talents, abilities, and capacities

I misuse the strength of Excellence when I:

- Approach making improvements in an overly meticulous way, placing a higher emphasis on making things perfect than I do on treating others with courtesy and kindness
- Act inflexibly and impatiently with my achievements or myself
- Maintain an attitude of superiority towards others
- Act intolerant of someone or something that does not meet my standards
- Use competition with others as my only means of motivating my achievement

Spiritual Reflection: ...in this world, aspirants may find enlightenment by two different paths. For the contemplative is the path of knowledge: for the active is the path of selfless action.[19]

❧ *Faithfulness* ❧

Faithfulness is being steadfast and maintaining commitments, particularly to a partner, but also to a set of beliefs or to an organization.

I am practicing Faithfulness effectively when I:

- Stay loyal and trustworthy in my thoughts, speech, and actions
- Respect the bond I have with a partner and maintain the chastity, unity, and integrity of our relationship
- Practice my beliefs in an honest, sincere, and forthright manner
- Keep going on a course I commit to follow

I need to strengthen Faithfulness when I:

- Share or connect my time, money, body, mind, heart, or soul inappropriately with someone when I am committed to another person
- Fail to practice my spiritual beliefs or speak out against them in a way that shakes the faith of others

I misuse the strength of Faithfulness when I:

- Put more importance on superficial relationships with others than with a partner and family
- Follow religious beliefs unquestioningly without investigating their truth
- Show unwavering support for a harmful relationship or friendships that are disloyal to a partner

Spiritual Reflection: ...faithfully observe their trusts and their covenants....[20]

✎ *Flexibility* ✎

Flexibility is adjusting to life as it happens and embracing changes as needed, while remaining true to values, beliefs, and appropriate priorities.

I am practicing Flexibility effectively when I:
- Detach from plans as needed
- Appreciate the joys and benefits that come with the unplanned and unexpected happenings in life
- Enthusiastically participate in a spontaneous activity
- Stay open to new ideas, creative options, innovative approaches, and alternative perspectives
- Adjust my thoughts and attitudes as needed to respond to new information or difficulties as they arise
- Gently bend to changes in people and circumstances without resistance, fear, or anger
- Am open to changing myself, including engaging in character growth

I need to strengthen Flexibility when I:
- Stubbornly insist that nothing should ever change
- Refuse to change myself, my beliefs, my patterns of living, or where I live, even when there are compelling reasons to do so
- Become upset due to changes in plans or unforeseen circumstances

I misuse the strength of Flexibility when I:
- Resist having any schedules, plans, structures, or goals
- Abandon or ignore my principles and good judgment to respond to a partner's request or to give in to peer pressure
- Change my mind regularly and quickly for no good reason
- Shy away from making choices or fail to stick with my previous thoughtful choices

Spiritual Reflection: If it be Thy pleasure, make me to grow as a tender herb in the meadows of Thy grace, that the gentle winds of Thy will may stir me up and bend me into conformity with Thy pleasure, in such wise that my movement and my stillness may be wholly directed by Thee.[21]

❧ *Forgiveness* ❧

Forgiveness is pardoning someone for saying or doing something hurtful, while giving up any desire for revenge or holding their actions against them.

I am practicing Forgiveness effectively when I:

- Accept what happened as unchangeable and release my feelings of anger, resentment, or pain
- Give others and myself the opportunity to resolve issues, reconcile, and start over anew
- Seek to understand the viewpoints of others
- Do not focus on the faults of others
- Commit to restore integrity and love in a relationship after a hurtful experience
- Know that harmony within myself and unity with others is far more important than holding onto negative feelings about the past
- Pray for assistance with pardoning the wrongdoer

I need to strengthen Forgiveness when I:

- Hold onto bitterness
- Seek revenge against someone
- Refuse to accept an apology when someone else has made a mistake or make amends when I do
- Hold grudges and resentment and bring the problem back up repeatedly with others
- Withhold forgiveness until the other person specifically asks me for it
- Criticize others or myself for words or actions

I misuse the strength of Forgiveness when I:

- Accept unjust, abusive, or harmful actions from someone without resolution
- Avoid holding others or myself accountable for words or actions
- Freely behave poorly because I presume automatic forgiveness

Spiritual Reflection: Bear with each other and forgive whatever grievances you may have against one another. Forgive as the Lord forgave you.[22]

❧ *Friendliness* ❧

Friendliness is having an outgoing and positive social attitude and practices that connect people.

I am practicing Friendliness effectively when I:
- Greet and include others in a warm, pleasant, and inviting way
- Smile at others, and share thoughts, ideas, and laughter with them
- Spend time with and help people during good times and difficulties
- Show welcoming and courteous hospitality at my home or as a host in a public place
- Take an interest in others and listen carefully to them, acknowledging and validating what they say or do, and keeping private what they share
- Remember and use others' names

I need to strengthen Friendliness when I:
- Behave in a cool, distant, or reserved way toward others
- Frown or greet others coldly
- Avoid extending hospitality
- Isolate myself from others or wait for others to be friendly toward me first
- Gossip, backbite, or spread slander about a partner or others [See chapter 12 for explanations.]

I misuse the strength of Friendliness when I:
- Connect only with others who can increase my status and importance
- Spend an excessive amount of time with friends, allowing them to overly influence me
- Neglect my responsibilities and family in order to spend time with friends
- Act inappropriately sexually seductive and intimate with someone
- Manipulate people into pitying me for being alone

Spiritual Reflection: Two are better off than one…. For should they fall, one can raise the other….[23]

❦ *Generosity* ❧

Generosity is being open-hearted and open-handed in giving away or sharing what I have, such as spirituality, ideas, time, resources, possessions, or money.

I am practicing Generosity effectively when I:

- Give joyfully, willingly, or sacrificially without expecting to receive anything in return
- Openly acknowledge the best in others and share my best self with them
- Share words and emotions from my heart
- Acknowledge the abundance of gifts I have in my life to share with others

I need to strengthen Generosity when I:

- Hoard what I have or am miserly or stingy with my heart, time, talents, money, or possessions
- Loan but never give to others
- Withhold love or important emotions and information from a partner
- Live and act as if everything is scarce or unavailable

I misuse the strength of Generosity when I:

- Give to the point where I neglect my future or my responsibilities to a partner, family, or friends
- Live in an extravagant or wasteful way
- Gamble with my resources, putting important aspects of my life at risk

Spiritual Reflection: Give of the good things which ye have (honorably) earned, and of the fruits of the earth which We have produced for you....[24]

❧ *Gentleness* ❧

Gentleness is expressing consideration from the heart in words that honor the feelings of others, and being soft and careful when physically touching.

I am practicing Gentleness effectively when I:
- Use self-awareness and self-discipline to moderate and control my words and actions so that they are sensitive to the feelings of others
- Touch an animal or person in a way that expresses affection and tenderness
- Act in ways that promote feelings of safety and security for others
- Protect things from breaking, and animals and people from harm or injury
- Think positive thoughts instead of critical ones

I need to strengthen Gentleness when I:
- Treat something roughly or someone cruelly
- Yell loudly or speak harshly, forcefully, or sarcastically
- Watch violent television shows or movies, or play violent video games
- Become angry and violent with others or myself

I misuse the strength of Gentleness when I:
- Avoid firmly handling an issue or dealing with someone's harsh words or violent actions
- Act in an overly submissive, unassertive, docile way, which allows others to manipulate or take advantage of me

Spiritual Reflection: Satisfy the necessities of life like the butterfly that sips the flower, without destroying its fragrance or its texture.[25]

✌ *Helpfulness* ✎

Helpfulness is understanding someone's needs or problems and taking appropriate action to address or solve them.

I am practicing Helpfulness effectively when I:

- Assist others as needed or requested in ways that make life easier or less stressful for them
- Perform tasks for others that they cannot do for themselves
- Consciously observe my surroundings and listen to the people around me to understand what needs to be done
- Create solutions that solve problems and promptly do what needs to be done to benefit others
- Discern if my actions are needed, wanted, and if they will create a positive outcome
- Ask for the assistance of others as appropriate

I need to strengthen Helpfulness when I:

- Focus only on my own needs, while remaining oblivious to the needs of others
- Avoid taking action even when someone asks me to or it is obvious that someone wants or needs assistance
- Hold an unwilling, begrudging, or selfish attitude about assisting others

I misuse the strength of Helpfulness when I:

- Ignore my own values or principles in order to assist someone
- Selectively aid only those who may do me or someone close to me a favor in return
- Enable someone to avoid their responsibilities or avoid the consequences for their actions
- Do not think through the assistance that I offer to make certain the outcome is positive and truly meets the needs of my partner or others

Spiritual Reflection: ...as we have opportunity, let us do good to all people....[26]

৶ *Honesty* ৶

Honesty is speaking and acting consistently with one's true self and high standards, even in the face of strong temptation to do otherwise.

I am practicing Honesty effectively when I:
- Act according to civil laws when handling money, property, and issues affecting others
- Speak forthrightly and openly to let others know who I am and what I think and believe; in other words, say what I mean and mean what I say
- Speak clearly and directly with others, including sharing feelings and thoughts with a partner, and information that is important to a relationship
- Base my words, actions, and choices upon my beliefs and principles
- Share genuine remorse and apologies after doing something hurtful or inappropriate

I need to strengthen Honesty when I:
- Withhold important information about myself and my actions, manipulate others by giving them false information, or allow others to believe something about me that is not true
- Conceal my behavior from those who have a legitimate interest in it
- Cheat, steal, take credit for the work of others, defraud people, or make false promises
- Present aspects of myself inaccurately, including temporarily changing my appearance to create a false impression deliberately
- Minimize or hide my beliefs and principles

I misuse the strength of Honesty when I:
- Speak or act without discretion, timeliness, or wisdom
- Participate in slander (calumny), backbiting, or gossip [See chapter 12 for explanations.]
- Speak in a blunt, harsh, or cruel way that upsets or hurts others

Spiritual Reflection: He who...speaks uprightly, spurns profit from fraudulent dealings, waves away a bribe instead of grasping it, ...shall dwell in lofty security....[27]

❧ *Humility* ❧

Humility is seeing one's true self, strengths, abilities, and accomplishments in perspective, acknowledging the greatness of the Creator and the strengths, abilities, and accomplishments of others.

I am practicing Humility effectively when I:

- Pray and maintain a relationship with a Higher Power greater than I am
- Keep my ego in check and stay modest or quiet about my accomplishments
- Give respect and high regard to others and their needs
- Serve others to the best of my ability
- Admit my mistakes to those I harm, learn from the experience, and make amends as appropriate
- Acknowledge my limitations, willingly accept assistance from others, and request help when needed

I need to strengthen Humility when I:

- Treat others as inferior to me, and maintain a superior attitude as if I have all the answers
- Brag and boast about my accomplishments
- Believe I do not make mistakes and am usually right
- Criticize others for their mistakes and shortcomings
- Engage in overly intense and inappropriate competition with others
- Consistently put my own needs before the needs of others

I misuse the strength of Humility when I:

- Allow others to treat me poorly out of a belief that I am unworthy of respect
- Focus my attention excessively on myself
- Show a lack of confidence and am excessively self-critical
- Confuse it with humiliation, which is degrading and shaming of others

Spiritual Reflection: ...enter...with humility, in posture and in words, and We shall forgive you your faults....[28]

❧ *Idealism* ❧

Idealism is dreaming of what is possible to accomplish, thinking beyond what currently exists, and taking action toward or advocating beneficial changes.

I am practicing Idealism effectively when I:

- Create a vision for what I want in a relationship for the future and for the future of my family
- Seek effective and sustainable changes and solutions to meet the needs and injustices of people in the world
- Choose solutions that result in benefit to all concerned
- Hold a vision of the world as a better place in the future and work to realize the vision
- Work to transform any situation from negative into positive
- Strive to increasingly understand and practice spiritual guidance in my life

I need to strengthen Idealism when I:

- Fail to see what needs improvement in my character, my life, and in the world around me
- Hold a pessimistic or hopeless attitude about the state of the world, my community, my family, or myself
- Settle for poor circumstances or complain, rather than take action to improve the situation

I misuse the strength of Idealism when I:

- Hold such high ideals that I become a perfectionist and totally intolerant of imperfection in anyone or in any aspect of life
- Neglect my current responsibilities while dreaming of how things could have been or should be
- Become too serious about fixing every little detail in life
- Rush into excessively ambitious plans without enough realistic planning and preparation

Spiritual Reflection: Let your acts be a guide unto all mankind.... It is through your deeds that ye can distinguish yourselves from others. Through them the brightness of your light can be shed upon the whole earth.[29]

∾ *Integrity* ∾

Integrity is achieving a state of balance and wholeness in life and character, and acting consistently with one's deepest beliefs and highest values.

I am practicing Integrity effectively when I:

- Act and speak in harmony with my ideals, beliefs, and intentions
- Stay true to my word and keep my commitments
- Am reliable, which shows others that they can count on my consistent behavior
- Practice a high standard of ethics in my workplace
- Use my character qualities consistently in my relationships with a partner, relatives, coworkers, neighbors, and in my community service
- Handle my responsibilities and pay my bills in a timely way

I need to strengthen Integrity when I:

- Break agreements and promises and do not respect and honor my word
- Maintain a low standard of behavior for myself and do not make corrections to improve my behavior
- Act immorally, unethically, or illegally
- Attempt to avoid the natural consequences of my harmful actions

I misuse the strength of Integrity when I:

- Act quickly with poorly thought-out motives
- Place trust inappropriately in others, and allow myself to be easily fooled or to be led astray
- Act with such rigid and strict concern that I become overly fussy or critical and focused on being perfect or making my efforts perfect

Spiritual Reflection: May integrity and uprightness watch over me....[30]

᷒ *Joyfulness* ᷒

Joyfulness is being in a state of high-spirited and ecstatic delight, gladness, and jubilation.

I am practicing Joyfulness effectively when I:
- Celebrate the wonder of life
- Smile, laugh, and enjoy life, even when I am experiencing difficulties
- Include and share humor and light-hearted fun appropriately in my life, with a partner, and with others
- Immerse myself in prayer and meditation, and feel spiritually inspired and uplifted
- Excitedly share new knowledge and insights with others
- Am very pleased that I have done my best and made wise choices
- Optimistically look for the best in my life and others

I need to strengthen Joyfulness when I:
- Grumble, whine, or complain about my life
- Look at life and experiences with a pessimistic attitude, sharing my expectation of negative outcomes with others
- Fail to be happy for the blessings others receive or the ones that come into my own life
- Avoid happy and fun people, places, and experiences because of a negative attitude

I misuse the strength of Joyfulness when I:
- Act in an insensitive way to a sorrowful situation, or invalidate the sad feelings of others
- Appreciate getting my own way with others through flattery, manipulation, or enticement
- Am glad or laugh when others suffer or are harmed by their experiences or difficulties

Spiritual Reflection: ...we also rejoice in our sufferings, because we know that suffering produces perseverance; perseverance, character; and character, hope.[31]

❧ *Justice* ❧

Justice is equitably assessing all the facts, feelings, principles, and laws in a situation, avoiding bias and all forms of prejudice, and then making a fair and correct decision.

I am practicing Justice effectively when I:

- Maintain balance in my relationship with a partner, so that neither of us feel the give and take between us is unfair over time
- Search for truth and form my opinions based on objective facts
- Treat others fairly
- Search for equitable solutions and reach impartial decisions
- Give aid, comfort, and/or assistance to those who have been neglected, abused, or mistreated
- Practice social activism and stand up for my own rights and the rights of others, seeking to prevent the mistreatment of others
- Work to restore integrity in situations where there have been unwise, unlawful, or unfair activities
- Reject the misbehavior of others, such as lying, cheating, or stealing, as unacceptable and subject to applicable laws

I need to strengthen Justice when I:

- Assume a partner will accommodate my needs without my also accommodating theirs
- Act unfairly or disrespectfully trample on the rights of others
- Violate fair standards or break laws
- Mistreat, harm, or injure someone
- Make decisions without careful thought or based on prejudice or bias
- Fail to look for or discern the facts of a situation
- Dominate someone, or use my strength, words, or actions to hurt or overcome the person

I misuse the strength of Justice when I:

- Try to be so fair that I become indecisive or insensitive to the nuances of a particular situation, or to the differences between situations
- Defend others inappropriately

Spiritual Reflection: Speak the truth to one another, render true and perfect justice....[32]

❧ *Kindness* ❧

Kindness is being considerate in a deliberately warm-hearted and sympathetic way that benefits others.

I am practicing Kindness effectively when I:
- Look outside myself and pay attention to the needs and interests of others
- Show a warm, pleasant, and considerate attitude toward others
- Share positive and uplifting words and gestures that calm, comfort, or assist someone
- Speak understanding words that comfort someone in the difficulties they are experiencing

I need to strengthen Kindness when I:
- Act as if people deserve severe consequences for their mistakes
- Live a self-centered life, ignoring the needs and wishes of those around me
- Behave in a harsh, mean, or critical way
- Hold a resentful, grudging, or bitter attitude toward others
- See others' needs and choose not to take action

I misuse the strength of Kindness when I:
- Accept and am easily fooled when others pretend they need me
- Naively let others take advantage of my willingness to help them
- Pretend to care while instead manipulating others
- Only act when it is to my own advancement or benefit

Spiritual Reflection: ...greater than all is lovingkindness. As the light of the moon is sixteen times stronger than the light of all the stars, so lovingkindness is sixteen times more efficacious in liberating the heart than all other religious accomplishments taken together.[33]

❧ *Love* ❧

Love is being connected at the levels of body, mind, heart, and soul with others, and acting in positive emotional ways with them that draw on the powerful magnetic and caring force that the Creator provides in the universe.

I am practicing Love effectively when I:

- Use my words, gestures, and actions to communicate warm and affectionate feelings toward a partner or others
- Respect that a partner is worthy of affection and consistently express it to them in the ways that mean the most to them*
- Maintain a healthy and unified relationship
- Make all my actions based in genuine caring for quality, commitment to benefiting others, and with appreciation for the best in others
- Pray and meditate to maintain a spiritual bond of love with the Creator

I need to strengthen Love when I:

- Act in a self-centered or careless way
- Hesitate to take any risk to build a bond with a partner and others
- Hold a bitter, critical, contemptuous, hateful, or condemning attitude toward others
- Treat people generally as if they are opponents or enemies
- Backbite, gossip, or slander the character of others [See chapter 12 for explanations.]
- Ignore someone's request for me to express affection to them in a specific way*

I misuse the strength of Love when I:

- Smother someone with so much attention that they have no space or time to be themselves or live their own life
- Fail to set boundaries and allow love to blind me to someone's poor character or unjust actions
- Manipulate or punish someone through giving and then withholding affection

Spiritual Reflection: Do everything in love.[34]

*See Chapter 15, "Love Languages"

ᴇᴇᴇ *Loyalty* ᴇᴇᴇ

Loyalty is honoring and connecting to someone or something beyond oneself, such as to a friend, partner, family, employers, organizations, community, religion, or country.

I am practicing Loyalty effectively when I:
- Honor and defend a partner, their actions, and others who are close to me
- Keep the people and causes I value as a high priority, even when they disappoint or hurt me
- Speak positively and respectfully about what I belong to or have an allegiance to, work to advance its interests, and defend it as needed
- Support the well-being of those I care about

I need to strengthen Loyalty when I:
- Backbite, gossip, or slander the character of a partner, friends, or relatives [See chapter 12 for explanations.]
- Undermine someone's legitimate authority
- Betray others or fail to keep my promises
- Let go of relationships easily for minor reasons

I misuse the strength of Loyalty when I:
- Hold allegiance to someone who is negative or destructive toward me, or those close to me, such as to someone who habitually treats us unjustly, falsely, or poorly or who involves us in negative activities, such as backbiting or criticism, that hurt others
- Blindly obey or follow someone who is acting unwisely or illegally
- Act jealously or possessively toward my friends or partner and not allow them the freedom to have other friendships and connections with people and activities

Spiritual Reflection: ...we...should on no account slacken our efforts to be loyal, sincere and men of good will. ... [W]e must be constant in our faithfulness and trustworthiness....[35]

❧ *Mercy* ❧

Mercy is being gentle, lenient, tolerant, and accepting that someone has made a mistake, and relieving their distress, even if it is undeserved or they seem unworthy.

I am practicing Mercy effectively when I:

- Give someone the opportunity to start over or accept what has happened and continue with a relationship
- Kindly accept others' apologies and amends
- Detach from and forgive the mistakes of others
- Tenderly allow others and myself to learn from our mistakes
- Let someone else have something they seem to need more than I do
- Give others the freedom to live their lives as they choose to without my commentary or interference

I need to strengthen Mercy when I:

- Constantly remind others of their failures
- Focus strongly and rigidly on what is right or just without tolerance for human failings
- Hold grudges and resentments
- Annoy others with repeated comments, complaints, or requests

I misuse the strength of Mercy when I:

- Tolerate and enable unkind, harmful, or unjust behavior from someone
- Allow others to get away with negative actions without consequences, such as legal repercussions or loss of money or property

Spiritual Reflection: Be ye therefore merciful, as your Father also is merciful.[36]

❧ *Moderation* ❧

Moderation is recognizing the extremes that are possible in speech, behavior, and choices and seeking the balance that creates positive outcomes.

I am practicing Moderation effectively when I:

- Assess how I use my time, attention, and resources and then set appropriate priorities and boundaries that respect my own health and wellbeing and that of others
- Include a partner, family, work, service, spirituality, and leisure in my life in appropriate balance
- Evaluate my schedule and commitments and then prioritize as needed
- Take time to share my thoughts and feelings, lower my stress level, and be more rested
- Respond calmly to situations and avoid being on an emotional roller coaster
- Use more than one character quality at the same time to guide my actions and make decisions appropriately

I need to strengthen Moderation when I:

- Fluctuate wildly from one extreme to another, creating conflict or causing harm
- Fail to take appropriate actions or make necessary choices to balance my words and actions
- Work too hard, becoming regularly exhausted and unable to participate in routine activities or spend time with a partner
- Give too much to others, talk too much, participate only in frivolous activities, or indulge my appetite and overeat

I misuse the strength of Moderation when I:

- Regard enjoyment of entertainment, food, and good company as frivolous
- Act in an overly cautious, timid, or reserved manner in a relationships or when making choices

Spiritual Reflection: Let a man be moderate in his eating and his recreation, moderately active, moderate in sleep and in wakefulness.[37]

ᴄᴏ *Patience* ᴄᴏ

Patience is staying in steady control of thoughts and actions and willingly taking the time to handle any difficult, inconvenient, delaying, or troublesome situations in a calm way without complaint.

I am practicing Patience effectively when I:
- Hold back a hasty reply, and think before speaking
- Show acceptance and tolerance of differences and limitations in others
- Tolerate a delay and wait for what is in motion to proceed or any difficulties to be resolved
- Accept what I cannot change calmly and with humor
- Give the attention, time, and practice needed to develop my character, learn new skills, and accomplish a task well
- Listen attentively
- Maintain quiet hope for positive outcomes
- Work carefully through a task that has many steps

I need to strengthen Patience when I:
- Act in an unreasonable, irrational, or short-tempered way because things do not go the way I want
- Force someone to rush, or push something to happen faster than is wise
- Complain, criticize, agitate, yell, or become anxious about the pace of something or the actions of others that I judge as being too slow
- Speak impulsively or rush ahead or into a situation without assessing it or having necessary discussions with others, and therefore cause harm

I misuse the strength of Patience when I:
- Cause delays, passively ignore issues, or act too slowly or not at all to address important matters or needs
- Wait an unreasonable amount of time to respond to trouble or danger, resulting in greater harm or injury
- Make a demand and then withhold affection and attention for extended lengths of time to wait out the other person and get my own way

Spiritual Reflection: The end of a matter is better than the beginning of it. Better a patient spirit....[38]

ᘛ *Peacefulness* ᘚ

Peacefulness is being emotionally calm and serene, while working to reduce conflict and build harmony between people.

I am practicing Peacefulness effectively when I:

- Seek points of agreement and harmony between myself, a partner, our families, or with others, and see this as one of the building blocks for global peace
- Communicate in respectful, loving, and positive ways, seeing in all interactions the seeds of peace
- Handle my responsibilities and any issues that arise in my life, rather than feeling anxiety about what is not being done
- Maintain an inner sense of calm, tranquility, and happiness
- Practice regular gratitude, meditation, and prayer
- Focus on love and reconciliation between people
- Listen to music or go to places that increase my serenity
- Stop discussions that are becoming a source of dissension with a partner, and replace thoughts of conflict with thoughts of harmony

I need to strengthen Peacefulness when I:

- Fight, argue, and provoke disagreements with a partner or others
- Criticize, judge, or attempt to dominate others
- Backbite, gossip, slander, or abuse others
- Attempt to manage other people's responsibilities [See chapter 12 for explanations.]
- Anxiously worry about potential negative outcomes
- See violent action as the only solution to an issue

I misuse the strength of Peacefulness when I:

- Suppress my emotions to avoid appropriate anger about injustice and neglect decisive action to seek resolution through appropriate authorities
- Become so calm and mellow that I cannot even feel positive or appropriate emotions such as happiness or excitement
- Fail to act in situations that need strength and decisive actions

Spiritual Reflection: …A word spoken in wrath is the sharpest sword….[39]

᯽ *Perseverance* ᯽

Perseverance is using strength and resources to persist and press onward in reaching worthwhile goals, particularly in the face of challenges or adversity.

I am practicing Perseverance effectively when I:
- Finish what I start
- Value my goals and focus on achieving them
- Stay in relationships long enough to fully determine whether they could be successful and attempt to work through issues together
- Steadfastly commit to and act according to my values and beliefs, even when it is difficult
- Continue my character and relationship development over time
- Make plans to overcome obstacles in the way of accomplishments
- Carry on even after crushing blows and crippling grief

I need to strengthen Perseverance when I:
- Stop progressing on tasks or important goals at the first sign of trouble or obstacles
- Skip from one activity or task to another without completing any of them
- Abandon my values and beliefs when someone challenges them, or it is hard to do what I believe is right
- Discount the importance of finishing what I started

I misuse the strength of Perseverance when I:
- Refuse to reconsider a goal, change directions, or seek advice and assistance after multiple challenges
- Stubbornly persist in doing something even when it is clearly unwise or causes significant harm or disunity

Spiritual Reflection: Those who patiently persevere will truly receive a reward without measure![40]

❧ *Purity* ❧

Purity is maintaining physical cleanliness, an orderly environment, uplifting and chaste thoughts, positive words, honest motivations for actions, and a spiritual heart and soul.

I am practicing Purity effectively when I:
- Maintain good personal hygiene
- Keep my clothes, vehicles, possessions, property, and home tidy, organized, and clean
- Replace degrading, destructive, or inappropriate sexual thoughts with those that are uplifting, noble, or spiritual, or allow them space in your mind only briefly without inviting them to stay
- Pray and meditate
- Have honest, selfless motives for my actions and choices
- Resist the temptation to participate in something harmful as soon as I recognize the feeling inside of myself
- Keep my body free of non-medicinal alcohol and drugs
- Eat healthy food and drink clean water that nourish my body and keep it functioning smoothly

I need to strengthen Purity when I:
- Pollute my body, mind, heart, or spirit with what is harmful
- Clutter up or avoid cleaning my environment
- Fill my mind with violent or sexual images
- Hold anger, hate, or jealousy in my mind and heart and hurt others and myself with them
- Speak or act with manipulative motives
- Swear or use words in hurtful, degrading, or defamatory ways
- Give into temptation or abandon spiritual practices or principles

I misuse the strength of Purity when I:
- Obsess about cleanliness and neatness so that others cannot relax and live normally around me
- Intolerantly lecture others about their harmful lifestyles
- Promote my high standards as better than those of other people

Spiritual Reflection: A man who is born with tendencies toward the Divine, is fearless and pure in heart.[41]

❧ *Purposefulness* ❧

Purposefulness is having meaningful and vital activities and goals in life and relationships and the determination to accomplish them.

I am practicing Purposefulness effectively when I:

- Take the time to set useful and valuable goals that fulfill my purposes in life or joint purposes with a partner, and act to achieve them
- Use determination, efficiency, and effectiveness to work toward my goals and dreams, including a partner wherever possible and practicable
- Focus on developing all aspects of my mind, talents, skills, and character, and encourage a partner to do the same
- Work persistently to accomplish improvements in my life and community
- Set up my environment in ways that support me in my goals, such as by reducing distractions
- Arrange for people to be around me who assist me with completing my tasks and achieving my goals
- Work diligently at both assigned and chosen tasks
- Use visualization and concentration to picture successful outcomes, including for a relationship

I need to strengthen Purposefulness when I:

- Wander aimlessly through life without any idea of where I am going or what I will do once I get there
- Spend my days lazily doing only what brings me momentary pleasure or allows me to live in the moment
- Ignore issues or tasks and do not act when it is timely and appropriate
- Avoid identifying my relationship expectations and discussing them with a partner

I misuse the strength of Purposefulness when I:

- Focus so much on my goals that I neglect a partner, family, or friends, or fail to meet the legitimate needs of others
- Am intolerant or rude toward those who stand in my way when I am trying to accomplish a task or goal
- Refuse to flexibly bend or change plans as needed when new information or circumstances arise

Spiritual Reflection: A season is set for everything, a time for every experience under heaven…A time for planting and a time for uprooting the planted; …A time for tearing down and a time for building up; A time for weeping and a time for laughing…A time for embracing and a time for shunning embraces; …A time for keeping and a time for discarding; …A time for loving…and a time for peace.[42]

✎ *Respect* ✎

Respect is interacting with every human being, and what they value, as worthy of fair treatment, consideration, and esteem.

I am practicing Respect effectively when I:

- Treat my body, mind, heart, soul, and belongings, and those of a partner and others, with dignity, care, appreciation, and gentleness
- Practice character qualities with consistency, and acknowledge the character qualities that a partner and others practice
- Speak, act, listen, and touch in ways that honor others, especially a partner, parents, and friends, and consider their personal limits, wishes, and comfort levels
- Allow others the right to practice their beliefs and values in the way they choose without interference, as long as their beliefs and values do not interfere with laws or with the just and legitimate rights of others
- Acknowledge the social and legal rights and personal boundaries of others
- Remember special dates, anniversaries, and occurrences in others' lives
- Give consideration to others even when their views, experiences, and perspectives are different from our own
- Obey and follow the rules, guidelines, and laws that apply to me

I need to strengthen Respect when I:

- Trample on the rights, property, boundaries, or needs of a partner or others
- Treat special or spiritual books and objects carelessly or irreverently
- Act immorally, unethically, or illegally
- Am critical or rude toward others or myself
- Intrude on others' privacy
- Am superior, proud, or arrogant toward others

I misuse the strength of Respect when I:

- Place such a high value upon a partner or others that I give them too much time or attention or defend and enable their unwise, cruel, or unjust behavior
- Try almost anything to win a partner's approval

Spiritual Reflection: ...all humanity must be looked upon with love, kindness and respect; for what we behold in them are none other than the signs and traces of God Himself.[43]

❧ *Responsibility* ❧

Responsibility is claiming personal accountability for one's own life, choices, happiness, commitments, and relationships with others.

I am practicing Responsibility effectively when I:

- Spend the time and attention needed to maintain and grow a relationship
- Use effective character choices to navigate through life
- Practice initiative, leadership, and empowerment with my relationships, education, job, and community
- Assess my words and actions every day, accepting credit or accountability as appropriate, and resolving any problems that I cause
- Study, learn, and seek to improve all facets of myself and achieve my potential
- Steadfastly keep all my promises and commitments
- Complete required tasks

I need to strengthen Responsibility when I:

- Blame a partner or others when I am partially or fully the one who caused a problem
- Defend my attitude, words, and actions even when I know they are harmful to a partner or others, or ignore the hurtful effect of my attitudes, words, and actions
- Break promises or laws, or ignore important rules
- Neglect my work, school, or service assignments and duties, or do not take action as needed to handle assigned tasks
- Do not apologize or make amends to a partner or others for my mistakes

I misuse the strength of Responsibility when I:

- Put my work or interests as higher priority than relationships with a partner, family, or friends, or act in ways that are contrary to the priorities that match my values
- Over-work myself, treating my whole life as serious and highly important, and rarely relax, have fun, or laugh
- Enable others to avoid performing tasks that they can and should do

Spiritual Reflection: He who tills his land shall have food in plenty, but he who pursues vanities is devoid of sense. ... One is repaid in kind for one's deeds.[44]

✆ *Self-Discipline* ✆

Self-Discipline is maintaining the inner control needed to fulfill one's goals and life purposes.

I am practicing Self-Discipline effectively when I:

- Monitor and control my thoughts, emotions, desires, and actions so they do not harm me, a partner, or others
- Stay in charge of my own behavior and govern myself to achieve what I want to accomplish or what requires my attention
- Establish structures and guidelines that keep me focused on my goals
- Act without needing reminders from a partner or others
- Speak and act in wise, calm, and timely ways
- Make healthy choices about my nutrition, exercise, and sleep
- Create routines, orderliness, and harmony in my environment
- Budget and control my spending of time and money appropriately
- Follow civil laws, such as speed limits, or religious laws, such as prayer or fasting

I need to strengthen Self-Discipline when I:

- Lose control of my thoughts, emotions, desires, temper, and reactions
- Set aside and act without following principles, rules, laws, commitments, beliefs, or cultural values
- Act without consideration for harm to my health, happiness, or future or those of a partner or others
- Give up on worthy goals for ones that are easier to achieve
- Spend my time only on what brings me instant and temporary pleasure

I misuse the strength of Self-Discipline when I:

- Act or speak rigidly or in an over-bearing manner
- Place more value on a set of rules than on other people or even my own self-respect
- Establish such a rigid personal or work schedule that I do not create space for relationships with a partner, friends, family, or Higher Power

Spiritual Reflection: ...show patience, firmness and self-control....[45]

⤷ *Service* ⤶

Service is being selfless or sacrificial in acting to make a significant difference in the quality of the lives of a partner, family, friends, or others.

I am practicing Service effectively when I:

- Proactively offer my time, talents, skills, and attention to a partner, friends, family, religion, employer, and community
- Work to complete tasks quietly and with humility, without any expectation of notice, reward, or appreciation
- Joyfully and willingly put the needs and comforts of a partner or others before my own
- Make contributions of time, resources, and opportunities that improve the health, happiness, well-being, and prosperity of others
- Assist or encourage people to participate in activities that benefit others, especially inviting a partner to work along with me

I need to strengthen Service when I:

- Expect people to wait on me, other than those paid to do so
- Let others do what needs to be done by everyone, while making no effort to participate
- Regard the requests, needs, and problems of others as too much trouble for me to try to answer, solve, or improve

I misuse the strength of Service when I:

- Enable others to act irresponsibly or to become unwisely dependent upon me
- Look with pride at my deeds of service
- Count on the attention and praise I receive
- Am so involved that I neglect important relationships, commitments, and responsibilities

Spiritual Reflection: ...serve one another in love. ... Love your neighbor as yourself.[46]

❧ *Sincerity* ❧

Sincerity is being genuine and earnest with motives, words, and actions.

I am practicing Sincerity effectively when I:

- Attain harmony, integrity, and honesty with my inner thoughts and outer words and actions
- Share my true self with partner and others in an authentic way
- Act with earnestness and integrity according to my beliefs, values, and character qualities
- Care deeply for others and show this in my words and actions
- Build trust between people with genuine words and deeds
- Let a partner and others know what I appreciate about them and what they do
- Say prayers with careful thought and genuine feeling

I need to strengthen Sincerity when I:

- Express love to get something from a partner, instead of as an unconditional and genuine emotion
- Manipulate someone
- Am dishonest about who I really am
- Fake my responses to others

I misuse the strength of Sincerity when I:

- Am naive and assume everyone is honest, allowing myself to be easily fooled or deceived
- Give so much serious attention to something that it prevents me from enjoying life
- Act impulsively without being certain whether my motives are honest and pure

Spiritual Reflection: Right speech will be his dwelling-place on the road. … Right efforts will be his steps: right thoughts his breath; and right contemplation will give him the peace that follows in his footprints.[47]

◦⟋ *Spirituality* ⟍◦

Spirituality is maintaining an interactive closeness and relationship with God or spiritual sources as divine guidance in my life.

I am practicing Spirituality effectively when I:

- Develop and practice character qualities effectively
- Converse with God in prayer
- Learn about God and spiritual topics through a variety of sources, such as faith communities, study groups, or books
- Use meditation to seek inspiration and make wise character and relationship choices
- Base my identity, words, and actions upon spiritual principles and values
- Feel inspired about particular activities or events
- Share spiritual insights and beliefs with a partner and others as requested or as appropriate, and respect theirs in return
- Treat spiritual books and places with reverence and awe
- Grow in steadfast faith in a Higher Power
- Participate in a spiritual or religious congregation or community and/or in interfaith activities

- s● Choose words and actions that reflect my lower nature instead of my higher one
- Focus my energy on material possessions or physical pleasures
- Lack confidence and trust that God will provide for my needs and guide me
- Resist character quality development, misuse qualities, or attack others' characters
- Try to force my beliefs on a partner or others

I misuse the strength of Spirituality when I:

- Isolate myself indefinitely to focus on my spiritual growth, while neglecting my responsibilities or the needs of a partner or others
- Think I have become too holy, lofty, or spiritual to associate with others

Spiritual Reflection: The need is very great, everywhere in the world...for a true spiritual awareness to pervade and motivate people's lives.[48]

‿6 *Strength* ‿

Strength is staying resolute in the face of challenges and difficulties, and overcoming them without breaking down.

I am practicing Strength effectively when I:

- Increase and reinforce the bonds I have with a partner, family, and friends so they are lasting, not temporary
- Support a partner when they are going through difficulties
- Develop and practice my character qualities until they consistently and effectively guide my choices
- Stand fast and firm in my beliefs, values, and convictions in making the best choices possible, even when they are difficult or unpopular
- Learn and grow as a person from managing problems effectively
- Do not give up easily, but keep going forward until it is clear that detachment is necessary
- Draw on appropriate resources to complete tasks and resolve difficulties, such as prayer, meditation, service, friendship, help from others, counseling, support groups, and thankfulness for blessings

I need to strengthen Strength when I:

- Let destructive fears and weaknesses hold me back from participating in a relationship and all of life
- Abandon solid friendships and relationships without first attempting to work through problems and find solutions
- Wallow in self-pity, complain, deny, run away from, or have excessive reactions to serious issues and problems
- Give in easily to unwise temptation or my desires
- Ignore or act contrary to my values or beliefs

I misuse the strength of Strength when I:

- Approach tasks or people in a rigid way
- Bully a partner or others who are weaker than I am
- Refuse stubbornly to reconsider or reassess poor plans and take different actions, or insist that I am right about how to handle whatever problems are arising
- Resist listening to someone's advice or input that is true and wise

Spiritual Reflection: …strengthen each other…that ye may prosper.[49]

❧ *Tactfulness* ❧

Tactfulness is choosing when to stay silent and when to speak gentle, kind words that do not offend others or hurt their feelings.

I am practicing Tactfulness effectively when I:
- Carefully assess what I am about to say to a partner or others, and communicate it with gentleness, courtesy, love, and sensitivity
- Ensure that my words, gestures, body language, and tone of voice are positive, truthful, timely, constructive, and wise
- Wait for my emotions to calm down before responding respectfully to the thoughts, opinions, or feelings of others
- Make requests of a partner or others rather than demands
- Stay silent or be brief when appropriate to avoid hurting another person's feelings

I need to strengthen Tactfulness when I:
- Respond hastily, hurt someone's feelings, and end up regretting my words and actions
- Speak unwisely or blurt out words without pausing to consider their effect on the listener, such as hurt or embarrassment
- Speak in a rude, insensitive, or inconsiderate way with a partner or others

I misuse the strength of Tactfulness when I:
- Keep silent because I am overly worried about someone's possible reaction
- Am so preoccupied with what to say that I find it difficult to talk to or be around a partner or others
- Take offense easily or am overly sensitive in response to what I think is tactless behavior of others

Spiritual Reflection: ...Not everything that a man knoweth can be disclosed, nor can everything that he can disclose be regarded as timely, nor can every timely utterance be considered as suited to the capacity of those who hear it.[50]

᎒Ꮙ *Thankfulness* ᏒᎧ

Thankfulness is expressing warm feelings of praise, appreciation, and gratitude for blessings, benefits, and kind gestures.

I am practicing Thankfulness effectively when I:
- Consciously appreciate what is good in my life
- Appreciate all that is good about a partner, my family, and my friends
- Accept and learn from the difficulties I experience, appreciating that they strengthen me and help me to develop my character
- Focus on the positive aspects of my life and the world around me
- Express gratitude to God for the blessings in my life
- Share with others how much I appreciate who they are and what they do
- See and understand that there is an abundance of good in the world

I need to strengthen Thankfulness when I:
- Refuse to acknowledge what others do for me, taking them for granted, and not saying thank you
- Wallow in self-pity, ignoring what is good in my life or circumstances
- Neglect to appreciate the beauty around me, such as nature, art, or music
- Act as if I deserve all the good things in my life without acknowledging those who provide them

I misuse the strength of Thankfulness when I:
- Use excessive compliments or flattering appreciation to manipulate others
- Provide favors to others to make them feel grateful and willing to give me a favor in return

Spiritual Reflection: Praise the Lord, for He is good; His steadfast love is eternal![51]

❧ *Thoughtfulness* ❧

Thoughtfulness is being deliberately and genuinely concerned about others' well-being and happiness, and acting in anticipation of, loving awareness of, and in response to their needs.

I am practicing Thoughtfulness effectively when I:
- Look for ways to meet the needs of a partner and others
- Act in considerate ways that make someone's life or tasks easier
- Plan positive and enjoyable activities for a partner and others
- Make choices based upon love, respect, and consideration for the interests, needs, and wishes of others
- Pay attention to the preferences of others, and keep these in mind when choosing activities, gifts, and communication styles
- Discuss plans with others before making decisions that involve or affect them
- Use careful, meditative, prayerful, and reasoned thinking about the consequences of my words, decisions, choices, and actions

I need to strengthen Thoughtfulness when I:
- Am impulsive in speech or actions and hurt others
- Ignore the wishes and needs of others
- Focus only on my own needs in a selfish and insensitive way

I misuse the strength of Thoughtfulness when I:
- Try too hard to assist someone and am intrusive or smothering
- Analyze details excessively, and attempt so strongly to take the right approach that I become fussy and absorbed with it

Spiritual Reflection: Good thoughts will produce good actions....[52]

❧ *Trustworthiness* ❧

Trustworthiness is handling all tasks, responsibilities, and private information in a reliable and honest way so that others have confidence in one's words and actions.

I am practicing Trustworthiness effectively when I:

- Consistently fulfill my agreements, promises, and commitments with a partner and others, including meeting agreed expectations and giving dependable service, thereby earning their confidence
- Listen carefully to personal sharing from a partner and keep it private
- Use good judgment and avoid being swayed by the opinions of others inappropriately
- Practice truthfulness, faithfulness, and loyalty in all my relationships
- Act with integrity, honesty, and a high standard of values, such as when handling money or responsibilities

I need to strengthen Trustworthiness when I:

- Use deceit, lies, or dishonesty to get things done
- Break promises by failing to do what I say I will
- Mishandle my responsibilities
- Avoid positions of leadership or service to others that I am capable of fulfilling because I fear being accountable to others
- Backbite, gossip, or slander the character of others [See chapter 12 for explanations.]

I misuse the strength of Trustworthiness when I:

- Attempt to keep someone happy no matter what the emotional or financial cost
- Exaggerate my worth to earn someone's confidence
- Value rules, policies, or my reputation more than the well-being of others and the strength of my relationships
- Rigidly try to keep what becomes a clearly harmful commitment or promise instead of renegotiating it

Spiritual Reflection: ...truly the best of men for thee to employ is the (man) who is strong and trusty....[53]

❦ *Truthfulness* ❦

Truthfulness is communicating accurately in a straightforward way that conveys one's best understanding of the facts.

I am practicing Truthfulness effectively when I:

- Promise a partner or others only what I can reliably fulfill
- Know and share my true self accurately and authentically with a partner and others
- Am careful and consistent with the accuracy of the words that I speak and write, which builds trust with a partner and others
- Fully investigate important facts independently and objectively before making decisions
- Speak what is factual in provable ways, and make it clear when I am voicing an opinion
- Admit to a partner and others when I make a mistake
- Share stories accurately and without exaggeration

I need to strengthen Truthfulness when I:

- Lie to or deceive others with false information
- Defend or cover up my actions with lies or partial truths
- Misuse my imagination or creativity to concoct stories so that they become inaccurate or misleading in order to gain attention from a partner or others, or to get what I want
- Slander the reputation of others or defame their characters
- Accept information from others without verifying its accuracy

I misuse the strength of Truthfulness when I:

- Speak the truth rudely, harshly, or hurtfully
- Backbite or gossip and defend my actions because the words are factual [See Chapter 12 for explanations.]

Spiritual Reflection: Jesus said, "If you hold to my teaching, you are really my disciples. Then you will know the truth, and the truth will set you free." [54]

↬ *Unity* ↫

Unity is consciously looking for and strengthening points of attraction and harmony and working together to build a strong foundation of oneness, love, commitment, and cooperation.

I am practicing Unity effectively when I:

- Draw out the diverse achievements, talents, and abilities of a partner or others and guide them to benefit others
- Build bonds of friendship with a partner, or others who are different from me, and invite them to be part of an ever-widening circle of fellowship and the most inclusive of loyalties
- Focus on points of agreement and eliminate points of conflict, reconciling differences with a partner or others in ways that bond us in love, harmony, and affinity
- Involve all those affected by a decision in the discussion, bringing a multiplicity of perspectives into concord and agreement
- Encourage full participation of everyone involved in an activity
- Encourage diverse individual initiative that results in benefit to others
- Practice justice and fairness in my relationships, service, and work

I need to strengthen Unity when I:

- Fail to protect a relationship, family, and friendships from attack and neglect
- Act with superiority and proudly separate myself from people who are different from me
- Give orders to a partner, friends, or coworkers instead of treating them as equals and collaborators
- Undermine group decisions or those made with a partner
- Act in lower nature ways that are hostile, indifferent, backbiting, gossiping, slanderous, cliquish, prideful, self-centered, biased, prejudiced, impatient, contentious, vengeful, jealous, disrespectful, unforgiving, argumentative, hateful, insulting, hasty, ill-tempered, violent, or manifest any other destructive, abusive, or negative attitude and behavior

I misuse the strength of Unity when I:

- Insist that everyone be the same or do the same thing in the same way
- Always defer to others in an effort to prevent dissension or conflict

Spiritual Reflection: …It behoveth man to adhere tenaciously unto that which will promote fellowship, kindliness and unity.[55]

✌ *Wisdom* ↣

Wisdom is drawing upon the knowledge learned from one's own experience and that of others, and determining the best choices for silence, words, or actions.

I am practicing Wisdom effectively when I:

- Learn from my mistakes, experiences, and problems, knowing better what to do in similar situations in the future
- Use listening, reflection, discernment, good judgment, experience, and common sense to assess whether my silence, words, or actions with a partner or others will be most timely and appropriate
- Patiently and thoroughly gather factual information from a variety of people and resources before making a decision
- Acknowledge my strengths and limitations, sharing my knowledge and understanding in respectful ways, but admitting when I do not know something, and I am willing to learn more about it
- Humbly discern when to request help from a partner or others, or provide assistance and guidance to them
- Calmly flow with the changes and occurrences with a partner and in the world, knowing that they are a natural part of life and often temporary

I need to strengthen Wisdom when I:

- Act without appropriate reflection and planning
- Take little or no responsibility for directing my life and actions, or for learning from the outcomes and consequences of my choices and improving them
- Ignore God and spiritual books as sources of wisdom and guidance
- Neglect to observe and learn from the experiences and knowledge of others

I misuse the strength of Wisdom when I:

- Talk to others in arrogant or prideful ways about how much more I know than they do, mercilessly critiquing, belittling, or judging them and trying to make them feel stupid or small
- Insist that a partner or others listen to my knowledge or advice
- Make simple things complicated or difficult to understand
- Share what I know without assessing its timeliness and consequences

Spiritual Reflection: Be humble, be harmless, have no pretension, be upright, forbearing...calmly encounter the painful, the pleasant...seek this knowledge and comprehend clearly why you should seek it...such, it is said, are the roots of true wisdom....[56]

The Next Step:
A Harmonious Dance—Considering Compatibility

As you reach the end of this book, you now have a solid understanding of the essentials for preparing yourself for a relationship. You know how to establish a *strong*, happy, and lasting relationship with someone by incorporating these key themes from *Can We Dance?* into your life:

1. Knowing and developing your own character and preparing yourself for a relationship
2. Finding a partner and accurately observing their character
3. Establishing a firm friendship
4. Learning essential communication skills that assist the two of you to maintain *unity*, including how to express both *encouragement* and *love* effectively

In addition, you have learned about the importance of making *excellent* choices and interacting with a partner with *equality*, *respect*, and all the character qualities. You also now know ways of exploring how *spirituality* can be part of your relationship. **When you have a relationship, and you go through all the stages and learning adventures presented in *Can We Dance?*, you then arrive at a transition point. Once you have established a serious friendship-based relationship with someone, you and your partner might choose to begin to talk about whether to marry each other. At this stage of your relationship, you are not necessarily making a *commitment* to marry, but seriously considering it.**

When marriage is a possibility between you and your partner, you enter a period called "courtship." This may sound like an out-of-date word, but courtship actually supports thoroughly preparing for marriage. It gives you time to ensure you are choosing a great partner, and your relationship has a solid foundation. **The knowledge, skills, and activities needed for courtship are the components of the next book in the Both Eyes Open™ series, *Can We Harmonize? Composing a Compatible Relationship*.** Just as the theme of this book was dance, its theme will be music.

When you share with others that you are in the courtship stage of a relationship, it communicates that the two of you are exclusive partners and considering marriage. Your goal in courtship is to determine if you and your partner are compatible—able to *respect* each other and work together in harmony to *create* a happy and lasting marriage. Can you work through your differences and still maintain the *integrity* of the bond between you and the *love* you feel for each other? Are there enough positive aspects of the relationship to sustain a long-term friendship and marriage together?

The genuine and effective ways in which you and your partner continue to practice character qualities with each other will be primary contributors to your ability to *create* the harmony essential for marriage. As John Bradshaw writes in *The Family*, a mature, healthy, and functional marriage has "…two people making music together. Both play their own instrument and use *their own unique skills*, but they play the same song."[1]

Although you have already begun to explore some of the following courtship topics, you may not have done so with a partner, or to the depth that will be required if you want to marry. Deeply understanding and exploring these areas of compatibility will *help* you and a partner determine whether to become engaged and whether you could live together harmoniously in a marriage. *Can We Harmonize?* will *help* you to imagine being married and discuss how the two of you will:

- Use in-depth communication tools for consultative decision-making
- Interact and build *love* and *unity* with family members
- Add and raise children
- Arrange your roles and tasks to include all aspects of *equality*
- Understand each other's experiences and views of sex and intimacy
- Expand the *spiritual* foundation between you
- Understand your cultural influences and build *unity*
- Earn and manage money
- Manage time choices and *service* commitments
- Handle difficulties of all kinds
- Set up and maintain a household

Acting and speaking *honestly* with each other will be even more vital for you and your partner during courtship. The clearer you are with each other about what is important, and the more *integrity* you both display in your words and actions, the better decisions you will make about your relationship. Once you clearly know that you can work together in harmony in all major areas, you will be in a position to become engaged. Then, the third book in this series will be *helpful* to you: *Can We Create? Designing an Inspirational Engagement*. Its theme will be art.

It is wise to maintain your character exploration throughout the entire time you are courting and engaged. You may have a difficult time ever being "100 percent sure" that marriage is the right thing to do, since all relationships involve a certain level of risk and uncertainty. However, one of the best ways to maximize your certainty in making

a lifetime commitment is to know your partner's character. Someone who consistently practices character qualities effectively with you will likely be an *excellent* partner.

After all your explorations of a partner and a relationship are complete, the decision to marry still requires an act of faith on the part of both you and your partner. This is not "blind *love*" or "blind faith," but faith based on conscious knowledge, since you (and hopefully your families) have thoroughly learned about each other. A truly healthy relationship occurs when both you and your partner have explored each other's lives with "both eyes open™," seeing each other clearly and knowing each other very well. Of course, you will not know everything, as marriage is a lifetime of discovery. However, you will know what is most important in determining that you can successfully go forward.

Making a knowledge-based *commitment* to each other will *help* you and your partner have a lasting, harmonious relationship filled with mutual *respect* and happiness. You will *commit* to nurturing and enriching your marriage together, empowering each other to develop character qualities, and sharing your lives together.

We wish you well on this journey! Together with our spouses, we keep you in our *encouraging* thoughts and supportive prayers.

Warm regards,

Susanne Alexander and John Miller

Appendices

Appendix A ~ Background and Research Notes

The theme throughout *Can We Dance?* is that of character—how to understand and develop your own character, how your character qualities affect your choices, and how to determine the character of a relationship partner. We weave the topic of character throughout self-discovery, learning from previous experiences, determining what you want in a partner, and building a friendship-based relationship. There is increasing attention occurring toward character and virtues as people search for meaning in their lives and ways to be happier. Therefore, many people are researching the topic of character, and we wish to acknowledge some of them here.

Bill Gothard and his book *Research in Principles of Life Basic Seminar Textbook*, started coauthor John Miller on his quest to understand character and the concept of misusing character qualities.

University-based researchers like Christopher Peterson, Professor of Psychology, University of Michigan, and Martin E. P. Seligman, Fox Leadership Professor of Psychology, University of Pennsylvania, are studying and classifying qualities such as *creativity*, *integrity*, and *kindness*. They are authors of *Character Strengths and Virtues: A Handbook and Classification*. Blaine Fowers at the University of Miami, and author of *Beyond the Myth of Marital Happiness*, focuses his work on the qualities of *loyalty*, *generosity*, *justice*, and *courage*. A team at Brigham Young University is developing ways to measure character in relationships and marriage.

Many other people globally are drawing people's attention to the importance of character. Among these is Linda Kavelin Popov of The Virtues Project™ (www.virtuesproject.com). She and her husband, Dan Popov, Ph.D., of WellSpring International Educational Foundation, have studied the world's religious scriptures and identified in them hundreds of qualities that guide human attitudes, words, and actions. Linda Kavelin Popov has incorporated the virtues into her books, *The Family Virtues Guide*, *The Virtues Project™ Educator's Guide*, and *A Pace of Grace*. As the Popovs travel internationally, they are finding universal application of these qualities for families, religious organizations, businesses, governments, youth organizations, and more. Some of their research and their encouragement have supported the development of our work.

Character education is also developing and spreading throughout the world's education systems, particularly at the primary school levels. In homes, parents are learning how to support the development of their children's characters. How character applies to relationships and marriage, however, is in the early stages of both university research and incorporation into relationship education.

This book, and our earlier one for married couples, *Pure Gold: Encouraging Character Qualities in Marriage* (second edition 2005), help to bring character into the mainstream of consideration as a foundation for happy, lasting relationships.

Appendix B ~ Sources, Copyright Notices, and Permissions
This page constitutes an extension to the copyright page.

Note: Every effort has been made to give credit and obtain permission where required and not a size where accepted fair use standards apply. Any omissions are completely unintentional. Upon notification, the publisher will be happy to make corrections in future editions of this work.

Understanding the Components of *Can We Dance?*

1. From *The Truth About Love: The Highs, the Lows, and How You Can Make It Last* by Pat Love, Ed.D., p. 61. Copyright © 2001 by Patricia Love. Reprinted by permission of Simon & Schuster Adult Publishing Group.

Part One—*Dance Lessons:* Preparing Yourself for a Great Relationship

Chapter 1: *Basic Footwork*—Understanding Character

1. From "Meditations with Native American Elders" by Don Coyhis (Mohican Nation), September 19, 2005. Copyright © 2006. Available from White Bison, Inc. at www.whitebison.org. Reprinted by permission.
2. Christopher Peterson and Martin E. P. Seligman, *Character Strengths and Virtues: A Handbook and Classification*, pp. 23-30. Copyright © 2004 by Values in Action Institute. Published by American Psychological Association.
3. Bahá'u'lláh, *Tablets of Bahá'u'lláh*, p. 36. Copyright © 1978 by The Universal House of Justice. Published by the Bahá'í World Centre.
4. *The Holy Bible* (New International Version); 1 Corinthians, 13:4, 5, 8. Copyright © 1984 and published by International Bible Society.
5. Translated by Abdullah Yúsuf 'Alí, *The Qur'án*, XLII-43. Copyright © 1946 by Khalil Al-Rawaf.
6. Confucius, *Confucius: The Analects*, Book IX, p. 99. Copyright © 1979 by D. C. Lau. Published by Penguin Books.
7. Blaine J. Fowers, Ph.D., *Beyond the Myth of Marital Happiness*, p. 116. Copyright © 2000 by Jossey-Bass Inc., Publishers. Reprinted with permission of John Wiley & Sons, Inc.
8. 'Abdu'l-Bahá, *Paris Talks*, p. 60. Copyright © 1971 and published by Bahá'í Publishing Trust.
9. Caroline Myss, Ph.D., *Anatomy of the Spirit,* p. 224. Copyright © 1996 by Caroline Myss. Harmony Books, a division of Random House, Inc. Used with permission.
10. Khalil A. Khavari, *Spiritual Intelligence*, p. 83. Copyright © 2000 by Khalil A. Khavari, Ph.D. Reprinted with permission of Khalil A. Khavari. Published by White Mountain Publications.
11. Joseph Hall, *Christian Moderation*, introduction.
12. Linda Kavelin Popov, *A Pace of Grace*, p. 139. Copyright © 2004 by Linda Kavelin Popov. Published by Plume, an imprint of Penguin Group (USA), Inc. Used with permission of author.

Chapter 2: *Your Part First*—Discovering Your Own Character

1. Taken from *Purpose Driven® Life* by Rick Warren, pp. 27-29. Copyright © 2002 by Rick Warren. Used by permission of The Zondervan Corporation.
2. 'Abdu'l-Bahá, *Selections from the Writings of 'Abdu'l-Bahá*, p. 35. Copyright © 1978 by The Universal House of Justice. Published by the Bahá'í World Centre.
3. Compiled by Paul Carus, *The Gospel of Buddha*, I:7. Copyright © 1915 and published by Open Court Publishing Company.
4. *Tanakh*, Mishlei (Proverbs) 2:2, 9. Copyright © 1985 and published by The Jewish Publication Society. Used with permission.
5. Howard Colby Ives, *Portals to Freedom,* p. 13. Copyright © 1976 by George Ronald, Publisher. Reprinted with permission of publisher.
6. *The Bible* (New International Version), Galatians 6:4.
7. William Shakespeare, *Hamlet*, Act I, scene iii.
8. Taken from *Relationships* by Dr. Les Parrott III; Leslie Parrott, p. 32. Copyright © 1998 by Les and

Leslie Parrott. Used by permission of The Zondervan Corporation.

9. Susan M. Campbell, Ph.D, *Beyond the Power Struggle*, p. 86. Copyright © 1984 by Susan M. Campbell. Published by Impact Publishers.
10. Linda Kavelin Popov, *A Pace of Grace*, p. 93.
11. *More African Proverbs*, p. 17. Copyright © 2002. Published by Bookcraft LTD. Used with permission of publisher.
12. Confucius, *Confucius, The Analects*, I:8.

Chapter 3: *Stepping Forward*—Developing Your Character

1. Michelle Weiner-Davis, *Divorce Busting*, pp. 92-94. Copyright © 1992 by Michelle Weiner-Davis, MSW, CSW. Published by Simon & Schuster.
2. Mother Teresa, Quoted by Michael Collopy, *Architects of Peace: Visions of Hope in Words and Images*, p. 31. Copyright © 2000 by Michael Collopy. Used with permission.
3. Taken from *Purpose Driven® Life* by Rick Warren, p. 179. Copyright © 2002 by Rick Warren. Used by permission of The Zondervan Corporation.
4. Dan Popov, Ph.D., of the WellSpring International Educational Foundation. Used with permission.
5. Bahá'u'lláh, *Gleanings from the Writings of Bahá'u'lláh*, p. 260. Copyright © 1952 by The National Spiritual Assembly of the Bahá'ís of the U.S. Published by Bahá'í Publishing Trust.
6. Joan Barstow Hernández, *Love, Courtship, and Marriage*, pp. 41-42. Published in South America. Reprinted with permission of author.
7. Compiled by Paul Carus, *The Gospel of Buddha*, XVII:2.
8. Henri Stendhal
9. Joan Barstow Hernández, *Love, Courtship, and Marriage*, p. 28. Reprinted with permission of author.
10. 'Abdu'l-Bahá, *Paris Talks*, p. 51.
11. Linda Kavelin Popov, *The Family Virtues Guide*, p. 250, Copyright © 1997 by Linda Kavelin Popov. Published by Plume, an imprint of Penguin Group (USA), Inc. Used with permission of author.
12. Alcoholics Anonymous, www.aa.org. Copyright © Alcoholics Anonymous World Services, Inc.
13. Natalie Jenkins quoted in Scott M. Stanley, *The Power of Commitment*, p. 205. Copyright © 2005 by Scott M. Stanley. Reprinted with permission of John Wiley & Sons, Inc.
14. Taken from *When Bad Things Happen to Good Marriages* by Dr. Les Parrott III; Leslie Parrott, p. 142. Copyright © 2001 by Les and Leslie Parrott. Used by permission of The Zondervan Corporation.
15. Howard J. Markman, Scott M. Stanley, Susan L. Blumberg, Natalie H. Jenkins, and Carol Whiteley, *12 Hours to a Great Marriage*, p. 207. Copyright © 2004 by John Wiley & Sons, Inc. Reprinted with permission of John Wiley & Sons, Inc.

Chapter 4: *Slips, Trips, and Falls*—Choosing, Learning, and Moving On

1. Some quotes drawn from the October 2004 Marriage Transformation LLC singles survey. Used with permission.
2. John Kolstoe, *Developing Genius*, pp. 197, 201. Copyright © 1995 by John Kolstoe. Reprinted with permission of George Ronald, Publisher.
3. Compiled by Paul Carus, *The Gospel of Buddha*, LX:25.
4. From the book *Living On Purpose* p. 186. Copyright © 2000 by Dan Millman. Reprinted with permission of New World Library, Novato, CA. 800/972-6657 ext. 52 or www.newworldlibrary.com.
5. Susan Jeffers, *The Feel the Fear Guide to Lasting Love*, pp. 24-25. Copyright © 2005 by Susan Jeffers, Ph.D. Published by Jeffers Press. Used with permission.

Chapter 5: *Gaining Confidence*—Claiming Commitment

1. W. H. Murray, *The Scottish Himalayan Expedition*
2. Some quotes drawn from the October 2004 Marriage Transformation LLC singles survey. Used with permission.
3. Rúhíyyih Rabbani, *Prescription for Living (Revised Edition)*, pp. 48-49. Copyright © 1978 by Rúhíyyih Rabbani. Reprinted with permission of George Ronald, Publisher.

4. Barbara Dafoe Whitehead and David Popenoe, *The State of Our Unions: The Social Health of Marriages in America*, Copyright © 2005 by Barbara Dafoe Whithead and David Popenoe, http://marriage.rutgers.edu. Used with permission.

5. Joan Barstow Hernández, *Love, Courtship, and Marriage*, p. 31.

6. Justice St. Rain, *Spiritual Guide to Great Sex*, p. 7. Copyright © 2003 Justice St. Rain; published by Interfaith Resources division of Special Ideas.

7. Laura M. Brotherson, CFLE, *And They Were Not Ashamed—Strengthening Marriage through Sexual Fulfillment* as quoted in "God's Wedding Gift: Why Save Sex for Marriage," p. 14, Meridian Magazine, August 2, 2005, www.ldsmag.com/familyconnections/050802gift.html. Used with permission of author.

8. Susanne M. Alexander with Craig A. Farnsworth and John S. Miller, *Pure Gold: Encouraging Character Qualities in Marriage*. Copyright © 2005 by Marriage Transformation LLC. Published by Marriage Transformation LLC; Susanne M. Alexander, *What's Character Got To Do With It? Enhancing Sexual Intimacy in Your Marriage*, Copyright © 2004 and published by Marriage Transformation LLC.

9. Reprinted from *Sacred Sex: A Spiritual Celebration of Oneness in Marriage*, pp. 4-5. Copyright © 2002 by Tim Alan Gardner. WaterBrook Press, Colorado Springs, CO. All rights reserved. Used with permission.

10. Dr. Paul Coleman, *How to Say It for Couples, Communicating with Tenderness, Openness and Honesty*, p. 204. Copyright © 2002 by Paul Coleman, Ph.D. Published by Penguin Books (Prentice Hall Press).

11. From *Dating Sucks*, pp. 177-178. Copyright © 2005, Joanne Kimes. Used by permission of Adams Media. All rights reserved.

12. The National Marriage Project; http://marriage.rutgers.edu/

13. Compiled by Paul Carus, *The Gospel of Buddha*, XLVI:6.

14. Rúhíyyih Rabbani, *Prescription for Living (Revised Edition)*, pp. 88-89.

15. Lauren Winner, *Real Sex, The Naked Truth About Chastity*, p. 23. Copyright © 2005 by Lauren F. Winner. Published by Brazos Press.

16. On behalf of the Universal House of Justice, *The Compilations of Compilations, Vol. I*, p. 51. Copyright © 1991 by Bahá'í Publications Australia. Published by The National Spiritual Assembly of the Bahá'ís of Australia.

17. Agnes Ghaznavi, *Sexuality, Relationships and Spiritual Growth*, p. 36-37. Copyright © 1995 by Agnes Ghaznavi. Reprinted with permission of George Ronald, Publisher.

18. Mary Baker Eddy, *Science and Health*, p. 57.

Chapter 6: *Both Eyes Open*—Discerning Your Expectations
1. Bahá'u'lláh, *Gleanings from the Writings of Bahá'u'lláh*, p. 194

2. William Lederer, *Creating a Good Relationship*, p. 56. Copyright © 1984 by William J. Lederer. Published by W. W. Norton Publishers.

3. Summary based on Khalil Khavari and Sue Khavari, *Together Forever*, pp. 33-35. Copyright © 1993 by Khalil and Sue Khavari. Reprinted with permission of authors. Published by Oneworld.

4. M. Scott Peck, M.D., *The Road Less Traveled*, p. 91. Copyright © 1978 by M. Scott Peck, M.D. Published by Simon & Schuster, Inc.

5. Some quotes drawn from the October 2004 Marriage Transformation LLC singles survey. Used with permission.

6. Taken from *Saving Your Second Marriage Before It Starts* by Dr. Les Parrott III; Leslie Parrott, p. 44. Copyright © 2001 by Les and Leslie Parrott. Used by permission of The Zondervan Corporation.

Chapter 7: *Partner Possibilities*—Determining a Match
1. *More African Proverbs*, p. 84.

2. Harville Hendrix, Ph.D., *Getting the Love You Want*, p. 14. Copyright © 1988 by Harville Hendrix. Published by Henry Holt and Company. Used with permission.

3. Rabbi Dov Heller, *10 Ways to Marry the Wrong Person*, November 25, 2001, www.aish.com. Used with permission.

4. 'Abdu'l-Bahá, *The Secret of Divine Civilization*, p. 19. Copyright © 1970 by The National Spiritual

Assembly of the Bahá'ís of the United States. Published by Bahá'í Publishing Trust.

5. St. Clement of Alexandria

Part Two—*It Takes Two:* Creating a Lasting Friendship-Based Relationship
Chapter 8: *First Dance*—Establishing a Friendship

1. John Gottman, Ph.D. and Nan Silver of *The Seven Principles for Making Marriage Work*, pp. 19-20. Copyright © 1999 by John Gottman, Ph.D., and Nan Silver. Published by Three Rivers Press. Used with permission.
2. Kahlil Gibran, *The Prophet*, p. 59. Copyright © 1951 by Kahlil Gibran. Published by Alfred A. Knopf, Inc.
3. Agnes Ghaznavi, *Sexuality, Relationships and Spiritual Growth*, p. 26.
4. Bill Gothard, *Research in Principles of Life Basic Seminar Textbook*, p. 167. Copyright © 1981 by Institute in Basic Life Principles, Inc. Published by Institute in Basic Life Principles, Inc.
5. Joan Barstow Hernández, *Love, Courtship, and Marriage*, p. 32.
6. Ibid., p. 34.
7. Gary Chapman, *The Five Love Languages for Singles*, p. 167. Copyright © 2004 by Gary Chapman. Published by Northfield Publishing. Used with permission.
8. On behalf of Shoghi Effendi, *Compilation of Compilations, Vol. II*, p. 3. Copyright © 1991 by Bahá'í Publications Australia. Published by The National Spiritual Assembly of the Bahá'ís of Australia.
9. Blaine J. Fowers, Ph.D., *Beyond the Myth of Marital Happiness*, p. 125, 128. Copyright © 2000 by Jossey-Bass Inc., Publishers. Reprinted with permission of John Wiley & Sons, Inc.
10. *More African Proverbs*, p. 12.
11. The National Marriage Project, "Ten Important Research Findings on Marriage and Choosing a Marriage Partner, Helpful Facts for Young Adults," http://marriage.rutgers.edu
12. Dale Carnegie, *How to Stop Worrying and Start Living*, p. 147. Copyright © 1948 by Dale Carnegie. Published by Simon & Schuster.
13. From *Dating Sucks*, p. 53.
14. Ibid., p. 1.
15. *More African Proverbs*, p. 70.

Chapter 9: *A Consistent Partner*—Shifting to a Serious Relationship

1. *The Bible* (New International Version), Galatians 5:13-14.
2. Linda Kavelin Popov, *A Pace of Grace*, p. 204-205.
3. 'Abdu'l-Bahá: *Paris Talks*, pp. 179-181.
4. Justice St. Rain, *Falling into Grace*, p. 112. Copyright © 1999 by Special Ideas. Published by Special Ideas. Used with permission.
5. From *A Wayfarer's Guide to Bringing the Sacred Home* by Joseph Sheppherd (Bahá'í Publishing 2002, pp. 95-97). Copyright © 2002 by National Assembly of the Bahá'ís of the United States. Reprinted with permission of the Bahá'í Publishing Trust, Wilmette, IL.
6. United Nations (www.un.org) and the Council of Europe, (www.coe.int/t/e/Human_Rights/Equality/).
7. Les Parrott III, *7 Secrets of a Healthy Dating Relationship*, p. 95. Copyright © 1995 by Beacon Hill Press of Kansas City. Published by Beacon Hill Press of Kansas City. Used with permission.
8. *More African Proverbs*, p. 49.
9. 'Abdu'l-Bahá, *Selections from the Writings of 'Abdu'l-Bahá*, p. 302.
10. Agnes Ghaznavi, Sexuality, Relationships and Spiritual Growth, p. 20.
11. From "Meditations with Native American Elders" by Don Coyhis (Mohican Nation), Copyright © 2006. Available from White Bison, Inc. at www.whitebison.org. Reprinted by permission.

Chapter 10: *Dips and Twirls*—Observing Your Partner's Moves

1. 'Abdu'l-Bahá, *Promulgation of Universal Peace*, p. 293. Copyright © 1982 by the National Assembly of the Bahá'ís of the United States. Published by Bahá'í Publishing Trust.
2. *Tanakh*, Mishlei (Proverbs), 18:15.

3. Linda Kavelin Popov, *A Pace of Grace*, p. 62.
4. Confucius, *Confucius, The Analects*, XVI:6.
5. Charlie Michaels (author of *Mastering Marriage*). Copyright © 2005 by Charlie Michaels and Mike Brown. Used with permission.
6. Confucius, *Confucius, The Analects*, II:10.
7. Confucius, *Confucius, The Analects*, V:10.

Chapter 11: *Advanced Practice*—Gaining Communication Skills

1. *The Bible* (New International Version), James 1:19
2. Oliver Wendell Holmes, *The Poet at the Breakfast Table*.
3. Summary based on Kathlyn Hendricks, Ph.D., and Gay Hendricks, Ph.D, *The Conscious Heart*, pp. 267-272. Copyright © 1997 by Kathlyn Hendricks and Gay Hendricks. Published by Random House. Used with permission of authors; www.hendricks.com.
4. Ibid., pp. 265-266.
5. Gary Chapman, *The Five Love Languages: How to Express Heartfelt Commitment to Your Mate*, pp. 42, 45. Copyright © 1995 by Gary D. Chapman. Published by Northfield Publishing. Used with permission.
6. John M. Gottman, Ph.D. and Joan DeClaire, *The Relationship Cure: A 5 Step Guide to Strengthening Your Marriage, Family, and Friendships*, p. 209. Copyright © 2001 by John M. Gottman, Ph.D. and Joan DeClaire. Published by Three Rivers Press.
7. *More African Proverbs*, p. 47.
8. This practice is also known as "Speaking the Language of the Virtues," as named by Linda Kavelin Popov of The Virtues Project™, www.virtuesproject.com.

Chapter 12: *Intricate Steps*—Sharing and Resolving Sensitive Matters

1. Taken from *Relationships* by Dr. Les Parrott III; Leslie Parrott, p. 82. Copyright © 1998 by Les and Leslie Parrott. Used by permission of The Zondervan Corporation.
2. Reprinted with the permission of Simon and Schuster Adult Publishing Group from *In the Meantime* by Iyanla Vanzant. Copyright © 1998 by Iyanla Vanzant, p. 211.
3. Susan Page, *The 8 Essential Traits of Couples Who Thrive*, p. 192. Copyright © 1994 by Susan Page. Published by Dell Publishing, a division of Bantam Doubleday Dell Publishing Group, Inc.
4. Translated by Abdullah Yúsuf 'Alí, *The Qur'án*, Introduction and Summary: Sura CIV.
5. Bahá'u'lláh, *Gleanings from the Writings of Bahá'u'lláh*, p. 265.
6. *More African Proverbs*, p. 87.
7. Pamphlet on Intimate Partner Violence, © 2006 The Cleveland Clinic Foundation.
8. Tina B. Tessina, Ph.D., *It Ends With You: Grow Up and Out of Dysfunction*, p. 201. Used with permission of author.
9. Compiled by Paul Carus, *The Gospel of Buddha*, XLVIII:15.
10. Taken from *Relationships* by Dr. Les Parrott III; Leslie Parrott, p. 136. Copyright © 1998 by Les and Leslie Parrott. Used by permission of The Zondervan Corporation.
11. Agnes Ghaznavi, *Sexuality, Relationships and Spiritual Growth*, p. 25.
12. Gary Chapman, *The Five Love Languages for Singles*, p. 113.

Chapter 13: *New Dances*—Exploring Some Differences

1. Joel Crohn, Ph.D., *Mixed Matches*, p. 30. Copyright © 1995 by Joel Crohn. Published by Ballantine Books.
2. D. Osher & B. Mejia. Overcoming barriers to intercultural relationships: A culturally competent approach, quoted in *Reaching Today's Youth*, 3(2), 48-52, 1999. *The Community Circle of Caring Journal*, National Educational Service, Center for Effective Collaboration and Practice, www.cecp.air.org.
3. Joel Crohn, Ph.D., *Mixed Matches*, p. 22.
4. 'Abdu'l-Bahá, *The Advent of Divine Justice*, p. 31. Copyright © 1966 (1971 edition) and published by The National Spiritual Assembly of the Bahá'ís of the United States.
5. Dugan Romano, *Intercultural Marriage*, pp. 183-184. Copyright © 1988,1997 by Dugan Romano. Published by Intercultural Press, Inc.

6. Reginald Newkirk and Nathan Rutstein, *Racial Healing: The Institutes for the Healing of Racism*, pp. 101-102. Copyright © 2000 and published by by National Resource Center for the Healing of Racism. Used with permission of Reginald Newkirk.
7. Translated by Abdullah Yúsuf 'Alí, *The Qur'án*, II:3.
8. Helen Neville, Ph.D., http://bdl.uoregon.edu.

Chapter 14: *Unified Movement*—Preventing Communications Missteps
1. *Tanakh*, Mishlei (Proverbs), 15:1,4.
2. Summary based on John Gottman, Ph.D. and Nan Silver of *The Seven Principles for Making Marriage Work*, Ch. 2.
3. Erik Blumenthal, *To Understand and Be Understood,* p. 37. Copyright © 1987 and published by Oneworld Publications.
4. Confucius, *Confucius, The Analects*, IV: 25.
5. Khalil A. Khavari, Ph.D., *Spiritual Intelligence*, p. 237.
6. 'Abdu'l-Bahá, quoted in Shoghi Effendi, *The Advent of Divine Justice*, p. 26.
7. Mehri Sefidvash, *Coral and Pearls,* p. 100.
8. Bahá'u'lláh, *Tablets of Bahá'u'lláh*, p. 157.

Chapter 15: *Smooth Dancing*—Strengthening Unity and Love
1. Bahá'u'lláh, *Gleanings from the Writings of Bahá'u'lláh*, p. 217.
2. Translated by Abdullah Yúsuf 'Alí, *The Qur'án*, II:148.
3. *The Bible (New International Version)*, I John, 3:18.
4. Summary based on Gary Chapman, *The Five Love Languages for Singles.*
5. Gary Chapman, *The Five Love Languages for Singles,* p. 149.
6. Summary based on Gary Chapman, *The Five Love Languages for Singles,* p. 128-138.
7. Summary based on Michele Weiner-Davis, *Divorce Busting*, Ch. 5.
8. From "Meditations with Native American Elders" by Don Coyhis (Mohican Nation), October 5. Copyright © 2006. Available from White Bison, Inc. at www.whitebison.org. Reprinted by permission. Elder's Meditation of the Day October 5, www.whitebison.org.
9. Honoré De Balzac, *Seraphita*, Ch. VI.
10. Drs. Les and Leslie Parrott, *The Love List* p. 34. Copyright © 2002 by Les and Leslie Parrott. Used with permission.
11. Howard J. Markman, Scott M. Stanley, Susan L. Blumberg, Natalie H. Jenkins, and Carol Whiteley, *12 Hours to a Great Marriage*, Ch. 6.
12. Linda Kavelin Popov, *A Pace of Grace*, p. 245.
13. *Tanakh*, Mishlei (Proverbs), 27:6.
14. Mehri Sefidvash, *Coral and Pearls*, pp. 11-12.

Part Three—*The Best Dance:* Exploring Powerful Character Qualities
1. *The Bible* (New International Version), Romans, 12:18.
2. 'Abdu'l-Bahá, *The Promulgation of Universal Peace*, p. 293.
3. Compiled by Paul Carus, *The Gospel of Buddha*, XXIV:4.
4. Translated by Abdullah Yúsuf 'Alí, *The Qur'án*, IV:36.
5. A newly translated extract from an unpublished Tablet revealed by 'Abdu'l-Bahá in the Persian language, cited in a letter dated November 26, 2003 from the Universal House of Justice to the members of the Bahá'í community in Iran.
6. *The Bible* (King James Version), Romans, 4:19,21.
7. Swami Prahavananda, *The Song of God: Bhagavad-Gita,* XII. Copyright © 1972 and published by The Vendanta Society of Southern California. Used with permission.
8. *Tanakh*, Mishlei (Proverbs) 28:1.
9. *The Bible* (King James Version), Hebrews 13:5.
10. 'Abdu'l-Bahá, *The Promulgation of Universal Peace*, p. 98.
11. Compiled by Paul Carus, *The Gospel of Buddha*, I:3.

12. Translated by Abdullah Yúsuf 'Alí, *The Qur'án*, IV:86.
13. 'Abdu'l-Bahá, *Selections from the Writings of 'Abdu'l-Bahá*, p. 145.
14. Swami Prahavananda, *The Song of God: Bhagavad-Gita*, II.
15. *Tanakh*, Mishlei (Proverbs) 2:2, 9.
16. The Universal House of Justice, *Wellspring of Guidance*, p. 39. Copyright © 1969 by The National Spiritual Assembly of the Bahá'ís of the United States. Published by Bahá'í Publishing Trust.
17. Martin Luther, *The Precious Sacred Writings of Martin Luther*, Vol. 11, "The Parable of the Sower." Copyright © 1906 and published by the Lutherans of All Lands (Minneapolis, MN).
18. 'Abdu'l-Bahá, *Paris Talks*, p. 162.
19. Swami Prahavananda, *The Song of God: Bhagavad-Gita*, III.
20. Translated by Abdullah Yúsuf 'Alí, *The Qur'án*, XXIII:8.
21. *Prayers and Meditations by Bahá'u'lláh*, p. 240. Copyright © 1938 by The National Spiritual Assembly of the Bahá'ís of the United States. Published by Bahá'í Publishing Trust.
22. *The Bible* (New International Version), Colossians, 3:13.
23. *Tanakh*, Kohelet (Ecclesiastes) 4:9-10.
24. Translated by Abdullah Yúsuf 'Alí, *The Qur'án*, II:267.
25. Compiled by Paul Carus, *The Gospel of Buddha*, XCIV:17.
26. *The Bible* (New International Version), Galatians 6:10.
27. *Tanakh*, Nevi'im (Isaiah), 33:15-16.
28. Translated by Abdullah Yúsuf 'Alí, *The Qur'án*, II:58.
29. Bahá'u'lláh, *Gleanings from the Writings of Bahá'u'lláh*, p. 305.
30. *Tanakh*, Tehillim (Psalms) 25:21.
31. *The Bible* (New International Version), Romans, 5:3-4.
32. *Tanakh*, Zecharia (Zechariah) 8:16.
33. Compiled by Paul Carus, *The Gospel of Buddha*, XX:22.
34. *The Bible* (New International Version), 1 Corinthians 16:14.
35. 'Abdu'l-Bahá, *Selections from the Writings of 'Abdu'l-Bahá*, p. 294.
36. *The Bible* (King James Version), Luke 6:36.
37. Swami Prahavananda, *The Song of God: Bhagavad-Gita*, VI.
38. *Tanakh, Kohelet* Ecclesiastes 7:8.
39. Compiled by Paul Carus, *The Gospel of Buddha*, LVIII:3.
40. Translated by Abdullah Yúsuf 'Alí, *The Qur'án*, XXXIX:10.
41. Swami Prahavananda, *The Song of God: Bhagavad-Gita*, XVI.
42. *Tanakh*, Kohelet Ecclesiastes 3:1-8.
43. 'Abdu'l-Bahá, *The Promulgation of Universal Peace*, p. 231.
44. *Tanakh*, Mishlei (Proverbs) 12:11, 14.
45. Translated by Abdullah Yúsuf 'Alí, *The Qur'án*, III:17.
46. *The Bible* (New International Version), Galatians 5:13-14.
47. Compiled by Paul Carus, *The Gospel of Buddha*, XVI:21.
48. On behalf of Shoghi Effendi, *Compilation of Compilations*, Vol. II, p. 14.
49. Translated by Abdullah Yúsuf 'Alí, *The Qur'án*, III:200.
50. Bahá'u'lláh, *Gleanings from the Writings of Bahá'u'lláh*, p. 176.
51. *Tanakh,* Tehillim (Psalms) 107:1.
52. Compiled by Paul Carus, *The Gospel of Buddha*, XLVIII:12.
53. Translated by Abdullah Yúsuf 'Alí, *The Qur'án*, XXVIII:26.
54. *The Bible* (New International Version), John 8:31-32.
55. Bahá'u'lláh, *Tables of Bahá'u'lláh*, p. 90.
56. Swami Prahavananda, *The Song of God: Bhagavad-Gita*, XIII.

The Next Step: *A Harmonious Dance*—Considering Compatibility

1. John Bradshaw, *The Family*, p. 51. Copyright © 1996 by John Bradshaw. Published by and reprinted with permission of Health Communications.

Appendix C ~ About the Authors and Publisher

Susanne M. Alexander and *Craig A. Farnsworth* are principals of **Marriage Transformation LLC**, a relationship and marriage education and publishing company (www.marriagetransformation.com). They are creating practical resources and powerful learning opportunities that empower people globally to create happy, lasting, and spiritually-based relationships and marriages. They have been married since August 1999, a second marriage for both of them. Between them, they have more than 50 years of marriage experience, four adult children, a son-in-law, and a granddaughter.

Susanne and Craig are relationship coaches, Character Development Consultants, and marriage educators, certified by Life Innovations, Inc. in PREPARE/ENRICH and by FranklinCovey in "The 8 Habits of a Successful Marriage." Susanne has also been trained by PREP Inc. The couple facilitates relationship, marriage preparation, and marriage enrichment workshops internationally with people of all ages. Their first book, published in 2003, was *Marriage Can Be Forever—Preparation Counts!* They are also coauthors of *Pure Gold: Encouraging Character Qualities in Marriage.*

৪৩৫৪

Susanne Alexander holds a B.A. in Communications from Baldwin-Wallace College in Ohio. Her articles as a journalist have been published in *Strengthening Marriage, First Years, Newsweek Japan, The (Cleveland) Plain Dealer, Crain's Cleveland Business, Writer's Digest,* and *Massage Magazine* among others. Susanne is a member of the American Society of Journalists and Authors. She is part of an author team that has written a college textbook, *College & Career Success Simplified,* published in July 2003.

৪৩৫৪

John S. Miller is a Character Coach and holds a B.S. in Psychology from Union College, Lincoln, Nebraska. He is coauthor of *Pure Gold: Encouraging Character Qualities in Marriage.* In 1994, John married his best friend, Cindy, a second marriage for both of them. While college honed his writing, research, and intellectual abilities, John considers the best classroom to be real-life experience combined with the quest for truth. He comes from five successive generations ravaged by divorce, so he is an expert at understanding how divorce destroys families.

Within the context of an inherent personal need to find better ways for relationships to function, John has spent 25 years studying character and conflict. He and his wife founded Solving Conflicts LLC (www.solvingconflicts.com) in 2005 to offer their unique system of character assessment. It comes from their own personal use of character to solve conflicts and John's research into the meaning of character strengths. John and Cindy attribute the success of their twelve-year marriage to this focus. It is John and Cindy's mission to make this cutting-edge system of character education and assessment available to all people.

Appendix D ~ Information on Marriage Transformation Books

PURE GOLD:
ENCOURAGING CHARACTER QUALITIES IN MARRIAGE

Susanne M. Alexander
with Craig A. Farnsworth and John S. Miller

You want a happy, lasting marriage filled with character qualities such as *trustworthiness, loyalty, truthfulness, love, courage,* and *generosity.* Marriage research shows that preventing destructive character attacks, and understanding and practicing these positive character qualities and more in your relationship are vital for the success of your marriage.

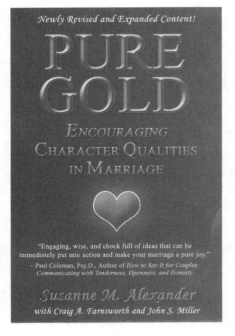

Inside *Pure Gold,* you will:

- Explore many ways to have a **loving, supportive relationship** that includes these qualities and more

- **Enrich and strengthen your marriage** with powerful character and communication skills

- Discover how more than 50 qualities empower you in creating an **extraordinary marriage** through engaging activities, examples, and quotations from experts and spiritual sources

ISBN: 0-9726893-5-4 or 978-0-9726893-5-9
Published by Marriage Transformation LLC

**Buy your copies today at your favorite bookstore
or online at www.marriagetransformation.com!**

Can We Harmonize?
Composing a Compatible Relationship

Planned for 2007!

Susanne M. Alexander

Couples determine whether they can pair their lives harmoniously together and are compatible enough for marriage. Topics focus on areas such as spirituality, children, handling challenges, equality, communications, family issues, household management, and much more.

Can We Create?
Designing an Inspirational Engagement

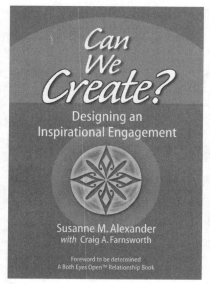

Planned for 2008!

Susanne M. Alexander

Couples discover how to successfully maintain their relationship and build family unity during the engagement period. They also continue getting to know one another's character, create a spiritual bond together, and use the wedding plan time to prepare for their marriage, not just the wedding day.

www.marriagetransformation.com

Appendix E ~ Please Contact Us

It will be a gift to us to hear back from you about your experiences with this book, and for you to share anything that would improve its usefulness in future editions. We also welcome hearing your relationship experiences and about what future material would be useful for you.

Please contact us as follows:

Marriage Transformation LLC
P. O. Box 23085, Cleveland, OH 44123, USA
E-mail: susanne@marriagetransformation.com
Website: www.marriagetransformation.com
Telephone: 216-383-9943; FAX: 216-383-9953
(9:30 a.m. to 8:00 p.m. Eastern U.S. Time Zone)

Please be sure to visit our website for announcements of exciting new books, products, services, and recommended resources for relationship and marriage education. Sets of worksheets from various books are also often available for purchase through:
www.marriagetransformation.com/store.htm

Please subscribe, on our website home page, to our free monthly e-newsletter, which is filled with great information for you about relationships, marriage, new books, and book sales.

Our books are also available through your favorite local or on-line bookseller!